AF765656

British Virgin Islands Offshore Business Laws

International Law & Taxation Publishers
London

British Virgin Islands Offshore Business Laws

ISBN 1-893713-37-7

International Law & Taxation Publishers
London

http://www.internationallawandtaxationpublishers.com

Contents

COMPANIES ACT (as amended)

ARRANGEMENT OF SECTIONS

Part I - Constitution and Incorporation

Unlimited Liability of Directors

Reduction of Capital

Subdivision of Shares

Articles of Association

General Provisions

Part II - Distribution of Capital and Liability of Members

Reserve Capital

Liability of Members

Calls Upon Shares

Transfer of Shares

Share Warrants to Bearer

Contracts

Part III -Management and Administration Provisions for Protection of Creditors

Winding up by Court

Official Liquidator

Ordinary Powers of Court

Extraordinary Powers of Court

Enforcement of and Appeal from Orders

Voluntary Winding up of Company

Winding up Subject to the Supervision of the Court

Supplemental Provisions

Striking Companies off Register

Procedure in Winding up by Court

Part V - Constitution of Registration Office

Part VI - Companies Authorized to Register

Part VII - Private Companies

Part VIII - Unregistered Companies

Part IX - Companies Established Outside the Territory

Part X

Part XI - Miscellaneous

Short title

1.This Act may be cited as the Companies Act.

Interpretation

2.In this Act the expression -

"Act of the Territorial Legislature" means any Act or Act in force in the Territory;

"the Court" means the Supreme Court or a Judge thereof. A Judge of the Supreme Court may do in Chambers any act which the Court is by this Act authorized to do so;

"private company" means a company which by its articles -

(a) restricts the right to transfer its shares;

(b) limits the number of its members (exclusive of persons who are in the employment of the company and of persons who having been formerly in the employment of the company, were while in such employment and have continued after the determination of such employment to be members of the company) to fifty: Provided that where two or more persons hold one or more shares in a company jointly they shall for the purpose of this definition be treated as a single member;

(c) prohibits any invitation to the public to subscribe for any shares or debentures of the company.

"Registrar" means the Registrar of Companies holding office as such under section 207.

Prohibition of partnership exceeding certain number

3.No company, association or partnership consisting of more than twenty persons shall be exceeding certain formed, for the purpose of carrying on any business that has for its object the acquisition or number gain by the company, association or partnership, or by the individual members thereof, unless it is registered as a company under this Act, or if formed in pursuance of some Act of the Imperial Parliament, or of the Legislature of the Territory, or by Royal Charter or Letters Patent; but this Act shall not apply to persons associated together for the purpose of banking or insurance.

Application to private companies

4.Save as herein otherwise expressly provided the provisions of this Act shall apply to private companies in like manner as they apply to public companies.

Application to banks

4A.(1) No company that has the word “bank” or “banking” as part of its name shall be registered under this Act unless there is issued in respect of that company a licence under the Banking Act.

(2) For the purposes of this section “bank” means a bank within the context of the Banking act, 1972 and “banking” has a corresponding meaning.

(3) A company that, at the date of the commencement of this section, would otherwise be registered in contravention of subsection (1) continues to be so registered for a period of three months from that date after which it ceases to be so registered; but application may be made under the Banking Act for registration of the Company under that Act.

PART I - Constitution And Incorporation

Memorandum of Association

Mode of forming company

5.Any five or more persons (or where the company to be formed will be a private company, any two or more persons) associated for any lawful purpose may, by subscribing their names to a Memorandum of Association, and otherwise complying with the requisitions of this Act in respect of registration, form an incorporated company, with or without limited liability.

Restriction on carrying on insurance business

5A.(1) After the date on which this section comes into force, and notwithstanding the provisions of carrying on insurance section 5, no person shall incorporate a company for carrying on the business of insurance, unless, prior approval for such incorporation has been obtained from the Ministry of Finance

(2) In this section "Business of Insurance"-

(a) means the assumption of the obligations of an insurer in any class of insurance business; and

(b) includes re-insurance business.

Mode of limiting liability of members

6.The liability of the members of a company formed under this Act may, according to the Memorandum of Association, be limited either to the amount, if any, unpaid on the shares respectively held by them, or to such amount as the members may respectively undertake by the Memorandum of Association to contribute to the assets of the Company in the event of its being wound up.

Memorandum of Association of a company limited by shares

7.Where a company is formed on the principle of having the liability of its members limited to the Association of an amount unpaid on their shares, hereinafter referred to as a company limited by shares, the Memorandum of Association shall contain the following things that is to say -

(a) The name of the proposed company, with the addition of the word "Limited" as the last word in such name;

(b) the place within the Territory in which the registered office of the company is proposed to be situate;

(c) the object for which the proposed company is to be established;

(d) a declaration that the liability of the members is limited;

(e) the amount of capital with which the company proposes to be registered, divided into shares of a certain fixed amount:

Provided: -

(i) that no subscriber shall take less than one share;

(ii) that each subscriber of the Memorandum of Association shall write opposite to his name, the number of shares he takes.

Memorandum of Association of a company limited by guarantee

8.Where a company is formed on the principle of having the liability of its members limited to such amount as the members respectively undertake to contribute to the assets of the company in the event of the same being wound up, hereinafter referred to as a company limited by guarantee, the Memorandum of Association shall contain the following things, that is to say -

(a) the name of the proposed company, with the addition of the word "Limited" as the last word in such name;

(b) the place within the Territory in which the registered office of the company is proposed to be situate;

(c) the objects for which the proposed company is to be established;

(d) a declaration that each member undertakes to contribute to the assets of the company, in the event of the same being wound up during the time that he is a member, or within one year afterwards, for payment of the debts and liabilities of the company contracted before the time at which he ceases to be a member, and of the costs, charges and expenses of winding up the company, and for the adjustment of the rights of the contributories amongst themselves, such amount as may be required, not exceeding a specified amount.

Memorandum of Association of an unlimited company

9.Where a company is formed on the principle of having no limit placed on the liability of its members, hereinafter referred to as an unlimited company, the Memorandum of Association shall contain the following things, that is to say

(a) the name of the proposed company;

(b) the place within the Territory in which the registered office of the company is proposed to be situate;

(c) the objects for which the proposed company is to be established.

Signature and effect of Memorandum of Association

10. The Memorandum of Association shall be signed by each subscriber in the presence of, and be attested by, one witness at the least, and the attestation shall be sufficient attestation for all purposes under the Registration and Records Act. It shall, when registered, bind the company and the members thereof, to the same extent as if each member had subscribed his name and affixed his seal thereto, and there were in the Memorandum contained, on the part of himself, his heirs, executors and administrators, a covenant to observe all the conditions of such Memorandum, subject to the provisions of this Act.

Power to alter Memorandum of Association

11. Any company may by special resolution modify the conditions contained in its Memorandum of Association, if authorized to do so by its regulations as originally framed, or as altered by special resolution in manner hereinafter mentioned.

Restriction of registration of companies by certain names

12.(1) No company shall be registered by a name which -

(a) is identical with that by which a company in existence is already registered or so nearly resembles that name as to be calculated to deceive, except where the company in existence is in the course of being dissolved and signifies its consent in such manner as the Registrar requires; or

(b) contains the words "Chamber of Commerce", unless the company is a company which is to be registered under a licence granted in pursuance of the next following section of the word "Limited" to its name; or

(c) contains the words "Building Society".

(2) Except with the consent of the Registrar no company shall be registered by a name which -

(a) contains the words "Royal" or "Imperial" or in the opinion of the Registrar suggests, or is calculated to suggest, the patronage of Her Majesty or of any member of the Royal Family or connection with Her Majesty's Government or any department thereof; or

(b) contains the words "Municipal" or "Chartered" or in the opinion of the Registrar suggests, or is calculated to suggest, connection with any municipality or other local authority or with any society or body incorporated by Royal Charter; or

(c) contains the words "Co-operative".

Power to dispense with "Limited" in name of charitable and other companies

13.(1) Where it is proved to the satisfaction of the Registrar that an association about to be formed as a limited company is to be formed for promoting commerce, art, science, religion, charity, other or any other useful object, and intends to apply its profits, if any, or other income in promoting its objects, and to prohibit the payment of any dividend to its members, the Registrar may by licence direct that the association may be registered as a company with limited liability, without the addition of the word "Limited" to its name, and the association may be registered accordingly.

(2)A licence by the Registrar under this section may be granted on such conditions and subject to such regulations as the Registrar thinks fit, and those conditions and regulations shall be binding on the association, and shall, if the Registrar so directs, be inserted in the Memorandum and Articles, or in one of those documents.

(3) The association shall on registration enjoy all the privileges of limited companies, and be subject to all of their obligations, except those of using the word "Limited" as any part of its name, and of its publishing its name, and of sending lists of members to the Registrar.

(4) A licence under this section may at any time be revoked by the Registrar, and upon revocation the Registrar shall enter the word "Limited" at the end of the name of the association upon the register, and the association shall cease to enjoy the exemptions and privileges granted by this section:

Provided that, before a licence is so revoked, the Registrar shall give to the association notice in writing of his intention, and shall afford the association and opportunity of being heard in opposition to the revocation.

(5) Where the name of the association contains the words "Chamber of Commerce", the notice shall be given as aforesaid shall include a statement of the effect of the provisions of subsection (3) of the next following section.

Change of name

14.(1) A company may, by special resolution and with the approval of the Registrar signified in writing, change its name.

(2) If a company, through inadvertence or otherwise, is, without such consent as is mentioned in paragraph (a) of subsection (1) of section 12, registered by a name which is identical with that by which a company in existence is previously registered or which so nearly resembles that name as to be calculated to deceive, the first-mentioned company may change its name with the sanction of the Registrar.

(3) Where a licence granted in pursuance of the last foregoing section of this Act to a company the name of which contains the words "Chamber of Commerce" is revoked, the company shall, within a period of six weeks from the date of the revocation or such longer period as the Registrar may think fit to allow, change its name to a name which does not contain those words. If a company makes default in complying with the requirements of this subsection, it shall be liable to a fine not exceeding twenty-four dollars for every day during which the default continues.

(4) Where a company changes its name, the Registrar shall enter the new name on the register in place of the former name, and shall issue a certificate of incorporation altered to meet the circumstances of the case.

(5) The change of name shall not affect any rights or obligations of the company, or render defective any legal proceedings by or against the company, and any legal proceedings that might have been continued or commence against it by its former name may be continued or commenced against it by its new name.

Unlimited Liability Of Directors

Companies may have directors with unlimited liability

15. Where a company is formed as a limited company under this Act, the liability of the directors or managers of such company, or the managing director, unlimited may, if so provided by the Memorandum of Association, be unlimited.

Liability of director, past and present, where liability is unlimited

16. The following modification shall be made in section 62 with respect to the contributions to respect to the contributions to required, in the event of the winding up of a limited company under this Act, from any director or manager whose liability is, in pursuance of this Act, unlimited -

(a) subject to the provisions hereinafter contained, any such director or manager, whether past or present shall, in addition to his liability, if any, to contribute as an ordinary member, be liable to contribute as if he were, at the date of the commencement of such winding up, a member of an unlimited company;

(b) no contribution required from any past director or manager, who has ceased to hold such office for a period of one year or upwards prior to the commencement of the winding up, shall exceed the amount, if any, which he is liable to contribute as an ordinary member of the company;

(c) no contribution required from any past director or manger, in respect of any debt or liability of the company contracted after the time at which he ceased to hold such office, shall exceed the amount, if any, which he is liable to contribute as an ordinary member of the company;

(d) subject to the provisions contained in the regulations of the company, no contribution required from any director or manager shall exceed the amount, if any, which he is liable to contribute as an ordinary member, unless the

Court deems it necessary to require such contribution in order to satisfy the debts and liabilities of the company and the costs, charges, and expenses of the winding up.

Director with unlimited liability may have set off as under s.135

17. In the event of the winding up of any limited company, the Court, if it thinks fit, may make to any director or manager of such company, whose liability is unlimited, the same allowance by way of set-off as, under section 135 it may make to a contributory where the company is not limited.

Notice to be given to director, on his election, that his liability will be unlimited

18.(l) In any limited company in which the liability of a director or manager, is unlimited, the directors or managers of the company, if any, and the member who proposes any persons for election or appointment to such office, shall add to such proposal a statement that the liability of the person holding such office will be unlimited, and the promoters, directors, managers and secretary, if any, of such company, or one of them, shall before such person accepts such office or acts therein give him notice in writing that his liability will be unlimited.

(2) If any director, manager, or proposer make default in adding such statement, or if any promoter, director, manager, or secretary make default in giving such notice, he shall be liable to a penalty not exceeding four hundred and eighty dollars, and shall also be liable for any damage which the person so elected or appointed may sustain from such default, but the liability of the person elected or appointed shall not be affected by such default.

Existing limited companies may by special resolution make liability of directors unlimited

19. Any limited company, may by special resolution, if authorized to do so by its regulations as originally framed or as altered by special resolution, from time to time modify the conditions contained in its Memorandum of Association so far as to render unlimited the liability of its directors or managers, or of the managing director; and such special resolution shall be the same validity as if it had been originally contained in the Memorandum of Association, and a copy thereof shall be embodied in or annexed to every copy of the Memorandum of Association which is issued after the passing of the resolution and any default in this respect shall be deemed to be a default in complying with the provisions of section 93, and shall be punished accordingly.

Reduction Of Capital

Construction of "capital" and powers to reduce capital

20. The word capital, as used in the next following sections, shall include paid up capital, and the powers hereby conferred to reduce capital shall include a power to cancel any lost any capital unrepresented by available assets, or to pay off any capital which may be in excess of the wants of the company; and paid up capital may be reduced either with or without extinguishing or reducing the liability, if any, remaining on the shares of the company, and to the extent to which such liability is not extinguished or reduced, it shall be deemed to be preserved notwithstanding anything hereinafter contained.

Power of company to reduce capital

21. Any company limited by shares may, by special resolution, so far modify the conditions contained in its Memorandum of Association, if authorized so to do by its regulations as originally framed or as altered by special resolution, as to reduce its capital; but no such resolution for reducing the capital of any company shall come into operation until an Order of the Court is registered by the Registrar as is hereinafter mentioned.

Company to add "and reduced" to its name for a limited period

22. The company shall, after the date of the passing of any special resolution for reducing its capital, add to its name, until such date as the Court may fix, the words "and reduced" as the last words in its name, and those words shall, until such date, be deemed to be part of the name of the company within the meaning of this Act.

Company to apply to the Court for an order confirming reduction

23.A company which has passed a special resolution for reducing its capital may apply to the Court, by petition, for an order confirming the reduction, and on the hearing of the petition, the Court, if satisfied, that, with respect to every creditor of the company who, under the provisions of this Act, is entitled to object to the reduction, either his consent to the reduction has been obtained, or his debt or claim has been discharged or has determined, or has been secured as hereinafter provided, may make an order confirming the reduction on such terms and subject to such conditions as it deems fit.

Creditors may object to reduction and list of objecting creditors to be settled by the Court

24.(1) Where a company proposes to reduce its capital, every creditor of the company, who, at the date fixed by the Court, is entitled to any debt or claim which, if that date were the commencement of the winding up of the company, shall be entitled, to object to the proposed reduction, and to be entered in the list of creditors who are so entitled to object.

(2) The Court shall settle a list of such creditors, and, for that purpose, shall ascertain as far as possible, without requiring an application from any creditor, the names of such creditors and the nature and amount of their debts or claims, and may publish notices fixing a certain day or days within which creditors of the company, who are not entered on the list are to claim to be so entered, or to be excluded from the right of objecting to the proposed reduction.

Court may dispense with consent of creditor on security being given for his debt

25. Where a creditor, whose name is entered on the list of creditors, and whose debt or claim is not discharged or determined, does not consent to the proposed reduction, the Court may, if it thinks fit, dispense with such consent, on the company securing the payment of the debt claim of such creditor, by setting apart and appropriating, in such manner as the Court may direct, a sum of such amount as is hereinafter mentioned, that is to say -

(a) if the full amount of the debt or claim of the creditor is admitted by the

company, or, though not admitted, is such as the company is willing to set apart and appropriate, then the full amount of the debt or claim shall be set apart and appropriated;

(b) if the full amount of the debt or claim of the creditor is not admitted by the company, and is not such as the company are willing to set apart and appropriate, or if the amount is contingent or not ascertained, then the Court may, if it thinks fit, enquire into and adjudicate upon the validity of such debt of claim, and the amount for which the company may be liable in respect thereof, in the same manner as if the company were being wound up by the Court, and the amount fixed by the Court on such inquiry and adjudication shall be set apart and appropriated.

Order and minute to be registered

26. (1) The Registrar upon the production to him of an order of the Court confirming the reduction of the capital of a company, and the delivery to him of a copy of the order and of a minute (approved by the Court), showing with respect to the capital of the company, as altered by the order, the amount of such capital, the number of shares in which it is to be divided, and the amount of each share, shall register the order and minute, and, on the registration, the special resolution confirmed by the order so registered shall take effect.

(2) Notice of such registration shall be published in such manner as the Court may direct.

(3) The Registrar shall certify under his hand the registration of the order and minute, and his certificate shall be conclusive evidence that all the requisitions of this Act with respect to the reduction of capital have been complied with, and that the capital of the company is such as is stated in the minute.

Minute to form part of Memorandum of Association

27. The minute, when registered, shall be deemed to be substituted for the corresponding part of the Memorandum of Association of the company, and shall be of the same validity and subject to the same alterations as if it had been originally contained in the Memorandum of Association, and subject as in this Act mentioned, no member of the company, whether past or present, shall be liable, in respect of any share, to any call or contribution exceeding in amount the difference, if any, between the amount which has been paid on such share and the amount of the share as fixed by the minute.

Savings of rights of creditors who are ignorant of proceedings

28. If any creditor who is entitled in respect of any debt or claim to object to the reduction of the capital of a company under this Act is, in consequence of his ignorance of the proceedings taken with a view to such reduction, or of their nature and effect with respect to his claim, not entered on the list of creditors, and after such reduction the company is unable, within the meaning of section

116 to pay the creditor the amount of such debt or claim, every person who was a member of the company at the date of registration of the order and minute relating to the reduction of the capital of the company shall be liable to contribute for the payment of such debt or claim an amount not exceeding the amount which he would have been liable to contribute if the company had commenced to be wound up on the day prior to such registration; and on the company being wound up the Court, on the application of such creditor, and on proof that he was ignorant of the proceedings taken with a view to the reduction, or of their nature and effect with respect to his claim, may if it thinks fit, settle a list of such contributories accordingly, and make and enforce calls and orders on the contributories settled in such list in the same manner in all respects as if they were ordinary contributories in winding up; but the provisions of this section shall not affect the rights of the contributories of the company among themselves.

Copy of registered minute

29. A minute, when registered, shall be embodied in every copy of the Memorandum of Association issued after its registration, and if any company makes default in complying with the provisions of this section, it shall incur a penalty not exceeding four dollars and eighty cents for each copy in respect of which such default is made, and every director and manager of the company, who shall knowingly and wilfully authorize or permit such default, shall incur the like penalty.

Penalty on concealment of name of creditor

30. If any director, manager or officer of the company wilfully conceals the name of any creditor of the company, who is entitled to object to the proposed, or wilfully misrepresents the nature or amount of the debt or claim of any creditor of the company, or if the director or manager of the company aids or abets in or is privy to any such concealment or misrepresentation as aforesaid, every such director, manager, or officer shall be guilty of a misdemeanour.

Further provisions as to reduction of capital

31.(1) Where the reduction of the capital of a company does not involve either the diminution of any liability in respect of unpaid capital, or the payment to any shareholder of any paid up capital -

(a) the creditors of the company shall not unless the Court otherwise directs, be entitled to object or required to consent to the reduction; and

(b) it shall not be necessary before the presentation of the petition for confirming the reduction to add, and the Court may, if it thinks it expedient to do so, dispense altogether with the addition of the words "and reduced" as hereinbefore mentioned.

(2) In any case in which the Court thinks fit so to do, it may require the company to publish, in such manner as it thinks fit, the reasons for the reduction of its capital, or such other information in regard to the reduction of its capital, as the Court may think expedient with a view to give proper information to the public in relation to the reduction of its capital by a company, and, if the Court thinks fit, the causes which led to such reduction.

(3) The minute required to be registered in the case of the reduction shall show, in addition to the other particulars required by law, the amount, if any, at the date of registration of the minute, proposed to be deemed to have been paid up on each share.

Power to reduce capital by the cancellation of unissued shares

32. Any company limited by shares may so far modify the conditions contained in its Memorandum of Association, if authorized so to do by its regulations as originally framed, or as altered by special resolution, as to reduce its capital by cancelling any shares, which at the date of the passing of such resolution, have not been taken or agreed to be taken by any person; and the provisions of sections 21 to 30 shall not apply to any reduction of capital made in pursuance of the section.

Accumulated profits may be returned to shareholders in reduction of capital

33.(1) When any company has accumulated a sum of undivided profits, which, with the consent of shareholders, may be distributed among the shareholders in the form of a dividend or bonus, it shall be lawful for the company, by special resolution, to return the same, or any part thereof, to the shareholders in reduction of the paid up capital of the company, the unpaid capital being thereby increased by a similar amount.

(2) The powers vested in the directors of making calls upon the shareholders, in respect of moneys unpaid on their shares, shall extend to the amount of unpaid capital as augmented by such reduction.

No resolution to take effect until particulars have been registered

34. No such special resolution as aforesaid shall take effect until a Memorandum, showing the particulars required by law in the case of a reduction of capital by order of the Court, shall have been produced to and registered by the Registrar.

Power to any shareholder within one month after passing of resolution, to require company to retain moneys paid upon shares held by such person

35. Upon any reduction of paid up capital made in pursuance of the last two preceding sections, it shall be lawful for any one or more of several joint shareholders, within one month after the passing of the special resolution for such reduction, to require the company to retain, and the company shall retain accordingly, the whole of the moneys actually paid upon the shares held by such person, either alone or jointly with any other person or persons, and which, in consequence of such reduction, would otherwise be returned to him or them; and, thereupon, the shares in respect of which the said moneys shall be so retained shall, in regard to the payment of dividends thereon, be deemed to be paid up to the same extent only as the shares on which payment, as aforesaid, has been accepted by the shareholders in reduction of their paid up capital; and the company shall invest and keep invested the moneys so retained, in such securities authorized for investment by trustees as the company shall determine, and upon the money so invested, or upon so much thereof as, from time to time, exceeds the amount of calls subsequently made upon the shares in respect of which such moneys shall have been retained, the company shall pay such interest as shall be received by them, from time to time, on such securities, and the amount so retained and invested shall be held to represent the future calls which may be made to replace the capital so reduced on those shares, whether the amount obtained on sale of the whole, or such proportion thereof as represents the amount of any call when made, produces more or less than the amount of such call.

Company to specify amounts which shareholders have required them to retain under s.35; also to specify amounts of profits returned to shareholders

36. From and after such reduction of capital under sections 33 and 34, the company shall specify in the annual lists of members to be made by them in pursuance of the last preceding section, and the company shall also specify in the statements of account laid before any general marketing of the company the amount of the undivided profits of the company which shall have been returned to the shareholders in reduction of the paid up capital of the company under sections 33 and amounts of 34.

Power to issue redeemable shares

36A.(1) Subject to the provisions of this section, a company limited by shares may, if so authorized by its Articles of Association, issues shares which are, or at the option of the company are to be liable, to be redeemed: -

Provided that no such shares shall be redeemed unless a director or manager shall first have filed with the Registrar a declaration that the proposed redemption will leave unimpaired capital or other assets of not less than the paid up value of the shares which are not to be redeemed or are not redeemable in addition to such sum as at the date of the proposed redemption would be required to meet the liabilities of the company.

(2) Subject to the provisions of this section, the redemption of shares thereunder may be effected on such terms and in such manner as may be provided by the Articles of Association of the company.

(3) The redemption of shares under this section by a company shall not be taken as reducing the amount of the company's authorized share capital.

(4) Where in pursuance of this section a company has redeemed or is about to redeem any shares, it shall have power to issue shares up to the nominal amount of the shares redeemed or to be redeemed as if those shares had never been issued.

(5) The capital redemption reserve fund may, notwithstanding anything in this section, be applied by the company in paying up unissued shares of the company to be issued to members of the company as fully paid bonus shares.

Subdivision Of Shares

Shares may be divided into shares of smaller amount

37. Any company limited by shares may, by special resolution, so far modify the conditions contained in its Memorandum of Association, if authorized so to do by its regulations as originally framed or as altered by special resolution, as by subdivision of its existing shares or any of them, to divide its capital, or part thereof, into shares of smaller amount than is fixed by its Memorandum of Association:

Provided that, in the subdivision of existing shares, the proportion between the amount which is paid and the amount, if any, which is unpaid on each share of reduced amount shall be the same as it was in the case of the existing share or shares from which the share of reduced amount is derived.

Special resolution to be embodied in Memorandum of Association

38. The statement of the number and amount of shares into which the capital of the company is divided, contained in every copy of the Memorandum of Association issued after the passing of any such special resolution, shall be in accordance with such resolution; and any company which makes default in complying with the provisions of this section shall incur a penalty not exceeding four dollars and eighty cents for each copy in respect of which such default is made; and every director and manager of the company who knowingly or wilfully authorized or permits such default shall incur the like penalty.

Articles Of Association

Regulations to be prescribed by Articles of Association

39. The Memorandum of Association may, in the case of a company limited by shares, and shall, in the case of a company limited by guarantee or unlimited, be accompanied, when registered, by Articles of Association, signed by the subscribers to the Memorandum of Association and prescribing such regulations for the company as the subscribers to Memorandum of Association deem expedient. The Articles shall be expressed in separate paragraphs, numbered arithmetically. They may adopt all or any of the provisions contained in the table marked A in the First Schedule. They shall, in the case of a company, whether limited by guarantee or unlimited, that has a capital divided into shares, state the amount of capital with which the company proposes to be registered, and, in the case of a company, whether limited by guarantee or unlimited, that has not a capital divided into shares, state the number of members with which the company proposes to be registered, for the purpose of enabling the Registrar to determine the fees payable on registration. In a company limited by guarantee or unlimited, and having a capital divided into shares, each subscriber shall take one share at the least, and shall write opposite to his name in the Memorandum of Association the number of shares he takes.

Application of Table A.

40. In the case of a company limited by shares, if the Memorandum of Association is not accompanied by Articles of Association, or in so far as the Articles do not exclude or modify the regulations contained in the table marked A in the First Schedule, the last-mentioned regulations shall, so far as the same are applicable, be deemed to be the regulations of the company, in the same manner and to the same extent as if they had been inserted in the Articles of Association and the Articles had been duly registered.

Signature and effect of Articles of Association Cap.67.

41. The Articles of Association shall be printed and shall be signed by each subscriber in the presence of, and be attested by, one witness at the least, and such attestation shall be a sufficient attestation for all purposes under the Registration and Records Act; when registered they shall bind the company and the members thereof to the same extent as if each member had subscribed his name and affixed his seal thereto, and there were in such Articles contained a covenant on the part of himself, his heirs, executors, and administrators to conform to all the regulations contained in such Articles, subject to the provisions of this Act; and all moneys payable by any member to the company, in pursuance of the conditions and regulations of the company, or any of such conditions or regulations, shall be deemed to be a specialty debt due from such member to the company.

General Provisions

Registration of Memorandum and Articles

42. The Memorandum of Association and the Articles of Association, if any, shall be delivered to the Registrar, who shall retain and register the same. There shall be paid to the Registrar by a company having a capital divided into shares, in respect of the several matters mentioned in the table marked B in the First Schedule, the several fees therein specified, or such smaller fees as the Governor aforesaid may from time to time direct; and all fees paid to the said Registrar in pursuance of this Act shall be paid into the Treasury to be applied as is hereinafter provided.

Effect of registration.

43. Upon the registration of the Memorandum of Association, and of the Articles of Association in cases where Articles of Association are required by this Act or by the desire of the parties to be registered, the Registrar shall certify under his hand that the company is incorporated, and, in the case of a limited company, that the company is limited. The subscribers of the Memorandum of Association, together with such other persons as may from time to time become members of the company, shall thereupon be a body corporate by the name contained in the Memorandum of Association, capable forthwith of exercising all the functions of an incorporated company, and having perpetual succession and a common seal, with power to hold and to sue and to be sued, but with such liability on the part of the members to contribute to the assets of the company in the event of the same being wound up as is hereinafter mentioned. A certificate of the incorporation of any company, given by the Registrar, shall be conclusive evidence that all the requisitions of this Act in respect of registration have been complied with: Provided that any certificate of the incorporation of any company, given by the Registrar for the time being, shall be received in evidence as if it were the original certificate, and any copy of, or extract from, any of the documents or part of the documents, kept and registered at the office for the registration of joint stock companies, if duly certified to be a true copy under the hand of the Registrar for the time being, and whom it shall not be necessary to prove to be the Registrar, shall, in all legal proceedings, civil or criminal, and in all cases whatsoever, be received in evidence as of equal validity with the original document.

Copies of Memorandum and Articles to be given to members.

44.A copy of the Memorandum of Association, having annexed thereto the Articles of Association, if any, shall be forwarded to every member, at his request, on payment of the sum of twenty-four cents for each copy; and if any company makes default in forwarding a copy of the Memorandum of Association and Articles of Association, if any, to a member in pursuance of this section, the company so making default shall for each offence incur a penalty not exceeding four dollars and eighty cents.

PART II - Distribution Of Capital And Liability Of Members.

Distribution Of Capital

Nature and interest in company

45. The shares or other interest of any member in a company under this Act shall be personal state, capable of being transferred in manner provided by the regulations of the company, and shall not be of the nature in real estate; and each share shall, in case of a company having a capital divided into shares, be distinguished by its appropriate number.

Definition of "member".

46. The subscribers of the Memorandum of Association of any company under this Act shall be deemed to have agreed to become members of the company whose Memorandum they have subscribed, and, upon the registration of the Company, shall be entered as members on the register of members hereinafter mentioned; and every other person who has agreed to become a member or a company under this Act, and whose name is entered on the register or members; shall be deemed to be a member of the company.

Transfer by personal representative.

47. Any transfer of the share or other interest of a deceased member of a company under this Act, made by his personal representative, shall, notwithstanding such personal representative may not himself be a member, be of the same validity as if he had been a member at the time of execution of the instrument of transfer.

Register of members.

48.(1) Every company under this Act shall cause to be kept in one or more books a register of its members, and there shall be entered therein the following particulars -

(a) the names and addresses, and the occupations, if any, of the members of the company, with the addition, in the case of a company having a capital divided into shares, of a statement of the shares held by each member, distinguishing each share by its number, and of the amount paid, or agreed to be considered as paid, on the shares of each member;

(b) the date at which the name of any person was entered in the register as a member;

(c) the date at which any person ceased to be a member.

(2) Any company acting in contravention of this section shall incur a penalty not exceeding twenty-four dollars for every day during which its default in complying with the provisions of this section continues, and every director or manager of the company who shall knowingly and wilfully authorize and permit such contravention shall incur the like penalty.

Annual list of members and summary.

49.(1) Every company having a share capital shall make a list of all persons who on the 30th day following the date of incorporation of the company and subsequently on the 30th day of June in every year following the year of incorporation of the company are members of the company, and of all persons who have ceased to be members since the date of the last return or, in the case of the first return, of the incorporation of the company.

(2) The list shall state the names, addresses, and occupations of all past and present members therein mentioned, and the numbers of shares held by each of the existing members at the date of the return specifying shares transferred since the last return or (in the case of the first return) of the incorporation of the company by persons who are still members and have ceased to be members respectively and the dates of registration of the transfers, and shall contain a summary distinguishing between shares issued for cash and shares issued as fully or partly paid up otherwise than in cash, and specifying the following particulars: -

(a) the amount of the share capital of the company, and the number of the shares into which it is divided;

(b) the number of shares taken from the commencement of the company up to the date of the return;

(c) the amount called up on each share;

(d) the total amount of calls received;

(e) the total amount of calls unpaid;

(f) the total amount of the sums (if any) paid by way of commission in respect of any shares or debentures, or allowed by way of discount in respect of any debentures, since the date of the last return;

(g) the total number of share forfeited;

(h) the total amount of shares or stock for which share warrants are outstanding at the date of the return;

(i) the total amount of share warrants issued and surrendered respectively since the date of the last return;

(j) the number of shares or amount of stock comprised in each share warrant;

(k) the names and addresses of the persons who at the date of the return are the directors of the company, or occupy the position of directors, by whatever name called; and

(l) the total amount of debt due from the company in respect of all mortgages and charges which are required to be registered with the Registrar under this Act.

(3) The summary shall also (except where the company is a private company) include -

(a) a statement made up to such date as may be specified in the statement, in the form of a Balance Sheet, audited by the company's auditors, and containing a summary of its share capital, its liabilities and its assets, giving such particulars as will disclose the general nature of these liabilities and assets, and how the values of the fixed assets have been arrived at;

(b) a further statement showing what part, if any, of the issued capital of the company consists of redeemable shares and the earliest date on which the company has power to redeem those shares.

(4) The above list and summary must be contained in a separate part of the register of members and not later than thirty days of the date of the first return and not later than the 30th day of September in each year following the year of incorporation the company shall forward to the Registrar a copy signed by a director or manager or secretary of the company.

Penalty on company not forwarding list to Registrar.

50. Any company under this Act, having a capital divided into shares, makes default in complying with the provisions of this Act, with respect to forwarding such list of members or summary as is hereinbefore mentioned to the Registrar, such company will incur the penalties specified hereinafter -

Period of Default	Penalty V per Centum
Not exceeding 1 month	20% fee payable for filing such document.
Exceeding 1 month but not exceeding 3 months	50% of fee payable for filing such document.
Exceeding 3 months but not exceeding 12 month	100% of fee payable for filing such document.
Exceeding 12 months each year of default,	100% of fee payable for filing such document for

and every director and manager of the company who shall knowingly and wilfully authorize or permit such default shall incur the like penalty.

Company to give notice of consolidation or of conversion of capital into stock

51. Every company under this Act, having a capital divided into shares, that has consolidated and divided its capital into shares of larger amount than its existing shares, or converted any portion of its capital into stock, shall give notice to the Registrar, of such consolidation, division, or conversion, specifying the shares so consolidated, divided, or converted.

Effect of conversion of shares into stock.

52. Where any company under this Act, and having a capital divided into shares, has converted any portion of its capital into stock, and given notice of such conversion to the Registrar, all the provisions of the provisions of this Act which are applicable to shares only shall cease as to so much of the capital as is converted into stock; and the register of members to be forwarded to the Registrar, shall show the amount of stock held by each member in the list, instead of the amount of shares and the particulars relating to shares hereinbefore required.

No trusts on register.

53. No notice of any trust expressed, implied or constructive, shall be entered on the register, or be receivable by the Registrar, in the case of companies registered under this Act.

Certificate of shares or stock.

54.A certificate, under the common seal of the company, specifying any share or shares or stock held by any member of a company, shall be prima facie evidence of the title of the member to the share or shares or stock therein specified.

Inspection of register

55. The register of members, commencing from the date of the registration of the company, shall be kept at the registered office of the company hereinafter mentioned; except when closed as hereinafter mentioned, it shall during business hours, but subject to such reasonable restrictions as the company in general meeting may impose, so that not less than two hours in each day be appointed for inspection, be open to the inspection of any member gratis, and to the inspection of any other person on the payment of twenty-four cents, or such less sum as the company may prescribe, for, each inspection; and every such member or other person may require a copy of such register, or of any part thereof, or of such list or summary of members as in hereinbefore mentioned, on payment of twelve cents for every hundred words required to be copied. If such inspection or copy is refused, the company shall incur for each refusal a penalty not exceeding nine dollars and sixty cents for every day during which such refusal continues and every director and manager of the company who shall knowingly authorize or permit such refusal shall incur the like penalty; and, in addition to the above penalty, the Court may, by order, compel an immediate inspection of the register.

Power to close register

56. Any company under this Act may, upon giving notice by advertisement in the Gazette or other paper used for official notification, and in some paper, if any, circulating in the Territory, close the register of members for any time or times not exceeding in the whole thirty days in each year.

Notice of increase of capital and of members to be given to Registrar

57. Where a company has a capital divided into shares, whether such shares may or may not have been converted into stock, notice of any increase in such capital beyond the registered capital, and where a company has not a capital divided into shares, notice of any increase in the number of members beyond the registered number, shall be given to the Registrar, in the case of an increase in capital, within thirty days from the date of the passing of the resolution by which such increase has been authorized; and, in the case of an increase of members, within thirty days from the time at which such increase of members has been resolved on or has taken place, and the Registrar shall forthwith record the amount of such increase of capital or members. If such notice is not given within the time period aforesaid, the company in default shall incur a penalty not exceeding one hundred dollars for every day during which such neglect to give notice continues; and every director and manager of the company who shall knowingly and wilfully authorize or permit such default shall incur the like penalty.

Remedy for improper entry, or omission of entry, in register.

58. If the name of any person is, without sufficient cause entered in or omitted from the register of members of any company under this Act, or if default is made or unnecessary delay takes place in entering on the register the fact of any person having ceased to be a member of the company, the person or member aggrieved, or any member of the company, or the company itself, may apply to the Court for an order that the register may be rectified; and the Court may either refuse such application, with or without cost, to be paid by the applicant, or may, if satisfied of the justice of the case, make an order for the rectification of the register, and may direct the company to pay all the costs of such motion, application or petition, and any damages the party aggrieved may have sustained. The Court may, in any proceeding under this section, decide on any question relating to the title of any person who is a party to such proceeding to have his name entered in or omitted from the register, whether such question arises between two or more members or alleged members, or between any members or alleged members and the company, and generally the Court may in any such proceeding decide any question that it may be necessary or expedient to decide for the rectification of the register: Provided that the Court may direct an issue to be tried, on the trial of which any question of law may be raised for the decision of the Court of Appeal.

Notice to Registrar of rectification of register.

59. Whenever any order has been made rectifying the register, in the case of a company hereby required to send a list of its members to the Registrar, the Court shall, by order, direct that due notice of such rectification be given to the Registrar.

Register to be evidence.

60. The register of members shall be prima facie evidence of any matters by this Act directed or authorized to be inserted therein.

Reserve Capital

Reserve capital of company, how provided.

61.(1) An unlimited company may, by the resolution passed by the members when assenting to registration as a limited company under this Act, and for the purpose of such registration or otherwise, increase the nominal amount of its capital by increasing the nominal amount of each of its shares:

Provided that no part of such increased capital shall be capable of being called up, except in the event, and for the purposes, of the company being wound up.

(2) In cases where no such increase of nominal capital may be resolved upon, an unlimited company may, by such resolution as aforesaid, provide that a portion of its uncalled capital shall not be capable of being called up except in the event, and for the purposes of the company being wound up.

(3) A limited company may, by special resolution, declare that any portion of its capital which has not been already called up shall not be capable of being called up, except in the event, and for the purposes, of the company being wound up; and, thereupon, such portion of capital shall not be capable of being called up, except in the event, and for the purposes, of the company being wound up.

Liability Of Members

Liability of present and past members of company.

62. In the event of a company formed under this Act being wound up, every present and past member of such company shall be liable to contribute to the assets of the company to an amount sufficient for payment of the debts and liabilities of the company, and the costs, charges, and expenses of the winding up, and for the payment of such sums as may be required for the adjustment of the rights of the contributories amongst themselves, with the qualifications following, that is to say -

(a) No past member shall be liable to contribute to the assets of the company if he has ceased to be a member for a period of one year or upwards prior to the commencement of the winding up;

(b) No past member shall be liable to contribute in respect of any debt or liability of the company contracted after the time at which he ceased to be a member;

(c) No past member shall be liable to contribute to the assets of the company unless it appears to the Court that the existing members are unable to satisfy the contributions required to be made by them in pursuance of this Act;

(d) In the case of a company limited by shares, no contribution shall be required from any member exceeding the amount, if any, unpaid on the shares in respect of which he is liable as a present or past member;

(e) In the case of a company limited by guarantee, no contribution shall be required from any member exceeding the amount of the undertaking entered into on his behalf by the Memorandum of Association;

(f) Nothing in this Act contained shall invalidate any provision contained in any

contract whereby the liability of individual members upon any such contract is restricted, or whereby the funds of the company are alone made liable in respect of such contract;

(g) No sum due to any member of a company, in his character of a member, by way of dividends, profits or otherwise, shall be deemed to be a debt of the company, payable to such member, in a case of competition between himself and any other creditor not being a member of the company; but any such sum may be taken into account, for the purposes of final adjustment of the rights of the contributories amongst themselves.

Calls Upon Shares

Company may have some shares fully paid and others not.

63. Nothing contained in this Act shall be deemed to prevent any company under this Act, if authorized by its regulations as originally framed, or as altered by special resolution, from doing any one or more of the following things -

(a) making arrangements on the issue of shares for a difference between the holders of such shares in the amount of calls to be paid, and in the time of payment of such calls;

(b) accepting from any member of the company who assents thereto the whole or part of the amount remaining unpaid on any share or shares held by him, either in discharge of the amount of a call payable in respect of any other share or shares held by him, or without any call having been made;

(c) paying dividends in proportion to the amount paid up in each share in cases where a larger amount is paid up on some shares than on others.

Manner in which shares are to be issued and held

64. Every share in any company shall be deemed and taken to have been issued and to be held subject to the payment of the whole amount thereof in cash, unless the same shall have been otherwise determined by a contract duly made in writing and filed with the Registrar within thirty days of the issue of such shares:

Provided that in case of default in delivering to the Registrar within thirty days of such issue of any document required to be delivered by this section, the company or any officer liable for default may apply to the Court for relief, and the Court, if satisfied that the omission to deliver was accidental or due to inadvertence or that it is just and equitable to grant relief may make an order extending the time for the delivery of the document for such period as the Court may think proper.

Transfer Of Shares

Transfer may be registered at request of transferor.

65. A company shall, on the application of the transferor of any share or interest in the company enter in its register of members the name of the transferee of such share or interest, in the same manner and subject to the same conditions as if the application for such entry were made by the transferee.

Share Warrants To Bearer

Warrant of limited shares fully paid up may be issued in name of bearer

66. In the case of a company limited by shares, the company, if authorized so to do by its regulations as originally framed, or as altered by special resolution, and subject to the provisions of such regulations, may, with respect to any share which is fully paid up, or with respect to stock, issue under their common seal a warrant stating that the bearer of the warrant is entitled to the share or shares of stock therein specified, and may provide, by coupons or otherwise, for the payment of the future dividends on the share or shares of stock included in such warrant, hereinafter referred to as a share warrant.

Effect of share warrant

67.A share warrant shall entitle the bearer of such warrant to the shares or stock specified in it and such shares or stock may be transferred by the delivery of the share warrant.

Re-registration of bearer of a share warrant in the register

68. The bearer of a share warrant shall, subject to the regulations of the company, be entitled, on surrendering such warrant for cancellation, to have his name entered as a member in the register of members, and the company shall be responsible for any loss incurred by any person by reason of the company entering in its register of members the name of any bearer of a share warrant in respect of the shares or stock specified therein without the share warrant being surrendered and cancelled.

Regulations of the company may make the bearer of a share warrant a member

69. The bearer of a share warrant may, if the regulations of the company so provide, be deemed to be a member of the company within the meaning of this Act, either to the full extent or for such purposes as may be prescribed by the regulations:

Provided that the bearer of a share warrant shall not be qualified in respect of the shares or stock specified in such warrant for being a director or manager of the company in cases where such a qualification is prescribed by the regulations of the company.

Entries in register where share warrant issued

70.(1) On the issue of a share warrant in respect of any share or stock, the company shall strike out of its register of members the name of the member then entered therein as holding such share or stock, as if he had ceased to be a member, and shall enter in the register the following particulars -

(a) the fact of the issue of the warrant;

(b) a statement of the shares or stock included in the warrant, distinguishing each share by its number;

(c) the date of the issue of the warrant.

(2) Until the warrant is surrendered, the above particulars shall be deemed to be the particulars which are required by section 48 to be entered in the register of members of a company; and on the surrender of a warrant, the date of such surrender shall be entered as if it were the date at which a person ceased to be a member.

Particulars to be contained in annual summary

71. After the issue by the company of a share warrant, the annual summary required by section 49, shall contain the following particulars: the total amount of shares or stock for which share warrants are outstanding at the date of the summary, and the total amount of share warrants which have been issued and surrendered respectively since the last summary was made, and the number of shares or amount of stock comprised in each warrant.

Penalties on persons committing forgery

72. Whosoever forges, or alters, or offers, utters, disposes of, or puts off, knowing the same to be forged or altered, any share warrant or coupon, or any document purporting to be share warrant or coupon, issued in pursuance of this Act, or demands or endeavours to obtain or receive any share or interest of or in any company under this Act, or to receive any dividend or money payable in respect thereof, by virtue of any such forged or altered share warrant, coupon or document, purporting as aforesaid, knowing the same to be forged or altered, with intent in any of the cases aforesaid to defraud, shall be guilty of felony, and shall be liable to be imprisoned for any term not exceeding two years with or without hard labour.

Penalties on person falsely personating owner of shares

73. Whosoever falsely and deceitfully personates any owner of any share or interest of or in any company, or of any share warrant or coupon issued in pursuance of this Act, and thereby obtains or endeavours to obtain any such share or interest, or share warrant or coupon, or receives or endeavours to receive any money due to any such owner, as if such offender were the true and lawful owner, shall be guilty of felony, and shall be liable to be imprisoned for any term not exceeding two years with or without hard labour.

Penalties on persons engraving plates, etc.

74. Whosoever, without lawful authority or excuse, the proof whereof shall be on the party accused, engraves or makes upon any plate, wood, stone or other material any share warrant or coupon, purporting to be a share warrant or coupon issued or made by any particular company under and in pursuance of this Act, or to be a blank share warrant, or coupon issued or made as aforesaid or to be a part of such a share warrant or coupon, or uses any such plate, wood, stone or other material, for the making or printing any such share warrant or coupon, or any such blank share warrant or coupon or any part thereof respectively, or knowingly has in his custody or possession any such plate, wood, stone, or other material, shall be guilty of felony, and shall be liable to be imprisoned for any term not exceeding two years with or without hard labour.

Contracts

Contracts how made

75.(1) Contracts on behalf of any company under this Act may be made as follows, that is to say -

(a) Any contract which, if made between private persons, would be by law required to be in writing, and, if made according to the law in the Territory, to be under seal, may be made on behalf of the company in writing under the common seal of the company, and such contract may be in the same manner varied or discharged;

(b) Any contract which, if made between private persons, would be by law required to be in writing, and signed by the parties to be charged therewith, may be made on behalf of the company in writing signed by any person acting under the express or implied authority of the company, and such contract may in the same manner be varied or discharged;

(c) Any contract which, if made between private persons, would by law be valid, although made by parole only, and not reduced into writing, may be made by parole on behalf of the company by any person acting under the express or implied authority of the company, and such contract may be in the same way varied or discharged.

(2) All contracts made according to the provisions herein contained shall be effectual in law, and shall be binding upon the company and their successors, and all other parties thereto their heirs, executors, or administrators as the case may be.

Prospectus, etc. to specify dates and names of parties to any contract made prior to issue of such prospectus, etc.

76. Every prospectus of a company, and every notice inviting persons to subscribe for shares in any joint stock company, shall specify the dates and the names of the parties to any contract entered into by the company, or the promoters, directors, or trustees thereof, before the issue of such prospectus or notice, whether subject to adoption by the directors or the company, or otherwise; and any prospectus or notice not specifying the same shall be deemed fraudulent on the part of the promoters, directors, and officers of the company knowingly issuing the same, as regards any person taking shares in the company on the faith of such prospectus, unless he shall have had notice of such contract.

PART III - Management And Administration

Provisions For Protection Of Creditors

Registered office of company

77. Every company under this Act shall have a registered office, to which all communications and notices may be addressed. If any company under this Act carries on business without having such an office, it shall incur a penalty not exceeding twenty-four dollars for every day during which business is so carried on.

Notice of situation of registered office.

78. Notice of the situation of such registered office, and of any change therein, shall be given to the Registrar, and recorded by him. Until such notice is given the company shall not be deemed to have complied with the provisions of this Act with respect to having a registered office.

Publication of name by a limited company.

79. Every limited company under this Act, whether limited by shares or by guarantee, shall paint or affix, and keep painted or affixed, its name on the outside of every office or place which the business of the company is carried on, in a conspicuous position, in letters easily legible, and shall have its name engraved in legible characters on its seal, and shall have its name engraved in legible characters in all notices, advertisements, and other official publications of such company, and in all bills of exchange, promissory notes, endorsements, cheques, and orders for money or goods purporting to be signed by or on behalf of such company, and in all bills of parcels, invoices, receipts and letters of credit of the company.

Penalties on non-publication of name

80. If any limited company under this Act does not paint or affix, and keep painted or affixed, its name in manner by this Act, it shall be liable to a penalty not exceeding twenty-four dollars for not so painting or affixing its name, for every day during which such name is not so kept painted or affixed; and every director and manager of the company who shall knowingly and wilfully authorize or permit such default shall be liable to the like penalty; and if any director, manager, or officer of such company, or any person on its behalf, uses or authorizes the use of any seal purporting to be the seal of the company whereon its name is not so engraven as aforesaid, or issues or authorizes the issue of any notice, advertisement, or other official publication of such company, or signs or authorizes to be signed on behalf of such company any bill of exchange, promissory note, endorsement, cheque, order for money or goods, or issues or authorizes to be issued any bill of parcels, invoice, receipt, or letter of credit of the company, wherein its name is not mentioned in manner aforesaid, he shall be liable to a penalty of two hundred and forty dollars, and shall further be personally liable to the holder of any such bill of exchange, promissory note, cheque, or order for money or goods, for the amount thereof, unless the same is duly paid by the company.

Register of mortgages

81. Every limited company under this Act shall keep a register of all mortgages and charges specifically affecting property of the company, and shall enter in such register, in respect of each mortgage or charge, a short description of the property mortgaged or charged, the amount of charge created, and the names of the mortgagees or persons entitled to such charge. If any property of the company is mortgaged or charged without such entry as aforesaid being made, every director, manager, or other officer of the company, who knowingly and wilfully authorizes or permits the omission of such entry, shall incur a penalty not exceeding two hundred and forty dollars. The register of mortgages required by this section shall be open to inspection by any creditor or member of the company at all reasonable times; and if such inspection is refused, any officer of the company refusing the same, and every director and manager of the company authorizing or wilfully and knowingly permitting such refusal, shall incur a penalty not exceeding twenty-four dollars, and a further penalty not exceeding nine dollars and sixty cents for every day during which such refusal continues; and, in addition to the above penalty, the Court may, by order, compel an immediate inspection of the register.

Certain companies to publish statement entered in First Schedule

82.(1) Every deposit, provident or benefit society under this Act shall, before it commences business, and also on the first Monday of February and the first Monday in August in every year during which it carries on business, make a statement in the table marked D in the First Schedule, or as near thereto as circumstances will admit; and a copy of such statement shall be put up in a conspicuous place in the registered office of the company, and in every branch office or place where the business of the company is carried on; and, if default is made in compliance with the provisions of this section, the company shall be liable to a penalty not exceeding twenty-four dollars for every day during which such default continues, and every director or manager of the company who shall knowingly and wilfully authorize or permit such default shall incur the like penalty.

(2) Every member and every creditor of any company mentioned in this section shall be entitled to a copy of the above-mentioned statement on payment of a sum not exceeding twelve cents.

List of directors to be sent to Registrar.

83. Every company under this Act, and not having a capital divided into shares, shall keep at its registered office, a register containing the names and addresses and the occupations of its directors or managers, and shall send to the Registrar a copy of such register, and shall from time to time notify to the Registrar any change that takes place in such directors or managers.

Penalty on company not keeping register of directors.

84. If any company under this Act, and not having a capital divided into shares, makes default in keeping a register of its directors and managers, or in sending a copy of such register to the Registrar in compliance with the foregoing rules, or in notifying to the Registrar any change that takes place in such directors or managers, such delinquent company shall incur a penalty not exceeding twenty-four dollars for every day during which such default continues, and every director or manager of the company who shall knowingly and wilfully authorize or permit such default shall incur the like penalty.

Promissory notes and bills of exchange.

85. A promissory note or bill of exchange shall be deemed to have been made, accepted, or endorsed on behalf of any company under this Act, if made, accepted or endorsed in the name of the company by any person acting under the authority of the company, or if made, accepted, or endorsed by or on behalf or on account of the company, by any person acting under the authority of the company.

Prohibition against carrying on business with less than a certain number of members

86. If at any time the number of members of a company is reduced, in the case of a private company, below two, or, in the case of any other company below five, and it carries on business for a period of six months while the number is so reduced, every person who is a member of the company during the time that it so carries on less than a business after such period of six months and is cognizant of the fact that it is carrying on business with fewer than two members, or five members, as the case may be, shall be severally liable for the payment of the whole debts of the company contracted during such time, and may be sued for the same without joinder in the action of any other member.

Provisions For Protection Of Members

Company to hold meeting within four months after registration.

87. Every company formed under this Act shall hold a general meeting within four months after its Memorandum of Association is registered, and, if such meeting is not held, the company shall be liable to a penalty not exceeding twenty-four dollars a day for every day after the expiration of such four months until the meeting is held, and every director or manager of the company, and every subscriber of the Memorandum of Association, who knowingly authorizes or permits such default, shall be liable to the same penalty.

General meeting of company.

88.A general meeting of every company under this Act shall be held once at the least in every year.

Power to alter regulations by special resolution.

89. Subject to the provisions of this Act, and to the conditions contained in the Memorandum of Association, any company formed under this Act, may in general meeting, from time to time by passing a special resolution in manner hereinafter mentioned, alter all or any of the regulations of the company contained in the Articles of Association, or in the table marked A in the First Schedule where such table is applicable to the company, or make new regulations to the exclusion of, or in addition to, all or any of the regulations of the company; and any regulations so made by special resolution shall be deemed to be regulations of the company, of the same validity as if they had been originally contained in the Articles of Association, and shall be subject in like manner to be altered or modified by any subsequent special resolution.

Definition of special resolution.

90.A resolution passed by a company under this Act, shall be deemed to be special whenever a resolution has been passed by a majority of not less than three-fourths of such members of the company, for the time being entitled according to the regulations of the company to vote, as may be present, in person or by proxy (in cases where by the regulations of the company, proxies are allowed), at any general meeting of which notice specifying the intention to propose such resolution has been duly given. At any meeting mentioned in this section, unless a poll is demanded by at least two members, a declaration of the chairman that the resolution has been carried shall be deemed conclusive evidence of the fact, without proof of the number or proportion of the votes recorded in favour of or against the same. Notice of any meeting shall, for the purposes of this section, be deemed to be duly given, and the meeting to be duly held, whenever such notice is given and the meeting held in manner prescribed by the regulations of the company. In computing the majority under this section, when a poll is demanded, reference shall be made to the number of votes to which each

Provision where no regulations as to meetings.

91. In default of any regulations as to voting every member shall have one vote, and in default of any regulations as to summoning general meetings, a meeting shall be held to be duly summoned of which seven days notice in writing has been served on every member in manner in which notices are required to be served by the table marked A in the First Schedule; and in default of any regulations as to the persons to summon meetings, two members shall be competent to summon the same, and in default of any regulation as to who is to be chairman of such meeting, it shall be competent for any person elected by the members present to preside.

Registry of special resolutions.

92. A copy of any special resolution that is passed by any company under this Act shall be printed and forwarded to the Registrar of Joint Stock Companies and be recorded by him. If such copy is not so forwarded within fifteen days from the date of confirmation of the resolution, the company shall incur the penalties specified hereinafter -

Period of Delay	Penalty per Centum
Not exceeding 1 month	20% of the fee for recording the resolution.
Exceeding 1 month but not exceeding 3 months	50% of the fee for recording the resolution.
Exceeding 3 months but not exceeding 12 months	100% of the fee for recording the resolution.
Exceeding 12 months each year of default.	100% of the fee for recording the resolution for

Copies of special resolutions.

93. Where Articles of Association have been registered, a copy of every special resolution for the time being in force shall be annexed to or embodied in every copy of the Articles of Association that may be issued after the passing of such resolution. Where no Articles of Association have been registered, a copy of any special resolution shall be forwarded to any member requesting the same on payment of twenty-four cents; or such less sum as the company may direct; and if any company makes default in complying with the provisions of this section, it shall incur a penalty not exceeding four dollars and eighty cents for each copy in respect of which such default is made; and every director and manager of the company who shall knowingly and wilfully authorize or permit such default, shall incur the like penalty.

Execution of deeds abroad.

94. Any company under this Act may, by instrument in writing under its common seal, empower any person, either generally, or in respect of any specified matters, as its attorney, to execute deeds on its behalf in any place not situate in the Territory; and every deed signed by such attorney, on behalf of the company, and under his seal, shall be binding on the company, and have the same effect as if it were under the common seal of the company.

Examination of affairs of company by inspectors.

95. The Governor may appoint one or more competent inspectors to examine into the affairs of any company under this Act, and to report thereon in such manner as the Governor may direct, upon the application following, that is to say

(a) in the case of any company that has a capital divided into shares, upon the application of members holding not less than one-fifth part of the whole shares of the company for the time being issued;

(b) in the case of any company not having a capital divided into shares, upon the application of members being in number not less than one-fifth part of the whole number of persons for the time being entered on the register of the company as members.

Application for inspection to be supported by evidence.

96. The application shall be supported by such evidence as the Governor may require for the purpose of showing that the applicants have good reason for requiring such investigation to be made, and that they are not actuated by malicious motives in instituting the same. The Governor may also require the applicants to give security for payment of the cost of the enquiry before appointing any inspector or inspectors.

Inspection of books.

97.(1) It shall be the duty of all officers and agents of the company to produce for the examination of the inspectors all books and documents in their custody or power, and any inspector may examine upon oath the officers and agents of the company in relation to its business and administer such oath accordingly.

(2) If any officer or agent refuses to produce any book or document hereby directed to be produced, or to answer any question relating to the affairs of the company, he shall incur a penalty not exceeding twenty-four dollars in respect of each offence.

Result of examination how dealt with.

98. Upon the conclusion of the examination, the inspectors shall report their opinion to the Governor; and such report shall be written or printed as the Governor directs; a copy shall be forwarded to the registered office of the company, and a further copy shall, at the request of the members upon whose application the inspection was made, be delivered to them or to any one or more of them. All expenses of and incidental to any such examination as aforesaid shall be defrayed by the members upon whose application the inspectors were appointed, unless the Governor shall direct the same to be paid out of the assets of the company, which he is hereby authorized to do so.

Power of company to appoint inspectors.

99. Any company under this Act, may, by special resolution, appoint inspectors for the purposes of examining into the affairs of the company, and the inspectors so appointed shall have the same powers and perform the same duties as inspectors appointed by the Governor, with this exception, that instead of making their report to the Governor, they shall make the same in such manner and to such persons as the company in general meeting directs; and the officers and agents of the company shall incur the same penalties, in case of any refusal to produce any book or document hereby required to be produced to such inspectors, or to answer any question, as they would have incurred if such inspector had been appointed by the Governor.

Report of inspectors to be evidence.

100. A copy of the report of any inspectors appointed under this Act, authenticated by the seal into whose affairs they have made inspection, shall be admissible in any legal proceeding as evidence of the opinion of the inspectors in relation to any matter contained in such report.

Notices

Service of notices on company.

101. Any summons, notice, order or other document required to be served upon the company, may be served by leaving the same, or sending it through the post in a prepaid letter addressed to the company at their registered office.

Rules as to notices by letter.

102. Any document to be served by post on the company shall be posted in such time as to admit of its being delivered in the due course of delivery, within the period, if any, prescribed for the service thereof; and, in proving service of such document, it shall be sufficient to prove that such document was properly directed, and that it was put as a prepaid letter into the post office.

Authentication of notices of company.

103. Any summons, notice, order or proceeding of requiring authentication by the company may be signed by any director, secretary, or other authorized officer of the company, and need not be under the common seal of the company, and the same may be in writing or in print, or partly in writing and partly in print.

Legal Proceedings

Recovery of penalties.

104. All offences under this Act made punishable by any penalty shall be punishable on summary conviction.

Application of penalties.

105. The Magistrate imposing any penalty under this Act may direct the whole or any part thereof to be applied in or towards payment of the costs of the proceedings, or in or towards rewarding the person upon whose information or at whose suit such penalty has been recovered; and, subject to such direction, all penalties shall be paid into the Treasury.

Evidence of proceedings at meetings.

106. Every company under this Act shall cause minutes of all resolutions and proceedings of general meetings of the company, and of the directors or managers of the company in cases where there are directors or managers, to be duly entered in books to be from time to time provided for the purpose; and any such minute as aforesaid, if purporting to be signed by the chairman of the meeting at which such resolutions were passed or proceedings had, or by the chairman as evidence of the next succeeding meeting, shall be received as evidence in all legal proceedings; and, until the contrary is proved, every general meeting of the company or meeting of directors or managers in respect of the proceedings of which minutes have been so made shall be deemed to have been duly held and convened, and all resolutions passed thereat, or proceedings had, to have been duly passed and had, and all appointments of directors, managers or liquidators shall be deemed to be valid, and all acts done by such directors, managers or liquidators shall be valid, notwithstanding any defect that may afterwards be discovered in their appointment or qualifications.

Provisions as to costs in actions brought by certain limited companies.

107. Where a limited company is plaintiff in any action, suit, or other legal proceeding, the Court may, if it appear by any credible testimony that there is reason to believe that, if the defendant be successful in his defence, the assets of the company will be insufficient to pay his costs, require sufficient security to be given for such costs, and may stay all proceedings until such security is given.

Declaration in action against members.

108. In any action or suit brought by the company against any member to recover any call or other moneys due from such member in his character of member, it shall not be necessary to set forth the special matter, but it shall be sufficient to allege that the defendant is a member of the company, and is indebted to the company in respect of a call made, or other moneys due, whereby an action or suit has accrued to the company.

Arbitration

Power for companies to refer matters to arbitration.

109. Any company under this Act may from time to time, by writing under its common seal, agree to refer, and may refer, to arbitration any difference, question, or other matter whatsoever in dispute between itself and any other company or person, and the companies, parties to the arbitration, may delegate to the person or persons to whom the reference is made power to settle any terms or to determine any matter capable of being lawfully settled or determined by the companies themselves, or by the directors or other managing body of such companies.

Provisions of Arbitration Act 1976 to apply.

110. All arbitrations authorized or directed by this Act shall be conducted in accordance with the Arbitration Act 1976.

Part IV - Winding Up

Preliminary

Meaning of contributory.

111. The term "contributory" shall mean every person liable to contribute to the assets of a company under this Act in the event of the same being wound up; it shall also, in all proceedings for determining the persons who are to be deemed contributories, and in all proceedings prior to the final determination of such persons, include any person alleged to be a contributory.

Nature and liability of contributory.

112. The liability of any person to contribute to the assets of a company under this Act, in the event of the same being wound up, shall be deemed to create a debt of the nature of a specialty accruing due from such person at the time when his liability commenced, but payable at the time or respective times when calls are made, as hereinafter mentioned, for enforcing such liability; and it shall be lawful in the case of bankruptcy of any contributory to prove against his estate the estimated value of his liability to future calls as well as calls already made.

Contributories in case of death.

113. If any contributories dies, either before or after he has been placed on the list of contributories hereinafter mentioned, his personal representatives, heirs and devisees shall be liable, in a due course of administration, to contribute to the assets of the company in discharge of the liability of such deceased contributory, and such personal representatives, heirs and devisees shall be deemed to be contributories accordingly.

Contributories in case of bankruptcy.

114. If any contributory becomes bankrupt either before or after he has been placed on the list of contributories, his trustee shall be deemed to represent such bankrupt for all the purposes of winding up, and shall be deemed to be contributory accordingly, and may be called upon to admit proof against the estate of such bankrupt, or otherwise to allow to be paid out of his assets, in due course of law, any moneys due from such bankrupt in respect of his liability to contribute to the assets of the company being wound up.

Winding Up By Court

Circumstances under which company may be wound up by Court.

115.A company under this Act may be wound up by the Court under the following circumstances, that company may be is to say -

(a) whenever the company has passed a special resolution requiring the company to be wound up by the Court;

(*b*) whenever the company does not commence its business within a year from its incorporation, or suspends its business for the space of a whole year;

(*c*) whenever the members are reduced in number to less than five;

(*d*) whenever the company is unable to pay its debts;

(*e*) whenever the Court is of opinion that it is just and equitable that the company should be wound up.

Company when deemed unable to pay its debts

116. A company under this Act shall be deemed to be unable to pay its debts

(*a*) whenever a creditor, by assignment or otherwise, to whom the company is indebted, at law or in equity, in a sum exceeding two hundred and forty dollars then due, has served on the company, by leaving the same at the principal place of business of the company, or by delivering to the secretary or some director or principal officer of the company, or by otherwise serving the same in such manner as the Court may approve or direct, a demand under his hand requiring the company to pay the sum so due, and the company has, for the space of three weeks succeeding the service of such demand, neglected to pay such sum or to secure or compound for the same to the reasonable satisfaction of the creditor;

(*b*) whenever execution or other process issued on a judgment, decree, or order obtained in any Court in favour of any creditor, at law or in equity, in any proceeding instituted by such creditor against the company, is returned unsatisfied in whole or in part;

(*c*) whenever it is proved to the satisfaction of the Court that the company that the company is unable to pay its debts.

Application for winding up to be made by petition.

117. Any application to the Court for winding up of a company under this Act shall be by petition and such petition may be presented by the company or by one or more creditor or creditors, contributory or contributories, of the company, or by any of the above parties, together or separately; and every order which may be made on any such petition shall operate in favour of all the creditors and all the contributories of the company in the same manner as if it had been made upon the joint petition of a creditor and contributory;

Provided that no contributory of a company under this Act shall be capable of presenting a petition for winding up such company unless the members of the company are reduced in number to less than five, or unless the shares in respect of which he is a contributory, or some of them, either were originally allotted to him, or have been held by him and registered in his name for a period of at least six months during the eighteen months previously to the commencement of the winding up, or have devolved upon him through the death of a former holder.

Commencement of winding up by Court.

118. A winding up of a company by the Court shall be deemed to commence at the time of the presentation of the petition for the winding up.

Court may grant injunction.

119. The Court may, at any time after the presentation of a petition for winding up a company under this Act, and before making an order for winding up the company, upon the application of the company, or of any creditor, or contributory of the company, restrain further proceedings in any action, suit or proceeding against the company, upon such terms as the Court thinks fit; the Court may also, at any time after the presentation of such petition, and before the first appointment of liquidators, appoint provisionally an official liquidator of the estate and effects of the company.

Course to be pursued by Court on hearing petition.

120. Upon hearing the petition the Court may dismiss the same with or without costs, may adjourn the hearing conditionally or unconditionally, and may make any interim order, or any other order that it deems just.

Actions and suits to be stayed after order for winding up.

121. When an order has been made for winding up a company under this Act, no suit, action or other proceeding shall be proceeded with or commenced against the company except with the leave of the Court, and subject to such terms as the Court may impose.

Copy of order to be forwarded to Registrar.

122. When an order has been made for winding up a company under this Act, a copy of such order shall forthwith be forwarded by the company to the Registrar who shall make a minute thereof in his books relating to the company.

Power of Court to stay proceedings.

123. The Court may at any time after an order has been made for winding up a company, upon the application by motion of any creditor or contributory of the company, and upon proof to the satisfaction of the Court that all proceedings in relation to such winding up ought to be stayed, made an order staying the same, either altogether or for a limited time, on such terms and subject to such conditions as it deems fit.

Effect of order on share capital of company limited by guarantee.

124. When an order has been made for winding up a company limited by guarantee, and having a capital divided into shares, any share capital that may not have been called up shall be deemed to be assets of the company, and to be a debt of the nature of a specialty due to the company from each member to the extent of any sums that may be unpaid on any shares held by him, and payable at such time as may be appointed by the Court.

Court may have regard to wishes of creditors or contributories.

125. The Court, may, as to all matters relating to the winding up, have regard to the wishes of creditors or contributories, as proved to it by any sufficient evidence, and may, if it thinks it expedient, direct meetings of the creditors or contributories to be summoned, held and conducted in such manner as the Court direct, for the purpose of ascertaining their wishes, and may appoint a person to act as chairman of any such meeting, and to report the result of such meeting to the Court; in the case of creditors, regard is to be had to the value of the debts due to each creditor, and in the case of contributories, to the number of votes conferred on each contributory by the regulations of the company.

Official Liquidator

Appointment of official liquidator.

126. For the purpose of conducting the proceedings in winding up a company, and assisting the Court therein, there may be appointed a person or persons to be called an official liquidator or official liquidators; and the Court may appoint such person or persons, either provisionally or otherwise, as it thinks fit, to the office of official liquidator or official liquidators; in all cases if more persons than one are appointed to the office of official liquidator, the Court shall declare whether any act hereby required or authorized to be done by the official liquidator is to be done by all or any one or more of such persons. The Court may also determine whether any and what security is to be given by an official liquidator on his appointment. If no official liquidator is appointed, or during any vacancy in such appointment, all the property of the company shall be deemed to be in the custody of the Court.

Resignations, removals, filling up vacancies, and compensation of official liquidator

127. Any official liquidator may resign or be removed by the Court on due cause shown; and any vacancy in the office of an official liquidator appointed by the Court shall be filled by the Court. There shall be paid to the official liquidator such salary or remuneration, by the way of percentage or otherwise as the Court may direct; and, if more liquidators than one are appointed, such remuneration shall be distributed amongst them, in such proportions as the Court directs.

Style and duties of official liquidator

128. The official liquidator or liquidators shall be described by the style of the official liquidator or official liquidators of the particular company in respect of which he is or they are appointed, and not by his or their individual name or names. He or they shall take into his or their custody, or under his or their control, all the property, effects and things in action to which the company is or appears to be entitled, and shall perform such duties in reference to the winding up of the company as may be imposed by the Court.

Powers of official liquidator

129. The official liquidator shall have power, with the sanction of the Court, to do the following things -

(a) to bring or defend any action, suit or prosecution, or other legal proceeding, civil or criminal, in the name and on behalf of the company;

(b) to carry on the business of the company so far as may be necessary for the beneficial winding up of the same;

(c) to sell the real and personal property, effects and things in action of the company by public auction or private contract, with power to transfer the whole thereof to any person or company, or to sell the same in parcels;

(d) to do all acts and to execute, in the name and on behalf of the company, all deeds, receipts, and other documents, and for that purpose to use, when necessary, the company's seal;

(e) to prove, rank, claim, and draw a dividend, in the matter of the bankruptcy of any contributory, for any balance against the estate of such contributory, and to take and receive dividends in respect of such balance, in the matter of bankruptcy, as a separate debt due from such bankrupt, and rateably with other separate creditors;

(f) to draw, accept, make and endorse any bill of exchange or promissory note in the name and on behalf of the company, also to raise upon the security of the assets of the company from time to time any requisite sum or sums of money; and the drawing, accepting, making or endorsing of every such bill of exchange or promissory note as aforesaid on behalf of the company shall have the same effect with respect to the liability of such company as if such bill or note had been drawn, accepted, made or endorsed by or on behalf of such company in the course of carrying on the business thereof;

(g) to do in his official name any act that may be necessary for obtaining payment of any moneys due from a contributory or from his estate, and which act can not be conveniently done in the name of the company; and, in all cases where he uses his official name for obtaining payment of any moneys due from a contributory, such moneys shall, for the purpose of enabling him to recover such moneys; be deemed to be due to the official liquidator himself;

(h) to do and execute all such other things as may be necessary for winding up the affairs of the company, and distributing its assets.

Discretion of official liquidator

130. The Court may provide by any order that the official liquidator may exercise any of the above powers without the sanction or intervention of the Court, and, where an official liquidator is provisionally appointed, may limit and restrict his powers by the order appointing him.

Solicitor to assist official liquidator

131. The official liquidator may, with the sanction of the Court, appoint a solicitor to assist him in the performance of his duties.

Ordinary Powers Of Court

Collection and application of assets

132. As soon as may be after making an order for winding up the company, the Court shall settle a list of contributories, with power to rectify the register of members in all cases where such rectification is required in pursuance of this Act, and shall cause the assets of the company to be collected, and applied in discharge of its liabilities.

Provision as to representative contributories

133. In settling the list of contributors the Court shall distinguish between persons who are contributories in their own right and persons who are contributories as being representatives of or being liable to the debts of others. It shall not be necessary, where the personal representative of any deceased contributory is placed on the list, to add the heirs or devisees of such contributory, nevertheless such heirs or devisees may be added as and when the Court thinks fit.

Power of Court to require delivery of property

134. The Court may, at any time after making an order for winding up a company, require any contributory for the time being settled on the list of contributories, or any trustee, receiver, banker or agent, or officer of the company to pay, deliver, convey, surrender or transfer forthwith, or within such time as the Court directs, to or into the hands of the official liquidator any sum or balance, books, papers, estate or effects which happen to be in his hands for the time being, and to which the company is prima facie entitled.

Power of Court to order payment of debts by contributories

135. The Court may, at any time after making an order for winding up the company, make an order on any contributory for the time being settled on the list of contributories, directing payment to be made, in manner in the said order mentioned, of any moneys due from him or from the estate of the person whom he represents to the company, exclusive of any moneys which he or the estate of the person whom he represents may be liable to contribute by virtue of any call made or to be made by the Court in pursuance of this part; and it may, in making such order, when the company is not limited, allow to such contributory by way of set off any moneys due to him, or the estate which he represents, from the company on any independent dealing or contract with the company, but not any moneys due to him as a member of the company in respect of any dividend or profit.

Provided that, when all the creditors of any company whether limited or unlimited are paid in full, any moneys due on any account whatever to any contributory from the company may be allowed to him by way of set-off against any subsequent call or calls.

Power of Court to make calls

136. The Court may, at any time after making an order for winding up a company, and either before or after it has ascertained the sufficiency of the assets of the company, make calls on and order payment thereof, to the extent of their liability, by all or any of the contributories for the time being settled on the list of contributories, for payment of all or any sums it deems necessary to satisfy the debts and liabilities of the company, and the costs, charges and expenses of winding it up, and for the adjustment of the rights of the contributories amongst themselves; and it may, in making a call, take into consideration the probability that some of the contributories upon whom the same is made may partly or wholly fail to pay their respective portions of the same.

Power of Court to order payment into bank

137. The Court may order any contributory, purchaser, or other person from payment whom money is due to the company to pay the same into a bank, or to some responsible person or persons to be named by the Court, to the account of the official liquidator, instead of to the official liquidator, and such order may be enforced in the same manner as it had directed payment to the official liquidator.

Regulation of account with Court

138. All moneys, bills, notes and other securities paid and delivered into such banks, or to such person or persons, in the event of a company being wound up by the Court, shall be subject to such order and regulation for the keeping of the account of such moneys and other effects, and for the payment and delivery in, or investment and payment and delivery out, of the same as the Court may direct.

Provision in case of representative contributory not paying moneys ordered

139. If any person made a contributory as personal representative of a deceased contributory makes default in paying any sum ordered to be paid by him, proceedings may be taken for administering the personal and real estates of such deceased contributory, or either of such estates, and of compelling payment there out of the moneys due.

Order conclusive evidence

140. Any order made by the Court in pursuance of this Act upon any contributory shall, subject to the provisions herein contained for appealing against such order, be conclusive evidence that the moneys, if any, thereby appearing to be due, or ordered to be paid, are due, and all other pertinent matters stated in such order are to be taken to be truly stated as against all persons, and in all proceedings whatsoever, with the exception of proceedings taken against the real estate of such deceased contributory, in which case such order shall only be prima facie evidence for the purpose of charging his real estate, unless his heirs or devisees were on the list of contributories at the time of the order being made.

Court may exclude creditors not proving within certain time

141. The Court may fix a certain day or certain days on or within which creditors of the company are to prove their debts or claims, or to be excluded from the benefit of any distribution made before such debts are proved.

Court to adjust rights of contributories

142. The Court shall adjust the rights of the contributories amongst themselves, and distribute any surplus that may remain amongst the parties entitled thereto.

Costs

143. The Court may, in the event of the assets being insufficient to satisfy the liabilities, make an order as to the payment, out of the estate of the company, of the costs, charges and expenses incurred in winding up any company, in such order or priority as the Court thinks just.

Dissolution of company

144. When the affairs of the company have been completely wound up, the Court shall make an order that the company be dissolved from the date of such order, and the company shall be dissolved accordingly.

Registrar to make minute of dissolution of company

145. Any order so made shall be reported by the official liquidator to the Registrar, who shall make a minute accordingly in his books of the dissolution of such company.

Penalty on not reporting dissolution of company

146. If the official liquidator makes default in reporting to the Registrar, in the case of a company being wound up by the Court, the order that the company be dissolved, he shall be liable to a penalty not exceeding twenty-four dollars for every day during which he is so in default.

Extraordinary Powers Of Court

Power of Court to summon before it persons suspected of having property of company

147. The Court may, after it has made an order for winding up the company, summon before it any officer of the company or supposed to be indebted to the company, or person known or suspected to have in his possession any of the estate or effects of the company, or supposed to be indebted to the company or any person whom the Court may deem capable of giving information concerning the trade, dealings, estate or effects of the company; and the Court may require any such officer or person to produce any books, papers, deeds, writings or other documents in his custody or power relating to the company, and if any person so summoned, after being tendered a reasonable sum for his expenses, refuses to come before the Court at the time appointed, having no lawful impediment (made known to the Court at the time of its sitting, and allowed by it), the Court may cause such person to be apprehended, and brought before the Court for examination; nevertheless, in cases where any person claims any lien on papers, deeds, or writings, or documents produced by him, such production shall be without prejudice to such lien, and the Court shall have jurisdiction in the winding up to determine all questions relating to such lien.

Examination of parties by Court

148. The Court may examine upon oath, either by word of mouth or upon written interrogatories, any person appearing or brought before it in manner aforesaid concerning the affairs, dealings, estate, or effects of the company, and may reduce into writing the answers of every such person, and require him to subscribe the same.

Power to arrest contributory about to abscond, or to remove or conceal any of his property

149. The Court may, at any time before or after it has made an order for winding up a company, upon proof being given that there is probable cause for believing that any contributory to, or to such company is about to quit the Territory, or otherwise to, or to remove or conceal any of his goods or chattels for the purpose of evading payment of calls, or for avoiding examination in respect of the affairs of the company, cause such contributory to be arrested, and his books, papers, money, securities for moneys, goods, and chattels to be seized, and him and them to be safely kept until such time as the Court may order.

Powers of Court cumulative

150. Any powers by this Act conferred on the Court shall be deemed to be in addition to, and not in restriction of, any other powers subsisting, either by law or equity, of instituting proceedings against any contributory, or the estate of any contributory, or against any debtor of the company, for the recovery of any call or other sums due from such contributory or debtor, or his estate, and such proceedings may be instituted accordingly.

Enforcement Of And Appeal From Orders

Power to enforce orders

151. All orders made by the Court under this Act may be enforced in the same manner in which orders of the Supreme Court made in any suit pending therein may be enforced.

Appeals from order

152. Re-hearings of and appeals from any order or decision made or given in the matter of the winding up of a company by the Court may be had to the Court of Appeal in the same manner and subject to the same conditions in and subject to which appeals may be had to the said Court of Appeal from any order or decision of the Supreme Court.

Affidavits, etc., sworn in UK, in the Territories or in foreign parts

153. Any affidavit, affirmation or declaration required to be sworn or made, under the provisions or for the purposes of this Part may be lawfully sworn or made in Great Britain or Northern or in any territory, island, plantation, or place under the dominion of Her Majesty, before any Court, Judge or persons lawfully authorized to take and receive affidavits, affirmations or declarations, or before any of Her Majesty's Consuls or Vice-Consuls, in any foreign parts out of Her Majesty's dominions; and all Courts, Judges, Justices, Commissioners, and persons acting judicially shall take judicial notice of the seal, or stamp, or signature (as the case may be) of any such Court, Judge, person, Consul or Vice-Consul, attached, appended, or subscribed to any such affidavit, affirmation or declaration, or to any other document to be used for the purposes of this Part.

Voluntary Winding Up Of Company

Circumstances under which company may be wound up voluntarily

154.(1) A company under this Act may be wound up voluntarily may -

(a) whenever the period, if any, fixed for the duration of the company by the Articles of Association expires, or whenever the event, if any, occurs upon the occurrence of which it is provided by the Articles of Association that the company is to be dissolved, and the company in general meeting has passed a resolution requiring the company to be wound up voluntarily;

(b) whenever the company has passed a special resolution requiring the company to be wound up voluntarily;

(c) whenever the company has passed an extraordinary resolution to the effect that it has been proved to their satisfaction that the company can not, by reason of its liabilities, continue its business, and that it is advisable to wind up the same.

(2) For the purposes of this Act any resolution shall be deemed to be extraordinary which is passed in such manner as would if it had been confirmed by a subsequent meeting, have constituted a special resolution as hereinbefore defined.

Commencement of voluntary winding up

155. A voluntary winding up shall be deemed to commence at the time of the passing of the resolution authorizing such winding up.

Effect of voluntary winding up on status of company

156. Whenever a company is wound up voluntarily, the company shall from the date of the commencement of such winding up, cease to carry on its business except in so far as may be required for the beneficial winding up thereof, and all transfers of shares, except transfers made to or with the sanction of the liquidators, or alterations in the status of the members of the company taking place after the commencement of such winding up, shall be void; but its corporate state and all its corporate powers shall, notwithstanding it is otherwise provided

Notice of resolution to wind up voluntarily

157. Notice of any special resolution or extraordinary resolution passed for winding up a company voluntarily shall be given by advertisement in the Gazette and, if there is no Gazette in the territory, then in such other manner as shall at the time be usual.

Consequences of voluntary winding up

158. The following consequences shall ensue upon the voluntary winding up of a company -

(a) The property of the company shall be applied in satisfaction of its liabilities, pari passu, and, subject thereto, shall, unless it be otherwise provided by the regulations of the company, be distributed among the members according to their rights and interests in the company;

(b) Liquidators shall be appointed for the purpose of winding up the affairs of the company and distributing the property;

(c) The company in general meeting shall appoint such person or persons as it thinks fit to be liquidators or a liquidator, and may fix the remuneration to be paid to them or him;

(d) If one person only is appointed, all the provisions herein contained in reference to several liquidators shall apply to him;

(e) Upon the appointment of liquidators, all the powers of the directors shall cease, except in so far as the company in general meeting or the liquidators may sanction the continuance of such powers;

(f) When several liquidators are appointed, every power hereby given may be exercised by such one or more of them as may be determined at the time of their appointment or in default of such determination by any number not less than two;

(g) The liquidators may, without the sanction of the Court, exercise all powers by this Act given to the official liquidator;

(h) The liquidators may exercise the powers hereinbefore given to the Court of settling the list of contributories of the company, and any list so settled shall be prima facie evidence of the liability of the persons named therein to be contributories;

(i) The liquidators may, at any time after the passing of the resolution for winding up the company, and before they have ascertained the sufficiency of the assets of the company, call on all or any of the contributories for the time being settled on the list of contributories, to the extent of their liabilities, to pay all or any sums they deem necessary to satisfy the debts and liabilities of the company, and the cost, charges and expenses of winding it up, and for the adjustment of the rights of the contributories amongst themselves; and the liquidators may, in making a call, take into consideration the probability that some of the contributories upon whom the same is made may partly or wholly fail to pay their respective portions of the same;

(j) The liquidators shall pay the debts of the company, and adjust the rights of the contributories amongst themselves.

Effect of winding up on share capital of company limited by guarantee

159. Where a company limited by guarantee, and having a capital divided into shares, is being wound up voluntarily, any share capital that may not have been called up shall be deemed to be assets of the company, and to be a specialty debt due from each member to the company, to the extent of any sums that may be unpaid on any shares held by him, and payable at such time as may be appointed by the liquidators.

Power of company to delegate authority to appoint liquidators

160. A company about to be wound up voluntarily, or in the course of being wound up voluntarily, may by an extraordinary resolution, delegate to its creditors, or to any committee of its creditors, the power of appointing liquidators or any of them, and supplying any vacancies in the appointment of liquidators, or may, by a like resolution, enter into any arrangement with respect to the powers to be exercised the liquidators and the manner in which they are to be exercised; and any act done by the creditors, in pursuance of such delegated power, shall have the same effect as if it had been done by the company.

Arrangement when binding on creditors

161. Any arrangement entered into between a company about to be wound up voluntarily, or in the course of being wound up voluntarily, and its creditors, shall be binding on the company if sanctioned by an extraordinary resolution, and on the creditors if acceded to by three-fourths in number and value of the creditors, subject to such right of appeal as is hereinafter mentioned.

Power of creditor or contributory to appeal

162. Any creditor or contributory of a company that has in manner aforesaid entered into any arrangement with its creditors, may, within three weeks from the date of the completion of such arrangement, appeal to the Court against such arrangement, and the Court may upon, as it thinks just amend, vary, or confirm the same.

Power of liquidators or contributories in voluntary winding up to apply to Court

163. Where a company is being wound up voluntarily the liquidators or any contributory of the company may apply to the Court to determine any question arising in the matter of such winding up, or to exercise, as respects the enforcing of calls, or in respect of any other matter, all or any of the powers which the Court might exercise if the company were being wound up by the Court; and the Court, if satisfied that the determination of such question, or the required exercise of power will be just and beneficial, may accede, wholly or partially, to such application, on such terms, and subject to such conditions, as the Court thinks fit, or it may make such other order or decree on such application as the Court thinks just.

Power of liquidators to call general meeting

164. Where a company is being wound up voluntarily, the liquidators may, from time to time, during the continuance of such winding up, summon general meetings of the company for the purpose of obtaining the sanction of the company by special resolution or extraordinary resolution, or for any other purposes they think fit; and, in the event of the winding up continuing for more than one year, the liquidators shall summon a general meeting of the company at the end of the first year, and of each succeeding year, from the commencement of the winding up, or as soon thereafter as may be convenient, and shall lay before such meeting an account showing their acts and dealings, and the manner in which the winding up has been conducted during the preceding year.

Power to fill vacancy in liquidators

165. If any vacancy occurs in the office of liquidator appointed by the company, by death, resignation, or otherwise, the company in general meeting may, subject to any arrangement they may have entered into with their creditors, fill up such vacancy, and a general meeting for the purpose of filling up such vacancy may be convened by the continuing liquidators, if any, or by an contributory of the company, and shall be deemed to have been duly held if held in manner prescribed by the regulations of the company, or in such other manner as may, on application by the continuing liquidator, if any, or by any contributory of the company, be determined by the Court.

Power of Court to appoint liquidators

166. If, from any cause whatever, there is no liquidator acting in the case of a voluntary winding up, the Court may, on the application of a contributory, appoint a liquidator or liquidators; the Court may also, on due cause shown, remove any liquidator, and appoint another liquidator to act in the matter of a voluntary winding up.

Liquidators on conclusion of winding up to make up an account

167. As soon as the affairs of the company are fully wound up, the liquidator shall make up an account showing the manner in which such winding up has been conducted, and the property of the company disposed of; and thereupon they shall call a general meeting of the company for the purpose of having the account laid before them and hearing any explanation that may be given by the liquidators. The meeting shall be called by advertisement, specifying the time, place and object of such meeting; and such advertisement shall be published one month at least previously to the meeting, in the Gazette and one or more newspapers, if such be published, in the Territory.

Liquidators to report meeting to Registrar

168. The liquidators shall make a return to the Registrar of such meeting having been held, and of the meeting date at which the same was held; and on the expiration of three months from the date of the registration of such return the company shall be deemed to be dissolved; and, if the liquidators make default in making such return to the Registrar, they shall incur a penalty not exceeding twenty-four dollars for every day during which such default continues.

Costs of voluntary liquidation

169. All costs, charges and expenses properly incurred in the voluntary winding up of a company, including the remuneration of the liquidators, shall be payable out of the assets of the company in priority to all other claims.

Saving of rights of creditors

170. The voluntary winding up of a company shall not be a bar to the right of any creditor of such company to have the same wound up by the Court, if the Court is of opinion that the rights of such creditor will be prejudiced by a voluntary winding up.

Power of Court to adopt proceedings of voluntary winding up

171. Where a company is in course of being wound up voluntarily, and proceedings are taken for the purpose of having the same wound up by the Court, the Court may, if it thinks fit, notwithstanding that it makes an order directing the company to be wound up by the Court, provide in such order, in any order, for the adoption of all or any of the proceedings taken in the course of the voluntary winding up.

Winding Up Subject To The Supervision Of The Court

Power of Court on application to direct winding up subject to supervision

172. When a resolution has been passed by a company to wind up voluntarily, the Court may make an order directing that the voluntary winding up shall continue, but subject to such supervision of the Court, and with such liberty for creditors, contributories, or others to apply to the Court, and generally upon such terms and subject to such conditions as the Court thinks just.

Petition for winding up subject to supervision

173. A petition, praying wholly or in part that a voluntary winding up should continue, but subject to the supervision of the Court, and which winding up is herein after referred to as a winding up subject to the supervision of the court, shall, for the purpose of giving jurisdiction to the Court over suits and actions, be deemed to be a petition for winding up the company by the Court.

Court may have regard to wishes of creditors

174. The Court may, in determining whether a company is to be wound up altogether by the Court or subject to the supervision of the Court, in the appointment of a liquidator or liquidators and in all other matters relating to the winding up subject to supervision, have regard to the wishes of the creditors or contributories as proved to it by any sufficient evidence; and may direct meetings of the creditors or contributories to be summoned, held and regulated in such manner as the Court directs for the purpose of ascertaining their wishes, and may appoint a person to act as chairman of any such meeting, and to report the result of such meeting to the Court. In the case of creditors, regard shall be had to the value of the debts due to each creditor, and in the case of contributories, to the number of votes conferred on each contributory by the regulations of the company.

Power of Court to appoint additional liquidators in winding up subject to supervision

175. Where any order is made by the Court for a winding up subject to the supervision of the Court, the Court may, in such order, or in any subsequent order, appoint any additional liquidator or liquidators, and any liquidators so appointed by the Court shall have the same powers, be subject to the same obligations, and in all respects stand in the same position as if they had been appointed by the company; the Court may from time to time remove any liquidators so appointed by the Court and fill up any vacancy occasioned by such removal, or by death or resignation.

Effect of order of Court for winding up subject to supervision

176. Where an order is made for the winding up, subject to the supervision of the Court, the liquidators appointed to conduct such winding up may, subject to any restrictions imposed by the Court, exercise all their powers without the sanction or intervention of the Court, in the same manner as if the company were being wound up altogether voluntarily; but save as aforesaid, any order made by the Court for a winding up subject to the supervision of the Court shall, for all purposes, including the staying of actions, suits, and other proceedings, be deemed to be an order of the Court for winding up the company by the Court, and shall confer full authority on the Court to make calls, or to enforce calls made by liquidators, and to exercise all other powers which it might have exercised if an order had been made for winding up the company altogether by the Court; and in the construction of the provisions whereby the Court is empowered to direct any act or thing to be done to or in favour of the official liquidators, the expression "official liquidators", shall be deemed to mean the liquidators conducting the winding up subject to the supervision of the Court.

Appointment in certain cases of voluntary liquidators to office of official liquidators

177. Where an order has been made for the winding up of a company subject to the supervision of the Court, and such order is afterwards superseded by an order directing the company to be wound up compulsorily, the Court may, in such last mentioned order or in any subsequent order, appoint the voluntary liquidators or any of them, either provisionally or permanently, and either with or without the addition of any other persons to be official liquidators.

Supplemental Provisions

Dispositions after the commencement of the winding up to be void

178. Where any company is being wound up by the Court or subject to the supervision of the Court, all dispositions of the property, effects and things in action of the company, and every transfer of shares, or alteration in the status of the members of the company, made between the commencement of the winding up and the order for winding up shall, unless the Court otherwise orders, be void.

The books of the company to be evidence

179. Where any company is being wound up, all books, accounts and documents of the company and of the liquidators shall, as between the contributories of the company, be prima facie evidence of the truth of all matters purporting to be therein recorded.

As to disposal of books, accounts and documents of the company

180. Where any company has been wound up under this Act, and is about to be dissolved, the books, accounts and documents of the company and of the liquidator may be disposed of in the following way, that is to say: Where the company has been wound up by or subject to the supervision of the Court, in such way as the Court directs; and where the company has been wound up voluntarily, in such way as the company by an extraordinary resolution directs; but after the lapse of five years from the date of such dissolution, no responsibility shall rest on the company, or the liquidators, or any one to whom the custody of such books, accounts and documents has been committed, by the reason that the same, or any of them, can not be made forthcoming to any party or parties claiming to be interested therein.

Inspection of books

181. Where an order has been made for winding up a company by the Court, or subject to the supervision of the Court, the Court may make such order for the inspection by the creditors and contributories of the company of its books and papers as the Court thinks just; and any books and papers in the possession of the company may be inspected by creditors or contributories in conformity with the order of the Court, but no further or otherwise.

Power of assignee to sue

182. Any person to whom anything in action belonging to the company is assigned in pursuance of this Act, may bring or defend any action or suit relating to such thing in action in his own name.

Proof of debts in winding up

183. In the event of any company being wound up under this Act, all debts payable on a contingency, and all claims against the company, present or future, certain contingent, ascertained or sounding only in damages, shall be admissible to proof against the company, a just estimate being made, so far as is possible, of the value of all such debts or claims as may be subject to any contingency or sound only in damages, or, for some other reason, do not bear a certain value:

Provided that the same rules shall prevail and be observed as to the respective rights of secured and unsecured creditors, and as to the debts and liabilities provable, and as to the valuation of annuities and future and contingent liabilities respectively, as may be in force for the time being under the law of bankruptcy, with respect to the estates of persons adjudged bankrupt; and all persons who in any such case would be entitled to prove for and receive dividends out of the assets of any such company, may come in under the winding up of such company, and make such claims as they may respectively be entitled to.

General scheme of liquidation may be sanctioned

184. The liquidators may, with the sanction of the Court, where the company is being wound by the Court or subject to the supervision of the Court, and with the sanction of an extraordinary resolution of the company where the company is being wound up altogether voluntarily, pay any classes of creditors in full, or make such compromise or other arrangement as the liquidators may deem expedient with creditors or persons claiming to be creditors, or persons having or alleging themselves to have any claim, present or future, certain or contingent, ascertained or sounding only in damages against the company, or whereby the company may be rendered liable.

Power to compromise

185. The liquidators may, with the sanction of the Court, where the company is being wound up by the Court, or subject to the supervision of the Court, and with the sanction of an extraordinary resolution of the company where the company is being wound up altogether voluntarily, compromise all calls and liabilities to calls, debts, liabilities capable of resulting in debts, and all claims, whether present or future, certain or contingent, ascertained or sounding only in damages, subsisting or supposed to subsist, between the company and any contributory or alleged contributory, or other debtor or person apprehending liability to the company, and all questions in any way relating to or affecting the assets of the company or the winding up of the company, upon receipt of such sums, payable at such times, and generally upon such terms as may be agreed upon, with power for the liquidators to take any security for the discharge of such debts or liabilities, and to give complete discharges in respect of all or any such calls, debts, or liabilities.

Where compromise proposed, Court may order a meeting of creditors, etc. to decide as to such compromise

186. Where any compromise or arrangement shall be proposed between a company which is in the course of being wound up, either voluntarily or by under the supervision of the Court, and the creditors of such company, or any class of such creditors, it shall be lawful for the court, in addition to any other of its powers, on the application in a summary way of any creditor or the liquidator, to order that a meeting or class of creditors shall be summoned in such manner as the Court shall direct; and if a majority in number representing three-fourths in value of such creditors or class of creditors present either in person or by proxy at such meeting, shall agree to any arrangement or compromise, such arrangement or compromise shall, if sanctioned by an order of the Court, be binding on all such creditors or class of creditors, as the case may be, and also on the liquidator and contributories of the said company.

Powers for liquidators to accept shares etc., as a consideration for sale of property of company

187. Where any company is proposed to be, or is in the course of being, wound up altogether the whole or a portion of its business or property is proposed to be transferred or sold to another company, the liquidators of the first mentioned company may, with the sanction of a special resolution of the company by whom they were appointed, of conferring either a general authority on the liquidators, or an authority in respect of any particular arrangement, receive, in compensation or part compensation for such transfer or sale, shares, policies, or other like interests in such other company, for the purpose of distribution amongst the members of the company being wound up, or may enter into any other arrangements whereby the members of the company being wound up may, in lieu of receiving cash, shares, policies, or other like interests, or in addition thereto, participate in the profits of, or receive any other benefit from, the purchasing company, and any sale made or arrangement entered into by the liquidators in pursuance of this section shall be binding on the members of the company being wound up, subject to this provision, that, if any member of the company being wound up, who has not voted in favour of the special resolution passed by the company of which he is a member at either of the meetings held for passing the same, expresses his dissent from any such special resolution, in writing addressed to the liquidators or one of them, and left at the registered office of the company not later than seven days after the date of the meeting at which such special resolution was passed, such dissentient member may require the liquidators to do one of the following things as the liquidators may prefer, that is to say: either to abstain from carrying such resolution into effect, or to purchase the interest held by such dissentient member at a price to be determined in manner hereinafter mentioned, such purchase money to be paid before the company is dissolved, and to be raised by the liquidators in such manner as may be determined by special resolution; no special resolution shall be deemed invalid for the purposes of this section by reason that it is passed antecedently to, or concurrently with, any resolution for winding up the company, or for appointing liquidators; but if an order be made within a year for winding up the company by, or subject to the supervision of, the Court, such resolution shall not be of any validity unless it is sanctioned by the Court.

Mode of determining price

188. The price to be paid for the purchase of the interest of any dissentient member may be determined by agreement, but if the parties dispute about the same, such dispute shall be settled by arbitration in manner hereinbefore provided.

Certain attachments, sequestration and executions to be void saving rights of Crown

189. Where any company is being wound up by the Court, or subject to the supervision of the Court, any attachment, sequestration, distress, or execution put in force against the estate or effects of the after the commencement of the winding up shall be void to all intents: provided that this section shall not apply where such attachment, sequestration, distress, or execution shall be on behalf of the Crown.

Fraudulent preference

190. Any such conveyance, mortgage, delivery of goods, payment, execution, or other act relating to property as would, if made or done by or against an individual be deemed, in the event of his bankruptcy, to have been made or done by way of undue or fraudulent preference of his creditors, shall, if made or done by or against any company, be deemed, in the event of such company being wound up under this Act, to have been made or done by way of undue or fraudulent preference of the creditors of such company, and shall be invalid accordingly; and, for the purposes of this section, the presentation of a petition for winding up a company shall, in the case of a company being wound up by the Court, or subject to the supervision of the Court, and a resolution for winding up the company shall, in case of a voluntary winding up, be deemed to correspond with the act of bankruptcy in the case of an individual; and any conveyance or assignment, made by any company formed under this Act, of all its estate and effects to trustees for the benefit of all its creditors shall be void to all intents.

Power of Court to assess damages against delinquent directors and officers

191. Where, in the course of the winding up of any company under this Act, it appears that any past or present director, manager, official or other liquidator, or any officer of such company has misapplied, or retained in his own hands, or become liable or accountable for, any moneys of the company or been guilty of any misfeasance or breach of trust in relation to the company, the Court may, on the application of any liquidator, or of any creditor or contributory of the company, notwithstanding that the offence is one for which the offender is criminally responsible, examine into the conduct of such director, manager, or other officer, and compel him to repay any moneys so misapplied or retained, or for which he has become liable or accountable, together with interest after such rate as the Court thinks just, or to contribute such sums of money to the assets of the company by way of compensation in respect to such misapplication, retainer, misfeasance, or breach of trust as the Court thinks just.

Penalty on falsification of books

192. If any director, officer, or contributory of any company wound up under this Act, destroys, mutilates, alters or falsifies any books, papers, writings or securities, or makes or is privy to the making of any false or fraudulent entry in any register, book of account, or other document belonging to the company with intent to defraud or deceive any person, every person so of fending shall be deemed to be guilty of a misdemeanour, and shall be liable to imprisonment for any term not exceeding two years with or without hard labour.

Prosecution of delinquent directors, etc. in case of winding up by Court

193. Where any order is made for winding up a company by the Court or subject to the supervision of the Court, if it appear in the course of such winding up that any past or present director, manager, officer, or member of such company has been guilty of any offence in relation to the company for which he is criminally responsible, the Court may, on the application of any persons interested in such winding up, or of its own motion, direct the official liquidator, or the liquidators (as the case may be), to institute and conduct a prosecution or prosecutions for such offence, and may order the cost and expenses to be paid out of the assets of the company.

Prosecution of delinquent directors etc. in case of voluntary winding up by Court

194. Where a company is being wound up altogether voluntarily, if it appear to the liquidators conducting such winding up that any past or present director, manager, officer or member of such company has been guilty of any offence in relation to the company for which he is criminally responsible, it shall be lawful for the liquidators, with the previous sanction of the Court, to prosecute such offender, and all expenses properly incurred by them in such prosecution shall be payable out of the assets of the company in priority to all other liabilities.

Penalty of perjury

195. If any person, upon any examination upon oath or affirmation authorized under this Act, or in any affidavit, deposition or solemn affirmation, in or about the winding up of any company under this Act, or otherwise in or about any matter arising under this Act, wilfully and corruptly gives false evidence, he shall be liable to the penalties of wilful perjury.

Wages and salary to be preferential claims

196. In the distribution of the assets of any company being wound up under this Act there shall be paid in priority to other debts claims -

(a) all wages and salary of any clerk or servant in respect of service rendered to the company during four months before the commencement of the winding up, not exceeding two hundred and forty dollars; and

(b) all wages of any workman or labourer in respect of services rendered to the company during two months before the commencement of the winding up.

Such claims to rank equally

197. The foregoing debts shall rank equally among themselves, and shall be paid in full unless the assets of the company are insufficient to meet them, in which case they shall abate in equal proportions among themselves.

Liquidator to discharge same on receipt of sufficient assets

198. Subject to the retention of such sums as may be necessary for the costs of administration or otherwise, the liquidator or liquidators or official liquidator shall discharge the foregoing debts forthwith, so far as the assets of the company are and will be sufficient to meet them, as and when assets come into the hands of such liquidator or liquidators, or official liquidator.

Striking Companies Off Register

Power of Registrar to strike names of defunct companies off register

199. Where the Registrar has reasonable cause to believe that a company, whether registered before or after the passing of this Act, is not carrying on business or in operation, he shall send to the company by post a letter inquiring whether the company is carrying on business or in operation.

Notice to be sent to company by Registrar

200. If the Registrar does not, within one month of sending the letter, receive any answer thereto, he shall, within fourteen days after the expiration of the month, send to the company by post a registered letter referring to the first letter, and stating that no answer thereto has been received by the Registrar, and that if an answer is not received to the second letter within one month from the date thereof, a notice will be published in the Gazette with a view to striking the name of the company off the register.

Notice in Gazette

201. If the Registrar either receives an answer from the company to the effect that Gazette it is not carrying on business or in operation, or does not, within one month after sending the second letter, receive any answer thereto, the Registrar may publish in the Gazette and send to the company a notice that, at the expiration of three months from the date of that notice, the name of the company mentioned therein will, unless cause is shown to the contrary, be struck off the register and the company will be dissolved.

Name to be struck off register and company dissolved

202. At the expiration of the time mentioned in the notice, the Registrar may, unless cause to the contrary is previously shown by such company, strike the name of such company off the register, and shall publish notice thereof in the Gazette and, on the publication in the Gazette of such last-mentioned notice, the company whose name is so struck off shall be dissolved: Provided that the liability, if any, of every director, managing officer, and member of the company shall continue and may be enforced as if the company had not been dissolved.

Court may order restoration of name and company

203. If any company or member thereof feels aggrieved by the name of such company having been struck off the register in pursuance of this section, the company or member may apply to the Court; and the Court, if satisfied that the company was, at the time of the striking off, carrying on business or in operation, and that it is just company so to do, may order the name of the company to be restored to the register, and thereupon the company shall be deemed to have continued in existence as if the name thereof had never been struck off; and the Court may, by the order, give such directions and make such provisions as seem just for placing the company and all other persons in the same position, as nearly as may be, as if the name of the company had never been struck off.

Property of dissolved company to be bona vacantia

203A.(1) When a company is dissolved, all property and rights whatsoever vested in or held on trust for the company immediately before its dissolution (including leasehold property, but not including property held by the Company on trust for any other person), are deemed to be bona vacantia and -

(a) accordingly belong to the Crown, and

(b) vest and may be dealt with in the same manner as other bona vacantia accruing to the Crown.

(2) The provisions of subsection (1) shall have effect subject and without prejudice to any order which may at any time be made by the Court under provisions of section 203.

Effect of Section 203 of company's revival after dissolution

203B.(1) Where any property or right is vested in the Crown by section 203A, the company's Crown may dispose of, or of an interest in that property or right notwithstanding that an order may be made under section 203.

(2) Where an order is made under section 203 -

(a) it does not effect the disposition (but without prejudice to the order so far as it relates to any other property or right previously vested in or held on trust for the company), and

(b) the Crown shall pay to the company an amount equal to -

(i) the amount of any consideration received for the property or right, or interest therein, or

(ii) the value of any such consideration at the time of the disposition, or if no consideration was received, an amount equal to the value of the property, right or interest disposed of, as at the date of the disposition.

Crown disclaimer of property vesting as bona vacantia

203C.(l) Where any property vests in the Crown under section 203A, the Crown's title thereto under that section may be disclaimed by a notice signed by the Governor in Council.

(2) Where a notice of disclaimer under this section is executed as respects any property, that property shall be deemed not to have vested in the Crown under section 203A.

(3) The right to execute a notice of disclaimer under this section may be waived by or on behalf of the Crown either expressly or by taking possession or other act evincing that intention.

(4) A notice of disclaimer under this section shall be of no effect unless it is executed within twelve months of the date on which the vesting of the property as aforesaid came to the notice of the Governor in Council or, if an application in writing is made to the Governor in Council by any person interested in the property requiring him to decide whether he will or will not disclaim, within a period of three months after the receipt of the application or such further period as may be allowed by the court which would have had jurisdiction to wind up the company if it had not been dissolved.

(5) A statement in a notice of disclaimer of any property under this section that the vesting of the property came to the notice of the Governor in Council on, a specified date or that no such application as aforesaid was received by him with respect to the property before a specified date shall, until the contrary is proved, be sufficient evidence of the fact stated.

(6) A notice of disclaimer under this section shall be delivered to the Registrar and retained and registered by him, and copies thereof shall be published in the Gazette and sent to any person who have given the Governor in Council notice that they claim to be interested in the property.

Notice by post in above cases

204. A letter or notice authorized or required for the purposes of this section to be sent to a company may be sent by post addressed to the company at its registered, if no office has been registered, addressed to the care if some director or officer of the company, or if there be no director, or officer of the company whose name and address are known to the Registrar, the letter or notice (in identical form) may be sent to each of the persons who subscribed the Memorandum of Association, addressed to him at the address mentioned in that memorandum.

Registrar to conform to regulations of Governor

205. In the execution of his duties under the six preceding sections, the Registrar shall conform to any regulations which may be, from time to time, made by the Governor.

Procedure In Winding Up By Court

Procedure in winding up by Court

206. Rules for the purposes of this Act may from time to time be made in like manner as Rules of the Supreme Court may be made, and, subject to any such rules, the Rules of the Supreme Court for the time being in force shall apply to and govern the practice and procedure in the winding up of companies by the Court.

PART V - Constitution Of Registration Office

Appointment of Registrar of companies etc.

207.(1) The Governor may appoint a Registrar of Companies and such other officers as be, necessary for the administration of this Act.

(2) The Governor may make regulations with respect to the duties to be performed by such Registrar and may determine the place or places at which an office or offices for the registration of companies is or are to be established.

(3) There shall be paid to the Registrar in respect of the several matters mentioned in the table marked, in the First Schedule, the several fees therein specified, and all fees authorized by and paid under this Act shall be paid into the Treasury.

(4) Any person may inspect the documents kept by the Registrar, and may require a certificate of the incorporation on any company, or extract of any document or part of a document to be certified by the Registrar, and there shall be paid for such inspection, and for such certificate of incorporation, or certified copy or extract, the respective fees specified in the table marked B in the First Schedule, and such certificate of incorporation or certified copy or extract shall be prima facie evidence of the matters therein contained in all legal proceedings whatever.

(5) The Registrar of High Court shall be ex-officio the Registrar of Companies, until an appointment is made under subsection (1).

Power of company to keep registers in UK or British Territories

208.(1) Any company whose objects comprise the transaction of business in the United Kingdom, or in any British Territory, may, if authorized to do so by its regulations as originally framed or as altered by special resolution, cause to be kept in that part of the United Kingdom or in any such Territory in which it transacts business a branch register or registers of members resident in the United Kingdom, or in such Territory.

(2) The company shall given to the Registrar notice of the situation of the office where any such branch register (in this section called a British register) is kept, and of any change therein, and of the discontinuance of any such office in the event of the same being discontinued.

(3) A British register shall, as regards the particulars entered therein, be deemed to be a part of the company's register of members, and shall be prima facie evidence of all particulars entered therein. Any such register shall be kept in the manner provided by this Act, with this qualification, that the advertisement mentioned in section 56 shall be inserted in some newspaper circulating in the district wherein the register to be closed is kept, and that any competent Court in the United Kingdom or such Territory where such register is kept, shall be entitled to exercise the same jurisdiction of rectifying the same as is by section 58 vested in the Supreme Court of the Territory, and that all offences under section 55 may, as regards a British register, be prosecuted summarily before any tribunal in the United Kingdom or such Territory where such register is kept, having summary criminal jurisdiction.

(4) The company shall transmit to its registered office a copy of every entry in its British register or registers as soon as may be after such entry is made, and the company shall cause to be kept at its registered office, duly entered up from time to time, a duplicate or duplicates of its British register or registers. The provisions of section 55 shall apply to every such duplicate, and every such duplicate shall, for all the purposes of this Act, be deemed to be part of the register of members of the company.

(5) Subject to the provisions of this Act with respect to the duplicate register, the shares registered in a British register shall be distinguished from the shares registered in the principal register, and no transaction with respect to any shares registered in a British register shall, during the continuance of the registration of such shares in such British register, be registered in any other register.

(6) The company may discontinue to keep any British register, and there upon all entries in that register shall be transferred to some other British register kept by the company in the United Kingdom or in such Territory, or to the register of members kept at the registered office of the company.

(7) Subject to the provisions of this section, any company may, by its regulations as originally framed or as altered by special resolution, make such provisions as it may think fit respecting the keeping of British registers.

PART VI - Companies Authorized To Register

Registration of existing companies

209.(1) The following regulations shall be observed with respect to the registration of companies under this Part, that is to say, save as hereinafter provided -

(*a*) No company having the liability of its members limited by Act of the Imperial Parliament or Legislature of the Territory, or by letters patent, and not being a joint stock company as hereinafter defined, shall register under this Act in pursuance of this Part;

(*b*) No company having the liability of its members limited by Act of the Imperial Parliament or Legislature of the Territory, or by letters patent, shall register under this Act in pursuance of this Part as an unlimited company, or as a company limited by guarantee;

(*c*) No company that is not a joint stock company as hereinafter defined, shall, in pursuance of this Part register under this Act as a company limited by shares;

(*d*) No company shall register under this Act, in pursuance of the Part, unless an assent to its so registering is given by a majority of such of its members as may be present personally or by proxy, in cases where proxies are allowed by the regulations of the company at some general meeting summoned for the purpose;

(*e*) Where a company not having the liability of its members limited by Act of the Imperial Parliament or Legislature of the Territory, or letters patent, is about to register as a limited company, the majority required to assent as aforesaid shall consist of not less than three-fourths of the members present, personally or by proxy, at such last mentioned general meeting;

(*f*) Where a company is about to register as a company limited by guarantee, the assent to its being so registered shall be accompanied by a resolution declaring that each member undertakes to contribute to the assets of the company, in the event of the same being wound up during the time that he is a member, or within one year afterwards, for payment of the debts and liabilities of the company, contracted before the time at which he ceased to be a member and of the costs, charges, and expenses of winding up the company, and for the adjustment of the rights of the contributories amongst themselves, such amount as may be required not exceeding a specified amount.

(2) In computing any majority under this section when a poll is demanded, regard shall be had to the number of votes to which each member is entitled according to the regulations of the company of which he is a member.

Companies capable of being registered

210. With the above exceptions and subject to the foregoing regulations, every company existing at the time of the commencement of this Act, consisting of five or more members, and any company hereafter formed in pursuance of any Act of the imperial Parliament or Act of the Legislature of the Territory, other than this Act, or by Royal Charter or letters patent, or being otherwise duly constituted by law, and consisting of five or more members, may, at any time hereinafter, register itself under this Act as an unlimited company, or a company limited by shares, or a company limited by guarantee; and no such registration shall be invalid by reason that it has taken place with a view to the company being wound up.

Definition of joint stock company

211. For the purposes of this Part, so far as the same relates to the description of companies empowered to register as companies limited by shares, a joint stock company shall be deemed to be a company having a permanent paid-up or nominal capital of fixed amount, divided into shares also of fixed amount, or held and transferable as stock, or dividend and held partly in one way and partly in the other, and formed on the principle of having for its members the holders of shares in such capital, or the holders of such stock, and no other person; and such company, when registered with limited liability under this Act, shall be deemed to be a company limited by shares.

Requisitions for registration by companies

212. Previously to the registration in pursuance of this Part of any joint stock company there shall be delivered to the Registrar the following documents that is to say -

(a) a list showing the names, addresses and occupations of all persons who, on a day named in such list, and not being more than six clear days before the day of registration, were members of such company, with the addition of the shares held by such persons respectively, distinguishing, in cases where such shares are numbered, each share by its number;

(b) a copy of any Act of the Imperial Parliament or Legislature of the Territory, Royal Charter, letters patent, deed of settlement, contract or copartners or other instrument constituting or regulating the company;

(c) if any joint stock company is intended to be registered as a limited company, the above list and copy shall be accompanied by a statement specifying the following particulars; that is to say -

(i) the nominal capital of the company and the number of shares into which it is divided;

(ii) the number of shares taken and the amount paid on each share;

(iii) the name of the company, with the addition of the word "Limited" as the last word thereof; with the addition, in the case of a company intended to be registered as a company limited by guarantee, of the resolution declaring the amount of the guarantee.

Requisitions for registration by existing company not being a joint stock company

213. Previously to the registration in pursuance of this Part of any company not being a joint stock company, there shall be delivered to the Registrar a list showing the names, addresses, and occupations of the directors or other managers, if any, of the company, also a copy of any Act of the Imperial Parliament or Legislature of the Territory, letters patent, deed of settlement, contract or copartnery or other instrument constituting or regulating the company, with the addition, in the case of a company intended to be registered as a company limited by guarantee, of the resolution declaring the amount of the guarantee.

Power for existing company to register amount of stock instead of shares

214. There a joint stock company, authorized to register under this Act, has the whole or any portion of its capital converted into stock, such company shall, as to the capital so converted, instead of delivering to the Registrar a statement of shares, deliver to the Registrar a statement of the amount of stock belonging to company, and the names of the persons who were holders of such stock, on same day to be named in the statement, not more than six clear days before the registration.

Authentication of statements of existing companies

215. The list of members and directors, and any other particulars relating to the company, hereby required to be delivered to the Registrar shall be verified by the declaration of the directors of the company delivering the same, or any two of them or of any two other principal officers of the company, made before the Registrar of the Supreme Court.

Registrar may require evidence as to nature of company

216. The Registrar may require such evidence as he thinks necessary for the purpose of satisfying himself whether an existing company is or not a joint stock company as hereinbefore defined.

Exemption of certain companies from payment of fees

217. No fees shall be charged in respect of the registration, in pursuance of this Part, of any company in cases where such company is not registered as a limited company, or where, previously to its registered as a limited company, the liability of the shareholders was limited by some other Act of the Imperial Parliament or Legislature of the Territory or by letters patent.

Power of company to change name

218. Any company authorized by this Part to register with limited liability shall, for the purpose of obtaining registration with limited liability, change its name, by adding thereto the word "Limited"

Certificate of registration of existing companies

219. Upon compliance with the requisitions in this Part contained with respect to registration, and on payment of such fees, if any, as are payable under the tables marked B and C in the First the Registrar shall certify under his hand that the company so applying for registration is incorporated as a company under this Act, and, in the case of a limited company, that it is limited and thereupon such company shall be incorporated, and shall have perpetual succession and a common seal, with power to hold lands and to exercise all the functions of an incorporated company.

Certificate to be evidence of compliance with Act

220. A certificate of incorporation given at any time to any company registered in pursuance of this Part shall be conclusive evidence that all the requisitions herein contained in respect of registration under this Act have been complied with, and that the company is authorized to be registered under this Act as a limited or unlimited company, as the case may be, and the date of incorporation mentioned in such certificate shall be deemed to be the date at which the company is incorporated under this Act.

Transfer of property to company

221. All such property, real and personal, including all interests and rights in, to, and out of property, real and personal, and including obligations and things in action as may belong to or be vested in the company at the date of its registration under this Act, shall, on registration pass to and vest in the company as incorporated under this Act for all the estate and interest of the company therein.

Registration not to affect obligations incurred previous to registration

222. The registration in pursuance of this Part of any company shall not affect or prejudice the liability of such company to have enforced against it, or its rights to enforce, any debt or obligation incurred, or any contract entered into, by, to, with, or on behalf of such company previously to such registration.

Continuation of existing actions

223. All such actions, suits and other legal proceedings as may, at the time of the registration of any company registered in pursuance of this Part, have commenced by or against such company, or the public officer or any member thereof, may be continued in the same manner as if such registration had not taken place; nevertheless, execution shall not issue against the effects of any individual member of such company upon any judgment, decree, or order obtained in any action, suit or proceeding so commenced as aforesaid; but in the event of the property and effects of the company being insufficient to satisfy such judgment, decree or order, an order may be obtained for winding up the company.

Effect of registration under Act

224.(1) When a company is registered under this Act in pursuance of this Part all provisions contained in any Act of the Imperial Parliament or Legislature of the Territory, deed of settlement, contract or copartnery, letters patent, or other instrument constituting or regulating the company, including, in the case of a company registered as a company limited by guarantee, the resolution declaring the amount of the guarantee, shall be deemed to be conditions and regulations of the company, in the same manner and with the same incidents as if they were contained in a registered Memorandum of Association and Articles of Association; and all the provisions of this Act shall apply to such company and the members, contributories, and creditors thereof in the same manner in all respects as if it had been formed under this Act, subject to the provisions following, that is to say -

(a) that Table A in the First Schedule shall not, unless adopted by special resolution, apply to any company registered under this Act in pursuance of this Part;

(b) that the provisions of this Act relating to the numbering of shares shall not apply to any joint stock company whose shares are not numbered;

(c) that no company shall have power to alter any provision contained in any Act of the Imperial Parliament or Legislature of the Territory relating to the company;

(d) that no company shall have power, without the sanction of the Governor, to alter any provision contained in any letters patent relating to the company;

(e) that in the event of the company being wound up, every person shall be a contributory, in respect of the debts and liabilities of the company contracted prior to registration, who is liable, at law or in equity, to pay or to contribute to the payment of any debt or liability of the company contracted prior to registration, or to pay or contribute to the payment of any sum for the adjustment of the rights of the members amongst themselves in respect of any such debt or liability; or to pay or to contribute to the payment of the cost, charges, and expenses of winding up the company, so far as related to such debts or liabilities as aforesaid; and every such contributory shall be liable to contribute to the assets of the company, in the course of the winding up, all sums due from him in respect of any such liability as aforesaid; and in the event of the death or bankruptcy of any such contributory as last aforesaid, the provisions hereinbefore contained with respect to the representatives, heirs and devisees of deceased contributories, and with reference to the trustees of bankrupt contributories, shall apply;

(f) that nothing herein contained shall authorize any company to alter any such provisions contained in any deed of settlement, contract of copartnery, letters patent, or other instrument constituting or regulating the company, as would, if such company had originally been formed under this Act, have been contained in the Memorandum of Association, and are not authorized to be

altered by this Act.

(2) Nothing herein contained shall derogate from any powers of altering its constitution or regulations which may be vested in any company registering under this Act in pursuance of this Part by virtue of any act of the Imperial Parliament or Legislature of the Territory, deed of settlement, contract of copartnery, letters patent, or other instrument constituting or regulating the company.

Power of Court to restrain further proceedings

225. The Court may, at any time after the presentation of a petition for winding up a company registered in pursuance of this Part, and before making an order for winding up the company, upon the application by motion of any creditor of the company, restrain further proceedings in any action, suit or legal proceeding against any contributory of the company, as well as against the company as hereinbefore provided, upon such terms as the Court thinks fit.

Order for winding up company

226. Where an order has been made for winding up a company registered in pursuance of this Part, in addition to the provisions hereinbefore contained it is hereby further provided that no suit, action, or other legal proceedings shall be commenced, or proceeded with against any contributory of the company in respect of any debt of the company, except with the leave of the Court, and subject to such terms as the Court may impose.

PART VII - Private Companies

Private company can convert into public company

227. A private company may, subject to anything contained in the Memorandum of Articles, by passing a special resolution, and by filing such resolution with the Registrar, turn itself into a public company.

Consequences attached to breach of certain Articles of private companies

228.(1) Where the articles of a company include the provisions which, by section 2 are required to be included therein in order to constitute a company a private company, and default is made in complying with any of those provisions, the company shall cease to be entitled to the privileges and exemptions conferred upon private companies hereunder and thereupon the provisions of this Act shall apply to the company as though it were not a private company.

(2) Where the Court is satisfied that the failure to comply with the conditions was accidental or due to inadvertence or some other sufficient cause, or that on other grounds it is just and equitable to grant relief, the Court may, on the application of the company, or any other person interested, and on such terms and conditions as seem to the Court just and expedient, order that the company be relieved from such consequences as aforesaid.

Annual list, summary and certificate to be sent to Registrar

229. Every private company shall send with the annual list of members and summary required to sent under section 49, a certificate, signed by a director or the secretary, that the company has not since the date of the last return, or in the case of a first return since the date of the incorporation of the company, issued any invitation to the public to subscribe for any shares or debentures of the company; and, where the list of members disclosed the fact that the number of members of the company exceeds fifty, also a certificate so signed that such excess consists wholly of persons who are under section 2, are to be excluded in reckoning the number of fifty.

PART VIII - Unregistered Companies

Winding up of unregistered companies, except Friendly Societies

230. Subject as hereinafter mentioned, any partnership, association, or company, except Friendly Societies established under the Friendly Societies' Acts for the time being in force in the Territory, consisting of more than five members, friendly and not registered under this Act, and hereinafter included under the term "unregistered company" may be wound up under this Act, and all the provisions of this Act with respect to winding up shall apply to such company, with the following exceptions and additions -

(a) No unregistered company shall be wound up under this Act voluntarily or subject to the supervision of the Court;

(b) The circumstances under which an unregistered company may be wound up are as follows, that is to say -

(i) whenever the company is dissolved, has ceased to carry on business, or is carrying on business only for the purpose of winding up its affairs;

(ii) whenever the company is unable to pay its debts;

(iii) whenever the Court is of opinion that it is just and equitable that the company should be wound up;

(c) An unregistered company shall, for the purposes of this Act, be deemed to be unable to pay its debts -

(i) whenever a creditor, by assignment or otherwise, to whom the company is indebted, at law or in equity, in a sum exceeding two hundred and forty dollars then due, has served on the company, by leaving the same at the principal place of business of the company, or by delivering to the secretary or some director or principal officer of the company, or by otherwise serving the same in such manner as the Court may approve or direct, a demand under his hand requiring the company to pay the sum so due, and the company has, for the space of three weeks succeeding the service of such demand, neglected to pay such sum, or to secure or compound for the same to the satisfaction of the creditor;

(ii) whenever any action, suit or other proceeding has been instituted against any member of the company for any debt or demand due, or claimed to be due, from the company, or from him in his character of member of the company, and notice in writing of the institution of such action, suit or other legal proceeding having been served upon the company, by leaving the same at the principal place of business of the company, or by delivering it to the secretary, or some director, manager or principal officer of the company, or by otherwise serving the same in such manner as the Court may approve or direct, the company has not within ten days after service of such notice paid, secured, or compounded for such debt or demand, or procured such action, suit, or other legal proceeding to be stayed, or indemnified the defendant, to his reasonable satisfaction, against such action, suit, or other legal proceeding, and against all cost, damages, and expenses to be incurred by him by reason of the same;

(iii) whenever execution or other process issued on a judgment, decree, or order obtained in any Court in favour of any creditor in any proceeding at law or in equity instituted by such creditor against the company, or any member thereof as such, or against any person authorized to be sued as nominal defendant on behalf of the company, is returned unsatisfied;

(iv) whenever it is otherwise proved to the satisfaction of the Court that the company is unable to pay its debts.

Who to be deemed a contributory in event of unregistered company being wound up

231. In the event of an unregistered company being wound up, every person shall be deemed to be a contributory who is liable, at law or in equity, to pay or contribute to the payment of any debt or liability of the company, or to pay or contribute to the payment of any sum for the adjustment of the rights of the members amongst themselves, or to pay or contribute to the payment of the costs, charges and expenses of winding up the company, and every such contributory shall be liable to contribute to the assets of the company, in the course of the winding up, all sums due from him in respect of any such liability as aforesaid; but, in the event of the death or bankruptcy of any contributory, the provisions hereinbefore contained with respect to the personal representatives, heirs and devisees of a deceased contributory, and to the trustee of a bankrupt contributory, shall apply.

Power of Court to restrain further proceedings

232. The Court, at any time after the presentation of a petition for winding up an unregistered company and before making an order for winding up the company, may, upon the application of any creditor of the company, restrain further proceedings in any action, suit or proceeding against any contributory of the company, or against the company, as hereinbefore provided, upon such terms as the Court thinks fit.

Effect of order for winding up unregistered company

233. Where an order has been made for winding up an unregistered company, in addition to the provisions hereinbefore contained in the case of companies formed under this Act, it is hereby further provided that no suit, action, or other legal proceeding shall be commenced or proceeded with against any contributory of the company in respect of any debt of the company, except with the leave of the Court, and subject to such terms as the Court may impose.

Further provision in case of unregistered company

234. If any unregistered company has no power to sue and be sued in a common name, or if for any reason it appears expedient, the Court may, by the order made for winding up such company, or by any subsequent order, direct that all such property, real and personal (including all interest, claims, and rights into and out of property, real and personal, and including things in action), as may belong to or be vested in the company, or to or in any person or persons on trust for or on behalf of the company, or any part of such property, is to vest in the official liquidator or official liquidators by his or their official name or names, and thereupon the same or such part thereof as may be specified in the order shall vest accordingly; and the official liquidator or official liquidators, may, in his or their official name or names, or in such name or names and after giving such indemnity as the Court directs, bring or defend any actions, suits, or other legal proceedings necessary to be brought or defended for the purposes of effectually winding up the company and recovering the property thereof.

Provisions in this Part of Act cumulative

235. The provisions made by this Part with respect to unregistered companies shall be deemed to be made in addition to and not in restriction of any provisions hereinbefore contained with respect to winding up companies by the Court, and the Court or official liquidator may, in addition to anything contained in this Part, exercise any powers or do any act in the case of unregistered companies which might be exercised or done by it or him in winding up companies formed under this Act; but an unregistered company shall not, except in the event of its being wound up, be deemed to be a company under this Act, and then only to the extent provided for by this Part.

PART IX - Companies Established Outside The Territory

Requirements as to companies established outside the Territory

235A.(l) Every company incorporated outside the Territory which establishes a place of business within the Territory shall within one month from the establishment of such place of business, and every such company which before the coming into outside the operation of this section established a place of business within the Territory, shall within six months from the coming into operation of this section file with the Registrar for registration -

(a) a certified copy of the charter, statutes, or Memorandum of Association and Articles of Association of the company, or other instrument constituting or defining the constitution of the company, and, if the instrument is not written in the English language, a certified translation thereof;

(b) a list of the directors and secretary of the company containing the particulars mentioned in subsection (2) of this section;

(c) the names and addresses of some one or more persons resident in the Territory authorized to accept on behalf of the company service of process and any notices required to be served on the company; and in the event of any alterations being made in any such instrument or in the directors or in the names or addresses of any such persons as herein required, the company shall within fifteen days from the date of such alteration file with the Registrar a notice of the alteration.

(2) The list referred to in paragraph (b) of subsection (1) of this section shall contain the following particulars, that is to say -

(a) with respect to each director -

(i) in the case of an individual, his Christian name and surname and any former Christian name or surname, his usual residential address, his nationality and his business occupation, if any, or if he has no business but holds any other directorship or directorships, particulars of that directorship or of those directorships; and

(ii) in the case of a corporation, its corporate name and registered or principal office;

(b) with respect to the secretary or, where there are joint secretaries, with respect to each of them -

(i) in the case of an individual, his present Christian name and surname, any former Christian name and surname and his usual residential address; and

(ii) in the case of a corporation or a Scottish firm, its corporate or firm name and registered or principal office.

(3) Any process or notice required to be served on the company shall be sufficiently served if addressed to any person whose name has been so filed as aforesaid and left at or sent by post to the address which has been so filed.

(4) Every company to which this section applies shall in every year file with the Registrar such a statement in the form of a Balance Sheet as would, if it were a company formed and registered under this act and having a share capital, be required under this Act to be included in the annual summary.

(5) Every company to which this section applies, and which uses the word "Limited" as part of its name, or whose liability is otherwise limited, shall -

(a) in every prospectus inviting subscriptions for its shares or debentures in the Territory, state the country in which the company is incorporated; and

(b) conspicuously exhibit on every place where it carries on business in the Territory, the name of the company and the country in which the company is incorporated;

(c) have the name of the company and of the country in which the company is incorporated mentioned in legible characters in all bill-heads and letter paper, and, in all notices, advertisements and other official publications of the company.

(6) If any company to which this section applies fails to comply with any of the requirements of this section the company, and every officer or agent of the company, shall be guilty of an offence and shall be liable on summary conviction to a fine not exceeding two hundred and fifty dollars in the currency of the United States of America, or, in the case of a continuing offence, twenty-five dollars in the currency of the United States of America for every day during which the default continues.

(7) For the purposes of this section -

the expression "certified" means certified by a director or secretary of the company to be a true copy or a correct translation;

the expression "director" includes any person occupying the position of director, by whatever name called; and

the expression "prospectus" means prospectus, notice, circular, advertisement or other invitation offering to the public for subscription or purchase any shares or debentures of the company.

(8) There shall be paid to the Registrar-

(a) for registering any document as required under paragraph (a) of subsection (1) of this section a fee of one hundred dollars in the currency of the United States of America;

(b) for registering any other document required by this section to be filed with him a fee of ten dollars in the currency of the United States of America.

PART X

Forms in Second Schedule

236. The forms set forth in the Second Schedule, or forms as near thereto as circumstances admit, shall be used in all matters to which such forms refer. The Governor may, from time to time, make such alterations in the tables and forms contained in the First Schedule, so that it does not increase the amount of fees payable to the Registrar in the said Schedule mentioned, and in the forms in the Second Schedule, or make such additions to the last-mentioned forms, as he deems requisite. Any such table or form, when altered, shall be published in the Gazette, and upon such publication being made, such table or form shall have the same force as if it were included in the Schedule, but no alteration made by the Governor in the table marked A contained in the First Schedule shall affect any company registered prior to the date of such alteration; or repeal, as respects such company, any portion of such table.

Right of appeal to the High Court

237.(1) Whenever any person shall be aggrieved by any decision of the Registrar in any matter governed by this Act, such person shall have the right, within ninety days of such decision, to appeal to the High Court against such decision and may for that purpose require the Registrar to state and sign a case, setting forth the matter in dispute and requesting the High Court to make a ruling therein.

(2) The Registrar shall, within thirty days of receipt of the request pursuant to subsection (1), state and sign a case accordingly and deliver the same to the person by whom it is required and, on his application, such case shall be set down for hearing by the High Court.

PART XI - Miscellaneous

Interpretation

238. In this Part unless the context otherwise requires -

"assets" means the gross assets of the company as shown in the Balance Sheet of the company if any has been prepared on the basis of normal accounting principles as at the 31st day of December next preceding the licence date or if none has been so prepared then the gross assets of the company which would be shown in a Balance Sheet prepared on such basis and as at such date but always excluding from such assets the assets of the company in the Territory;

"assets in the Territory" means all assets which are physically situate in the Territory, vessels and aircraft registered in the Territory, shares in any company incorporated in the Territory and chooses in action which by law are deemed situate in the Territory;

"resident company" means a company which during the year ending on the 31st day of December last preceding the licence date -

(a) has availed itself of the provisions of any Income Tax (Double Taxation Relief) Order in Council made by the Government of the United Kingdom and applicable to the Territory implementing the terms of any Double Taxation Relief agreement entered into between the Government of the United Kingdom and the Government of any other country and for this purpose a company shall be taken to have availed itself of the provisions of such an Order if it shall have been entitled to pay or shall have paid any dividend or interest free of any tax which would have been imposed on such dividend or interest if such an Order had not been made;

(b) is a company the affairs of which were controlled and managed in the Territory at any time during such year other than during the thirty days next following its incorporation and without limiting the generality of the foregoing definition the affairs of the company shall be deemed to be so controlled and managed wherever on or after the effective date of this act more than half the members of the Board of Directors are resident in the Territory; or

(c) is a company incorporated on or after the lst December in such year and which on or before the licence date shall have notified the Registrar in the prescribed manner that it desires to be classified as resident;

"non-resident company" means any company which is not a resident company;

"licence date" means 30th April in any year.

Licence fee

239. Every company incorporated under the provision of this Act and every company registered to do business in the Territory under the provisions of Part IX shall on or before the licence date make a return to the Registrar in the prescribed form and shall on the licence date pay to the Registrar an annual licence fee in respect of the twelve months immediately following the licence date as follows: -

For non resident companies	$ 250.00
For resident companies whose assets do not exceed $10,000	$ 25.00
exceed $10,000 but do not exceed $50,000	$ 50.00
exceed $50,000 but do not exceed $100,000	$ 100.00
exceed $100,000 but do not exceed $200,000	$ 200.00
exceed $200,000 but do not exceed $300,00	$ 300.00
exceed $300,000 but do not exceed $400,000	$ 400.00
exceed $400,000 but do not exceed $500,000	$ 500.00
exceed $500,000 but do not exceed $600,000	$ 600.00
exceed $600,000 but do not exceed $700,000	$ 700.00
exceed $700,000 but do not exceed $800,000	$ 800.00
exceed $800,000 but do not exceed $900,000	$ 900.00
exceed $900,000 but do not exceed $1,500,000	$ 1,000.00
exceed $1,500,000 but do not exceed $2,000,000	$ 1,500.00
exceed $2,000,000 but do not exceed $2,500,000	$ 2,000.00
exceed $2,500,000 but do not exceed $3,000,000	$ 2,500.00
exceed $3,000,000 but do not exceed $3,500,000	$ 3,000.00
exceed $3,500,000 but do not exceed $4,000,000	$ 3,500.00
exceed $4,000,000 but do not exceed $5,000,000	$ 5,000.00

exceed $5,000,000 but do not exceed $6,000,000	$ 6,000.00
exceed $6,000,000 but do not exceed $7,000,000	$ 7,000.00
exceed $7,000,000 but do not exceed $8,000,000	$ 8,000.00
exceed $8,000,000 but do not exceed $9,000,000	$ 9,000.00
exceed $9,000,000	$10,000.00

Provided that were any company has failed to pay the licence fee due on or before the 31st day of July next following the licence date the licence fee due and payable for such company shall be 110% of the amounts stated above, if such fee is paid between the 31st day of July and the 31st day of October next following the licence date, and shall be 150% of the amounts stated above if such licence fee is paid between the 31st day of December next following the licence date.

(Note - up to 31st December 1981 the fee was abated by such sum as the company shall have paid in the twelve months immediately preceding the due date in respect of any licence under the Trade Licensing Act, 1963 or the Banking Act, 1972).

Striking off for failure to pay fee

240.(1) If a company in any year fails to pay its annual licence fee by the 3lst December, the Registrar shall forthwith strike the name of the company off the register and in the case of a company registered under Part IX, shall cancel its registration.

(2) Where the name of a company has been struck off the register or where its registration has been cancelled for non-payment of the annual licence fee, the Registrar may, upon application made to him and subject to payment of the fees set forth in subsection (3), restore the name of the company to the register; and, where the name of a company is so restored, it shall be deemed never to have been struck off the register.

(3) The fees payable upon any application to the Registrar under subsection (2) are as follows:

(a) all fees payable in terms of section 239; and

(b) if the application for restoration of the name of the company is made.

(i) within 6 months of the date on which the name of the company was struck off $250.00

(ii) later than 6 months after that date $500.00

(4) For the avoidance of doubt it is hereby stated that

(a) the fees referred to in paragraph (a) of subsection (3) are the unpaid annual licence fees payable by the company in respect of each year prior to the year of restoration of its name to the register together with 50% of each annual licence fee; and

(b) the fees specified in paragraph (b) of the subsection are the fees that are payable in respect of the application for restoration of the company's name to the register.

Regulations

241. The Governor may make such regulations as he may deem necessary or expedient for the better carrying out, administration and enforcement of this Part of the Act.

FIRST SCHEDULE

Ss. 39, 40, 89, 91, 224, 236

TABLE A

Regulations For Management Of A Company Limited By Shares

1) If several persons are registered as joint holders of any share, any one of such persons may give effectual receipts for any dividend payable in respect of such share.

2) Every member shall, on payment of twenty-four cents, or such less sum as the company in general meeting may prescribe, be entitled to a certificate, under the common seal of the company, specifying the share or shares held by him, and the amount paid up thereon.

3) If such certificate is worn out or lost, it may be renewed on payment of twenty-four cents, or such less sum as the company in general meeting may prescribe.

Calls On Shares

4) The directors may, from time to time, make such calls upon the members in respect of all moneys unpaid on their shares as they think fit, provided that twenty-one days notice at least is given of each call, and each member shall be liable to pay the amount of calls so made to the persons, and at the times and places, appointed by the directors.

5) A call shall be deemed to have been made at the time when the resolution of the directors authorizing such call was passed.

6) f the call payable in respect of any shares is not paid before or on the day appointed for payment thereof, the holder for the time being of such share shall be liable to pay interest for the same at the rate of six per cent per annum from the day appointed for the payment thereof to the time of the actual payment.

7) The directors may, if they think fit, receive from any member willing to advance the same, all or any part of the moneys due upon the shares held by him beyond the sums actually called for; and upon the moneys so paid in advance, or so much thereof as from time to time exceeds the amount of the calls then made upon the shares in respect of which such advance has been made, the company may pay interest at such rate as the member paying such sum in advance and the directors agree upon.

Transfer Of Shares

8) The instrument of transfer of any share in the company shall be executed both by the transferor and transferee and the transferor shall be deemed to remain a holder of such share until the name of the transferee is entered in the register book in respect thereof.

9) Shares in the company shall be transferred in the following form -

I, A.B., of, _____________ in consideration of the sum of _____ dollars, paid to me by C.D., of , do hereby transfer to the said C.D. the share (or shares) numbered _______________ standing in my name in the books of the _____________ company, to hold unto the said C.D., his executors, administrators, and assigns, subject to the several conditions on which I held the same at the time of the execution hereof; and I, the said C.D., do hereby agree to take the said share (or shares) subject to the same conditions. As witness our hands the ____________ day of ____________.

10) The company may decline to register any transfer of shares made by a member who is indebted to them.

11) The transfer books shall be closed during the fourteen days immediately preceding the ordinary general meeting in each year.

Transmission Of Shares

12) The executors or administrators of a deceased member shall be the only persons recognized by the company as having any title to his share.

13) Any person becoming entitled to a share in consequence of the death or bankruptcy of any member may be registered as a member upon such evidence being produced as may, from time to time, be required by the company.

14) Any person who has become entitled to a share in consequence of the death or bankruptcy of any member may, instead of being registered himself, elect to have some person named by him registered as a transferee of such share.

15) The person so becoming entitled shall testify such election by executing to his nominee an instrument of transfer of such share.

16) The instrument of transfer shall be presented to the company, accompanied with such evidence as the directors may require to prove the title of the transferor, and thereupon the company shall register the transferee as a member.

Forfeiture Of Shares

17) If any member fails to pay any call on the day appointed for payment thereof, the directors may, at any time thereafter, during such time as the call remains unpaid, serve a notice on him, requiring him to pay such call, together with interest and any expenses that may have accrued by reason of such non-payment.

18) The notice shall name a further day on or before which such call, and all interest and expenses that have accrued by reason of such nonpayment, are to be paid; and shall also name the place where payment is to be made (the place so named being either the registered office of the company, or some other place at which calls of the company are usually made payable). The notice shall also state that, in the event of non-payment at or before the time and at the place appointed, the shares in respect of which such call was made will be liable to be forfeited.

19) If the requisitions of any such notice as aforesaid are not complied with, any share in respect of which such notice has been given may, at any time thereafter before the payment of all calls, interest and expenses due in respect thereof has been made, be forfeited by a resolution of the directors to that effect.

20) Any share so forfeited shall be deemed to be the property of the company and may be disposed of in such manner as the company in general meeting thinks fit.

21) Any member whose shares have been forfeited shall notwithstanding, be liable to pay the company all calls owing upon such shares at the time of the forfeiture.

22) A statutory declaration in writing that the call in respect of a share was made and notice thereof given, and that default in payment of the call was made, and that the forfeiture of the share was made by a resolution of the directors to that effect, shall be sufficient evidence of the facts therein stated, as against all persons entitled to such share; and such declaration and the receipt of the company for the price of such share, shall constitute a good title to such share, and a certificate of proprietorship shall be delivered to a purchaser, and thereupon he shall be deemed the holder of such share discharged from all calls due prior to such purchase, and he shall not be bound to see to the application of the purchase money, nor shall his title to such share be affected by any irregularity in the proceedings in reference to such sale.

Conversion Of Shares Into Stock

23) The directors may, with the sanction of the company previously given in general meeting, convert any paid up shares into stock.

24) When any shares have been converted into stock, the several holders of such stock may thenceforth transfer their respective interests therein or any part of such interests, in the same manner and subject to the same regulations as and subject to which any shares in the capital of the company may be transferred, or as near thereto as circumstances admit.

25) The several holders of stock shall be entitled to participate in the dividends and profits of the company according to the amount of their respective interests in such stock and such interests shall, in proportion to the amount thereof, confer on the holders thereof respectively the same privileges and advantages for the purpose of voting at meetings of the company, and for other purposes, as would have been conferred by shares of equal amount in the capital of the company; but so that none of such privileges or advantages, except the participation in the dividends and profits of the company, shall be conferred by any such aliquot part of consolidated stock as would not, if existing in shares, have conferred such privileges or advantages.

Increase In Capital

26) The directors may, with the sanction of a special resolution of the company previously given in general meeting increase its capital by the issue of new shares, such aggregate increase to be of such amount, and to be divided into shares of such respective amounts, as the company in general meeting directs, or if no direction is given, as the directors think expedient.

27) Subject to any direction to the contrary, that may be given by the meeting that sanctions the increase of capital, all new shares shall be offered to the members in proportion to the existing shares held by them, and such offer shall be made by notice specifying the number of shares to which the member is entitled, and limiting a time within which the offer, if not accepted, will be deemed to be declined, and after the expiration of such time, or on the receipt of an intimation from the member to whom such notice is given that he declines to accept the shares offered, the directors may dispose of the same in such manner as they think most beneficial to the company.

28) Any capital raised by the creation of new shares shall be considered as part of the original capital, and shall be subject to the same provisions with reference to the payment of calls, and the forfeiture of shares on non-payment of calls, or otherwise, as if it had been part of the original capital.

General Meetings

29) The first general meeting shall be held at such time, not being more than six months after the registration of the company, and at such place as the directors may determine.

30) Subsequent general meetings shall be held at such time and place as may be prescribed by the company in general meeting; and if no other time or place is prescribed, a general meeting shall be held on the first Monday in February in every year, at such place as may be determined by the directors.

31) The above-mentioned general meetings shall be called ordinary meetings; all other general meetings shall be called extra-ordinary.

32) The directors may, whenever they think fit, and they shall, upon a requisition made in writing by not less than one-fourth in number of the members of the company, convene an extraordinary general meeting.

33) Any requisition made by the members shall express the object of the meeting proposed to be called, and shall be left at the registered office of the company.

34) Upon the receipt of such requisition the directors shall forthwith proceed to convene an extraordinary meeting. If they do not proceed to convene the same within twenty-one days from the date of the requisition, the requisitionists, or any other members amounting to the required number, may themselves convene an extraordinary general meeting.

Proceedings At General Meetings

35) Seven days notice at the least, specifying the place, the day, and the hour of meeting, and, in case of special business, the general nature of such business, shall be given to the members in manner hereinafter mentioned, or in such other manner, if any, as may be prescribed by the company in general meeting; but the non-receipt of such notice by any member shall not invalidate the proceedings at any general meeting.

36) All business shall be deemed special that is transacted at an extraordinary meeting, and all that is transacted at any ordinary meeting, with the exception of sanctioning a dividend and the consideration of accounts, balance sheet, and the ordinary report of the directors.

37) No business shall be transacted at any general meeting, except the declaration of a dividend, unless a quorum of members is present at the time when the meeting proceeds to business; and such quorum shall be ascertained as follows, that is to say: if the persons who have taken shares in the company at the time of the meeting do not exceed five in number, the quorum shall be three, if they exceed five there shall be added to the above quorum one for every five-additional members up to fifty and one for every ten additional members after fifty, with this limitation, that no quorum shall in any case exceed twenty.

38) If within one hour from the time appointed for the meeting, a quorum is not present, the meeting, if convened upon the requisition of members, shall be dissolved; in any other case, it shall stand adjourned to the same day in the next week, at the same time and place; and if, at such adjourned meeting, a quorum is not present, it shall be adjourned sine die.

39) The chairman, if any, of the board of directors shall preside as chairman at every general meeting of the company.

40) If there is no such chairman, or if at any meeting he is not present within fifteen minutes after the time appointed for holding the meeting, the members present shall choose some one of their number to be chairman.

41) The chairman may, with the consent of the meeting, adjourn any meeting from time to time, and from place to place, but no business shall be transacted at any adjourned meeting other than the business left unfinished at the meeting from which the adjournment took place.

42) At any general meeting, unless a poll is demanded by at least three members, a declaration by the chairman that a resolution has been carried, and an entry to that effect in the book of proceedings of the company, shall be sufficient evidence of the fact, without proof of the number or proportion of the votes recorded in favour of or against such resolution.

43) If a poll is demanded by three or more members, it shall be taken in such manner as the chairman directs, and the result of such poll shall be deemed to be the resolution of the company in general meeting; and in the case of an equality of votes at any general meeting, the chairman shall be entitled to a second or casting vote.

Votes Of Members

44) Every member shall have one vote for every share up to ten; he shall have an additional vote for every five shares beyond the first ten shares up to one hundred, and an additional vote for every ten shares beyond the first hundred shares.

45) If any member is a lunatic or idiot he may vote by his committee.

46) If two or more persons are jointly entitled to a share or shares the members whose name stands first in the Register of members as one of the holders of such share or shares, and no other shall be entitled to vote in respect of the same.

47) No member shall be entitled to vote at any general meeting unless all calls due from him have been paid, and no member shall be entitled to vote, in respect of any share that he has acquired by transfer, at any meeting held after the expiration of three months from the registration of the company, unless he has been possessed of the share in respect of which he claims to vote for at least three months previously to the time of holding the meeting at which he proposes to vote.

48) Votes may be given either personally or by proxy.

49) The instrument appointing a proxy shall be in writing under the hand of the appointer, or such appointer is a corporation, under their common seal, and shall be attested by one or more witness or witnesses. No person shall be appointed a proxy who is not a member of the company.

50) The instrument appointing a proxy shall be deposited at the registered office of the company not less than seventy-two hours before the time for holding the meeting at which the person named in such instrument proposes to vote, but no instrument appointing a proxy shall be valid after the expiration of twelve months from the date of its execution, unless it purports to appoint a proxy to act for the appointer during his absence from the Territory.

51) An instrument appointing a proxy shall be in the following form -

Company, Limited.

I, ____________ of ____________, in the Territory of ____________, being a member of the Company, Limited, and entitled to vote (or, votes), hereby appoint ___________ of ___________, as my proxy, to vote for me and on my behalf at the ordinary (or extraordinary, as the case may be) general meeting of the company to be held on the ___________ day of ___________, and at any adjournment thereof (or at any meeting of the Company that may be held during my absence from the Territory of ____________).

As witness my hand this ____________ day of ____________ .

Signed by the said ____________ in the presence of ____________ .

Directors

52) The number of the directors, and the names of the first directors, shall be determined by the subscribers of the Memorandum of Association.

53) Until directors are appointed the subscribers of the Memorandum of Association shall be deemed to be directors.

54) The future remuneration of the directors, and their remuneration for services performed previously to the first general meeting, shall be determined by the company in general meeting.

Powers Of Directors

55) The business of the company shall be managed by the directors, who may pay all expenses incurred in getting up and registering the company, and may exercise all such powers of the company as are not by the foregoing Act, or by these articles, required to be exercised by the company in general meeting; subject, nevertheless, to any regulations of these articles, to the provisions of the foregoing Act, and to such regulations, being not inconsistent with the aforesaid regulations or provisions, as may be prescribed by the company in general meeting; but no regulation made by the company in general meeting shall invalidate any prior act of the directors which would have been valid if such regulations had not been made.

56) The continuing directors may act notwithstanding any vacancy in their body.

Disqualification Of Directors

57) The office of a director shall be vacated -

If he becomes bankrupt; or

If he is concerned in, or participates in, the profits of any contract with the company.

But the above rule shall be subject to the following exception: That no director shall vacate his office by reason of his being a member of any company which has entered into contracts with or done any work for, the company of which he is director; nevertheless, he shall not vote in respect of such contract or work, and, if he does so vote, his vote shall not be counted.

Rotation Of Directors

58) At the first ordinary meeting after the registration of the company, the whole of the directors shall retire from office; and at the first ordinary meeting in every subsequent year, one-third of the directors for the time being; or if their number is not a multiple of three, then the nearest number to one-third shall retire from office.

59) The one-third or other nearest number to retire during the first and second years ensuing the first ordinary meeting of the company shall, unless the directors agree amongst themselves, be determined by ballot. In every subsequent year the one-third or other nearest number who have been longest in office shall retire.

60) A retiring director shall be re-eligible.

61) The company, at the general meeting at which any directors shall retire in manner aforesaid, shall fill up the vacated offices by electing a like number of persons.

62) If at any meeting at which an election of directors ought to take place the places of the vacating directors are not filled up, the meeting shall stand adjourned till the same day in the next week, at the same time and place; and if at such adjourned meeting the places of the vacating directors are not filled up the vacating directors, or such of them as have not had their places filled up, shall continue in office until the ordinary meeting in the next year, and so on from time to time until their places are filled up.

63) The company may from time to time, in general meeting, increase or reduce the number of directors, and may also determine in what rotation such increased or reduced number is to go out of office.

64) Any casual vacancy occurring in the board of directors may be filled up by the directors, but any person so chosen shall retain his office so long only as the vacating director would have retained the same if no vacancy had occurred.

65) The company, in general meeting, may, by special resolution, remove any director before the expiration of his period of office, and may by an ordinary resolution appoint another person in his stead; the person appointed shall hold office during such time only as the director in whose place he is appointed would have held the same if he had not been removed.

Proceedings Of Directors

66) The directors may meet together for the dispatch of business, adjourn, and otherwise regulate their meetings as they think fit, and determine the quorum necessary for the transaction of business. Questions arising at any meeting shall be decided by a majority of votes; in case of an equality of votes the chairman shall have a second or casting vote: a director may at any time summon a meeting of the directors.

67) The directors may elect a chairman of their meetings, and determine the period for which he is to hold office; but if no such chairman is elected, or if at any meeting the chairman is not present at the time appointed for holding the same, the directors present shall choose some one of their number to be the chairman of such meeting.

68) The directors may delegate any of their powers to committees consisting of such member or members of their body as they think fit; any committee so formed shall in the exercise of the powers so delegated, conform to any regulations that may be imposed on them by the directors.

69) A committee may elect a chairman of their meetings; if no such chairman is elected, or if he is not present at the time appointed for holding the same, the members present shall choose one of their number to be chairman of such meeting.

70) A committee may meet and adjourn as they think proper. Questions arising at any meeting shall be determined by a majority of votes of the members present; and in case of an equality of votes, the chairman shall have a second or casting vote.

71) All acts done by any meeting of the directors, or of a committee of directors, or by any person acting as director, shall, notwithstanding that it be afterwards discovered that there was some defect in the appointment of any such directors or persons acting as aforesaid, or that they or any of them were disqualified, be as valid as if every such person had been duly appointed and was qualified to be a director.

Dividends

72) The directors may, with the sanction of the company in general meeting, declare a dividend to be paid to the members in proportion to their shares.

73) No dividend shall be payable except out of the profits arising from the business of the company.

74) The directors may, before recommending any dividend, set aside out of the profits of the company such sum as they think proper as a reserve fund to meet contingencies or for equalizing dividends, or for repairing or maintaining the works connected with the business of the company, or any part thereof; and the directors may invest the sum so set apart as a reserve fund upon such securities as they may select.

75) The directors may deduct from the dividends payable to any member all such sums of money as may be due from him to the company on account of calls or otherwise.

76) Notice of any dividend that may have been declared shall be given to each member in manner hereinafter mentioned; and all dividends unclaimed for three years, after having been declared, may be forfeited by the directors for the benefit of the company.

77) No dividends shall bear interest as against the company.

Accounts

78) The directors shall cause true accounts to be kept -

Of the stock in trade of the company;

Of the sums of money received and expended by the company, and the matter in respect of which such receipts and expenditures takes place; and

Of the credit and liabilities of the company.

The books of account shall be kept at the registered office of the company, and subject to any reasonable restrictions as to the time and manner of inspecting the same that may be imposed by the company in general meeting, shall be open to the inspection of the members during the hours of business.

79) Once at the least in every year the directors shall lay before the company in general meeting a statement of the income and expenditure for the past year made up to a date not more than three months before such meeting.

80) The statement so made shall show, arranged under the most convenient heads, the amount of gross income, distinguishing the several sources from which it has been derived, and the amount of gross expenditure, distinguishing the expense of the establishment, salaries and other like matters; every item of expenditure fairly chargeable against the year's income shall be brought into account, so that a just balance of profit and loss may be laid before the meeting; and in cases where any item of expenditure, which may in fairness be distributed over several years, has been incurred in any one year, the whole amount of such item shall be stated, with the addition of the reasons why only a portion of such expenditure is charged against the income of the year.

81) A Balance Sheet shall be made out in every year, and laid before the company in general meeting, and such Balance Sheet shall contain a summary of the property and liabilities of the company, arranged under heads appearing in the form annexed to this table, or as near thereto as circumstances admit.

82) A printed copy of such Balance Sheet shall, seven days previously to such meeting, be served on every member in the manner in which notices are hereinafter directed to be served.

Audit

83) Once at the least in every year the accounts of the company shall be examined, and the correctness of the Balance Sheet ascertained by one or more auditor or auditors.

84) The first auditors shall be appointed by the directors: subsequent auditors shall be appointed by the company in general meeting.

85) If one auditor only is appointed, all the provisions herein contained relating to auditors shall apply to him.

86) The auditors may be members of the company, but no person is eligible as an auditor who is interested, otherwise than a member, in any transaction of the company; and no director or other officer of the company is eligible during his continuance in office.

87) The election of auditors shall be made by the company at their ordinary meeting in each year.

88) The remuneration of the first auditors shall be fixed by the directors; that of subsequent auditors shall be fixed by the company in general meeting.

89) Any auditor shall be re-eligible on his quitting office.

90) If any casual vacancy occurs in the office of any auditor appointed by the company, the directors shall forthwith call an extraordinary general meeting for the purpose of supplying the same.

91) If no election of auditors is made in manner aforesaid the Governor may, on the application of not less than five members of the company, appoint an auditor for the current year, and fix the remuneration to be paid to him by the company for his services.

92) Every auditor shall be supplied with a copy of the Balance Sheet, and it shall be his duty to examine the same with the accounts and vouchers relating thereto.

93) Every auditor shall have a list delivered to him of all books kept by the company, and shall at all reasonable times have access to the books and accounts of the company; he may, at the expense of the company, employ accountants or other persons to assist him in investigating such accounts, and he may, in relation to such accounts, examine the directors or any other officer of the company.

94) The auditors shall make a report to the members upon the Balance Sheet and Accounts, and in every such report they shall state whether, in their opinion, the Balance Sheet is a full and fair Balance Sheet, containing the particulars required by these regulations, and properly drawn up so as to exhibit a true and correct view of the state of the company's affairs, and in case they have called for explanations or information from the directors, whether such explanations or information have been given by the directors, and whether they have been satisfactory; and such report shall be read, together with the report of the directors, at the ordinary meeting.

Notices

95) A notice may be served by the company upon any member either personally, or by leaving the same either at his registered place of abode or place of business in the town where the company's principal office is situate, or by posting it in a prepaid letter addressed to him at his registered place of abode when elsewhere than in such town.

96) All notices directed to be given to the members shall, with respect to any share to which persons are jointly entitled, be given to whichever of such persons is named first in the register of members; and notice so given shall be sufficient notice to all the holders of such share.

97) Any notice, if served by post, shall be deemed to have been served at the time when the letter containing the same would be delivered in the ordinary course of the post, and, in proving such service, it shall be sufficient to prove that the letter containing the notices was properly addressed and put into the post office.

Balance Sheet (1) Of The Co. Made Up To 19

Capital And Liabilities

Property And Assets

Capital: Showing -

1) The number of shares ...

2) The amount paid per share Dr.

3) If any arrears of calls, the nature of the arrears and the names of any defaulters ...

4) The particulars of any forfeited shares

II - Debts and Liabilities of the Company: Showing -

5) The amount of loans on mortgages or debenture bonds.

6) The amount of debts owing by the company, distinguishing -

a) Debts for which acceptances have been given...

b) Debts to tradesmen for supplies of stock-in-trade or other articles

c) Debts for law expenses ...

d) Debts for interest on debentures or other loans ...

e) Unclaimed dividends

f) Debts not enumerated above

Property held by the Company: Showing -

7) Immovable property,

distinguishing -

a) Freehold lands

b) Freehold buildings

c) Leasehold buildings

8) Movable property, distinguishing -

d) Stock in trade...

e) Plant...

The cost to be stated with deductions for deterioration in value as charged to the reserve fund or profit and loss...

IV - Debts owing to the Company: Showing -

9) Debts considered good for which the company holds bills or other securities

10) Debts considered good for which the company holds no securities ...

11) Debts considered doubtful and bad. Any debt due from a director or other officer of the company to be separately stated.

V - Cash and Investments.

Showing -

12) The nature of investment and rate of investment

13) The amount of cash, where lodged, and if bearing interest

[--- Unable To Translate Graphic ---]

Contingent Liabilities -

Claims against the company not acknowledged as debts ....

Moneys for which the company is contingently liable ...

(1) See Regulation 81 in Table A.

VI - Reserve Fund: Showing -

The amount set aside from profits to meet contingencies

VII - Profit and Loss: Showing -

The disposable balance for payment of dividends, etc.

[--- Unable To Translate Graphic ---]

TABLE B Ss. 42, 49, 207, 219.

Tables Of Fees To Be Paid To The Registrar

By A Company Having A Capital Divided Into Shares

17/1981 For registration of a company whose nominal capital does not exceed $10,000, a fee of $ 200

17/1981 For registration of a Company whose nominal capital registration exceeds $10,000, the fee of $200 with the following additional fee of $15 for subsequent increase of every additional $10,000 of nominal capital or part thereof

17/1981 For filing annual returns $ 50

17/1981 For registering of any document hereby required or authorized to be registered, other than Memorandum of Association $ 10

17/1981 For making a record of any part hereby authorized or required to be recorded by the Registrar of Companies, a fee of $ 10

11/1988 For certified copy or extract of any document $ 10

11/1988 For an inspection of the documents kept by the Registrar pursuant to this Act $ 2

Table C Ss. 42, 219.

Table Of Fees To Be Paid To The Registrar By A Company Not Having A Capital Divided Into Shares

2/1976 For registration of a company not having a Capital divided into shares $ 100

For registering any document hereby required or authorized to be registered, other than the Memorandum of Association $ 5

34/1977 For making a record of any fact hereby authorized or required to be required to be recorded by the Registrar, a fee of $ 5

S. 82 table D

Form Of Statement Referred To In Part Iii Of This Act

*The capital of the company is $ ______________ , divided into ______________ shares of $ each.

The number of shares issued is ____________, calls to the amount of $ ____________ per share have been made, under which the sum of $ ____________ has been received.

The liabilities of the company on the lst day of ____________ , were -

Debts owing to sundry person by the company -

On judgment, $

On specialty, $

On notes or bills, $

On simple contracts, $

On estimated liabilities, $

The assets of the company on that day were

Government securities (stating them), $

Bills of exchange and promissory notes, $

Cash at the bankers, $ other securities, $

*If the company has no capital divided into shares, the portion of the statement relating to capital and shares must be omitted.

Second Schedule

S. 236

Form A

Memorandum Of Association Of A Company Limited By Shares

1st) The name of the company is "The Company, Limited"

2nd) The registered office of the company will be situate in

3rd) The object for which the company is established are

4th) The liability of the members is limited

5th) The capital of the company is $ ___________, divided into shares of $ _________ each.

We, the several persons whose names and addresses are subscribed, are desirous of being formed into a company, in pursuance of this, Memorandum of Association, and we respectively agree to take the number of shares in the capital of the company set opposite our respective names.

Names and addresses

Descriptions of Subscribers

Number of Shares taken by each

Subscriber

1)	John Jones of St. John's	Merchant	200
2)	John Smith of Basseterre	Planter	25
3)	Thomas Green of	Storekeeper	30
4)	John Thomspon of	Lawyer	40
5)	Caleb White of	Cattle Breeder	15
6)	Andrew Brown of	Grazier	5
7)	Caesar White of	Market Gardener	10
		TOTAL SHARES TAKEN	325

Dated the ____________ day of _____________ 19 __.

FORM B

Memorandum And Articles Of Association Of A Company Limited By Guarantee, And Not Having A Capital Divided Into Shares

Memorandum of Association

1st) The name of the company is

2nd) The registered office of the company will be situated in

3rd) The objects for which the company is established are

4th) Every member of the company undertakes to contribute to the assets of the company in the event of the same being wound up during the time that he is a member, or within one year afterwards, for payment of the debts and liabilities of the company contracted before the time at which he ceases to be a member, and the costs, charges and expenses of winding up the same, and for the adjustment of the rights of the contributories amongst themselves, such amount as may be required, not exceeding $48.00.

We, the several persons whose names and addresses are subscribed, are desirous of being formed into a company, in pursuance of this Memorandum of Association.

Names, Addresses, and Descriptions of Subscribers

1) John Jones, of , Merchant.

2) John Smith, of ,

3) Thomas Green, of ,

4) John Thompson, of ,

5) Caleb White, of ,

6) Andrew Brown, of ,

7) Caesar White, of ,

Date the ____________ day of ____________, 19___.

Witness to the above signatures.

A.B. (address to be added).

Articles Of Association To A Company Preceding Memorandum Of Association

1) The company, for the purpose of registration, is declared to consist of members.

2) The directors hereinafter mentioned may, whenever the business of the association requires it, register an increase of members.

Definition Of Members

3)Every person shall be deemed to have agreed to become a member of the company who insures any share in pursuance of the regulations hereinafter contained.

General Meetings

4) The first general meeting shall be held at such time not being more than three months after the incorporation of the company, and at such place, as the directors may determine.

5) Subsequent general meetings shall be held at such time and place as may be prescribed by the company in general meeting; and if no other time or place is prescribed, a general meeting shall be held on the first Monday in February in every year, at such place as may be determined by the directors.

6) The above-mentioned general meetings shall be called ordinary meetings; all other general meetings shall be called extraordinary.

7) The directors may, whenever they think f it, and they shall, upon a requisition made in writing by any three or more members, convene an extraordinary general meeting.

8) Any requisition made by the members shall express the object of the meeting proposed to be called, and shall be left at the registered office of the company.

9) Upon the receipt of such requisition, the directors shall forthwith proceed to convene a general meeting; if they do not proceed to convene the same within twenty-one days from the date of the requisition, the requisitionist, or any other three members, may themselves convene a meeting.

Proceedings At General Meetings

10) Seven days, notice at the least specifying the place, the day, and the hour of meeting, and in case of special business, the general nature of such business, shall be given to the members in manner hereinafter mentioned, or in such other manner, if any as may be prescribed by the company in general meeting; but the non receipt of such notice by any member shall not invalidate the proceedings at any general meeting.

11) All business shall be deemed special that is transacted at an extraordinary meeting, and all that is transacted at an ordinary meeting, with the exception of the consideration of the Accounts, Balance Sheets, and the ordinary report of the directors.

12) No business shall be transacted at any meeting except the declaration of dividend, unless a quorum of members is present at the commencement of such business; and such quorum shall be ascertained as follows: that is to say, if the members of the company at the time of the meeting do not exceed five in number, the quorum shall be three; if they exceed five, there shall be added to the above quorum one for every five additional members up to fifty, and one for every ten additional members after fifty, with this limitation, that no quorum shall in any case exceed thirty.

13) If within one hour from the time appointed for the meeting a quorum of members is not present, the meeting, if convened upon the requisition of the members, shall be dissolved; in any other case it shall stand adjourned to the same day in the following week at the same time and place; and if at such adjourned meeting a quorum of members is not present, it shall be adjourned sine die.

14) The chairman, if any, of the directors shall preside as chairman at every general meeting of the company.

15) If there is no such chairman, or if at any meeting he is not present at the time of holding the same, the members present shall choose some one of their number to be chairman of such meeting.

16) The chairman may, with the consent of the meeting adjourn any meeting from time to time and from place to place, but no business shall be transacted at any adjourned meeting other than the business left unfinished at the meeting from which the adjournment took place.

17) At any general meeting, unless a poll is demanded by at least three members, a declaration by the chairman that a resolution has been carried, and an entry to that effect in the book of proceedings of the company, shall be sufficient evidence of the fact, without proof of the number or proportion of the votes recorded in favour of or against such resolution.

18) If a poll is demanded in manner aforesaid, the same shall be taken in such manner as the chairman directs, and the results of such poll shall be deemed to be the resolution of the company in general meeting.

Votes Of Members

19) Every member shall have one vote and no more.

20) If any member is a lunatic or idiot he may vote by his committee.

21) No member shall be entitled to vote at any meeting unless all moneys due from him to the company have been paid.

22) Votes may be given either personally or by proxies. A proxy shall be appointed in writing under the hand of the appointer or if such appointer is a corporation, under its common seal.

23) No person shall be appointed a proxy who is not a member, and the instrument appointing him shall be deposited at the registered office of the company not less than forty-eight hours before the time of holding the meeting at which he proposes to vote.

24) Any instrument appointing a proxy shall be in the following form -

____________, Company, Limited

I, ____________ of ____________, in the Territory of ____________, being a member of the Company, Limited, hereby appoint __________ , of as my proxy, to vote for me and on my behalf at the (ordinary or extraordinary, as the case may be) general meeting of the company to be held on the ____________ day of ____________, and at any adjournment thereof.

As witness my hand this ____________ day of ____________ .

Signed by the said ____________ in the presence of ____________ .

Directors

25) The number of the directors, and the names of the first directors, shall be determined by the subscribers of the Memorandum of Association.

26) Until directors are appointed, the subscribers of the Memorandum of Association shall for all purposes of this Act be deemed to be directors.

Power Of Directors

27) The business of the company shall be managed by the directors, who may exercise all such powers of the company as are not hereby required to be exercised by the company in general meeting; but no regulation made by the company in general meeting shall invalidate any prior act of the directors which would have been valid if such regulation had not been made.

Election Of Directors

28) The directors shall be elected annually by the company in general meeting.

BUSINESS OF COMPANY

(Here insert rules as to mode in which business of is to be conducted).

29) The accounts of the company shall be audited by a committee of two members, to be called the audit committee.

30) The first audit committee shall be nominated by the directors out of the body of members.

31) Subsequent audit committees shall be nominated by the members at the ordinary general meeting in each year.

32) The audit committee shall be supplied with a copy of the Balance Sheet, and it shall be their duty to examine the same with the Accounts and vouchers relating thereto.

33) The audit committee shall have a list delivered to them of all books kept by the company, and they shall at all reasonable times have access to the books and accounts of the company; they may, at the expense of the company, employ accountants or other persons to assist them in investigating such accounts, and they may, in relation to such accounts, examine the directors or any other officer of the company.

34) The audit committee shall make a report to the members upon the Balance Sheet and Accounts, and in every such report they shall state whether in their opinion the Balance Sheet is a full and fair Balance Sheet, containing the particulars required by the regulations of the company, and properly drawn up, so as exhibit a true and correct view of the state of the company's affairs, and in case they have called for explanation or information from the directors, whether such explanation or information has been given by the directors, and whether it has been satisfactory, and such report shall be read together with the report of the directors at the ordinary meeting.

Notices

35) A notice may be served by the company upon any member either personally, or by leaving the same at his registered place of business, in the town where the company's principal office is situate, or by posting it in a prepaid letter addressed to him at his registered place of abode when elsewhere than in such town.

36) Any notice, if served by post, shall be deemed to have been served at the time when the letter containing the same would be delivered in the ordinary course of the post, and in proving such service it shall be sufficient to prove that the letter containing the notice was properly addressed and put into the post office.

Winding Up

37) The company shall be wound up voluntarily whenever an extraordinary resolution, as defined by the Companies Act, is passed, requiring the company to be would up voluntarily.

Names, Addresses, and Descriptions of Subscribers

1) John Jones, of , Merchant.

2) John Smith, of ,

3) Thomas Green, of ,

4) John Thompson, of ,

5) Caleb White, of ,

6) Andrew Brown, of ,

7) Caesar White, of ,

Date the ____________ day of ____________, 19___.

Witness to the above signatures.

A.B. (address to be added).

Form C

Memorandum And Articles Of Association Of A Company Limited By Guarantee, And Having A Capital Divided Into Shares

1st) The name of the company is

2nd) The registered office of the company will be situate in

3rd) The objects for which the company is established are

4th) Every member of the company undertakes to contribute to the assets of the company, in the event of the same being wound up during the time that he is a member, or within one year afterwards, for payment of the debts and liabilities of the company contracted before the time at which he ceases to be a member, and the costs, charges, and expenses of winding up the same; and for the adjustment of the rights of the contributories amongst themselves, such amount as may be required, not exceeding $96.00.

We, the several persons whose names and addresses are subscribed are desirous of being formed into a company in pursuance of this Memorandum of Association.

Names, Addresses, and Descriptions of Subscribers

1) John Jones, of , Merchant.

2) John Smith, of ,

3) Thomas Green, of ,

4) John Thompson, of ,

5) Caleb White, of ,

6) Andrew Brown, of ,

7) Caesar White, of ,

Date the ____________ day of ____________, 19___.

Witness to the above signatures.

A.B. (address to be added).

Articles Of Association To A Company Preceding Memorandum Of Association

1) The capital of the company shall consist of $ __________ divided into ___________ shares of $ ____________ each.

2) The directors may, with the sanction of the company in general meeting, reduce the amount of shares.

3) The directors may, with the sanction of the company in general meeting, cancel any shares belonging to the company.

4) All the Articles of Table A shall be deemed to be incorporated with these Articles, and to apply to the company.

We, the several persons whose names and addresses are subscribed, agree to take the number of shares in the capital of the company set opposite our respective names.

Names and addresses

Descriptions of Subscribers

Number of Shares taken by each

Subscriber

1)	John Jones of St. John's	Merchant	200
2)	John Smith of Basseterre	Planter	25
3)	Thomas Green of	Storekeeper	30
4)	John Thomspon of	Lawyer	40
5)	Caleb White of	Cattle Breeder	15
6)	Andrew Brown of	Grazier	5
7)	Caesar White of	Market Gardener	10
TOTAL SHARES TAKEN			325

Dated the ____________ day of ______________ 19 ___.

Witness to the above signatures,

A.B. (address to be added).

Form D

Memorandum And Articles Of Association Of An Unlimited Company, Having A Capital Divided Into Shares Memorandum Of Association

lst) The name of the company is

2nd) The registered office of the company will be situate in

3rd) The objects for which the company are established are

We, the several persons whose names are subscribed, are desirous of being formed into a company, in pursuance of this Memorandum of Association.

Names, Addresses, and Descriptions of Subscribers

1) John Jones, of, Merchant.

2) John Smith, of ,

3) Thomas Green, of ,

4) John Thompson, of ,

5) Caleb White, of ,

6) Andrew Brown, of ,

7) Caesar White, of ,

Date the ____________ day of ____________, 19___.

Witness to the above signatures.

A.B. (address to be added).

Articles Of Association To Accompany Preceding Memorandum Of Association Capital Of The Company

The capital of the Company is $ ____________ divided into shares of $ ____________ each.

Application of Table A

All the Articles of Table A shall be deemed to be incorporated with these Articles, and to apply to the company.

We, the several persons whose names and addresses are subscribed, agree to take the number of shares in the capital of the company set opposite our respective names.

Names and addresses

Descriptions of Subscribers

Number of Shares taken by each Subscriber

1)	John Jones of St. John's	Merchant	200
2)	John Smith of Basseterre	Planter	25
3)	Thomas Green of	Storekeeper	30
4)	John Thomspon of	Lawyer	40
5)	Caleb White of	Cattle Breeder	15
6)	Andrew Brown of	Grazier	5
7)	Caesar White of	Market Gardener	10
TOTAL SHARES TAKEN			325

Dated the ____________ day of _____________ 19 ___ .

Witness to the above signatures,

A.B. (address to be added).

Form E

As Required By The Second Part Of The Act Summary Of Capital And Shares Of The Company, Made Up To The ____________ Day Of ____________ 19__.

Nominal capital $ ____________, divided into ____________ shares of $ ____________ each.

Number of shares taken up to the ____________ day of ____________ .

There has been called up on each share $ ____________ .

Total amount of calls received $ ____________.

Total amount of calls unpaid $ ____________.

List of persons holding shares in the _________ Company on the _________ day of _________ , and of persons who have held shares therein at any time during the year immediately preceding the said ____________ day of ____________, showing their names and addresses, and on account of the shares so held.

Names, Addresses & Occupations Account of shares

Folio in Registrar Ledger containing particulars

Surname

Christian Name

Address

Occupation

Shares held by Existing Members during Preceding Year

Additional Shares held by Existing Members during Preceding Year

Number Date of transfer

Shares held by persons no longer members

Number Date of transfer

Remarks

COMPANY MANAGEMENT ACT, 1990

ARRANGEMENT OF SECTIONS

28. Commencement.

SCHEDULE

Short title

1. This Act may be cited as the Company Management Act, 1990.

PART I - Preliminary

Interpretation

2.(1) In this Act,

"auditor" means a person who

(a) is qualified as an accountant by examination conducted by one of the institutes of Chartered Accountants or Certified Accountants in England and Wales, Ireland, or Scotland, the Canadian Institute of Chartered Accountants or the American Institute of Certified Public Accountants and is a current member in good standing of one of those institutes; or

(b) possesses such other qualification in accountancy as the Governor in Council, by order, approves and is in good standing with respect to such qualification;

"business of company management" means the provision of company management services for profit or reward in or from within the Virgin Islands;

"Certificate of Compliance" means the Certificate of Compliance issue under paragraph (c) of subsection (1) of section 17;

"company management" means

(a) the registration of companies under the Companies Act or the International Business Companies Act;

(b) the provision of registered agent services for companies incorporated under the International Business Companies Act;

(c) the provision of registered office services for companies incorporated under the Companies Act or the International Business Companies Act;

(d) the provision of directors or officers for companies; and

(e) the provision of nominee shareholders of companies;

"financial year" means, in relation to a licensee under this Act,

(a) the period not exceeding 53 weeks at the end of which the balance of the licensee's account is struck; or

(b) if no such balance is struck, or if a period in excess of 53 weeks is used, then a calendar year;

"Governor" means the Governor in council;

"Inspector" means the Inspector of Company Managers appointed under section 14;

"licence" means a licence granted under subsection (3) of section 4;

"licensee" means a person holding a licence under this Act;

"Registrar" means the Registrar of the High Court.

(2) For the purposes of this Act and subject to subsection (5), a company is deemed to be a subsidiary of another if

(a) that other either

(i) is a member of it and controls the composition of its board of directors, or

(ii) holds more than half in nominal value of its equity share capital; or

(b) the first-mentioned company is a subsidiary of any company that is the other's subsidiary.

(3) For purposes of subsection (2), the composition of a company's board of directors is deemed to be controlled by another company if that other company by the exercise of some power exercisable by it without the consent or concurrence of any other person can appoint or remove the holders of all or a majority of the directorships.

(4) For purposes of subsection (3), the other company is deemed to have power to appoint to a directorship with respect to which any of the following conditions is satisfied:

(a) that a person cannot be appointed to it without the exercise in his favour by the other company of such a power as is mentioned in subsection (3);

(b) that a person's appointment to the directorship follows necessarily from his appointment as a director of the other company; or

(c) that the directorship is held by the other company itself or by a subsidiary of it.

(5) In determining whether one company is a subsidiary of another

(a) any shares held or power exercisable by the other in a fiduciary capacity are to be treated as not held or exercisable by it;

(b) subject to paragraphs (c) and (d), any shares held or power exercisable

(i) by any person as nominee for the other except where the other is concerned only in a fiduciary capacity, or

(ii) by, or by a nominee for, a subsidiary of the other not being a subsidiary which is concerned only in a fiduciary capacity, are to be treated as held or exercisable by the other;

(c) any shares held or power exercisable by any person by virtue of the provisions of any debentures of the first-mentioned company or of a trust deed securing any issue of such debentures are to be disregarded; and

(d) any shares held or power exercisable by, or by a nominee for, the other or its subsidiary, not being held or exercisable as mentioned in paragraph (c), are to be treated as not held or exercisable by the other if the ordinary business of the other or its subsidiary, as the case may be, includes the lending of money and the shares are held or the power is exercisable as above-mentioned by way of security only for the purposes of a transaction entered into in the ordinary course of that business.

(6) For purposes of this Act

(a) a company is deemed to be another's holding company if the other is its subsidiary; and

(b) a body corporate is deemed the wholly-owned subsidiary of another if it has no members except that other and that other's wholly owned subsidiaries and its or their nominees.

PART II - Licences

Requirement for licence

3. No person shall carry on the business of company management in or from within the Virgin Islands unless he has obtained a licence under this Act for the purpose.

Application for licence

4.(1) A licence is obtainable by making application therefor to the Governor in the prescribed form.

(2) An application under subsection (1) shall contain the particulars set out the Schedule and shall be accompanied by the fee set forth in section 5.

(3) If the Governor is satisfied that an application is not against the public interest and that the applicant is qualified to carry on the business of company management, he may grant the application and issue to the applicant a licence subject to such terms and conditions as appear to the Governor necessary.

(4) Any decision to refuse to grant a licence, other than a licence in respect of a business in existence at the date of the commencement of this Act, is final and is not subject to any appeal.

(5) The Governor shall cause notice of the grant of a licence under this Act to be published in the Gazette.

Fees

5.(1) An application under section 4 shall be accompanied by a fee of $200 which is not refundable.

(2) The issue of a licence under section 4 shall be subject to payment of

(a) a fee of $500 if the licence is issued on or before the 30th day of June in any year; or

(b) a fee of $250 if the licence is issued on or after the 1st day of July in any year.

Duration of licence

6. A licence issued under this Act is valid until the 31st December of the year in which it is issued but is renewable during the month of January in the following year for a further period of one year upon payment of

(a) a fee of $500; and

(b) a fee equivalent to $10 for each company registered under the Companies Act or International Business Companies Act, 1984, for which the licensee provides the registered office.

Exemptions from licences

7.(1) A person who is licensed under this Act is not required to be licensed under the Business, Professions and Trade Licences Act, 1989 to carry on the business of company management.

(2) This Act does not apply to a company licensed under the Banks and Trust Companies Act, 1990.

Existing businesses

8. A person who at the date of the commencement of this Act is carrying on the business of company management has a period of three months from that date within which to comply with the provisions of this Act.

Notification of change in particulars of licensee

9. Where a change occurs in the particulars of a licensee, as set out in the application for the licence, the licensee shall, as soon as possible thereafter, inform the Governor of the change.

Capitalization of company management companies

10. No licence shall be issued in respect of a company the paid up share capital of which is less than $25,000.

Display of licence

11. A licence issued under this Act shall be prominently displayed on the premises where the business of company management is carried on.

Surrender of licence

12.(1) A licensee who has ceased to carry on the business in respect of which the licence was granted may apply to the Governor to surrender his licence if the licensee

(a) produces evidence that he has repaid all deposits and has transferred al assets held or administered on behalf of companies managed by him; or

(b) being a company, is being wound up voluntarily and produces evidence that the company is solvent and is able on demand to repay all deposits held by it and all its other creditors and has transferred all assets held or administered on behalf of companies managed by it, and the Governor may thereupon approve the surrender.

(2) In the case of an application under paragraph (b) of subsection (1), the Attorney General may apply to the court for an order that the licensee be wound up either by the court, or be subject to the supervision of the court, and where the court so orders the provisions of the Companies Act relating to the winding up of a company by or subject to the supervision of the court, mutatis mutandis, apply.

PART III - Transferability of Shares and Changes in Directors

Shares, etc., not to be issued or transferred without approval

13.(1) No shares or other interests, whether legal or equitable, in a company or partnership licensed under this Act shall be issued, transferred or otherwise disposed of without the prior written approval of the Governor except that the Governor may exempt any company or partnership from the provisions of this section without approval subject to such terms and conditions as the Governor thinks fit.

(2) No appointment of directors of a company licensed under this Act shall be made without the prior written approval of the Governor.

PART IV - Administration

Inspector of Company Managers

14.(1) The Governor shall appoint a public officer to be known as the Inspector of Company Managers for the purpose of ensuring the proper administration of this Act.

(2) The functions of the Inspector are

(a) to maintain a general review of company management in the Virgin Islands;

(b) where he thinks fit or when required by the Governor, to examine in such manner as he considers for the purpose of satisfying himself that all provisions of this Act are being complied with and that the licensee is in a sound financial position and is carrying on his business in a satisfactory manner, and to report to the Governor the results of such examination;

(c) to report to the Governor regarding any documents or records examined by or produced to the Inspector in the course of the performance of his functions; and

(d) to examine and make recommendations to the Governor with respect to all applications for licences.

(3) In the performance of his duties under this Act and subject to the provisions of section 20, the Inspector may at all reasonable times

(a) require a licensee to produce for examination such of his books, records and other documents that the licensee is required to maintain pursuant to section 16; and

(b) require a licensee to supply such information or explanation, as the Inspector may reasonably require for the purpose of enabling him to perform his functions under this Act.

(4) Notwithstanding subsection (3), the Inspector does not have access to any document of a company managed by a licensee or to any information, matter or thing relating to or concerning the affairs of any such company without first having obtained

(a) the written consent of that company; or

(b) an order of the court made on the grounds that there are no other reasonable means of obtaining such document, matter or thing.

(5) The Inspector, with the written approval of the Governor, may authorize in writing any person to assist him in the performance of his functions under this Act.

Restrictions in use of certain terms

15.(1) No person other than a licensee shall

(a) use any word, either in English or in any other language, in the description or title under which he carries on business in or from within the Virgin Islands that, in the opinion of the Governor, suggests the business of company management; or

(b) make any representation in any document or in any other manner that is likely to suggest that he is carrying on the business of company management.

(2) The Governor may require a licensee who carries on the business of company management a name which is

(a) identical with that of any other person, whether within or outside the Virgin Islands, or which so nearly resembles that name as to be calculated to deceive;

(b) calculated to suggest falsely the patronage of or connection with some person whether within or outside the Virgin Islands; or

(c) calculated to suggest falsely that he has a special status in relation to or derived from the Government or has the official approval of, or acts on behalf of, the Government or of any of its departments or officials, forthwith to change his name and in default of compliance may revoke his licence.

Duties of licensee

16. A licensee shall maintain in respect of his business of company management

(a) such books and records as shall accurately reflect the business of the licensee;

(b) separate accounts in his books for each company the licensee manages and shall segregate the funds and other property of every such company from his own; and

(c) one or more separate bank accounts into which he shall deposit all monies held by him on behalf of each company he manages.

Annual returns, etc.

17.(1) A licensee shall within 6 months of the end of his financial year

(a) prepare annual accounts in accordance with generally accepted accounting principles, audited by an independent auditor;

(b) furnish to the Inspector his annual accounts together with written confirmation from an independent auditor that the annual accounts have been prepared as required under paragraph (a) hereof and whether or not the auditor's certificate for such accounts is unqualified and if qualified, the nature of the qualification; and

(c) furnish to the Inspector a Certificate of Compliance issued by an independent auditor that the information set out in the application for a licence, as modified by any subsequent notification of change in accordance with section 9, remains correct and gives an accurate summary of the business of the licensee.

(2) A licensee shall, at any time, if required by the Inspector furnish to the Inspector a Certificate of Compliance issued in accordance with paragraph (c) of subsection (1).

(3) A licensee shall, at any time, if required by the Inspector, produce to the Inspector such evidence as may be required as to the solvency or otherwise of his business and that the licensee has, in the case of a company, maintained the required minimum paid up share capital.

Power of search

18.(1) If a Judge or a magistrate is satisfied by information on oath, whether oral or written, given by the Inspector or a person authorized by the Inspector

(a) that a licence has been suspended under section 21;

(b) that there is reasonable ground for suspecting that an offence against this Act has been or is being committed and that evidence of the commission of the offence is to be found at any premises or in any vehicle, vessel or aircraft specified in the information; or

(c) that any documents, cash or securities that ought to have been produced under subsection (3) of section 14 and have not been produced are to be found at any premises or in any vehicle, vessel or aircraft specified in the information he may grant a search warrant authorizing the Inspector, together with any other person named in the warrant, to enter such premises or any premises at any such time within one month from the date of the warrant, and to search the premises or the vehicle, vessel or aircraft.

(2) The Inspector or any other person authorized by a warrant to search any premises or any vehicle, vessel or aircraft may search every person who is found in or whom he has reasonable ground to believe to have recently left or to be about to enter those premises, or that vehicle, vessel or aircraft, and may seize any document, cash or security found in the premises, or in the vehicle, vessel or aircraft which he has reasonable grounds for believing ought to have been produced under subsection (3) of section 14, except that no female shall, in pursuance of any warrant issued under this section, be searched except by a female.

(3) Where by virtue of this section a person has any power to enter any premises or a vehicle, vessel or aircraft, he may use such force as is reasonably necessary for the purpose of exercising that power.

PART V - Miscellaneous

Power of Inspector to require insurance

19. The Inspector may require a licensee to effect a policy of insurance with a reputable insurance company against to require

(a) losses arising out of claims of negligence or breach of duty by the licensee or by any employee;

(b) the dishonesty of employees or of the licensee;

(c) loss of documents; and

(d) such other risks as the Inspector may stipulate, in such amount and of such a nature as the Inspector may determine to be fit and proper, having due regard to the nature and type of business carried on by the licensee; and, in the event that the insurance is withdrawn, cancelled or not renewed, the licensee shall immediately notify the Inspector and shall cease to carry on his business until the insurance has been reinstated or replaced.

Preservation of secrecy

20.(1) Except for the purpose of the performance or exercise of his duties or functions under this Act or when lawfully required to do so by the court or under the provisions of any other law, neither the Inspector nor any person acting under his authority shall disclose any information relating to any application under the provisions of this Act, or to the affairs of a licensee or of a company managed by a licensee, which he has acquired in the performance or exercise of such duties or functions.

(2) Any person who contravenes subsection (1) is guilty of an offence and is liable on summary conviction to a fine not exceeding $2,500 or to imprisonment for a term not exceeding one year or both.

Suspension of licence

21.(1) Where the Governor is of the opinion that a licensee is

(a) carrying on the business of company management in a manner detrimental to the public interest, or to the interest of the companies being managed by him or any of them; or

(b) contravention of this Act or any other law, the Governor may require him forthwith to take such steps as may be necessary to rectify the matter, and may forthwith suspend the licence pending the receipt of information or any explanation under paragraph (b) of subsection (3) of section 14.

(2) A suspension shall not exceed a period of 30 days, unless extended from time to time by an order of the court on application of the Inspector on the grounds that it is in the public interest that the suspension continue and specifying the duration of such period of further suspension, which shall not itself exceed 30 days each at any one time.

Revocation of licence

22.(1) The Governor may revoke a licence

(a) if the licensee has ceased to carry on the business of company management;

(b) if the licensee
- **(i)** becomes bankrupt,
- **(ii)** goes into liquidation,
- **(iii)** is wound up, or
- **(iv)** is otherwise dissolved; or

(c) if, having received a report from the Inspector regarding the licensee under paragraph (b) of subsection (2) of section 14, he is of the opinion that it would be detrimental to the public interest for the licensee to continue to carry on the business of company management.

(2) An appeal under this section shall not operate as a suspension of the revocation.

Offences

23.(1) Any person who with intent to deceive, for any purpose of this Act makes any representation that he knows to be false or does not believe to be true, is guilty of an offence and is liable on summary conviction to a fine not exceeding $50,000 or to imprisonment for a term not exceeding 2 years or both.

(2) Subject to subsection (1), a person who with intent to deceive, by any act or omission contravenes any provision or requirement of this Act, is guilty of an offence and is liable on summary conviction to a fine not exceeding $25,000 or to imprisonment for a term not exceeding one year or both.

(3) Any licensee who advertises inviting either directly or indirectly other parties to commit breaches of the laws of the country in which such advertisement appears or to which such advertisement is directed is guilty of an offence and is liable on summary conviction to a fine not exceeding $1,000 or to imprisonment for a term not exceeding 6 months or both.

(4) Where a limited liability company is convicted of an offence under subsection (3), every director and every officer concerned with the management of the company is also liable to be convicted for that offence unless he satisfies the court that the offence was committed without his knowledge or consent or that he took all reasonable steps to prevent the commission of the offence.

(5) Any person who

(a) assaults or obstructs the Inspector or other person in the performance of his functions under this section;

(b) uses any insulting language to an Inspector or other person in the performance of his functions under this section;

(c) by the offer of any gratuity, bribe or other inducement prevents or attempts to prevent an Inspector or other person from performing his functions under this section; or

(d) contravenes any provision of this Act for which no punishment is specifically provided, is guilty of an offence and is liable on summary conviction to a fine not exceeding $1,000 or to imprisonment for a term not exceeding one year or both.

Appeals

24.(1) An appeal lies to the High Court from any decision of the Governor

(a) revoking a licence under subsection (2) of section 15 or under subsection (1) of section 22; or

(b) suspending a license or requiring a licensee to take certain steps which the Governor may specify under subsection (1) of section 21.

(2) An appeal against the decision of the Governor shall be by motion.

(3) The following procedure applies to appeals from the Governor.

(a) the appellant within 21 days after the day on which the Governor has given his decision, shall serve a notice in writing, signed by the appellant or his solicitor, on the Attorney General of his intention to appeal and of the general grounds of his appeal, except that any person aggrieved by a decision of the Governor may upon serving notice on the Attorney General apply to the court within 14 days after the day on which the Governor has given his decision for leave to extend the time within which notice of appeal prescribed by this section may be served, and the court upon hearing of the application may extend the time prescribed by this section as it deems fit;

(b) the Attorney General shall within 21 days of receiving the notice of appeal, obtain a copy of the Governor's decision and transmit to the Registrar without delay a copy thereof together with all papers relating to the appeal, except that the Governor is not compelled to disclose any information if he considers that the public interest would suffer by such disclosure and a certificate given

by the Governor under the Public Seal is conclusive that disclosure is not in the public interest;

(c) the Registrar shall set down the appeal for hearing on such day as is convenient, and shall cause notice of the hearing to be published, in such manner, as the court may direct; and

(d) the court may adjourn the hearing of any appeal and may, upon the hearing thereof, confirm, reverse, vary or modify the decision of the Governor or remit the matter with the opinion of the court thereon to the Governor.

(4) An appeal against a decision of the Governor shall not operate as a suspension of the decision of the Governor.

Immunity

25. No liability attaches to the Governor, the Inspector or any person acting under the authority of the Governor or the Inspector for an act done in good faith in the discharge or purported discharge of his functions under this Act.

Regulations

26. The Governor may make regulations generally for carrying the purpose and provisions of this Act into effect, and specifically

(a) prescribing anything by this Act authorized or required to be prescribed; and

(b) exempting any person or business, or class of person or business, from any provision of this Act.

Directions

27. Without limiting or affecting section 26, the Inspector may, from time to time, issue by publication in the Gazette, directions in relation to such matters as he may think fit and appropriate and failure by any licensee to comply with the directions shall be taken into consideration when any action is proposed to be taken under section 21 or 22.

Commencement

28. This Act comes into operation on such date as the Governor by proclamation published in the Gazette appoints.

Schedule

(Section 4(2))

Particulars To Be Specified In Applications

Every person or company applying for a licence under this Act shall furnish in writing to the Governor the following particulars which shall accompany the application:

(1) Name of applicant.

(2) Address in the Virgin Islands of principal office of applicant and, in the case of a company, its registered office.

(3) In the case of a company, the names and addresses of all directors.

(4) In the case of a company, the names and addresses of all shareholders.

(5) In the case of a partnership, the names and addresses of all partners.

(6) In the case of a company, the names and addresses of all officers and managers.

(7) Names and addresses of solicitors, if any, to the applicant, together with a letter from the solicitors confirming that they act for the applicant.

(8) Names and addresses of auditors of the applicant, together with a letter from auditors confirming that they act for the applicant.

(9) In the case of a company,

(a) the name and address of one of its officers who is the authorized agent in the Virgin Islands to accept on behalf of the applicant service of process and any notices required to be served on it; and

(b) the name and address of another of its officers who in the absence or inability to act for the officer named in subparagraph (a) is the authorized agent in the Virgin Islands of the applicant for the purposes of subparagraph (a).

(10) In the case of a company, evidence of the proper incorporation of the company in the Virgin Islands or in the country of incorporation, as the case may be.

(11) Evidence in writing that the applicant himself or some person or company directly or indirectly connected with the applicant is possessed of solid and practical experience in company management.

(12) The following:

(a) An undertaking in writing to provide and set apart a fully paid up capital before or at the time it commences business, such as the Governor may in his absolute discretion determine, or by a guarantee under seal of such sum given by a holding or parent or other company approved by the Governor; and

(b) The guarantee referred to in subparagraph (a) shall expressly provide that its formal validity, its essential validity, its interpretation and effect and the rights and obligations of the parties to it are governed exclusively by the law of the Virgin Islands and that the court of the Virgin Islands only shall be the forum for these purposes.

(13) Character references in writing, together with such other evidence as the Governor may require, that neither the applicant nor, if it is an applicant company, any director or officer of the company has a criminal record either in the Virgin Islands or elsewhere.

(14) Annual accounts of its holding company (if any), for the preceding 3 years and thereafter annually duly audited and certified by an independent auditor.

(15) Names of all subsidiary companies of the applicant with addresses of their registered offices.

(16) In the case of a company or partnership, a copy of the act, charter, certificate of incorporation or memorandum of association and articles of association or partnership agreement of the applicant, as may be appropriate, verified by an affidavit sworn by a director, secretary or partner and duly authenticated as follows:

(a) in the case of a company incorporated in the Virgin Islands, notarised; and

(b) in the case of a foreign company, certified and authenticated under the public seal of the country, city or place under the laws of which such company has been incorporated.

(17) References, including one from a bank or trust company.

(18) Statement of assets and liabilities at the end of the month prior to the submission of the application certified by a director or senior officer.

(19) Statement of capital of any other company held, directly or through a subsidiary, as an asset of the applicant.

INTERNATIONAL BUSINESS COMPANIES ACT, 1984

(as amended)

ARRANGEMENT OF SECTIONS

PART I - Short Title and Interpretation

PART II - Constitution of Companies

PART III Capital & Dividends

PART IV - Registered Office and Agent

PART V - Directors, Officers, Agents and Liquidators

PART VI - Protection of Members and Creditors

PART VII - Merger, Consolidation, Sale of Assets, Forced Redemptions, Arrangements and Dissenters

PART VIII - Continuation

INTERNATIONAL BUSINESS COMPANIES ACT

(as amended)

PART I - Short Title and Interpretation.

Short title.

1. This Act may be cited as the International Business Companies Act.

Interpretation.

2.(1) In this Act -

"articles" means the articles of association of a company incorporated under this Act"

"authorised capital" of a company means the sum of the aggregate par value of all shares with par value which the company is authorised by its memorandum to issue plus the amount, if any, stated in its memorandum as authorised capital to be represented by shares without par value which the company is authorised by its memorandum to issue;

"capital" of a company means the sum of the aggregate par value of all outstanding shares with par value of the company and shares with par value held by the company as treasury shares plus -

(a) the aggregate of the amounts designated as capital of all outstanding shares without par value of the company and shares without par value held by the company as treasury shares, and

(b) the amounts as are from time to time transferred from surplus to capital by a resolution of directors;

"Companies Act" means the Companies Act of the British Virgin Islands;

"continued" means continued within the context of Part VIII;

"court" means the High Court or a Judge thereof;

"licence fee payment date" means the date on which the company licence fee is paid pursuant to the provisions of section 105;

"licence fee final payment date" means 30th April or 31st October in any year;

"member" means a person who holds shares in a company;

"memorandum" means the memorandum of association of a company incorporated under this Act;

"person" includes a trust, the estate of a deceased individual, a partnership, or an unincorporated association of persons;

"person resident in the British Virgin Islands" means a person who ordinarily resides within the British Virgin Islands or carries on business from an office or other fixed place of business within the British Virgin Islands but does not include a company incorporated under this Act;

"Register" means the Register of International Business Companies maintained by the Registrar in accordance with subsection (1) of section 14;

"registered agent" means the person who is at any particular time performing the functions of registered agent of a company incorporated under this Act pursuant to subsection (1) of section 39;

"Registrar" means the Registrar of Companies appointed under the Companies Act and includes any other officer so appointed who acts, under the delegated authority of the Registrar pursuant to, section 207 (6) of the Companies Act;

"securities" means shares and debt obligations of every kind, and options, warrants and rights to acquire shares or debt obligations;

"surplus" in relation to a company, means the excess, if any, at the time of the determination, of the total assets of the company over the sum of its total liabilities, as shown in the books of account, plus its capital;

"treasury shares" means shares of a company that were previously issued but were repurchased, redeemed or otherwise acquired by the company and not cancelled.

(2) A reference to money in this Act is a reference to the currency of the United States of America.

(3) A company that is incorporated under the Companies Act or under the laws of a jurisdiction outside the British Virgin Islands shall be a company incorporated under this Act if it is continued as a company incorporated under this Act in accordance with Part VIII and references in this Act to a "company incorporated under this Act" shall be construed accordingly.

(4) A reference in this Act to voting in relation to shares shall be construed as a reference to voting by members holding the shares except that it is the votes allocated to the shares that shall be counted and not the number of members who actually voted and a reference to shares being present at a meeting shall be given a corresponding construction.

(5) Unless otherwise defined in the articles of a company incorporated under this Act, the expression "resolution of directors" means -

(a) a resolution approved at a duly constituted meeting of directors or of a committee of directors of a company, by affirmative vote of a simple majority or

such larger majority as may be specified in the articles, of the directors present at the meeting who voted and did not abstain; or

(b) a resolution consented to in writing by an absolute majority, or such larger majority as may be specified in the articles, of all the directors or of all the members of the committee, as the case may be;

but, where a director is given more than one vote in any circumstances, he shall in the circumstances be counted for the purpose of establishing majorities by the number of votes he casts.

(6) Unless otherwise defined in the articles of a company incorporated under this Act, the expression "resolution of members" means -

(a) a resolution approved at a duly constituted meeting of the members of a company by the affirmative vote of -

(i) a simple majority, or such larger majority as may be specified in the articles, of the votes of the shares that were present at the meeting and entitled to vote thereon and were voted and did not abstain, or

(ii) a simple majority, or such larger majority as may be specified in the articles of the votes of each class or series of shares which were present at the meeting and entitled to vote thereon as a class or series and were voted and not abstained and of a simple majority, or such larger majority as may be specified in the articles, of the votes of the remaining shares entitled to vote thereon that were present at the meeting and were voted and not abstained; or

(b) a resolution consented to in writing by -

(i) an absolute majority, or such larger majority as may be specified in the articles, of the votes of shares entitled to vote thereon, or

(ii) an absolute majority, or such larger majority as may be specified in the articles, of the votes of series of shares entitled to vote thereon as a class or series and of an absolute majority, or such larger majority as may be specified in the articles, of the votes of the remaining shares entitled to vote thereon.

PART II - Constitution of Companies

Incorporation.

3. Subject to the requirements of this Act, the registered agent named in the memorandum may, by subscribing to a memorandum and to articles, incorporate a company under this Act.

Restrictions on incorporation.

4. No company shall be incorporated under this Act unless immediately upon its incorporation the company is an international business company.

Requirements of international business companies.

5.(1) For purposes of this Act, an international business company is a company that does not -

(a) carry on business with persons resident in the British Virgin Islands;

(b) own an interest in real property situate in the British Virgin Islands, other than a lease referred to in paragraph (e) of subsection (2);

(c) carry on banking or trust business, unless it is licensed under the Banks and Trust Companies Act 1990;

(d) carry on business as an insurance or a reinsurance company, insurance agent or insurance broker, unless it is licensed under an enactment authorising it to carry on that business;

(e) carry on the business of company management unless it is licensed under the Company Management Act, 1990; or

(f) carry on the business of providing the registered office or the registered agent for companies incorporated in the British Virgin Islands.

(2) For purposes of paragraph (a) of subsection (1), an international business company shall not be treated as carrying on business with persons resident in the British Virgin Islands by reason only that -

(a) it makes or maintains deposits with a person carrying on banking business within the British Virgin Islands;

(b) it makes or maintains professional contact with solicitors, barristers, accountants, bookkeepers, trust companies, administration companies, investment advisers or other similar persons carrying on business within the British Virgin Islands;

(c) it prepares or maintains books and records within the British Virgin Islands;

(d) it holds, within the British Virgin Islands, meetings of its directors or members;

(e) it holds a lease of property for use as an office from which to communicate with members or where books and records of the company are prepared or maintained;

(f) it holds shares, debt obligations or other securities in a company incorporated under this Act or under the Companies Act; or

(g) shares, debt obligations or other securities in the company are owned by any person resident in the British Virgin Islands or by any company incorporated under this Act or under the Companies Act.

Effect of failure to satisfy requirement of section 5.

6.(1) Without affecting the operation of section 99, if a company is incorporated under this Act without having satisfied the requirements prescribed for an international business company under section 5, or if having satisfied the requirements it subsequently ceases to satisfy the requirements for a continuous period of more than 30 days, the company shall upon expiration of that period notify the Registrar of that fact.

(2) A company that wilfully contravenes subsection (1) is liable to a penalty of $100 for each day or part thereof during which the contravention continues, and a director who knowingly permits the contravention is liable to a like penalty.

Personal liability.

7. Subject to section 74, no member, director, officer, agent or liquidator of a company incorporated under this Act is liable for any debt, obligation or default of the company, unless specifically provided in this Act or in any other law for the time being in force in the British Virgin Islands, and except in so far as he may be liable for his own conduct or acts.

Business objects or purposes.

8. A company may be incorporated under this Act for any object or purpose not prohibited under this Act or under any other law for the time being in force in the British Virgin Islands.

Powers.

9.(1) Subject to any limitations or provisions to the contrary in its memorandum or articles, this Act or any other law for the time being in force in the British Virgin Islands, a company incorporated under this Act has the power, irrespective of corporate benefit, to perform all acts and engage in all activities necessary or conducive to the conduct, promotion or attainment of the objects or purposes of the company, including the power to do the following -

(a) issue registered shares or shares issued to bearer or both;

(b) issue the following -

(i) voting shares,

(ii) non-voting shares,

(iii) shares that may have more or less than one vote per share,

(iv) shares that may be voted only on certain matters or only upon the occurrence of certain events, and

(v) shares that may be voted only when held by persons who meet specified requirements;

(c) issue common shares, preferred shares, limited shares or redeemable shares;

(d) issue shares that entitle participation only in certain assets;

(e) issue options, warrants or rights, or instruments of a similar nature, to acquire any securities of the company;

(f) issue securities that, at the option of the holder thereof or of the company or upon the happening of a specified event, are convertible into, or exchangeable for, other securities in the company or any property then or to be owned by the company;

(g) purchase, redeem or otherwise acquire and hold its own shares;

(h) guarantee a liability or obligation of any person and to secure any of its obligations by mortgage, pledge or other charge, of any of its assets for that purpose;

(i) protect the assets of the company for the benefit of the company, its creditors and its members, and at the discretion of the directors, for any person having a direct or indirect interest in the company; and

(j) issue shares in any one or more currencies.

(2) For purposes of paragraph (i) of subsection (1), notwithstanding any other provision of this Act or of any other law for the time being in force in the British Virgin Islands or any rule of law to the contrary, the directors may cause the company, to transfer any of its assets in trust to one or more trustees, to any company, association, partnership, foundation or similar entity; and, with respect to the transfer, the directors may provide that the company, its creditors, its members or any person having a direct or indirect interest in the company, or any of them, may be the beneficiaries, creditors, members, certificate holders, partners or holders of any other similar interest.

(3) The rights or interests of any existing or subsequent creditor of the company in any assets of the company are not affected by any transfer under subsection (2), and those rights or interests may be pleaded against any transferee in any such transfer.

Validity of acts of company.

10.(1) No act of a company incorporated under this Act and no transfer of real or personal property by or to a company so incorporated is invalid by reason only of the fact that the company was without capacity or power to perform the act, or to transfer or receive the property, but the lack of capacity or power may be pleaded in the following cases-

(a) in proceedings by a member against the company to prohibit the performance of any act or the transfer of real or personal property by or to the company;

(b) in proceedings by the company, whether acting directly or through a receiver, trustee, or other legal representative, or through members in a derivative action, against the incumbent or former directors of the company for loss or damage due to their unauthorised act.

(2) For purposes of paragraph (a) of subsection (1), the court may set aside and prohibit the performance of a contract if -

(a) the unauthorised act or transfer sought to be set aside or prohibited is being, or is to be, performed or made under any contract to which the company is a party;

(b) all the parties to the contract are parties to the proceedings; and

(c) it appears fair and reasonable to set aside or prohibit the performance of the contract; and in so doing the court may, in applying this subsection, award to the company or to the other parties to the contract such compensation as may be reasonable except that in determining the amount of compensation the court shall not take into account anticipated profits to be derived from the performance of the contract.

Name.

11.(1) The word “Limited”, “Corporation”, “Incorporated”, “Societe Anonyme” or “Sociedad Anonima” or the abbreviation “Ltd”, “Corp”, “Inc” or “S.A.” must be part of the name of every company incorporated under this Act, but a company may use and be legally designated by either the full or the abbreviated form.

(2) No company shall be incorporated under this Act under a name that -

(a) is identical with that under which a company in existence is already incorporated under this Act or registered under the Companies Act or so nearly resembles the name as to be calculated to deceive, except where the company in existence gives its consent; or

(b) contains the words "Assurance", "Bank", "Building Society", "Chamber of Commerce", "Chartered", "Cooperative", "Imperial", "Insurance, "Municipal", "Royal", "Trust Company" and "Trustee company" or a word conveying a similar meaning, or any other word that, in the opinion of the Registrar, suggests or is calculated to suggest -

(i) the patronage of Her Majesty or that of a member of the Royal Family,

(ii) a connection with Her Majesty's Government or a department thereof, or

(iii) a connection with a municipality or other local authority or with a society or body incorporated by Royal Charter,
except with the approval of the Registrar in writing;

(c) is indecent, offensive or, in the opinion of the Registrar, objectionable.

(3) A company may amend its memorandum to change its name.

(4) If a company is incorporated under a name that -

(a) is identical with a name under which a company in existence was incorporated under this Act or registered under the Companies Act, or

(b) so nearly resembles the name as to be calculated to deceive,

the Registrar may, without the consent of the company in existence, give notice to the last registered company to change its name and if it fails to do so within 60 days from the date of the notice, the Registrar must amend the memorandum of the company to change its name to such name as the Registrar deems appropriate, and the Registrar must publish notice of the change in the Gazette.

(5) Subject to subsections (2) and (4), where a company changes its name, the Registrar must enter the new name on the Register in place of the former name, and must issue a certificate of incorporation indicating the change of name.

(6) A change of name does not affect any rights or obligations of a company, or render defective any legal proceedings by or against a company, and all legal proceedings that have been commenced against the company by its former name may be continued against it by its new name.

(7) Subject to subsection (2) the Registrar may, upon a request made by any person, reserve for 90 days a name for future adoption by a company under this Act.

Memorandum.

12.(1) The memorandum must include

(a) the name of the company;

(b) the address within the British Virgin Islands of the registered office of the company;

(c) the name and address within the British Virgin Islands of the registered agent of the company;

(d) the objects or purposes for which the company is to be incorporated;

(e) the currency in which shares in the company shall be issued;

(f) a statement of the authorised capital of the company setting forth the aggregate of the par value of all shares with par value that the company is authorised to issue and the amount, if any, to be represented by shares without par value that the company is authorised to issue;

(g) a statement of the number of classes and series of shares, the number of shares of each such class and series and the par value of shares with par value and that shares may be without par value, if that is the case;

(h) a statement of the designations, powers, preferences and rights, and the qualifications, limitations or restrictions of each class and series of shares that the company is authorised to issue, unless the directors are to be authorised to fix any such designations, powers, preferences, rights, qualifications, limitations and restrictions and in that case, an express grant of such authority as may be desired to grant to the directors to fix by a resolution any such designations, powers, preferences, rights, qualifications, limitations and restrictions that have not been fixed by the memorandum;

(i) a statement of the number of shares to be issued as registered shares and the number of shares to be issued as shares issued to bearer, unless the directors are authorised to determine at their discretion whether shares are to be issued as registered shares or to bearer, and in that case an express grant of

such authority as may be desired must be given to empower the directors to issue shares as registered shares or to bearer as they may determine by resolution of directors;

(j) whether registered shares may be exchanged for shares issued to bearer and whether shares issued to bearer may be exchanged for registered shares;

(k) if shares issued to bearer are authorised to be issued, the manner in which a required notice to members is to be given to the holders of shares issued to bearer; and

(l) a statement that the company may not carry on the activities set forth in subsection (1) of section 5 which statement shall set forth verbatim the activities described in that subsection, unless it is licensed to carry out any of the activities referred to in that subsection.

(2) For purposes of paragraph (d) of subsection (1), if the memorandum contains a statement either alone or with other objects or purposes that the object or purpose of the company is to engage in any act or activity that is not prohibited under any law for the time being in force in the British Virgin Islands, the effect of that statement is to make all acts and activities that are not illegal part of the objects or purposes of the company, subject to any limitations in the memorandum.

(3) The memorandum must be subscribed by the registered agent named in the memorandum in the presence of another person who must sign his name as a witness.

(4) The memorandum, when registered, binds the company and its members from time to time to the same extent as if each member had subscribed his name and affixed his seal thereto and as if there were contained in the memorandum, on the part of himself, his heirs, executors and administrators, a covenant to observe the provisions of the memorandum, subject to this Act.

Articles.

13.(1) The memorandum, when submitted for registration, must be accompanied by articles prescribing regulations for the company.

(2) The articles must be subscribed by the registered agent named in the memorandum in the presence of another person who must sign his name as a witness.

(3) The articles, when registered, bind the company and its members from time to time to the same extent as if each member had subscribed his name and affixed his seal thereto and as if there were contained in the articles, on the part of himself, his heirs, executors and administrators, a covenant to observe the provisions of the articles, subject to this Act.

Registration.

14.(1) The Registrar shall not register the memorandum or the articles delivered to him unless he is satisfied that all requirements of this Act in respect of registration have been complied with and

(a) a solicitor engaged in the formation of the company; or

(b) the registered agent named in the memorandum of the company to be the registered agent,

certifies in writing that the requirements of this Act in respect of registration have been complied with and the written certification delivered to the Registrar is sufficient evidence of compliance.

(2) Subject to subsection (1), the Registrar shall retain and register the memorandum and articles submitted to him in a Register to be maintained by him to be known as the Register of International Business Companies.

(3) Upon the registration of the memorandum and the articles, the Registrar shall issue a certificate of incorporation under his hand and seal certifying that the company is incorporated.

Certificate of incorporation.

15.(1) Upon the issue by the Registrar of a certificate of incorporation of a company, the company is, from the date shown on the certificate of incorporation, a body corporate under the name contained in the memorandum with the full capacity of an individual who is sui juris.

(2) A certificate of incorporation of a company incorporated under this Act issued by the Registrar is prima facie evidence of compliance with all requirements of this Act in respect of incorporation.

Amendment of memorandum articles.

16.(1) Subject to any limitations or provisions to the contrary in its memorandum or articles, a company incorporated under this Act may amend its memorandum or articles by a resolution of members or, where permitted by its memorandum or articles or by this Act, by a resolution of directors.

(2) A company that amends its memorandum or articles must submit to the Registrar an extract of the resolution of the members or the resolution of directors amending the memorandum or articles, as the case may be, certified as a true copy of the resolution amending the memorandum or articles by -

(a) the solicitor engaged in advising the company; or

(b) the registered agent named in the memorandum of the company, and the Registrar must retain and register the certified copy of the extract of the resolution.

(3) An amendment to the memorandum or articles has effect from the time the amendment is registered by the Registrar.

(4) A company that wilfully contravenes subsection (2) is liable to a penalty of $50 for each day or part thereof during which the contravention continues, and a director who knowingly permits the contravention is liable to a like penalty.

Copies of memorandum and articles to members.

17. A copy of the memorandum and a copy of the articles must be given to any member who requests a copy on payment by the member of such amount as the directors may determine to be reasonably necessary to defray the costs of preparing and furnishing them.

PART III - Capital and Dividends

Power to allot shares.

17A. Subject to any limitations or provisions to the contrary in its memorandum or articles, the unissued shares and treasury shares of a company incorporated under this Act shall be at the disposal of the directors who may, without limiting or affecting any rights previously conferred on the holders of any existing shares or class or series of shares, offer, allot, grant options over or otherwise dispose of shares to such persons, at such times and upon such terms as the company may, by resolution of directors, determine.

Shares to be fully paid.

18. No share in a company incorporated under this Act may be issued until the consideration in respect of the share is fully paid, and when issued the share is for all purposes fully paid and non-assessable save that a share issued for a promissory note or other written obligation for payment of a debt may be issued subject to forfeiture in the manner prescribed in section 19A.

Kind of consideration for shares.

19. Subject to any limitations or provisions to the contrary in its memorandum or articles each share in a company incorporated under this Act shall be issued for money, services rendered, personal property (including other shares, debt obligations or other securities in the company), an estate in real property, a promissory note or other binding obligation to contribute money or property, or any combination thereof.

Forfeiture of shares.

19A.(1) The memorandum or articles, or an agreement for the subscription of shares, of a company incorporated under this Act may contain provisions for the forfeiture of shares for which payment is not made pursuant to a promissory note or other written binding obligation for payment of a debt.

(2) Any provision in the memorandum or articles, or in an agreement for the subscription of shares of a company incorporated under this Act providing for the forfeiture of shares shall contain a requirement that written notice specifying a date for payment to be made be served on the member who defaults in making payment pursuant to a promissory note or other written binding obligation to pay a debt.

(3) The written notice referred to in subsection (2) shall name a further date not earlier than the expiration of 14 days from the date of service of the notice on or before which the payment required by the notice is to be made and shall contain a statement that in the event of non-payment at or before the time named in the notice the shares, or any of them, in respect of which payment is not made will be liable to be forfeited.

(4) Where a notice has been issued under this section and the requirements of the notice have not been complied with, the directors may, at any time before tender of payment, by resolution of directors forfeit and cancel the shares to which the notice relates.

(5) The company is under no obligation to refund any moneys to the member whose shares have been cancelled pursuant to subsection (4) and that member shall be discharged from any further obligation to the company.

Amount of consideration for shares.

20.(1) Subject to any limitations or provisions to the contrary in its memorandum or articles, shares in a company incorporated under this Act may be issued for such amount as may be determined from time to time by the directors, except that in the case of shares with par value, the amount shall not be less than the par value; and, in the absence of fraud, the decision of the directors as to the value of the consideration received by the company in respect of the issue is conclusive, unless a question of law is involved.

(2) A share issued by a company incorporated under this Act upon conversion of, or in exchange for, another share or a debt obligation or other security in the company, shall be treated for all purposes as having been issued for money equal to the consideration received or deemed to have been received by the company in respect of the other share, debt obligation or security.

(3) *Repealed*

Fractional shares.

21. Subject to any limitations or provisions to the contrary in its memorandum or articles, a company incorporated under this Act may issue fractions of a share and unless and to the extent otherwise provided in the memorandum or articles, a fractional share has the corresponding fractional liabilities, limitations, preferences, privileges, qualifications, restrictions, rights and other attributes of a whole share of the same class or series of shares.

Authorised capital in several currencies.

21A.(1) The authorised capital, if any, of a company incorporated under this Act may be stated in more that one currency in which case the par value of the shares, if any, shall be expressed in the same currencies.

(2) The Registrar may issue guidelines with respect to the calculation of fees payable pursuant to section 104 for companies with an authorised capital stated in a currency other than United States dollars.

Capital and surplus accounts.

22.(1) Upon the issue by a company incorporated under this Act of a share with par value, the consideration in respect of the share constitutes capital to the extent of the par value and the excess constitutes surplus.

(2) Subject to any limitations or provisions to the contrary in its memorandum or articles, upon the issue by a company incorporated under this Act of a share without par value, the consideration in respect of the share constitutes capital to the extent designated by the directors and the excess constitutes surplus, except that the directors must designate as capital an amount of the consideration that is at least equal to the amount that the share is entitled to as a preference, if any, in the assets of the company upon liquidation of the company.

(3) Upon the disposition by a company incorporated under this Act of a treasury share, the consideration in respect of the share is added to surplus.

Dividend of shares.

23.(1) A share issued as a dividend by a company incorporated under this Act shall be treated for all purposes as having been issued for money equal to the surplus that is transferred to capital upon the issue of the share.

(2) In the case of a dividend of authorised but unissued shares with par value, an amount equal to the aggregate par value of the shares shall be transferred from surplus to capital at the time of distribution.

(3) In the case of a dividend of authorised but unissued shares without par value, the amount designated by the directors shall be transferred from surplus to capital at the time of the distribution, except that the directors must designate as capital an amount that is at least equal to the amount that the shares are entitled to as a preference, if any, in the assets of the company upon liquidation of the company.

(4) A division of the issued and outstanding shares of a class or series of shares into a larger number of shares of the same class or series having a proportionally smaller par value does not constitute a dividend of shares.

Increase or reduction of authorised capital.

24.(1) Subject to any limitations or provisions to the contrary in its memorandum or articles, a company incorporated under this Act may amend its memorandum to increase or reduce its authorised capital, and in connection therewith, the company may -

(a) increase or reduce the number or shares which the company may issue;

(b) increase or reduce the par value of any of its shares; or

(c) effect any combination under paragraphs (a) and (b).

(2) Where a company reduces its authorised capital under subsection (1), then, for purposes of computing the capital of the company, any capital that immediately before the reduction was represented by shares but immediately following the reduction is no longer represented by shares shall be deemed to be capital transferred from surplus to capital.

(3) A company shall, in writing, inform the Registrar of any increase or decrease of its authorised capital.

Division and combination.

25.(1) A company incorporated under this Act may amend its memorandum -

(a) to divide the shares, including issued shares, of a class or series into a larger number of shares of the same class or series; or

(b) to combine the shares, including issued shares, of a class or series into a smaller number of shares of the same class or series.

(2) Where shares are divided or combined under subsection (1), the aggregate par value of the new shares must be equal to the aggregate par value of the original shares.

Character of a share.

26. Shares of a company incorporated under this Act are personal property and are not of the nature of real property.

Share certificates.

27.(1) A company incorporated under this Act must state in its articles whether or not certificates in respect of its shares shall be issued.

(2) If a company incorporated under this Act issues certificates in respect of its shares, the certificates -

(a) must be signed by two directors or two officers of the company, or by one director and one officer; or

(b) must be under the common seal of the company, with or without the signature of any director or officer of the company; and the articles may provide for the signatures or common seal to be facsimiles.

(3) A certificate issued in accordance with subsection (2) specifying a share held by a member of the company is prima facie evidence of the title of the member to the share specified therein.

Share register.

28.(1) A company incorporated under this Act shall cause to be kept one or more registers to be known as share registers containing -

(a) the names and addresses of the persons who hold registered shares in the company;

(b) the number of each class and series of registered shares held by each person;

(c) the date on which the name of each person was entered in the share register;

(d) the date on which any person ceased to be a member;

(e) in the case of shares issued to bearer, the total number of each class and series of shares issued to bearer; and

(f) with respect to each certificate for shares issued to bearer -

(i) the identifying number of the certificate;

(ii) the number of each class or series of shares issued to bearer specified therein; and

(iii) the date of issue of the certificate; but the company may delete from the register information relating to persons who are no longer members or information relating to shares issued to bearer that have been cancelled.

(2) The share register may be in any such form as the directors may approve but if it is in magnetic, electronic or other data storage form, the company must be able to produce legible evidence of its contents.

(3) *Repealed*

(4) The share register is prima facie evidence of any matters directed or authorised by this Act to be contained therein.

(5) A company that wilfully contravenes this section is liable to a penalty of $25 for each day or part thereof during which the contravention continues, and a director who knowingly permits the contravention is liable to a like penalty.

Rectification of share register.

29.(1) If -

(a) information that is required to be entered in the share register under section 28 is omitted therefrom or inaccurately entered therein; or

(b) there is unreasonable delay in entering the information in the share register, a member of the company, or any person who is aggrieved by the omission, inaccuracy or delay, may apply to the court for an order that the share register be rectified, and the court may either grant or refuse the application, with or

without costs to be paid by the applicant, or order the rectification of the share register, and may direct the company to pay all costs of the application and any damages the applicant may have sustained.

(2) The court may, in any proceedings under subsection (1), determine any question relating to the right of a person who is a party to the proceedings to have his name entered in or omitted from the share register, whether the question arises between-

(a) two or more members or alleged members; or

(b) between members or alleged members and the company;

and generally the court may in the proceedings determine any question that may be necessary or expedient to be determined for the rectification of the share register.

Transfer of registered shares.

30.(1) Subject to any limitations or provisions to the contrary in its memorandum or articles, registered shares of a company incorporated under this Act may be transferred by a written instrument of transfer signed by the transferor and containing the name and address of the transferee.

(2) In the absence of a written instrument of transfer mentioned in subsection (1), the directors may accept such evidence of a transfer of shares as they consider appropriate.

(3) A company shall not be required to treat a transferee of a registered share in the company as a member until the transferee's name has been entered in the share register.

(4) Subject to any limitations or provisions to the contrary in its memorandum or articles, a company incorporated under this Act must, on the application of the transferor or transferee of a registered share in the company, enter in its share register the name of the transferee of the share.

(5) A transfer of registered shares of a deceased, incompetent or bankrupt member of a company incorporated under this Act made by his personal representative, guardian or trustee, as the case may be, or a transfer of registered shares owned by a person as a result of a transfer from a member by operation of law, is of the same validity as if the personal representative, guardian, trustee or transferee had been the registered holder of the shares at the time of the execution of the instrument of transfer.

(6) For the purposes of subsection (5), what amounts to incompetence on the part of a person is a matter to be determined by the court after having regard to all the relevant evidence and the circumstances of the case.

Transfer of bearer shares.

31. A share issued to bearer is transferable by delivery of the certificate relating to the share.

Seizure.

32.(1) Where a government authority, whether it is legally constituted or not, in any jurisdiction outside the British Virgin Islands -

(a) by or in connection with a nationalisation, expropriation, confiscation, coercion, force or duress, or similar action; or

(b) by or in connection with the imposition of any confiscatory tax, assessment or other governmental charge,

takes or seizes any shares or other interest in a company incorporated under this Act, the company itself or a person holding shares or any other interest in the company, including an interest as a creditor, may apply to the court for an order that the company disregard the taking or seizure and continue to treat the person who would have held shares or any other interest in the company but for the taking or seizure of the share or other interest as continuing to hold the shares or other interest.

(2) Without affecting subsection (1), where a person whose shares or other interests have been taken or seized as referred to in subsection (1) is other than a natural person, the person making the application under subsection (1), or the company itself, may apply to the court for an additional order for the company to treat the persons believed by the company to have held the direct or indirect beneficial interests in the shares or other interests in the company as the holder of those shares or other interests.

(3) The court may, upon application made to it under subsection (1) or (2) -

(a) grant such relief as it considers equitable and proper; and

(b) order that any shares of or other interests in the company vest in such trustees as the court may appoint upon such trusts and for such purposes as the court determines.

Acquisition of own shares.

33.(1) Subject to any limitations or provisions to the contrary in its memorandum or articles, a company incorporated under this Act may purchase, redeem or otherwise acquire and hold its own shares but only out of surplus or in exchange for newly issued shares of equal value.

(1A) Subject to subsection (1), a company incorporated under this Act may not purchase, redeem or otherwise acquire its own shares without the consent of the member whose shares are to be purchased, redeemed or otherwise acquired, unless the company is permitted to purchase, redeem or otherwise acquire the shares without that consent by virtue of -

(a) the provisions of the memorandum or articles of the company;

(b) the designations, powers, preferences, rights, qualifications, limitations and restrictions with which the shares were issued; or

(c) the subscription agreement for the issue of the shares.

(2) No purchase, redemption or other acquisition permitted under subsection (1) shall be made unless the directors determine that immediately after the purchase, redemption or other acquisition -

(a) the company will be able to satisfy its liabilities as they become due in the ordinary course of its business; and

(b) the realisable value of the assets of the company will not be less than the sum of its total liabilities other than deferred taxes, as shown in the books of account, and its capital;

and, in the absence of fraud, the decision of the directors as to the realisable value of the assets of the company is conclusive, unless a question of law is involved.

(3) A determination by the directors under subsection (2) is not required where shares are purchased, redeemed or otherwise acquired -

(a) pursuant to a right of a member to have his shares redeemed or to have his shares exchanged for money or other property of the company;

(b) by virtue of a transfer of capital pursuant to paragraph (b) (iii) of section 35 (1);

(c) by virtue of the provisions of section 83; and

(d) pursuant to an order of the court.

(4) Subject to any limitations or provisions to the contrary in its memorandum or articles, shares that a company purchases, redeems or otherwise acquires may be cancelled or held as treasury shares unless the shares are purchased, redeemed or otherwise acquired by virtue of a reduction in capital in a manner that would be a contravention of the requirements of section 35 (3), in which case they shall be cancelled but they shall be available for reissue; and upon the cancellation of a share, the amount included as capital of the company with respect to that share shall be deducted from the capital of the company.

(5) A company incorporated under this Act may purchase, redeem or otherwise acquire the shares of the company at a price lower than fair value if permitted by, and then only in accordance with, the terms of -

(a) its memorandum or articles; or

(b) a written agreement for the subscription for the shares to be purchased, redeemed or otherwise acquired.

Treasury shares disabled.

34. Where shares in a company incorporated under this Act -

(a) are held by the company as treasury shares; or

(b) are held by another company of which the first company holds, directly or indirectly, shares having more than 50 per cent of the votes in the election of directors of the other company, the shares of the first company are not entitled to vote or to have dividends paid thereon and shall not be treated as outstanding for any purpose under this Act except for purposes of determining the capital of the first company.

Increase or reduction of capital.

35.(1) Subject to any limitations or provisions to the contrary in its memorandum or articles and subject to subsections (3) and (4), the capital of a company incorporated under this Act may, by a resolution of members or by resolution of directors, be -

(a) increased by transferring an amount out of the surplus of the company to capital; or

(b) reduced by transferring an amount out of capital of the company to surplus.

(2) *Repealed.*

(3) No reduction of capital shall be effected that reduces the capital of the company to an amount that is less than the sum of -

(a) the aggregate par value of -

(i) all outstanding shares with par value, and

(ii) all shares with par value held by the company as treasury shares; and

(b) the aggregate of the amounts designated as capital of -

(i) all outstanding shares without par value, and

(ii) all shares without par value held by the company as treasury shares that are entitled to a preference, if any, in the assets of the company upon liquidation of the company.

(4) No reduction of capital shall be effected under subsection (1) unless the directors determine that immediately after the reduction -

(a) the company will be able to satisfy its liabilities as they become due in the ordinary course of its business, and

(b) the realisable value of the assets of the company will not be less than its total liabilities, other than deferred taxes, as shown in the books of account, and its remaining capital;

and, in the absence of fraud, the decision of the directors as to the realisable value of the assets of the company is conclusive, unless a question of law is involved.

Dividends.

36.(1) Subject to any limitations or provisions to the contrary in its memorandum or articles, a company incorporated under this Act may, by a resolution of directors, declare and pay dividends in money, shares or other property.

(2) Dividends shall only be declared and paid out of surplus.

(3) No dividend shall be declared and paid unless the directors determine that immediately after the payment of the dividend -

(a) the company will be able to satisfy its liabilities as they become due in the ordinary course of its business; and

(b) the realisable value of the assets of the company will not be less than the sum of its total liabilities, other than deferred taxes, as shown in the books of account, and its capital;

and, in the absence of fraud, the decision of the directors as to the realisable value of the assets of the company is conclusive, unless a question of law is involved.

Appreciation of assets.

37. Subject to any limitations or provisions to the contrary in its memorandum or articles, a company incorporated under this Act may, by a resolution of directors, include in the computation of surplus for any purpose under this Act the net unrealised appreciation of the assets of the company, and, in the absence of fraud, the decision of the directors as to the value of the assets is conclusive, unless a question of law is involved.

Mortgages and charges of shares.

37A.(1) A mortgage or charge of shares of a company incorporated under this Act must be in writing signed by, or with the authority of, the holder of the bearer share or the registered holder of the registered share to which the mortgage or charge relates.

(2) In the case of a bearer share, a mortgage or charge thereof is not valid and enforceable unless the certificate for the share to be mortgaged or charged is deposited with the mortgagee or chargee but the deposit of the certificate with the mortgagee or chargee shall not constitute a transfer of the bearer share, title to which shall only pass upon due compliance with the provisions of law governing realisation of the security by the mortgagee or chargee.

(3) A mortgage or charge of shares of a company incorporated under this Act need not be in any specific form but it must clearly indicate -

(a) the intention to create a mortgage or charge; and

(b) the amount secured by the mortgage or charge or how that amount is to be calculated.

(4) A mortgage or charge of shares of a company incorporated under this Act may be governed by the law of a jurisdiction other than the British Virgin Islands, but if a law other than the law of the British Virgin Islands is specified as the governing law -

(a) the mortgage or charge must be in compliance with the requirements of its governing law in order for the mortgage or charge to be valid and binding on the company; and

(b) the remedies available to a mortgagee or chargee shall be governed by the governing law and the instrument creating the mortgage or charge save that the rights between the mortgagor or mortgagee as a member of the company and the company shall continue to be governed by the memorandum and the articles of the company and this Act.

(5) If no law is specified to govern a mortgage or charge of shares of a company incorporated under this Act, the instrument creating the mortgage or charge shall be governed by the laws of the British Virgin Islands and, in the case of a default by the mortgagor or chargor on the terms of the mortgage, the mortgagee or chargee is entitled to the following remedies:-

(a) subject to any limitations or provisions to the contrary in the instrument creating the mortgage or charge, the right to sell the shares; and

(b) the right to appoint a receiver who, subject to any limitations or provisions to the contrary in the instrument creating the mortgage or charge, may -

(i) vote the shares,

(ii) receive dividends and other payments in respect of the shares, and

(iii) exercise other rights and powers of the mortgagor or chargor in respect of the shares, until such time as the mortgage or charge is discharged.

(6) Subsection (5) also applies to a mortgage or charge of shares of a company incorporated under this Act where the law of the British Virgin Islands is specified as the governing law.

(7) Subject to any provisions to the contrary in the instrument of mortgage or charge of shares of a company incorporated under this Act, all amounts that accrue from the enforcement of the mortgage or charge shall be applied in the following manner -

(a) firstly, in meeting the costs incurred in enforcing the mortgage or charge;

(b) secondly, in discharging the sums secured by the mortgage or charge; and

(c) thirdly, in paying any balance due to the mortgagor or chargor.

(8) The remedies referred to in subsection (5) are not exercisable until -

(a) a default has occurred and has continued for a period of not less than 30 days, or such shorter period as may be specified in the instrument creating the mortgage or charge; and

(b) the default has not been rectified within 14 days from service of the notice specifying the default and requiring rectification thereof.

(9) In the case of the mortgage or charge of registered shares there may be entered in the share register of the company -

(a) a statement that the shares are mortgaged or charged;

(b) the name of the mortgagee or chargee; and

(c) the date on which the statement and name are entered in the share register.

PART IV - Registered Office and Agent

Registered office.

38. A company incorporated under this Act shall at all times have a registered office in the British Virgin Islands, and the registered office must be an office maintained in the British Virgin Islands by the company or its registered agent.

Registered agent.

39.(1) A company incorporated under this Act shall at all times have a registered agent in the British Virgin Islands.

(2) No person shall be a registered agent unless he has been licensed as a registered agent under the Company Management Act, 1990 or under the Banks and Trust Companies Act, 1990.

40. *Repealed*

Registered agents.

40A.(1) The Registrar shall maintain a register of licensed registered agents in which the following details shall be recorded -

(a) the name of the registered agent;

(b) the address of the registered agent;

(c) the names of the individuals authorised to sign on behalf of any firm or corporation that is a registered agent;

(d) the date when the first licence to act as a registered agent was issued pursuant to the Company Management Act, 1990 or the Banks and Trust Companies Act, 1990; and

(e) in a case where a registered agent ceases to be a registered agent -

(i) the date on which the registered agent ceased to be licensed, and

(ii) whether the cessation was due to failure to renew his licence, death or liquidation or revocation under the Company Management Act, 1990 or under the Banks and Trust Companies Act, 1990.

(2) The Registrar shall, during the month of February in each year, publish in the Gazette a list of registered agents as appeared on the register of licensed registered agents on 31st January in that year.

(3) Any change in the details kept by the Registrar in the register of registered agents pursuant to subsection (1) shall be notified immediately by the registered agent to the Registrar, and, upon payment of such fee as may be prescribed by the Governor in Council, the Registrar shall record the change in the register of registered agents.

(4) Where the registered agent of a company desires to cease to act as registered agent and the registered agent is unable to reach an agreement with the company for which he is registered agent concerning his replacement, the following provisions apply -

(a) the registered agent shall give not less than 90 days written notice to any director or officer of the company of which he is the registered agent at the director's or officer's last known address, or if the registered agent is not aware of the identity of any director or officer then the person from whom the registered agent last received instructions concerning the company, specifying the wish of the registered agent to resign as registered agent and shall together with the notice provide a list of all registered agents in the British Virgin Islands with their names and addresses;

(b) the registered agent shall submit to the Registrar a copy of the notice and list of registered agents referred to in paragraph (a);

(c) if, at the time of expiry of the notice, the company has not adopted a resolution to amend its memorandum to change its registered agent, the registered agent shall inform the Registrar in writing that the company has not changed its registered agent whereupon the Registrar shall publish a notice in the Gazette that the name of the company will be struck off the Register, unless the company, within 30 days from the date of the publication of the notice in the Gazette, registers with the Registrar a copy of a resolution amending the memorandum to change its registered agent; and

(d) if a company fails within 30 days from the date of the publication of the notice referred to in paragraph (c) to register with the Registrar a copy of a resolution amending its memorandum to change its registered agent, the Registrar shall strike the name of the company off the Register and shall publish in the Gazette a notice that the name of the company has been struck off the Register.

(5) Where the licence of a registered agent has been revoked under the Company Management Act, 1990 or the Banks and Trust Companies Act, 1990, or if a registered agent dies or fails to renew his licence the Inspector of Company Managers or the Inspector of Banks and Trust Companies, as the case may be, shall, for the purpose of changing the registered agent of the company, communicate with each company for which the person whose licence has been revoked or who has died or has failed to renew his licence is the registered agent and the provisions of subsection (4) have effect mutatis mutandis for the purpose of providing the procedures for changing the registered agent.

(6) A company that has been struck off the Register under this section remains liable for all claims, debts, liabilities and obligations of the company, and the striking-off does not affect the liability of any of its members, directors, officers or agents.

Penalty for contravention of sections 38 and 39.

41. A company that wilfully contravenes section 38 or 39 is liable to a penalty of $25 for each day or part thereof during which the contravention continues, and a director who knowingly permits the contravention is liable to a like penalty.

PART V - Directors, Officers, Agents and Liquidators

Management by directors.

42. Subject to any limitations or provisions to the contrary in its memorandum or articles, the business and affairs of a company incorporated under this Act shall be managed by a board of directors that consists of one or more persons who shall be individuals or companies.

Election, term and removal of directors.

43.(1) The first directors of a company incorporated under this Act shall be elected by the subscribers to the memorandum; and thereafter, the directors shall be elected by the members for such term as the members may determine, and where permitted by the memorandum or articles of a company incorporated under this Act, the directors may also elect directors for such term as the directors may determine.

(2) Each director holds office until his successor takes office or until his earlier death, resignation or removal.

(3) Subject to any limitations or provisions to the contrary in its memorandum or articles -

(a) a director may be removed from office by a resolution of members or by a resolution of directors; and

(b) a director may resign his office by giving written notice of his resignation to the company and the resignation has effect from the date the notice is received by the company or from such later date as may be specified in the notice.

(4) Subject to any limitations or provisions to the contrary in its memorandum or articles, a vacancy in the board of directors may be filled by a resolution of members or of a majority of the remaining directors.

Optional register of directors.

43A.(1) A company incorporated under this Act may keep a register to be known as a register of directors containing -

(a) the names and addresses of the persons who are directors of the company;

(b) the date on which each person whose name is entered in the register was appointed as a director of the company; and

(c) the date on which each person named as a director ceased to be a director of the company.

(2) The register of directors may be in such form as the directors approve, but if it is in magnetic, electronic or other data storage form, the company must be able to produce legible evidence of its contents.

(3) A copy of the register of directors, commencing from the date of the registration of the company, shall be kept at the registered office of the company referred to in section 38.

(4) The register of directors is prima facie evidence of any matters directed or authorised by this Act to be contained therein.

Number of directors.

44. The number of directors shall be fixed by the articles and, subject to any limitations or provisions to the contrary in its memorandum or articles, the articles may be amended to change the number of directors.

Powers of directors.

45. The directors have all the powers of the company that are not reserved to the members under this Act or in the memorandum or articles.

Emoluments of directors.

46. Subject to any limitations or provisions to the contrary in its memorandum or articles, the directors may, by a resolution of directors, fix the emoluments of directors in respect of services to be rendered in any capacity to the company.

Committees of directors.

47.(1) The directors may, by a resolution of directors, designate one or more committees, each consisting of one or more directors.

(2) Subject to any limitations or provisions to the contrary in its memorandum or articles, each committee has such powers and authority of the directors, including the power and authority to affix the common seal of the company, as are set forth in the resolution of directors establishing the committee, except that no committee has any power or authority with respect to the matters requiring a resolution of directors under sections 43 and 53.

Meetings of directors.

48.(1) Subject to any limitations or provisions to the contrary in its memorandum or articles, the directors of a company incorporated under this Act may meet at such times and in such manner and places within or outside the British Virgin Islands as the directors may determine to be necessary or desirable.

(2) A director shall be deemed to be present at a meeting of directors if -

(a) he participates by telephone or other electronic means; and

(b) all directors participating in the meeting are able to hear each other.

Notice of meetings of directors.

49.(1) Subject to a requirement in the memorandum or articles to give longer notice, a director shall be given not less than 3 days' notice of meetings of directors.

(2) Notwithstanding subsection (1), subject to any limitations or provisions to the contrary in its memorandum or articles, a meeting of directors held in contravention of that subsection is valid if all of the directors, or such majority thereof as may be specified in the memorandum or articles entitled to vote at the meeting, have waived the notice of the meeting; and, for this purpose, the presence of a director at the meeting shall be deemed to constitute waiver on his part.

(3) The inadvertent failure to give notice of a meeting to a director, or the fact that a director has not received the notice, does not invalidate the meeting.

Quorum for meetings of directors.

50. The quorum for a meeting of directors is that fixed by the memorandum or articles; but, where no quorum is so fixed, a meeting of directors is properly constituted for all purposes if at the commencement of the meeting one-half of the total number of directors are present in person or by alternate.

Consents of directors.

51. Subject to any limitations or provisions to the contrary in its memorandum or articles, an action that may be taken by the directors or a committee of directors at a meeting may also be taken by a resolution of directors or a committee of directors consented to in writing or by telex, telegram, cable or other written electronic communication, without the need for any notice.

Alternates for directors.

52.(1) Subject to any limitations or provisions to the contrary in its memorandum or articles, a director may by a written instrument appoint an alternate who need not be a director.

(2) An alternate for a director appointed under subsection (1) is entitled to attend meetings in the absence of the director who appointed him and to vote or consent in the place of the director.

Officers and agents.

53.(1) The directors may, by a resolution of directors, appoint any person, including a person who is a director, to be an officer or agent of the company.

(2) Subject to any limitations or provisions to the contrary in its memorandum or articles, each officer or agent has such powers and authority of the directors, including the power and authority to affix the common seal of the company, as are set forth in the articles or in the resolution of directors appointing the officer or agent, except that no officer or agent has any power or authority with respect to the matters requiring a resolution of directors under this Act.

(3) The resolution of directors appointing any person to be an agent of the company may authorise the agent to appoint one or more substitutes or delegates to exercise some or all of the powers conferred on the agent by the company.

(4) The directors may remove an officer or agent, appointed under subsection (1) and may revoke or vary a power conferred on him under subsection (2).

Standard of care.

54.(1) Every director, officer, agent and liquidator of a company incorporated under this Act, in performing his functions, shall act honestly and in good faith with a view to the best interests of the company and exercise the care, diligence and skill that a reasonably prudent person would exercise in comparable circumstances.

(2) No provision in the memorandum or articles of a company incorporated under this Act or in any agreement entered into by the company relieves a director, officer, agent or liquidator of the company from the duty to act in accordance with the memorandum or articles or from any personal liability arising from his management of the business and affairs of the company.

Reliance on records and reports.

55. Every director, officer, agent and liquidator of a company incorporated under this Act, in performing his functions, is entitled to rely upon the share register kept under section 28, the books of accounts and records and the minutes and copies of consents to resolutions kept under section 66 and any report made to the company by any other director, officer, agent or liquidator or by any person selected by the company to make the report.

Conflict of interests.

56.(1) Subject to any limitations or provisions to the contrary in its memorandum or articles, no agreement or transaction between -

(a) a company incorporated under this Act; and

(b) one or more of its directors or liquidators, or any person in which any director or liquidator has a financial interest or to whom any director or liquidator is related, including as a director or liquidator of that other person, is void or voidable for this reason only or by reason only that the director or liquidator is present at the meeting of directors or liquidators, or at the meeting of the committee of directors or liquidators, that approves the agreement or trans-

action or that the vote or consent of the director or liquidator is counted for that purpose.

(2) Subject to any limitations or provisions to the contrary in the memorandum or articles, an agreement or transaction referred to in subsection (1) is valid if -

(a) the material facts of the interest of each director or liquidator in the agreement or transaction and his interest in or relationship to any other party to the agreement or transaction are disclosed in good faith or are known by the other directors or liquidators; and

(b) the agreement or transaction is approved or ratified by a resolution of directors or liquidators that has been approved -

(i) without counting the vote or consent of any interested director or liquidator, or

(ii) by the unanimous vote or consent of all disinterested directors or liquidators if the votes or consents of all disinterested directors or liquidators is insufficient to approve a resolution of directors or liquidators.

(3) Subject to any limitations or provisions to the contrary in the memorandum or articles, an agreement or transaction referred to in subsection (1) is valid if -

(a) the material facts of the interest of each director or liquidator in the agreement or transaction and his interest in or relationship to any other party to the agreement or transaction are disclosed in good faith or are known by the members entitled to vote at a meeting of members; and

(b) the agreement or transaction is approved or ratified by a resolution of members.

(3A) Subject to any limitations or provisions to the contrary in the memorandum or articles, an agreement or transaction referred to in subsection (1) is valid unless it is shown that at the time the agreement or transaction was authorised, approved or ratified by resolution of directors or by resolution of members the agreement or transaction was unfairly prejudicial to one or more members of the company or to the creditors of the company except that no person who voted in favour of the resolution authorising, approving or ratifying the agreement or transaction shall be capable subsequently of impugning or objecting to the agreement or transaction.

(4) Subject to any limitations or provisions to the contrary in its memorandum or articles, a director or liquidator who has an interest in any particular business to be considered at a meeting of directors, liquidators or members may be counted for purposes of determining whether the meeting is duly constituted in accordance with section 50 or otherwise.

Indemnification.

57.(1) Subject to subsection (2) and any limitations in its memorandum or articles, a company incorporated under this Act may indemnify against all expenses, including legal fees, and against all judgments, fines and amounts paid in settlement and reasonably incurred in connection with legal, administrative or investigative proceedings any person who -

(a) is or was a party or is threatened to be made a party to any threatened, pending or completed proceedings, whether civil, criminal, administrative or investigative, by reason of the fact that the person is or was a director, an officer or a liquidator of the company; or

(b) is or was, at the request of the company, serving as a director, officer or liquidator of, or in any other capacity is or was acting for, another company or a partnership, joint venture, trust or other enterprise.

(2) Subsection (1) only applies to a person referred to in that subsection if the person acted honestly and in good faith with a view to the best interests of the company and, in the case of criminal proceedings, the person has no reasonable cause to believe that his conduct was unlawful.

(3) The decision of the directors as to whether the person acted honestly and in good faith and with a view to the best interests of the company and as to whether the person had no reasonable cause to believe that his conduct was unlawful is in the absence of fraud, sufficient for the purposes of this section, unless a question of law is involved.

(4) The termination of any proceedings by any judgment, order, settlement, conviction or the entering of a nolle prosequi does not, by itself, create a presumption that the person did not act honestly and in good faith and with a view to the best interests of the company or that the person had reasonable cause to believe that his conduct was unlawful.

(5) If a person referred to in subsection (1) has been successful in defence of any proceedings referred to in subsection (1), the person is entitled to be indemnified against all expenses, including legal fees, and against all judgments, fines and amounts paid in settlement and reasonably incurred by the person in connection with the proceedings.

Insurance.

58. A company incorporated under this Act may purchase and maintain insurance in relation to any person who is or was a director, an officer or a liquidator of the company, or who at the request of the company is or was serving as a director, an officer or a liquidator of, or in any other capacity is or was acting for, another company or a partnership, joint venture, trust or other enterprise, against any liability asserted against the person and incurred by the person in that capacity, whether or not the company has or would have had the power to indemnify the person against the liability under subsection (1) of section 57.

PART VI - Protection of Members and Creditors

Meetings of members.

59.(1) Subject to any limitations or provisions to the contrary in its memorandum or articles, the directors of a company incorporated under this Act may convene meetings of the members of the company at such times and in such manner and places within or outside the British Virgin Islands as the directors consider necessary or desirable.

(2) Subject to any limitations or provisions to the contrary in its memorandum or articles for a lesser percentage, upon the written request of members holding more than 50 per cent of the votes of the outstanding voting shares in the company, the directors shall convene a meeting of members.

(3) Subject to any limitations or provisions to the contrary in its memorandum or articles, a member shall be deemed to be present at a meeting of members if -

(a) he participates by telephone or other electronic means; and

(b) all members participating in the meeting are able to hear each other.

(4) A member may be represented at a meeting of members by a proxy who may speak and vote on behalf of the member.

(5) The following apply in respect of a joint ownership of shares -

(a) if two or more persons hold shares jointly each of them may be present in person or by proxy at a meeting of members and may speak as a member;

(b) if only one of them is present in person or by proxy he may vote on behalf of all of them; and

(c) if two or more are present in person or by proxy, they must vote as one.

Notice of meetings of members.

60.(1) Subject to a requirement in the memorandum or articles to give longer notice, the directors shall give not less than 7 days' notice of meetings of members to those persons whose names on the date the notice is given appear as members in the share register referred to in section 28 and are entitled to vote at the meeting.

(2) Notwithstanding subsection (1), and subject to any limitations or provisions to the contrary in its memorandum or articles, a meeting of members held in contravention of the requirement to give notice is valid if members holding a 90 per cent majority, or such lesser majority as may be specified in the memorandum or articles, of -

(a) the total number of shares entitled to vote on all the matters to be considered at the meeting; or

(b) the votes of each class or series of shares where members are entitled to vote thereon as a class or series together with an absolute majority of the remaining votes, have waived notice of the meeting; and, for this purpose, the presence of a member at the meeting shall be deemed to constitute waiver on his part.

(3) The inadvertent failure of the directors to give notice to a member, or the fact that a member has not received notice, does not invalidate the meeting.

Quorum for meetings of members.

61. The quorum for a meeting of members for purposes of a resolution of members is that fixed by the memorandum or articles; but, where no quorum is so fixed, a meeting of members is properly constituted for all purposes if at the commencement of the meeting there are present in person or by proxy one-half of the votes of the shares of each class or series of shares entitled to vote as a class or series thereon and the same proportion of the votes of the remaining shares entitled to vote thereon.

Voting by members.

62.(1) Except as otherwise provided in the memorandum or articles, all shares vote as one class and each whole share has one vote.

(2) The directors of a company incorporated under this Act may fix the date notice is given of a meeting as the record date for determining those shares that are entitled to vote at the meeting.

Voting trusts.

62A.(1) One or more members of a company incorporated under this Act may by agreement in writing deposit bearer shares with, or transfer registered shares to, any person authorised to act as trustee for the purpose of vesting in such person, who may be designated voting trustee, the right to vote thereon and the following provisions shall apply -

(a) the period of time for which the trustee may vote shall not exceed 10 years;

(b) subject to paragraph (a), the agreement may contain any other provisions not inconsistent with the purpose of the agreement;

(c) a copy of the agreement shall be filed at the registered office of the company and shall be open to the inspection of members of the company -

(i) in the case of any beneficiary of the trust under the agreement, daily during business hours, and

(ii) in the case of members of the company, subject to the provisions of section 67;

(d) where certificates for registered shares have been issued for shares that are to be transferred to a trustee pursuant to this section, new certificates shall be issued to the voting trustee to represent the shares so transferred and the certificates formerly representing the shares that have been transferred shall be surrendered and cancelled;

(e) where a certificate is issued to a voting trustee, an endorsement shall be made on the certificate that the shares represented thereby in the case of registered shares and the certificates in the case of bearer shares are held by the person named therein pursuant to an agreement;

(f) there shall be noted in the share register of the company against the record of the shares held by the trustee the fact that such an agreement exists;

(g) the voting trustee may vote the shares so issued or transferred during the period specified in the agreement;

(h) shares registered in the name of the voting trustee may be voted either in person or by proxy and, in voting the shares, the voting trustee shall not incur any liability as member or trustee, except in so far as he may be liable for his own conduct or acts;

(i) where two or more persons are designated as voting trustees and the right and method of voting any shares registered in their names at any meeting of members or on any resolution of members are not fixed by the agreement appointing the trustees, the right to vote shall be determined by a majority of the trustees, or if they are equally divided as to the right and manner of voting the shares in any particular case, the votes of the shares in such case shall be divided equally among the trustees;

(j) at any time within 2 years prior to the time of expiration of any voting trust agreement as originally fixed or as last extended as provided in this subsection, one or more beneficiaries of the trust under the voting trust agreement may, by written agreement and with the written consent of the voting trustee, extend the duration of the voting trust agreement for an additional period not exceeding 10 years from the expiration date of the trust as originally fixed or as last extended; and

(k) the voting trustee shall, prior to the time of expiration of a voting trust agreement, as originally fixed or as previously extended, as the case may be, file at the registered office of the company a copy of the extension agreement and of his consent thereto, and thereupon the duration of the voting trust agreement shall be extended for the period fixed in the extension agreement,

but no extension agreement shall affect the rights or obligations of persons not parties thereto.

(2) Two or more members of a company incorporated under this Act may by agreement in writing provide that in exercising any voting rights the shares held by them shall be voted -

(a) as provided by the agreement;

(b) as the parties may agree; or

(c) as determined in accordance with such procedure as they may agree upon.

(3) No agreement made pursuant to subsection (2) shall be effective for a period of more than 10 years from the date it is made, but at any time within the 2 years immediately preceding the date of the expiration of the agreement the parties may extend its duration for an additional period, not exceeding 10 years at any one time, as they may desire.

(4) The validity of any voting trust or other voting agreement is not affected during a period of 10 years from the date when it was created or last extended by reason only of the fact that under its terms it will or may last beyond a period of 10 years.

(5) This section shall be deemed not to invalidate any voting or other agreement among members or any irrevocable proxy that is not otherwise illegal.

Consents of members.

63. Subject to any limitations or provisions to the contrary in its memorandum or articles, an action that may be taken by members at a meeting of members may also be taken by a resolution of members consented to in writing or by telex, telegram, cable or other written electronic communication, without the need for any notice.

Service of notice on members

64.(1) Any notice, information or written statement required under this Act to be given by a company incorporated under this Act to members must be served -

(a) in the case of members holding registered shares -

(i) in the manner prescribed in the memorandum or articles, as the case may be, or

(ii) in the absence of a provision in the memorandum or articles, by personal service or by mail addressed to each member at the address shown in the share register; and *(b)* in the case of members holding shares issued to bearer, in the absence of a provision in the memorandum or articles, or if the notice, information or written statement can no longer be served as specified in the memorandum and articles by publishing the notice, information or written statement in a newspaper circulated in the British Virgin Islands and a newspaper in the place where the company has its principal office.

(2) Subject to a requirement in the memorandum or articles to give a specific length of notice, the directors must give sufficient notice of meetings of members to members holding shares issued to bearer to allow a reasonable opportunity for them to take action in order to secure or exercise the right or privilege, other than the right or privilege to vote, that is the subject of the notice.

(3) For purposes of subsection (2), what amounts to sufficient notice is a matter of fact to be determined after having regard to all the circumstances.

Service of process, etc. on company.

65.(1) Any summons, notice, order, document, process, information or written statement to be served on a company incorporated under this Act may be served by leaving it, or by sending it by registered mail addressed to the company, at its registered office, or by leaving it with, or by sending it by registered mail to, the registered agent of the company.

(2) Service of any summons, notice, order, document, process, information or written statement to be served on a company incorporated under this Act may be proved by showing that the summons, notice, order, document, process, information or written statement -

(a) was mailed in such time as to admit to its being delivered in the normal course of delivery, within the period prescribed for service; and

(b) was correctly addressed and the postage was prepaid.

Books, records and common seal.

66.(1) A company incorporated under this Act shall keep such accounts and records as the directors consider necessary or desirable in order to reflect the financial position of the company.

(2) A company incorporated under this Act shall keep -

(a) minutes of all meetings of -

(i) directors,

(ii) members,

(iii) committees of directors,

(iv) committees of officers, and

(v) committees of members, and

(b) copies of all resolutions consented to by -

(i) directors,

(ii) members,

(iii) committees of directors,

(iv) committees of officers, and

(v) committees of members.

(3) The books, records and minutes required by this section shall be kept at the registered office of the company or at such other place as the directors determine.

(3A) A company incorporated under this Act shall have a common seal and an imprint thereof shall be kept at the registered office of the company.

(4) A company that wilfully contravenes this section is liable to a penalty of $25 for each day or part thereof during which the contravention continues, and a director, who knowingly permits the contravention is liable to a like penalty.

Inspection of books and records.

67.(1) A member of a company incorporated under this Act may, in person or by attorney and in furtherance of a proper purpose, request in writing specifying the purpose to inspect during normal business hours the share register of the company or the books, records, minutes and consents kept by the company and to make copies or extracts therefrom.

(2) For purposes of subsection (1), a proper purpose is a purpose reasonably related to the member's interest as a member.

(3) If a request under subsection (1) is submitted by an attorney for a member, the request must be accompanied by a power of attorney authorising the attorney to act for the member.

(4) If the company, by a resolution of directors, determines that it is not in the best interest of the company or of any other member of the company to comply with a request under subsection (1), the company may refuse the request.

(5) Upon refusal by the company of a request under subsection (1), the member may before the expiration of a period of 90 days of his receiving notice of the refusal, apply to the court for an order to allow the inspection.

Contracts generally.

68.(1) Contracts may be entered into on behalf of a company incorporated under this Act as follows -

(a) a contract that, if entered into between individuals, is required by law to be in writing and under seal, may be entered into by or on behalf of the company in writing under the common seal of the company, and may, in the same manner, be varied or discharged;

(b) a contract that, if entered into between individuals, is required by law to be in writing and signed by the parties, may be entered into by or on behalf of the company in writing and signed by a person acting under the express or implied authority of the company, and may, in the same manner, be varied or discharged; and

(c) a contract that, if entered into between individuals, is valid although entered into orally, and not reduced to writing, may be entered into orally by or on behalf of the company by a person acting under the express or implied authority of the company, and may, in the same manner, be varied or discharged.

(2) A contract entered into in accordance with this section is valid and is binding on the company and its successors and all other parties to the contract.

(3) Without affecting paragraph (a) of subsection (1), a contract, agreement or other instrument executed by or on behalf of a company by a director or an authorised officer or agent of the company is not invalid by reason only of the fact that the common seal of the company is not affixed to the contract, agreement or instrument.

Contracts before incorporation.

69.(1) A person who enters into a written contract in the name of or on behalf of a company incorporated under this Act before the company comes into existence, is personally bound by the contract and is entitled to the benefits of the contract, except where -

(a) the contract specifically provides otherwise; or

(b) subject to any provisions of the contract to the contrary, the company adopts the contract under subsection (2).

(2) Within a reasonable time after a company incorporated under this Act comes into existence, the company may, by any action or conduct signifying its intention to be bound thereby, adopt a written contract entered into in its name or on its behalf before it came into existence.

(3) When a company adopts a contract under subsection (2) -

(a) the company is bound by, and entitled to the benefits of, the contract as if the company had been in existence at the date of the contract and had been a party to it; and

(b) subject to any provisions of the contract to the contrary, the person who acted in the name of or on behalf of the company ceases to be bound by or entitled to the benefits of the contract.

Contracts for payment or transfer.

70.(1) If any contract, agreement, deed or other instrument relating to the payment of a claim or the delivering or transferring of property, whether real or personal, wherever situate, is entered into by a company incorporated under this Act and the contract, agreement, deed or other instrument designates a payee or beneficiary to receive the payment or property -

(a) upon the death of the person making the designation;

(b) upon the death of another person; or

(c) upon the happening of any other event specified in the contract, agreement, deed or other instrument, then, any such payment, delivery or transfer, the rights of any payee or beneficiary, and the ownership of any property received, are not impaired or defeated by any law or rule of law governing the transfer of property by will, gift or intestacy.

(2) Subsection (1) applies to a contract, agreement, deed or other instrument referred to in that subsection notwithstanding anything to the contrary in the law of any other jurisdiction, including the law of any jurisdiction where the person making the designation referred to in subsection (1) resides or is domiciled, and notwithstanding that -

(a) the designation is revocable or subject to change; or

(b) the claim or property -

(i) is not yet payable or transferable, as the case may be, at the time the designation is made, or

(ii) is subject to withdrawal, collection or assignment by the person making the designation.

Optional register of mortgages and charges.

70A.(1) A company incorporated under this Act may create a mortgage, charge or other encumbrance over any of its assets situate in any part of the world in accordance with the law of any jurisdiction of the company's choice and the mortgage, charge or other encumbrance shall be binding on the company to the extent, and in accordance with the requirements, of the chosen law.

(2) A company incorporated under this Act may maintain at its registered office a register of mortgages, charges and other encumbrances in which there shall be entered particulars regarding each mortgage, charge and other encumbrance as follows -

(a) the sum secured;

(b) the assets secured;

(c) the name and address of the mortgagee, chargee or other encumbrancer;

(d) the date of creation of the mortgage, charge or other encumbrance; and

(e) the date on which the particulars specified in paragraphs (a) to (d) in respect of the mortgage, charge or other encumbrance are entered in the register.

(3) In the event that an application is made to a court in the British Virgin Islands to enforce any mortgage, charge or other encumbrance created by a company incorporated under this Act and there are assets of the company which are subject to two or more mortgages, charges or other encumbrances, then, notwithstanding the provisions of any other law, priorities shall be determined in accordance with the dates of entry in the register of mortgages and charges; and, unregistered mortgages, charges and other encumbrances created after 1st January, 1991 shall rank after registered mortgages, charges and other encumbrances, but unregistered mortgages, charges and other encumbrances created prior to 1st January, 1991 shall have priority over mortgages, charges and other encumbrances registered pursuant to this provision and shall rank in order of their creation.

Notes and bills of exchange.

71. A promissory note or bill of exchange shall be deemed to have been made, accepted or endorsed by a company incorporated under this Act if it is made, accepted or endorsed in the name of the company -

(a) by or on behalf or on account of the company; or

(b) by a person acting under the express or implied authority of the company; and if so endorsed, the person signing the endorsement is not liable thereon.

Power of attorney.

72.(1) A company incorporated under this Act may, by an instrument in writing, whether or not under its common seal, authorise a person, either generally or in respect of any specified matters, as its agent to act on behalf of the company and to execute contracts, agreements, deeds and other instruments on behalf of the company.

(2) A contract, agreement, deed or other instrument executed on behalf of the company by an agent appointed under subsection (1), whether or not under his seal, is binding on the company and has the same effect as if it were under the common seal of the company.

Authentication or attestation.

73.(1) A document requiring authentication or attestation by a company incorporated under this Act may be signed by a director, a secretary or by an authorised officer or agent of the company, and need not be under its common seal.

(2) If the signature of any director, officer or agent authenticating or attesting any document is verified in writing by the registered agent of a company the company is bound by the document.

Company without members.

74. If at any time there is no member of a company incorporated under this Act, any person doing business in the name of or on behalf of the company is personally liable for the payment of all debts of the company contracted during the time and the person may be sued therefor without joinder in the proceedings of any other person.

PART VII - Merger, Consolidation, Sale of Assets, Forced Redemptions, Arrangements and Dissenters

Interpretation for purposes of Part VII.

75. In this Part -

"consolidated company" means the new company that results from the consolidation of two or more constituent companies;

"consolidation" means the uniting of two or more constituent companies into a new company;

"constituent company" means an existing company that is participating in a merger or consolidation with one or more other existing companies;

"merger" means the merging of two or more constituent companies into one of the constituent companies;

"parent company" means a company that owns at least 90 per cent of the outstanding shares of each class and series of shares in another company;

"subsidiary company" means a company at least 90 per cent of whose outstanding shares of each class and series of shares are owned by another company;

"surviving company" means the constituent company into which one or more other constituent companies are merged.

Merger and consolidation.

76.(1) Two or more companies incorporated under this Act may merge or consolidate in accordance with subsections (3) to (5).

(2) One or more companies incorporated under this Act may merge or consolidate with one or more companies incorporated under the Companies Act in accordance with subsections (3) to (5), if the surviving company or the consolidated company will satisfy the requirements prescribed for an international business company under section 5.

(3) The directors of each constituent company that proposes to participate in a merger or consolidation must approve a written plan of merger or consolidation containing, as the case requires -

(a) the name of each constituent company and the name of the surviving company or the consolidated company;

(b) in respect to each constituent company -

(i) the designation and number of outstanding shares of each class and series of shares, specifying each such class and series entitled to vote on the merger or consolidation, and

(ii) a specification of each such class and series, if any, entitled to vote as a class or series;

(c) the terms and conditions of the proposed merger or consolidation, including the manner and basis of converting shares in each constituent company into shares, debt obligations or other securities in the surviving company or consolidated company, or money or other property, or a combination thereof;

(d) in respect of a merger, a statement of any amendment to the memorandum or articles of the surviving company to be brought about by the merger; and

(e) in respect of a consolidation, everything required to be included in the memorandum and articles for a company incorporated under this Act, except statements as to facts not available at the time the plan of consolidation is approved by the directors.

(4) Some or all shares of the same class or series of shares in each constituent company may be converted into a particular or mixed kind of property and other shares of the class or series, or all shares of other classes or series of shares, may be converted into other property.

(5) The following apply in respect of a merger or consolidation under this section -

(a) the plan of merger or consolidation must be authorised by a resolution of members and the outstanding shares of a class or series of shares are entitled to vote on the merger or consolidation as a class or series if the memorandum or articles so provide or if the plan of merger or consolidation contains any provisions that, if contained in a proposed amendment to the memorandum or articles, would entitle the class or series to vote on the proposed amendment as a class or series;

(b) if a meeting of members is to be held, notice of the meeting, accompanied by a copy of the plan of merger or consolidation, must be given to each member, whether or not entitled to vote on the merger or consolidation;

(c) if it is proposed to obtain the written consent of members, a copy of the plan of merger or consolidation must be given to each member, whether or not entitled to consent to the plan of merger or consolidation;

(d) after approval of the plan of merger or consolidation by the directors and members of each constituent company, articles of merger or consolidation must be executed by each company and must contain -

(i) the plan of merger or consolidation and, in the case of a consolidation, any statement required to be included in the memorandum and articles for a company incorporated under this Act;

(ii) the date on which the memorandum and articles of each constituent company were registered by the Registrar;

(iii) the manner in which the merger or consolidation was authorised with respect to each constituent company;

(e) the articles of merger or consolidation must be submitted to the Registrar who must retain and register them in the Register; and

(f) upon the registration of the articles of merger or consolidation, the Registrar shall issue a certificate under his hand and seal certifying that the articles of merger or consolidation have been registered.

(6) A certificate of merger or consolidation issued by the Registrar is prima facie evidence of compliance with all requirements of this Act in respect of the merger or consolidation.

Merger with subsidiary.

77.(1) A parent company incorporated under this Act may merge with one or more subsidiary companies incorporated under this Act or under the Companies Act, without the authorisation of the members of any company, in accordance with subsections (2) to (6), if the surviving company is a company incorporated under this Act and will satisfy the requirements prescribed for an international business company under section 5.

(2) The directors of the parent company must approve a written plan of merger containing -

(a) the name of each constituent company and the name of the surviving company;

(b) in respect to each constituent company -

(i) the designation and number of outstanding shares of each class and series of shares, and

(ii) the number of shares of each class and series of shares in each subsidiary company owned by the parent company; and

(c) the terms and conditions of the proposed merger, including the manner and basis of converting shares in each company to be merged into shares, debt obligations or other securities in the surviving company, or money or other property, or a combination thereof.

(3) Some or all shares of the same class or series of shares in each company to be merged may be converted into property of a particular or mixed kind and other shares of the class or series, or all shares of other classes or series of shares, may be converted into other property; but, if the parent company is not the surviving company, shares of each class and series of shares in the parent company may only be converted into similar shares of the surviving company.

(4) A copy of the plan of merger or an outline thereof must be given to every member of each subsidiary company to be merged unless the giving of that copy or outline has been waived by that member.

(5) Articles of merger must be executed by the parent company and must contain -

(a) the plan of merger;

(b) the date on which the memorandum and articles of each constituent company were registered by the Registrar; and

(c) if the parent company does not own all shares in each subsidiary company to be merged, the date on which a copy of the plan of merger or an outline thereof was made available to the members of each subsidiary company.

(6) The articles of merger must be submitted to the Registrar who must retain and register them in the Register.

(7) Upon the registration of the articles of merger, the Registrar shall issue a certificate under his hand and seal certifying that the articles of merger have been registered.

(8) A certificate of merger issued by the Registrar is prima facie evidence of compliance with all requirements of this Act in respect of the merger.

Effect of merger or consolidation.

78.(1) A merger or consolidation is effective on the date the articles of merger or consolidation are registered by the Registrar or on such date subsequent thereto, not exceeding 30 days, as is stated in the articles of merger or consolidation.

(2) As soon as a merger or consolidation becomes effective -

(a) the surviving company or the consolidated company in so far as is consistent with its memorandum and articles, as amended or established by the articles of merger or consolidation, has all rights, privileges, immunities, powers, objects and purposes of each of the constituent companies;

(b) in the case of a merger, the memorandum and articles of the surviving company are automatically amended to the extent, if any, that changes in its memorandum and articles are contained in the articles of merger;

(c) in the case of a consolidation, the statements contained in the articles of

consolidation that are required or authorised to be contained in the memorandum and articles of a company incorporated under this Act, are the memorandum and articles of the consolidated company;

(d) property of every description, including choses in action and the business of each of the constituent companies, immediately vests in the surviving company or the consolidated company; and

(e) the surviving company or the consolidated company is liable for all claims, debts, liabilities and obligations of each of the constituent companies.

(3) Where a merger or consolidation occurs -

(a) no conviction, judgment, ruling, order, claim, debt, liability or obligation due or to become due, and no cause existing, against a constituent company or against any member, director, officer or agent thereof, is released or impaired by the merger or consolidation; and

(b) no proceedings, whether civil or criminal, pending at the time of a merger or consolidation by or against a constituent company, or against any member, director, officer or agent thereof, are abated or discontinued by the merger or consolidation, but -

(i) the proceedings may be enforced, prosecuted, settled or compromised by or against the surviving company or the consolidated company or against the member, director, officer or agent thereof, as the case may be, or

(ii) the surviving company or the consolidated company may be substituted in the proceedings for the constituent company.

(4) The Registrar shall strike off the Register -

(a) a constituent company that is not the surviving company in a merger; or

(b) a constituent company that participates in a consolidation.

Merger or consolidation with foreign company.

79.(1) One or more companies incorporated under this Act may merge or consolidate with one or more companies incorporated under the laws of jurisdictions outside the British Virgin Islands in accordance with subsections (2) to (4), including where one of the constituent companies is a parent company and the other constituent companies are subsidiary companies, if the merger or consolidation is permitted by the laws of the jurisdictions in which the companies incorporated outside the British Virgin Islands are incorporated.

(2) The following apply in respect of a merger or consolidation under this section -

(a) a company incorporated under this Act shall comply with the provisions of this Act with respect to the merger or consolidation, as the case may be, of companies incorporated under this Act and a company incorporated under the laws of a jurisdiction outside the British Virgin Islands shall comply with the laws of that jurisdiction; and

(b) if the surviving company or the consolidated company is to be incorporated under the laws of a jurisdiction outside the British Virgin Islands, it must submit to the Registrar -

(i) an agreement that a service of process may be effected on it in the British Virgin Islands in respect of proceedings for the enforcement of any claim, debt, liability or obligation of a constituent company incorporated under this Act or in respect of proceedings for the enforcement of the rights of a dissenting member of a constituent company incorporated under this Act against the surviving company or the consolidated company;

(ii) an irrevocable appointment of the Registrar as its agent to accept service of process in proceedings referred to in sub-paragraph (i);

(iii) an agreement that it will promptly pay to the dissenting members of a constituent company incorporated under this Act the amount, if any, to which they are entitled under this Act with respect to the rights of dissenting members; and

(iv) a certificate of merger or consolidation issued by the appropriate authority of the foreign jurisdiction where it is incorporated; or, if no certificate of merger is issued by the appropriate authority of the foreign jurisdiction, then, such evidence of the merger or consolidation as the Registrar considers acceptable.

(3) The effect under this section of a merger or consolidation is the same as in the case of a merger or consolidation under section 76 if the surviving company or the consolidated company is incorporated under this Act, but if the surviving company or the consolidated company is incorporated under the laws of a jurisdiction outside the British Virgin Islands, the effect of the merger or consolidation is the same as in the case of a merger or consolidation under section 76 except in so far as the laws of the other jurisdiction otherwise provide.

(4) If the surviving company or the consolidated company is incorporated under this Act, the merger or consolidation is effective on the date the articles of merger or consolidation are registered by the Registrar or on such date subsequent thereto, not exceeding 30 days, as is stated in the articles of merger or consolidation; but if the surviving company or the consolidated company is incorporated under the laws of a jurisdiction outside the British Virgin Islands, the merger or consolidation is effective as provided by the laws of that other jurisdiction.

Disposition of assets.

80. Subject to any limitations or provisions to the contrary in its memorandum or articles, any sale, transfer, lease, exchange or other disposition other than a mortgage, charge or other encumbrance or the enforcement thereof, of more than 50 per cent of the assets of a company incorporated under this Act, other than a transfer pursuant to the power described in subsection (2) of section 9, if not made in the usual or regular course of business carried on by the company, shall be made as follows -

(a) the proposed sale, transfer, lease, exchange or other disposition must be approved by the directors;

(b) upon approval of the proposed sale, transfer, lease, exchange or other disposition, the directors must submit the proposal to the members for it to be authorised by a resolution of members;

(c) if a meeting of members is to be held, notice of the meeting, accompanied by an outline of the proposal, must be given to each member, whether or not he is entitled to vote on the sale, transfer, lease, exchange or other disposition; and

(d) if it is proposed to obtain the written consent of members, an outline of the proposal must be given to each member, whether or not he is entitled to consent to the sale, transfer, lease, exchange or other disposition.

Redemption of minority shares.

81.(1) Subject to any limitations or provisions to the contrary in its memorandum or articles -

(a) members holding 90 per cent of the votes of the outstanding shares entitled to vote; and

(b) members holding 90 per cent of the votes of the outstanding shares of each class and series of shares entitled to vote as a class or series, on a merger or consolidation under section 76, may give a written instruction to a company incorporated under this Act directing the company to redeem the shares held by the remaining members.

(2) Upon receipt of the written instruction referred to in subsection (1), the company shall redeem the shares specified in the written instruction irrespective of whether or not the shares are by their terms redeemable.

(3) The company must give written notice to each member whose shares are to be redeemed stating the redemption price and the manner in which the redemption is to be effected.

Arrangements.

82.(1) In this section, "arrangement" means -

(a) an amendment to the memorandum or articles;

(b) a reorganisation or reconstruction of a company incorporated under this Act;

(c) a merger or consolidation of one or more companies incorporated under this Act with one or more other companies, if the surviving company or the consolidated company is a company incorporated under this Act;

(d) a separation of two or more businesses carried on by a company incorporated under this Act;

(e) any sale, transfer, exchange or other disposition of any part of the property, assets or business of a company incorporated under this Act to any person in exchange for shares, debt obligations or other securities of that other person, or money or other property, or a combination thereof;

(f) any sale, transfer, exchange or other disposition of shares, debt obligations or other securities in a company incorporated under this Act held by the holders thereof for shares, debt obligations or other securities in the company or money or other property, or a combination thereof;

(g) a winding-up and dissolution of a company incorporated under this Act; and

(h) any combination of any of the things specified in paragraphs (a) to (g).

(2) If the directors of a company incorporated under this Act determine that it is in the best interests of the company or the creditors or members thereof, the directors of the company may, by a resolution of directors, approve a plan of arrangement that contains the details of the proposed arrangement, even though the proposed arrangement may be authorised or permitted by any other provision of this Act or otherwise permitted.

(3) Upon approval of the plan of arrangement by the directors, the company must make application to the court for approval of the proposed arrangement.

(4) The court may, upon an application made to it under subsection (3), make an interim or a final order that is not subject to an appeal unless a question of law is involved and in which case notice of appeal must be given within the period of 20 days immediately following the date of the order, and in making the order the court may -

(a) determine what notice, if any, of the proposed arrangement is to be given to any person;

(b) determine whether approval of the proposed arrangement by any person should be obtained and the manner of obtaining the approval;

(c) determine whether any holder of shares, debt obligations or other securities in the company may dissent from the proposed arrangement and receive payment of the fair value of his shares, debt obligations or other securities under section 83;

(d) conduct a hearing and permit any interested person to appear; and

(e) approve or reject the plan of arrangement as proposed or with such amendments as it may direct.

(5) Where the court makes an order approving a plan of arrangement, the directors of the company, if they are still desirous of executing the plan, shall confirm the plan of arrangement as approved by the court whether or not the court has directed any amendments to be made thereto.

(6) The directors of the company, upon confirming the plan of arrangement, shall -

(a) give notice to the persons to whom the order of the court requires notice to be given; and

(b) submit the plan of arrangement to those persons for such approval, if any, as the order of the court requires.

(7) After the plan of arrangement has been approved by those persons by whom the order of the court may require approval, articles of arrangement must be executed by the company and must contain -

(a) the plan of arrangement;

(b) the order of the court approving the plan of arrangement, and

(c) the manner in which the plan of arrangement was approved, if approval was required by the order of the court.

(8) The articles of arrangement must be submitted to the Registrar who must retain and register them in the Register.

(9) Upon the registration of the articles of arrangement, the Registrar shall issue a certificate under his hand and seal certifying that the articles of arrangement have been registered.

(10) A certificate of arrangement issued by the Registrar is prima facie evidence of compliance with all requirements of this Act in respect of the arrangement.

(11) An arrangement is effective on the date the articles of arrangement are registered by the Registrar or on such date subsequent thereto, not exceeding 30 days, as is stated in the articles of arrangement.

Rights of dissenters.

83.(1) A member of a company incorporated under this Act is entitled to payment of the fair value of his shares upon dissenting from -

(a) a merger, if the company is a constituent company, unless the company is the surviving company and the member continues to hold the same or similar shares;

(b) a consolidation, if the company is a constituent company;

(c) any sale, transfer, lease, exchange or other disposition of more than 50 per cent of the assets or business of the company, if not made in the usual or regular course of the business carried on by the company, but not including -

(i) a disposition pursuant to an order of the court having jurisdiction in the matter;

(ii) a disposition for money on terms requiring all or substantially all net proceeds to be distributed to the members in accordance with their respective interests within one year after the date of disposition; or

(iii) a transfer pursuant to the power described in subsection (2) of section 9;

(d) a redemption of his shares by the company pursuant to section 81; and

(e) an arrangement, if permitted by the court.

(2) A member who desires to exercise his entitlement under subsection (1) must give to the company, before the meeting of members at which the action is submitted to a vote, or at the meeting but before the vote, written objection to the action; but an objection is not required from a member to whom the company did not give notice of the meeting in accordance with this Act or where the proposed action is authorised by written consent of members without a meeting.

(3) An objection under subsection (2) must include a statement that the member proposes to demand payment for his shares if the action is taken.

(4) Within 20 days immediately following the date on which the vote of members authorising the action is taken, or the date on which written consent of members without a meeting is obtained, the company must give written notice of the authorisation or consent to each member who gave written objection or from whom written objection was not required, except those members who voted for, or consented to in writing, the proposed action.

(5) A member to whom the company was required to give notice who elects to dissent must, within 20 days immediately following the date on which the notice referred to in subsection (4) is given, give to the company a written notice of his decision to elect to dissent, stating -

(a) his name and address;

(b) the number and classes or series of shares in respect of which he dissents; and

(c) a demand for payment of the fair value of his shares; and a member who elects to dissent from a merger under section 77 must give to the company a written notice of his decision to elect to dissent within 20 days immediately following the date on which the copy of the plan of merger or an outline thereof is given to him in accordance with section 77.

(6) A member who dissents must do so in respect of all shares that he holds in the company.

(7) Upon the giving of a notice of election to dissent, the member to whom the notice relates ceases to have any of the rights of a member except the right to be paid the fair value of his shares.

(8) Within 7 days immediately following the date of the expiration of the period within which members may give their notices of election to dissent, or within 7 days immediately following the date on which the proposed action is put into effect, whichever is later, the company or, in the case of a merger or consolidation, the surviving company or the consolidated company, must make a written offer to each dissenting member to purchase his shares at a specified price that the company determines to be their fair value; and if, within 30 days immediately following the date on which the offer is made, the company making the offer and the dissenting member agree upon the price to be paid for his shares, the company shall pay to the member the amount in money upon the surrender of the certificates representing his shares.

(9) If the company and a dissenting member fail, within the period of 30 days referred to in subsection (8), to agree on the price to be paid for the shares owned by the member, within 20 days immediately following the date on which the period of 30 days expires, the following shall apply -

(a) the company and the dissenting member shall each designate an appraiser;

(b) the two designated appraisers together shall designate a third appraiser;

(c) the three appraisers shall fix the fair value of the shares owned by the dis-

senting member as of the close of business on the day prior to the date on which the vote of members authorising the action was taken or the date on which written consent of members without a meeting was obtained, excluding any appreciation or depreciation directly or indirectly induced by the action or its proposal, and that value is binding on the company and the dissenting member for all purposes; and

(d) the company shall pay to the member the amount in money upon the surrender by him of the certificates representing his shares.

(10) Shares acquired by the company pursuant to subsection (8) or (9) shall be cancelled but if the shares are shares of a surviving company, they shall be available for reissue.

(11) The enforcement by a member of his entitlement under this section excludes the enforcement by the member of a right to which he might otherwise be entitled by virtue of his holding shares, except that this section does not exclude the right of the member to institute proceedings to obtain relief on the ground that the action is illegal.

(12) Only subsections (1) and (8) to (11) shall apply in the case of a redemption of shares by a company pursuant to the provisions of section 81 and in such case the written offer to be made to the dissenting member pursuant to subsection (8) shall be made within 7 days immediately following the direction given to a company pursuant to section 81 to redeem its shares.

PART VIII - Continuation

Continuation.

84.(1) A company incorporated under the Companies Act or incorporated under the laws of a jurisdiction outside the British Virgin Islands may, if it will satisfy the requirements prescribed for an international business company under section 5, continue as a company incorporated under this Act as follows -

(a) articles of continuation, written in the English language or if written in a language other than the English language, accompanied by a certified translation into the English language, must be approved -

(i) by a majority of the directors or the other persons who are charged with exercising the powers of the company, or

(ii) in such other manner as may be established by the company for exercising the powers of the company;

(b) the articles of continuation must contain -

(i) the name of the company and the name under which it is being continued,

(ii) the jurisdiction under which it is incorporated,

(iii) the date on which it was incorporated,

(iv) the information required to be included in a memorandum under subsection (1) of section 12, and

(v) the amendments to its memorandum and articles, or their equivalent, that are to be effective upon the registration of the articles of continuation;

(c) the articles of continuation, accompanied by a copy of the memorandum and articles of the company, or their equivalent, written in the English language or if written in a language other than the English language, accompanied by a certified translation into the English language, and, in the case of a foreign company, evidence satisfactory to the Registrar that the company is in good standing, must be submitted to the Registrar who must retain and register them in the Register; and

(d) upon the registration of the articles of continuation, the Registrar shall issue a certificate of continuation under his hand and seal certifying that the company is incorporated under this Act.

(2) A company incorporated under the laws of a jurisdiction outside the British Virgin Islands is entitled to continue as a company incorporated under this Act notwithstanding any provision to the contrary in the laws of the jurisdiction under which it is incorporated.

(3) Notwithstanding any provisions of the Companies Act, a company incorporated under that Act may, by resolution of the directors, continue the incorporation of the company under this Act.

(4) Where a company incorporated under the Companies Act has continued its incorporation under this Act, the Registrar shall strike the name of the company off the Register maintained under that Act and publish notice of the striking-off in the Gazette.

Provisional registration.

85.(1) A company incorporated under the laws of a jurisdiction outside the British Virgin Islands that is permitted under section 84 to continue as a company incorporated under this Act, may, after complying with paragraphs (a) and (b) of subsection (1) of section 84, submit to the Registrar the following documents -

(a) articles of continuation, accompanied by a copy of its memorandum and articles, or their equivalent, written in the English language, or if written in a language other than the English language, accompanied by a certified translation into the English language; and

(b) a written authorisation designating one or more persons who may give notice to the Registrar, by telex, telegram, cable or by registered mail, that the articles of continuation should become effective.

(2) The Registrar shall not, prior to the receipt of the notice referred to in subsection (1), permit any person to inspect the documents referred to in subsection (1) and shall not divulge any information in respect thereof.

(3) Upon receipt of the notice referred to in subsection (1), the Registrar shall -

(a) register the documents referred to in subsection (1) in the Register; and

(b) issue a certificate of continuation under his hand and seal certifying that the company is incorporated under this Act.

(4) For purposes of subsection (3), the Registrar may rely on a notice referred to in subsection (1) sent, or purported to be sent, by a person named in the written authorisation.

(5) Prior to the registration of the documents referred to in subsection (1), a company may rescind the written authorisation referred to in subsection (1) by delivering to the Registrar a written notice of rescission.

(6) If the Registrar does not receive a notice referred to in subsection (1) from a person named in the written authorisation within one year immediately following the date on which the documents referred to in subsection (1) were submitted to the Registrar, the articles of continuation are rescinded.

(7) A company entitled to submit to the Registrar the documents referred to in subsection (1) may authorise the Registrar to accept as resubmitted the documents referred to in that subsection, before or after the documents previously submitted referred to in subsection (1) have been rescinded.

Certificate of continuation.

86. A certificate of continuation issued by the Registrar under paragraph (d) of subsection (1) of section 84 or under subsection (3) of section 85 is prima facie evidence of compliance with all requirements of this Act in respect of continuation.

Effect of continuation.

87.(1) From the time of the issue by the Registrar of a certificate of continuation under paragraph (d) of subsection (1) of section 84 or under subsection (3) of section 85 -

(a) the company to which the certificate relates -

(i) continues to be a body corporate, incorporated under this Act, under the name designated in the articles of continuation,

(ii) is capable of exercising all powers of a company incorporated under this Act, and

(iii) is no longer to be treated as a company incorporated under the Companies Act or a company incorporated under the laws of a jurisdiction outside the British Virgin Islands;

(b) the memorandum and articles of the company, or their equivalent, as amended by the articles of continuation, are the memorandum and articles of the company;

(c) property of every description, including choses in action and the business of the company, continue to be vested in the company; and

(d) the company continues to be liable for all of its claims, debts, liabilities and obligations.

(2) Where a company is continued under this Act -

(a) no conviction, judgment, ruling, order, claim, debt, liability or obligation

due or to become due, and no cause existing, against the company or against any member, director, officer or agent thereof, is released or impaired by its continuation as a company under this Act; and

(b) no proceedings, whether civil or criminal, pending at the time of the issue by the Registrar of a certificate of continuation under paragraph (d) of subsection (1) of section 84 or under subsection (3) of section 85 by or against the company, or against any member, director, officer or agent thereof, are abated or discontinued by its continuation as a company under this Act, but the proceedings may be enforced, prosecuted, settled or compromised by or against the company or against the member, director, officer or agent thereof, as the case may be.

(3) All shares in the company that were outstanding prior to the issue by the Registrar of a certificate of continuation under paragraph (d) of subsection (1) of section 84 or under subsection (3) of section 85 in respect to the company shall be deemed to have been issued in conformity with this Act, but a share that at the time of the issue of the certificate of continuation was not fully paid shall be paid up no later than one year immediately following the date of the issue of the certificate of continuation and until the share is paid up, the member holding the share remains liable for the amount unpaid on the share.

(4) If at the time of the issue by the Registrar of a certificate of continuation under paragraph (d) of subsection (1) of section 84 or under subsection (3) of section 85 in respect of the company any provisions of the memorandum and articles of the company do not in any respect accord with this Act -

(a) the provisions of the memorandum and articles continue to govern the company until the provisions are amended to accord with this Act or for a period of 2 years immediately following the date of the issue of the certificate of continuation, whichever is the sooner;

(b) any provisions of the memorandum and articles of the company that are in any respect in conflict with this Act cease to govern the company when the provisions are amended to accord with this Act or after the expiration of a period of 2 years after the date of issue of the certificate of continuation, whichever is the sooner; and

(c) the company shall make such amendments to its memorandum and articles as may be necessary to accord with this Act within a period that is not later than 2 years immediately following the date of the issue of the certificate of continuation.

Continuation under foreign law.

88.(1) Subject to any limitations or provisions to the contrary in its memorandum or articles, a company incorporated under this Act and for which the Registrar would issue a certificate of good standing pursuant to subsection (1) of section 114 may, by a resolution of directors or by a resolution of members, continue as a company incorporated under the laws of a jurisdiction outside the British Virgin Islands in the manner provided under those laws.

(2) A company incorporated under this Act that continues as a company incorporated under the laws of a jurisdiction outside the British Virgin Islands does not cease to be a company incorporated under this Act unless the laws of the jurisdiction outside the British Virgin Islands permit the continuation and the company has complied with those laws.

(2A) The registered agent of a company incorporated under this Act that continues as a company incorporated under the laws of a jurisdiction outside the British Virgin Islands may within 30 days of the continuation of the company under the laws of the foreign jurisdiction submit to the Registrar an affidavit to the effect that the company has continued its incorporation under the laws of the named foreign jurisdiction and the Registrar shall retain and register the affidavit.

(2B) Upon registration of the affidavit referred to in subsection (2A) the Registrar shall -

(a) strike the name of the company off the Register;

(b) issue a certificate of discontinuance; and

(c) publish the striking off in the Gazette.

(3) Where a company incorporated under this Act is continued under the laws of a jurisdiction outside the British Virgin Islands -

(a) the company continues to be liable for all of its claims, debts, liabilities and obligations that existed prior to its continuation as a company under the laws of the jurisdiction outside the British Virgin Islands;

(b) no conviction, judgment, ruling, order, claim, debt, liability or obligation due or to become due, and no cause existing, against the company or against any member, director, officer or agent thereof, is released or impaired by its continuation as a company under the laws of the jurisdiction outside the British Virgin Islands;

(c) no proceedings, whether civil or criminal, pending by or against the company, or against any member, director, officer or agent thereof, are abated or discontinued by its continuation as a company under the laws of the jurisdiction outside the British Virgin Islands, but the proceedings may be enforced, prosecuted, settled or compromised by or against the company or against the member, director, officer or agent thereof, as the case may be; and

(d) service of process may continue to be effected on the registered agent of the company in the British Virgin Islands in respect of any claim, debt, liability or obligation of the company during its existence as a company incorporated under this Act.

PART IX - Winding-Up, Dissolution, and Striking-Off

Compulsory winding-up and dissolution.

89. A company incorporated under this Act shall commence to wind up and dissolve by a resolution of directors upon expiration of such time as may be prescribed by its memorandum or articles for its existence or upon the happening of an event which has been specified in the memorandum or articles as an event that shall terminate the existence of the company.

Voluntary winding-up and dissolution.

90.(1) A company incorporated under this Act that has never issued shares may voluntarily commence to wind up and dissolve by a resolution of directors.

(2) Subject to any limitations or provisions to the contrary in its memorandum or articles, a company incorporated under this Act that has previously issued shares may voluntarily commence to wind up and dissolve by a resolution of members or by a resolution of directors.

Powers of directors in a winding-up and dissolution.

91. Upon the commencement of a winding-up and dissolution under section 89 or permitted under section 90, the directors may only -

(a) authorise a liquidator, by a resolution of directors, to carry on the business of the company if the liquidator determines that to do so would be necessary or in the best interests of the creditors or members of the company, and

(b) determine to rescind the articles of dissolution as permitted under paragraph (a) of subsection (1) of section 95.

Duties of liquidator.

92.(1) A liquidator shall, upon his appointment in accordance with this Part and upon the commencement of a winding-up and dissolution, proceed -

(a) to identify all assets of the company;

(b) to identify all creditors of and claimants against the company;

(c) to pay or provide for the payment of, or to discharge, all claims, debts, liabilities and obligations of the company;

(d) to distribute any surplus assets of the company to the members in accordance with the actions and transactions of the liquidator; and

(e) to prepare or cause to be prepared a statement of account in respect of the actions and transactions of the liquidator; and

(f) to send a copy of the statement of account to all members if so required by the plan of dissolution required by section 94.

(2) A transfer, including a prior transfer, described in subsection (2) of section 9 of all or substantially all of the assets of a company incorporated under this Act for the benefit of the creditors and members of the company, is sufficient to satisfy the requirements of paragraphs (c) and (d) of subsection (1).

Powers of liquidator.

93.(1) In order to perform the duties imposed on him under section 92, a liquidator has all powers of the company that are not reserved to the members under this Act or in the memorandum or articles, including, but not limited to, the power -

(a) to take custody of the assets of the company and, in connection therewith, to register any property of the company in the name of the liquidator or that of his nominee;

(b) to sell any assets of the company at public auction or by private sale without any notice;

(c) to collect the debts and assets due or belonging to the company;

(d) to borrow money from any person for any purpose that will facilitate the winding-up and dissolution of the company and to pledge or mortgage any property of the company as security for any such borrowing;

(e) to negotiate, compromise and settle any claim, debt, liability or obligation of the company;

(f) to prosecute and defend, in the name of the company or in the name of the liquidator or otherwise, any action or other legal proceedings;

(g) to retain solicitors, accountants and other advisers and appoint agents;

(h) to carry on the business of the company, if the liquidator has received authorisation to do so in the plan of liquidation or by a resolution of directors permitted under section 91, as the liquidator may determine to be necessary or to be in the best interests of the creditors or members of the company;

(i) to execute any contract, agreement or other instrument in the name of the company or in the name of the liquidator; and

(j) to make any distribution in money or in other property or partly in each, and if in other property, to allot the property, or an undivided interest therein, in equal or unequal proportions.

(2) Notwithstanding paragraph (h) of subsection (1), a liquidator shall not, without the permission of the court, carry on for a period in excess of 2 years the business of a company that is being wound up and dissolved under this Act.

Procedure on winding-up and dissolution.

94.(1) The directors of a company required under section 89 or proposing under section 90 to wind up and dissolve the company must approve a plan of dissolution containing -

(a) a statement of the reason for the winding-up and dissolving;

(b) a statement that the company is, and will continue to be, able to discharge or pay or provide for the payment of all claims, debts, liabilities and obligations in full;

(c) a statement that the winding up will commence on the date when articles of dissolution are submitted to the Registrar or on such date subsequent thereto, not exceeding 30 days, as is stated in the articles of dissolution;

(d) a statement of the estimated time required to wind up and dissolve the company;

(e) a statement as to whether the liquidator is authorised to carry on the business of the company if the liquidator determines that to do so would be necessary or in the best interests of the creditors or members of the company;

(f) a statement of the name and address of each person to be appointed a liquidator and the remuneration proposed to be paid to each liquidator; and

(g) a statement as to whether the liquidator is required to send to all members a statement of account prepared or caused to be prepared by the liquidator in respect of his actions or transactions.

(2) If a winding-up and dissolution is being effected in a case where subsection (2) of section 90 is applicable -

(a) the plan of dissolution must be authorised by a resolution of members, and the holders of the outstanding shares of a class or series of shares are entitled to vote on the plan of dissolution as a class or series only if the memorandum or articles so provide;

(b) if a meeting of members is to be held, notice of the meeting, accompanied by a copy of the plan of dissolution, must be given to each member, whether or not entitled to vote on the plan of dissolution; and

(c) if it is proposed to obtain the written consent of members, a copy of the plan

of dissolution must be given to each member, whether or not entitled to consent to the plan of dissolution.

(3) After approval of the plan of dissolution by the directors, and if required, by the members in accordance with subsection (2), articles of dissolution must be executed by the company and must contain -

(a) the plan of dissolution; and

(b) the manner in which the plan of dissolution was authorised.

(4) Articles of dissolution must be submitted to the Registrar who must retain and register them in the Register and within 30 days immediately following the date on which the articles of dissolution are submitted to the Registrar, the company must cause to be published, in the Gazette, in a publication of general circulation in the British Virgin Islands and in a publication of general circulation in the country or place where the company has its principal office, a notice stating -

(a) that the company is in dissolution;

(b) the date of commencement of the dissolution; and

(c) the names and addresses of the liquidators.

(5) A winding-up and dissolution commences on the date the articles of dissolution are registered by the Registrar or on such date subsequent thereto, not exceeding 30 days, as is stated in the articles of dissolution

(6) A liquidator shall, upon completion of a winding-up and dissolution, submit to the Registrar a statement that the winding-up and dissolution has been completed and upon receiving the notice, the Registrar shall -

(a) strike the company off the Register; and

(b) issue a certificate of dissolution under his hand and seal certifying that the company has been dissolved.

(7) Where the Registrar issues a certificate of dissolution under his hand and seal certifying that the company has been dissolved -

(a) the certificate is prima facie evidence of compliance with all requirements of this Act in respect of dissolution; and

(b) the dissolution of the company is effective from the date of the issue of the certificate.

(8) Immediately following the issue by the Registrar of a certificate of dissolution under subsection (6), the liquidator shall cause to be published in the Gazette a notice that the company has been dissolved and has been struck off the Register.

(9) A company that wilfully contravenes subsection (4) is liable to a penalty of $50 for every day or part thereof during which the contravention continues, and a director or liquidator who knowingly permits the contravention is liable to a like penalty.

Rescission of winding-up and dissolution.

95.(1) In the case of a winding-up and dissolution permitted under section 90, a company may, prior to submitting to the Registrar a notice specified in subsection (4) of section 94, rescind the articles of dissolution by -

(a) a resolution of directors in the case of a winding-up and dissolution under subsection (1) of section 90; or

(b) a resolution of members in the case of a winding-up and dissolution under subsection (2) of section 90.

(2) A copy of a resolution referred to in subsection (1) must be submitted to the Registrar who must retain and register it in the Register.

(3) Within 30 days immediately following the date on which the resolution referred to in subsection (1) has been submitted to the Registrar, the company must cause a notice stating that the company has rescinded its intention to wind up and dissolve to be published in the Gazette, in a publication of general circulation in the British Virgin Islands and in a publication of general circulation in the country or place where the company has its principal office.

Winding-up and dissolution of company unable to pay its claims, etc.

96.(1) Where -

(a) the directors or, as the case may be, the members of a company that is required under section 89 or permitted under section 90 to wind up and dissolve, at the time of the passing of the resolution to wind up and dissolve the company, have reason to believe that the company will not be able to pay or provide for the payment of or discharge all claims, debts, liabilities and obligations of the company in full; or

(b) the liquidator after his appointment has reason so to believe, then, the directors, the members or the liquidator, as the case may be, shall immediately give notice of the fact to the Registrar.

(2) Where notice has been given to the Registrar under subsection (1), all winding-up and dissolution proceedings after the notice has been given shall be in accordance with the provisions of the Companies Act relating to winding-up and dissolution and those provisions shall apply mutatis mutandis to the winding-up and dissolution of the company.

Winding-up and dissolution by the court.

97.(1) Notwithstanding the provisions of this Act relating to winding-up and dissolution, a company incorporated under this Act may be wound up by the court under any of the circumstances, in so far as they are applicable to a company incorporated under this Act, in which a company incorporated under the Companies Act may be wound up by the court and, in that case, the provisions of the Companies Act relating to winding-up and dissolution apply mutatis mutandis to the winding-up and dissolution of the company.

(2) Any person who, pursuant to the provisions of subsection (1), files, or causes to be filed, a petition for the winding up of a company incorporated under this Act, shall forthwith serve on the Registrar a notice that the petition has been filed, and the Registrar must retain and register the notice.

Receivers and managers.

98.(1) The provisions of the Companies Act regarding receivers and managers govern mutatis mutandis the appointment, duties, powers and liabilities of receivers and managers of the assets of any company incorporated under this Act.

(2) This section comes into operation on such date as the Governor may appoint by proclamation published in the Gazette.

Striking-off.

99.(1) Notwithstanding section 6, where the Registrar has reasonable cause to believe that a company incorporated under this Act no longer satisfies the requirements prescribed for an international business company under section 5, the Registrar must serve on the company a notice that the name of the company may be struck off the Register if the company no longer satisfies those requirements.

(2) If the Registrar does not receive a reply within 30 days immediately following the date of the service of the notice referred to in subsection (1), he must serve on the company another notice that the name of the company may be struck off the Register if a reply to the notice is not received within 30 days immediately following the date thereof and that a notice of the contemplated striking-off will be published in the Gazette.

(3) If the Registrar -

(a) receives from the company a notice stating that the company no longer satisfies the requirements prescribed for an international business company under section 5, in reply to a notice served on the company under subsection (1) or (2);

(b) does not receive a reply to a notice served on the company under subsection (2) as required by that subsection, he must publish a notice in the Gazette that the name of the company will be struck off the Register unless the company or another person satisfies the Registrar that the name of the company should not be struck off.

(4) At the expiration of a period of 90 days immediately following the date of the publication of the notice under subsection (3), the Registrar shall strike the name of the company off the Register, unless the company or any other person satisfies the Registrar that the name of the company should not be struck off, and the Registrar must publish notice of the striking-off in the Gazette.

(5) If a company fails to pay the increased licence fee due under subsection (3) of section 105 on or before the expiration period of a period of 2 months from the time specified in subsection (1) or (2), as the case may be, of section 105, the Registrar shall within 2 months from the expiration of the said period of 2 months send to the registered agent of the company a written notice that the name of the company will be struck off the Register if the licence fee specified in subsection (4) of section 105 is not paid on or before the next licence fee final payment date.

(6) If a company fails to pay the increased fee stated in the notice referred to in subsection (5) at or before the next licence fee final payment date, the Registrar shall strike the name of the company off the Register on the date immediately following the next licence fee final payment date.

(7) Within one month following each licence fee final payment date, the Registrar shall send to the registered agent of each company the name of which has been struck off the Register notice of striking off.

(8) Within 2 months following each licence fee final payment date, the Registrar shall publish in the Gazette the names of all companies struck off the Register on the date immediately following the licence fee final payment date.

(9) A company the name of which has been struck off the Register under this section remains liable for all claims, debts, liabilities and obligations of the company, and the striking off does not affect the liability of any of its members, directors, officers or agents.

(10) The striking off of a company shall not be affected by any failure on the part of the Registrar to serve a notice on the registered agent or to publish a notice in the Gazette.

(11) Subsections (5) to (8) do not apply to a company in the process of being wound up and dissolved.

Restoration to register.

100.(1) If the name of a company has been struck off the Register under subsection (4) of section 99, the company, or a creditor, member or liquidator thereof, may apply to the court to have the name of the company restored to the Register.

(2) If upon an application under subsection (1) the court is satisfied that -

(a) at the time the name of the company was struck off the Register, the company did satisfy the requirements prescribed for an international business company under section 5; and

(b) it would be fair and reasonable for the name of the company to be restored to the Register, the court may order the name of the company to be restored to the Register upon payment to the Registrar of all fees due under section 104 and all licence fees due under section 105 without any increase for late payment, and upon restoration of the name of the company to the Register, the name of the company is deemed never to have been struck off the Register.

(3) If the name of a company has been struck off the Register under subsection (6) of section 99, the company, or a creditor, member or liquidator thereof, may, within 10 years immediately following the date of the striking off, apply to the Registrar to have the name of the company restored to the Register, and upon payment of -

(a) all the fees due under section 104;

(b) the increased licence fee due under subsection (3) of section 105; and

(c) the increased licence fee due under subsection (3) of section 105 for each year during which the name of the company remains struck off the Register,

the Registrar shall restore the name of the company to the Register and upon restoration of the name of the company to the Register, the name of the company is deemed never to have been struck off the Register.

(3A) If the name of a company has been struck off the Register under subsection (5) or subsection (6) of section 40A, the company, or a creditor, member or liquidator thereof, may apply to the Registrar to have the name of the company restored to the Register.

(3B) If upon an application under subsection (3A) the Registrar is satisfied that-

(a) a licensed person has agreed to act as a registered agent of the company; and

(b) it would be fair and reasonable for the name of the company to be restored to the Register, the Registrar may restore the name of the company to the Register upon satisfaction of the conditions set forth in subsection (3C) and upon restoration of the name of the company to the Register, the name of the company is deemed never to have been struck off the Register.

(3C) The conditions referred to in subsection (3B) are as follows -

(a) the submission to the Registrar by the applicant for the restoration of a copy of the resolution amending the memorandum of the company to change the registered agent; and

(b) payment to the Registrar by the applicant for the restoration of -

(i) all fees due under section 104, and

(ii) all licence fees due under section 105 without increase for late payment.

(4) For purposes of this Part, the appointment of an official receiver under section 102 operates as an order to restore the name of the company to the Register.

Effect of striking-off.

101.(1) Where the name of a company has been struck off the Register, the company, and the directors, members, liquidators and receivers thereof, may not legally -

(a) commence legal proceedings, carry on any business or in any way deal with the assets of the company;

(b) defend any legal proceedings, make any claim or claim any right for, or in the name of, the company; or

(c) act in any way with respect to the affairs of the company.

(2) Notwithstanding subsection (1), where the name of the company has been struck off the Register, the company, or a director, member, liquidator or receiver thereof, may -

(a) make application for restoration of the name of the company to the Register;

(b) continue to defend proceedings that were commenced against the company prior to the date of the striking-off; and

(c) continue to carry on legal proceedings that were instituted on behalf of the company prior to the date of striking-off.

(3) The fact that the name of a company is struck off the Register does not prevent -

(a) the company from incurring liabilities;

(b) any creditor from making a claim against the company and pursuing the claim through to judgment or execution; or

(c) the appointment by the court of an official liquidator for the company under section 102.

Appointment of official liquidator.

102. The court may appoint a person to be the official liquidator in respect of a company the name of which has been struck off the Register.

Dissolution of company struck off.

103.(1) If the name of a company has been struck off the Register under section 99 and remains struck off continuously for a period of 10 years, the company shall be deemed to have been dissolved, but the Registrar may, if he determines that it is in the best interests of the Crown to do so, apply to the court on or before the expiration of the period of 10 years to have the company put into liquidation and a person appointed by the court shall be the official liquidator thereof.

(2) The duties of an official liquidator in respect of a company in liquidation pursuant to subsection (1) are limited to -

(a) identifying and taking possession of all assets of the company;

(b) calling for claims by advertisement in the Gazette and in such other manner as he deems appropriate, requiring all claims to be submitted to him within a period of not less than 90 days immediately following the date of the advertisement; and

(c) applying those assets that he recovers in the following order of priority -

(i) in satisfaction of all outstanding fees, licence fees and penalties due to the Registrar, and

(ii) in satisfaction pari passu of all other claims admitted by the official liquidator.

(3) In order to perform the duties with which he is charged under subsection (2), the official liquidator may exercise such powers as the court may as it considers reasonable confer on him.

(4) The official liquidator may require such proof as he considers necessary to substantiate any claim submitted to him and he may admit, reject or settle claims on the basis of the evidence submitted to him.

(5) When the official liquidator has completed his duties, he shall submit a written report of his conduct of the liquidation proceedings to the Registrar and, upon receipt of the report by the Registrar, all assets of the company, wherever situate, that are not disposed of, vest in the Crown and the company is dissolved.

(6) The official liquidator is entitled to such remuneration out of the assets of the company for his services as the court approves, but if the company is unable to discharge all of its claims, debts, liabilities and obligations, payment of the official liquidator's remuneration shall be a charge on the Consolidated Fund.

(7) No liability attaches to an official liquidator -

(a) to account to creditors of the company who have not submitted claims within the time allowed by him; or

(b) for any failure to locate any assets of the company.

PART X - Fees and Penalties

Fees.

104. There shall be paid to the Registrar fees as follows -

(a) $300 upon the registration by the Registrar of a company incorporated under this Act the authorised capital of which does not exceed $50,000 and all the shares of which have a par value;

(b) $1,000 upon the registration by the Registrar of a company incorporated under this Act the authorised capital of which exceeds $50,000;

(c) upon registration by the Registrar of a copy of a resolution of members or a resolution of directors amending the memorandum or articles of a company incorporated under this Act -

(i) $25 if the registration is within 30 days immediately following the passing of the resolution authorising the amendment,

(ii) $50 if the registration is within 60 days immediately following the passing of the resolution authorising the amendment,

(iii) $75 if the registration is within 90 days immediately following the passing of the resolution authorising the amendment, and

(iv) $100 if the registration is later than 90 days following the passing of the resolution authorising the amendment;

(d) $500 upon the registration by the Registrar of articles of merger or consolidation, but $700 in the case of articles of merger or consolidation that also constitute the memorandum of a company the authorised capital of which exceeds $50,000 or that amend the memorandum of a surviving company to increase the authorised capital from $50,000 or less to more than $50,000;

(e) $500 upon the registration by the Registrar of articles of arrangement, but $700 in the case of articles of arrangement that also constitute the memorandum of a company the authorised capital of which exceeds $50,000 or that amend the memorandum of a company to increase the authorised capital from $50,000 or less to more than $50,000;

(f) $250 upon the submission to the Registrar of articles of continuation for a company incorporated under the Companies Act the authorised capital of which does not exceed $50,000, and, in addition, in the case of a company that continues its incorporation under this Act before 30th April in any year, such sum as would have been payable by that company under the Compa-

nies Act if that company had not so continued its incorporation under this Act;

(g) $1,000 upon the submission to the Registrar of articles of continuation for a company incorporated under the Companies Act the authorised capital of which exceeds $50,000, and, in addition, in the case of a company that continues its incorporation under this Act before 30th April in any year, such sum as would have been payable by that company under the Companies Act if that company had not so continued its incorporation under this Act;

(h) $500 upon the submission to the Registrar of articles of continuation for a company not incorporated under the Companies Act the authorised capital of which does not exceed $50,000;

(i) $1,000 upon the submission to the Registrar of articles of continuation for a company not incorporated under the Companies Act the authorised capital of which exceeds $50,000;

(j) $100 upon the registration by the Registrar of articles of dissolution;

(k) $100 upon the registration by the Registrar of a resolution rescinding articles of dissolution;

(l) $25 upon the issue by the Registrar of a duplicate, or certified copy of a certificate of incorporation, merger, consolidation, arrangement, continuation, dissolution, discontinuance or good standing;

(m) $15 upon the issue by the Registrar of a copy or extract, whether or not certified, of a document or a part of a document, other than a certificate of incorporation, merger, consolidation, arrangement, continuation, dissolution or good standing;

(n) $10 for an inspection of the documents kept by the Registrar pursuant to this Act;

(o) upon restoration by the Registrar to the Register of a company incorporated under this Act, the name of which was struck off the Register -

(i) $300 if the restoration is applied for within 6 months immediately following the striking of the name off the Register; or

(ii) $600 if the restoration is applied for more than 6 months immediately following the striking of the name off the Register;

(p) $25 for the reservation of a name as provided for in subsection (7) of section 11;

(q) $10 for an inspection of each entry in the Register.

(r) $500 upon submission to the Registrar of documents referred to in subsection (1) of section 85;

(s) $100 upon resubmission to the Registrar of the documents referred to in subsection (7) of section 85;

(t) $350 upon the registration by the Registrar of a company incorporated under this Act -

(i) if the authorised capital of the company does not exceed $50,000 and some or all of its shares have no par value, or

(ii) the company has no authorised capital and all of its shares have no par value;

(u) $25 upon the registration by the Registrar of a notice of increase or decrease of authorised capital of a company incorporated under this Act, but $700 in the case of a notice of increase of authorised capital from $50,000 or less to more than $50,000;

(v) $50 upon initial registration by the Registrar of a copy of a share register, a register of directors or a register of mortgages;

(w) $50 upon registration by the Registrar of a copy of a share register, a register of directors or a register of mortgages and charges showing changes from the copy of the particular register a copy of which was last registered by the Registrar;

(x) $50 upon registration by the Registrar of a notice that a company has elected to cease to register a copy of a share register, a register of directors or a register of mortgages and charges showing changes from the copy of the particular register a copy of which was last registered with the Registrar;

(y) $100 upon the registration by the Registrar of an affidavit attesting to a company incorporated under this Act continuing its incorporation under the laws of another jurisdiction; and

(z) $50 upon registration by the Registrar of any document referred to in section 111B.

Licence fees.

105.(1) A company that is incorporated in the first 6 months of a year shall on or before 31st May in the following year and in each succeeding year pay to the Registrar a licence fee as follows -

(a) $300 if on the licence fee payment date its authorized capital does not exceed $50,000 and all its shares have par value;

(b) $1,000 if on the licence fee payment date its authorized capital exceeds $50,000; and

(c) $350 if on the licence fee payment date -

(i) its authorized capital does not exceed $50,000 and some or all of its shares have no par value, or

(ii) it has no authorized capital and all its shares have no par value.

(2) A company that is incorporated in the second 6 months of a year shall on or before 30th November in the following year and in each succeeding year pay to the Registrar a licence fee as follows -

(a) $300 if on the licence fee payment date its authorized capital does not exceed $50,000 and all its shares have par value;

(b) $1,000 if on the licence fee payment date its authorized capital exceeds $50,000; and

(c) $350 if on the licence fee payment date -

(i) its authorized capital does not exceed $50,000 and some or all of its shares have no par value; or

(ii) it has no authorized capital and all its shares have no par value.

(3) If a company fails to pay the amount due as the licence fee under subsection (1) or (2), as the case may be, by the time specified therein, then the licence fee increases by 10 per cent of that amount.

(4) If a company fails to pay the amount due as an increased licence fee under subsection (3) at or before the expiration of a period of 2 months from the time specified in subsection (1) or (2), as the case may be, then the licence fee increases by 50 per cent of that amount.

(5) This section does not apply to a company in the process of being wound up and dissolved.

Penalties to be paid to the Registrar.

106. Any penalty incurred under this Act shall to be paid to the Registrar.

Recovery of penalties, etc.

107. Any fee, licence fee or penalty payable under this Act that remains unpaid for 30 days immediately following the date on which demand for payment is made by the Registrar is recoverable at the instance of the Attorney General before a Magistrate in civil proceedings as a debt due to the Crown notwithstanding the amount sought to be recovered.

Company struck off liable for fees, etc.

108. A company incorporated under this Act continues to be liable for all fees, licence fees and penalties payable under this Act notwithstanding that the name of the company has been struck off the Register and all those fees, licence fees and penalties have priority to all other claims against the assets of the company.

Fees, etc. to be paid into Consolidated Fund.

109. All fees, licence fees and penalties paid under this Act shall be paid by the Registrar into the Consolidated Fund.

Fees payable to Registrar.

110.(1) The Registrar may refuse to take any action required of him under this Act for which a fee is prescribed until all fees have been paid.

(2) The Registrar may refuse to continue under this Act a company incorporated under the Companies Act until all fees prescribed as payable by the company under the Companies Act have been paid.

PART XI - Income Taxes, Stamp Duties and Registration of Documents

Exemptions from tax etc.

111.(1) Notwithstanding any provision of the Income Tax Act -

(a) a company incorporated under this Act;

(b) all dividends, interest, rents, royalties, compensations and other amounts paid by the company to persons who are not persons resident in the British Virgin Islands; and

(c) capital gains realised with respect to any shares, debt obligations or other securities of a company incorporated under this Act by persons who are not persons resident in the British Virgin Islands, are exempt from all provisions of the Income Tax Act.

(2) No estate, inheritance, succession or gift tax, rate, duty, levy or other charge is payable by persons who are not persons resident in the British Virgin Islands with respect to any shares, debt obligations or other securities of a company incorporated under this Act.

(3) Notwithstanding any provision of the Stamp Act -

(a) all instruments relating to transfers of property to or by a company incorporated under this Act;

(b) all instruments relating to transactions in respect of the shares, debt obligations or other securities of a company incorporated under this Act; and

(c) all instruments relating to other transactions relating to the business of a company incorporated under this Act, are exempt from the payment of stamp duty.

(4) Notwithstanding any provisions of the Registration and Records Act, all deeds and other instruments relating to -

(a) transfers of property to or by a company incorporated under this Act;

(b) transactions in respect of the shares, debt obligations or other securities of a company incorporated under this Act;

(c) other transactions relating to the business of a company incorporated under this Act, are exempt from the provisions of that Act.

Optional registration of registers.

111A.(1) A company incorporated under this Act may elect to submit for registration by the Registrar any of the following registers -

(a) its share register;

(b) its register of directors; or

(c) its register of mortgages and charges.

(2) A company that has elected to submit for registration a copy of a register shall, until it otherwise notifies the Registrar pursuant to subsection (3), submit for registration any changes in a register by substituting for registration a copy of the register containing the changes.

(3) A company that submits for registration a copy of a register with the Registrar may elect to cease registration of changes in the register by so informing the Registrar in writing.

(4) If a company elects to submit for registration any register pursuant to subsection (1), then, until such time as the company informs the Registrar pursuant to subsection (3) that it elects to cease to register changes in any register, the company is bound by the contents of each copy register submitted to the Registrar.

Optional registration of mortgages and charges.

111B. A company incorporated under this Act may submit to the Registrar for registration -

(a) any document or copy of a document creating a mortgage, charge or other encumbrance over some or all its assets;

(b) any document or copy of a document amending any document referred to in paragraph (a); and

(c) any document releasing or discharging a mortgage, charge or other encumbrance over any or all its assets, and the Registrar must retain and register the document or, as the case may be, the copy thereof.

PART XII - Miscellaneous

Regulations.

112.(1) The Governor in Council may make regulations with respect to the duties to be performed by the Registrar under this Act and in so doing may prescribe the place where the office for the registration of international business companies is located.

(2) Without limiting or affecting subsection (1), the Governor in Council may make regulations with respect to the conduct, duties and responsibilities of registered agents.

Form of certificate.

113. Any certificate or other document required to be issued by the Registrar under this Act shall be in such form as the Governor in Council may approve.

Certificate of good standing.

114.(1) The Registrar shall, upon request by any person, issue a certificate of good standing under his hand and seal certifying that a company incorporated under this Act is of good standing if the Registrar is satisfied that -

(a) the name of the company is on the Register; and

(b) the company has paid all fees, licence fees and penalties due and payable.

(2) The certificate of good standing issued under subsection (1) must contain a statement as to whether -

(a) the company has submitted to the Registrar articles of merger or consolidation that have not yet become effective;

(b) the company has submitted to the Registrar articles of arrangement that have not yet become effective;

(c) the company is in the process of being wound up and dissolved; or

(d) any proceedings to strike the name of the company off the Register have been instituted.

Inspection of documents.

115.(1) Except as provided in subsection (2) of section 85, a person may -

(a) inspect the documents kept by the Registrar pursuant to this Act; and

(b) require a certificate of incorporation, merger, consolidation, arrangement,

continuation, dissolution or good standing of a company incorporated under this Act, or a copy or an extract of any document or any part of a document of which he has custody, to be certified by the Registrar; and a certificate of incorporation, merger, consolidation, arrangement, continuation, dissolution or good standing or a certified copy or extract is prima facie evidence of the matters contained therein.

(2) A document or a copy or an extract of any document or any part of a document certified by the Registrar under subsection (1) is admissible in evidence in any proceedings as if it were the original document.

Jurisdiction.

116. For purposes of determining matters relating to title and jurisdiction but not for purposes of taxation, the situs of the ownership of shares, debt obligations or other securities of a company incorporated under this Act is in the British Virgin Islands.

Declaration by court.

117.(1) A company incorporated under this Act may, without the necessity of joining any other party, apply to the court, by summons supported by an affidavit, for a declaration on any question of interpretation of this Act or of the memorandum or articles of the company.

(2) A person acting on a declaration by the court as a result of an application under subsection (1) shall be deemed, in so far as regards the discharge of any fiduciary or professional duty, to have properly discharged his duties in the subject matter of the application.

Judge in Chambers.

118. A Judge of the High Court may exercise in Chambers any jurisdiction that is vested in the court by this Act and in exercise of that jurisdiction, the Judge may award costs as may be just.

Commencement

119. This Act, except for section 98, comes into operation on such day as the Governor appoints by proclamation in the Gazette.

BRITISH VIRGIN ISLANDS

THE PARTNERSHIP ACT, 1996

ARRANGEMENT OF SECTIONS

Part I - Short Title and Interpretation

Part II - Nature of Partnership

Part III - Relation of Partners to Persons Dealing With Them

Part IV- Relations of Partners to One Another

Part V - Dissolution of Partnership and its Consequences

Part VI - Limited Partnerships

Part VII -Miscellaneous

The Partnership Act, 1996

An Act to declare and amend the law of partnership and to declare the law relating to limited partnerships.

ENACTED by the Legislature of the Virgin Islands as follows:

PART I - Short Title and Interpretation

Short title and commencement

1. This Act may be cited as the Partnership Act, 1996 and shall come into force on the date which the Governor may appoint by proclamation published in the *Gazette.*

Interpretation

2. In this Act, unless the contrary intention appears,

"articles means the articles of partnership of a limited partnership formed under this Act;

"business" includes every trade, occupation or profession;

"court" means the High Court or a Judge thereof;

"firm" means the group of persons who have entered into partnership with one another;

"firm-name" means the name under which the business of a firm is carried on;

"general partner", in relation to a limited partnership, means a partner who is not a limited partner as defined herein;

"general partnership" means any partnership that is not a limited partnership;

"international limited partnership" means the limited partnership referred to in section 49 of this Act;

"limited partnership" means a partnership formed under Part VI of this Act referred to in section 47 of this Act;

"limited partner", in relation to a limited partnership, means a partner who does not take part in the control of the partnership business and whose liability is limited subject to the provisions of this Act;

"local limited partnership" means the limited partnership referred to in section 48 of this Act;

"memorandum" means the memorandum of partnership of a limited partnership formed under this Act;

"Minister" means the Minister responsible for finance;

"partner" in relation to a limited partnership includes a limited partner and a general partner;

"person" includes a natural person, a partnership general or limited, domestic or foreign, a company, trust, estate, association, custodian, nominee or any other individual or entity in its own or any representative capacity;

"register" means the register referred to in section 54 of this Act;

"Registrar" means the Registrar of Limited Partnerships referred to in section 52 of this Act;

"substituted limited partner" means a person who, after becoming an assignee of part or all of the interest of a limited partner, is admitted to the limited partnership pursuant to the provisions of its articles or, if the articles are silent on the issue, is admitted with the unanimous consent of the partners.

PART II - Nature Of Partnership

Definition of partnership

3.(1) Partnership is the relation which subsists between persons carrying on a business in common with a view of profit.

(2) The relation between members of any company or association which is -

(a) registered as a company under the Companies Act or incorporated as a company under the International Business Companies Act; or

(b) formed or incorporated by or in pursuance of any other Act, letters patent or Royal Charter,

is not a partnership within the meaning of this Act.

Rules for determining existence of partnership

4. In determining whether a partnership does or does not exist, regard shall be had to the following rules:

(a) all circumstances surrounding the contract are to be considered and the true intent of the parties is to be ascertained from their agreement, words and conduct;

(b) joint tenancy, tenancy in common, joint property, common property or part ownership does not of itself create a partnership as to anything so held or owned, whether the tenants or owners do or do not share any profits made by the use thereof;

(c) the sharing of gross returns does not of itself create a partnership, whether the persons sharing such returns have or have not a joint or common right or interest in any property from which or from the use of which the returns are derived; and

(d) the receipt by a person of a share of the profits of a business is *prima facie* evidence that he is a partner in the business, but receipt of such a share, or of a payment contingent on or varying with the profits of a business, goes not of itself make him a partner in the business; and in particular

(i) the receipt by a person of a debt or other liquidated amount by instalments or otherwise out of the accruing profits of a business does not of itself make him a partner in the business or liable as such;

(ii) a contract for the remuneration of a servant or agent of a person engaged in a business by a share of the profits of the business does not of itself make the servant or agent a partner in the business or liable as such;

(iii) a person being the widow or child of a deceased partner, and receiving by way of annuity a portion of the profits made in the business in which the deceased person was a partner, is not by reason only of such receipt a partner in the business or liable as such;

(iv) the advance of money by way of loan to a person engaged or about to engage in any business on a contract in writing with that person, signed by or on behalf of all the parties thereto, that the lender shall receive a rate of interest varying with the profits arising from carrying on the business, does not of itself make the lender a partner with the person or persons carrying on the business or liable as such; and

(v) a person receiving by way of annuity or otherwise a portion of the profits of a business in consideration of the sale by him of the goodwill of the business is not by reason only of such receipt a partner in the business or liable as such.

Postponement of rights of person lending or selling in consideration of share of profits in case of insolvency

5.(1) Where a person to whom money has been advanced by way of loan upon a contract as is mentioned in section 4(d)(iv) is adjudged bankrupt, enters into an arrangement to pay his creditors less than one hundred cents in the dollar or dies insolvent, the lender shall not be entitled to recover anything in respect of the loan until the claims of the borrower's other creditors for valuable consideration in money or money's worth have been satisfied.

(2) Where a person who, in consideration of a share of the profits of a business, has bought of its goodwill, is adjudged bankrupt, enters into an arrangement to pay his creditors less than one hundred cents in the dollar or dies insolvent, the seller of the goodwill shall not be entitled to recover anything in respect of the share of profits contracted for until the claims of the buyer's other creditors for valuable consideration in money or money's worth are satisfied.

(3) Nothing in this section shall operate so as to prevent a secured creditor from retaining or realising his security.

Nature of partner's interest in partnership

6. A partner's interest in a partnership within the meaning of this Act is personal property situate in the Territory.

PART III - Relations of Partners to Persons Dealing With Them

Power of partner to bind the firm

7.(1) Every partner is an agent of the firm and his other partners for the purpose of the business of the partnership.

(2) The acts of every partner who does any act for carrying on in the usual way business of the kind carried on by the firm of which he is a partner bind the firm and his partners, unless the partner so acting

(a) has in fact no authority to act for the firm in the particular matter; and

(b) the person with whom he is dealing either knows that he has no authority or does not know or believe him to be a partner.

Partners bound by acts on behalf of firm

8. An act or instrument relating to the business of the firm done or executed in the firm-name, or in any other manner showing an intention to bind the firm, by any person thereby authorised, whether a partner or not, is binding on the firm and all the partners except that this section shall not affect any general rule of law relating to the execution of deeds or negotiable instruments.

Partner using credit of firm for private purposes

9. Where one partner pledges the credit of the firm for a purpose apparently not connected with the firm's ordinary course of business, the firm is not bound, unless he is in fact specially authorised by the other partners, but this section does not affect any personal liability incurred by an individual partner.

Effect of notice that firm will not be bound by acts of partner

10. If it has been agreed between the partners that any restriction shall be placed on the power of any one or more of them to bind the firm, no act done in contravention of the agreement is binding on the firm with respect to persons having notice of the agreement.

Liability of partners for debts and obligations

11. Every partner in a firm is liable jointly with the other partners for all debts and obligations of the firm incurred while he is a partner, and after his death his estate is also severally liable in the due course of administration for such debts and obligations, so far as they remain unsatisfied, but subject to the prior payment of his separate debts.

Liability of the firm for wrongs

12. Where, by any wrongful act or omission of any partner acting in the ordinary course of the business of the firm, or with the authority of his co-partners, loss or injury is caused to any person not being a partner in the firm, or any penalty is incurred, the firm is liable therefor to the same extent as the partner so acting or omitting to act.

Misapplication of money or property received for or in custody of the firm

13. In the following cases, namely -

(a) where one partner acting within the scope of his apparent authority receives the money or property of a third person and misapplies it; and

(b) where a firm in the course of its business receives the money or property of a third person, and the money or property so received is misapplied by one or more of the partners while it is in the custody of the firm, the firm is liable to make good the loss.

Liability of partners for wrongs

14. Every partner is liable jointly and severally with his co-partners for everything for which the firm while he is a partner therein becomes liable under either section 12 or section 13.

Improper employment of trust property for partnership

15. If a partner, being a trustee of a trust which is not part of the business of the firm of which he is a partner, improperly employs the trust property in the business or on the account of the partnership, no other partner is liable for the trust property to the persons beneficially interested therein except that

(a) this section shall not affect any liability incurred by any partner by reason of his having notice of a breach of trust; and

(b) nothing in this section shall prevent trust money from being traced and recovered from the firm if still in its possession or under its control.

Persons liable by "holding out"

16.(1) Everyone who by words spoken or written or by conduct represents himself, or who knowingly suffers himself to be represented, as a partner in a particular firm is liable as a partner to any one who has on the faith of any such representation, given credit to the firm, whether the representation has or has not been made or communicated to the person so giving credit by or with the knowledge of the apparent partner making the representation or suffering it to be made.

(2) Notwithstanding subsection (1) where after a partner's death the partnership business is continued in the same firm-name, the continued use of that name or of the deceased partner's name as part thereof shall not of itself make his executors or administrators of his estate liable for any partnership debts contracted after his death.

Admissions and representations of partners

17. An admission or representation made by any partner concerning the firm's affairs, and in the ordinary course of its business, is evidence against the firm.

Notice to acting partner to be notice to the firm

18. Notice to any partner who habitually acts in the partnership business of any matter relating to partnership affairs operates as notice to the firm, except in the case of a fraud on the firm committed by or with the consent of that partner.

Liabilities of incoming and outgoing partners

19.(1) A person who is admitted as a partner into an existing firm does not thereby become liable to the creditors of the firm for anything done before he became a partner.

(2) A partner who retires from a firm does not thereby cease to be liable for partnership debts or obligations incurred before his retirement.

(3) A retiring partner may be discharged from any existing liabilities by an agreement to that effect between himself and the members of the firm as newly constituted and the creditors, and this agreement may be either expressed or inferred as a fact from the course of dealing between the creditors and the firm as newly constituted.

Revocation of continuing guarantee by change in firm

20. A continuing guarantee given either to a firm or to a third person in respect of the transactions of a firm is, in the absence of agreement to the contrary, revoked as to future transactions by any change in the constitution of the firm to which, or of the firm in respect of the transactions of which, the guarantee was given.

PART IV - Relations of Partners to One Another

Variation by consent of terms of partnership

21. The mutual rights and duties of partners, whether ascertained by agreement or defined by this Act, may be varied by the consent of all the partners, and such consent may be either express or inferred from a course of dealing.

Partnership property

22.(1) Subject to subsections (2) and (3) all property and rights and interests in property originally brought into the partnership stock or acquired, whether by purchase or otherwise, on account of the firm, or for the purposes and in the course of the partnership business, are called in this Act "partnership property" and shall be held and applied by the partners exclusively for the purposes of the partnership and in accordance with the partnership agreement.

(2) The legal estate or interest in any land which belongs to the partnership shall devolve according to the general rules of law thereto applicable, but in trust, so far as necessary, for the persons beneficially interested in the land under this section.

(3) Where co-owners of an estate or interest in any land, not being itself partnership property, are partners as to profits made by the use of that land or estate, and purchase other land or estate out of the profits to be used in like manner, the land or estate so purchased belongs to them, in the absence of an agreement to the contrary, not as partners but as co-owners for the same respective estates and interests as are held by them in the land first mentioned at the date of the purchase.

Property bought with partnership money

23. Unless the contrary intention appears, property bought with money belonging to the firm is deemed to have been bought on account of the firm.

Partnership property treated as personal or movable estate

24. Where land or any estate or interest therein has become partnership property, it shall, unless the contrary intention appears, be treated as between the partners (including the representatives of a deceased partner) , and also as between the heirs of a deceased partner and his executors or administrators, as personal or movable and not real estate.

Procedure against partnership property for a partner's separate judgment debt.

25.(1) A writ of execution shall not issue against any partnership property except on a judgment against the firm.

(2) A court may, on the application by summons of any judgment creditor of a partner, make an order charging that partner's interest in the partnership property and profits with payment of the amount of the judgment debt and interest thereon, and may by the same or a subsequent order -

(a) appoint a receiver of that partner's share of profits (whether already declared or accruing) and of any other money which may be coming to him in respect of the partnership; and

(b) direct all accounts and inquiries, and give all other orders and directions which might have been directed or given if the charge had been made in favour of the judgment creditor by the partner, or which the circumstances of the case may require.

(3) The other partner or partners shall be at liberty at any time to redeem the interest charged, or in the case of sale being directed, to purchase the same.

Rules as to interests and duties of partners subject to special agreement.

26. The interests of partners in the partnership property and their rights and duties in relation to the partnership shall be determined, subject to any agreement express or implied between the partners, by the following rules:

(a) all the partners are entitled to share equally in the capital and profits of the business and shall contribute equally towards the losses whether of capital or otherwise sustained by the firm;

(b) the firm shall indemnify every partner in respect of payments made and personal liabilities incurred by him;

(i) in the ordinary and proper conduct of the business of the firm, or

(ii) in or about anything necessarily done for the preservation of the business or property of the firm;

(c) a partner making, for the purpose of the partnership, any actual payment or advance beyond the amount of capital which he has agreed to subscribe is entitled to interest at the rate of 10 per centum per annum from the date of the payment or advance:

(d) a partner is not entitled, before the ascertainment of profits, to interest on the capital subscribed by him;

(e) every partner may take part in the management of the partnership business;

(f) no partner shall be entitled to remuneration for acting in the partnership business;

(g) no person may be introduced as a partner without the consent of all existing partners;

(h) any difference arising as to ordinary matters connected with the partnership business may be decided by a majority of the partners, but no change may be made in the nature of the partnership business without the consent of all existing partners; and

(i) the partnership books are to be kept at the place of business of the partnership, or the principal place of business, if there is more than one; and every partner may, when he thinks fit, have access to and inspect and copy any of them.

Expulsion of partner

27. No majority of the partners can expel any partner unless a power to do so has been conferred by express agreement between the partners.

Retirement from partnership at will

28.(1) Where no fixed term has been agreed upon for the duration of a partnership, any partner may determine the partnership at any time on giving notice of his intention so to do to all the other partners.

(2) Where the partnership has originally been constituted by deed or other instrument in writing, a notice in writing, signed by the partner giving it, shall be sufficient for this purpose.

Continuance on old terms presumed.

29.(1) Where a partnership entered into for a fixed term is continued after the term has expired, and without any express new agreement, the rights and duties of the partners remain the same as they were at the expiration of the term, so far as is consistent with the incidents of a partnership at will.

(2) A continuance of the business by the partners or such of them as habitually acted therein during the term, without any settlement or liquidation of the partnership affairs, is presumed to be a continuance of the partnership.

Duty of partners to render accounts, etc.

30. Partners are bound to render true accounts and full information of all things affecting the partnership to any partner, his agents or representatives.

Accountability of partners for private profits

31.(1) Every partner shall account to the firm for any benefit derived by him without the consent of the other partners

(a) from any transaction concerning the partnership; or

(*b*) from any use by him of the partnership property, name or business connection.

(2) This section applies also to transactions undertaken after a partnership has been dissolved by the death of a partner and before the affairs thereof have been completely wound up, either by any surviving partner or by the administrators of the deceased partner.

Duty of partner not to compete with firm

32. If a partner, without the consent of the other partners, carries on any business of the same nature as and competing with that of the firm, he must account for and pay over to the firm all profits made by him in that business.

Rights of assignee of share in partnership

33.(1) An assignment by any partner of his share in the partnership, either absolute or by way of mortgage or redeemable charge, does not, as against the other partners, entitle the assignee, during the continuance of the partnership to

(*a*) interfere in the management or administration of the partnership business or affairs,

(*b*) require any accounts of the partnership transactions; or

(*c*) inspect the partnership books,

but entitles the assignee only to receive the share of profits to which the assigning partner would otherwise be entitled, and the assignee must accept the account of profits agreed to by the partners.

(2) In case of a dissolution of the partnership, whether as respects all the partners or as respects the assigning partner, the assignee is entitled to receive the share of the partnership assets to which the assigning partner is entitled as between himself and the other partners, and, for the purpose of ascertaining that share, to an account as from the date of the dissolution.

PART V- Dissolution of Partnership and its Consequences

Dissolution by expiration or notice

34. Subject to any agreement between the partners, a partnership is dissolved

(a) if entered into for a fixed term, by the expiration of that term;

(b) if entered into for a single adventure or undertaking, by the termination of that adventure or undertaking; or

(c) if entered into for an undefined time, by any partner giving notice to the other or others of his intention to dissolve the partnership, in which case the partnership is dissolved as from the date mentioned in the notice as the date of dissolution, or, if no date is so mentioned, as from the date of the communication of the notice.

Dissolution by bankruptcy, death or charge

35.(1) Notwithstanding the provisions of section 21, every partnership is dissolved as regards all the partners by the death or bankruptcy of any partner unless all of the remaining partners vote within 90 days after the event giving rise to the dissolution to continue the partnership.

(2) A partnership may, at the option of the other partners, be dissolved if any partner suffers his share of the partnership property to be charged under this Act for his separate debt.

Dissolution by illegality

36. A partnership is in every case dissolved by the happening of any event which makes it unlawful for the business of the firm to be carried on or for the members of the firm to carry it on in partnership.

Dissolution by the court

37.(1) On application by a partner the court may decree a dissolution of the partnership in any of the following cases -

(a) when a partner is shown to the satisfaction of the court to be permanently of unsound mind in an application made on behalf of that partner by his committee or next friend or person having title to intervene or any other partner;

(b) when a partner, other than the partner suing, becomes in any way permanently incapable of performing his part of the partnership contract;

(c) when a partner, other than the partner suing, has been guilty of such conduct as, in the opinion of the court, regard being had to the nature of the business, is calculated prejudicially to affect the carrying on of the business;

(*d*) when a partner, other than the partner suing, wilfully or persistently commits a breach of the partnership agreement, or otherwise so conducts himself in matters relating to the partnership business that it is not reasonably practicable for the other partner or partners to carry on the business in partnership with him;

(*e*) when the business of the partnership can only be carried on at a loss;

(*f*) whenever in any case circumstances have arisen which, in the opinion of the court, render it just and equitable that the partnership be dissolved.

Rights of persons dealing with firm against apparent partners of firm

38.(1) Where a person deals with a firm after a change in its constitution he is entitled to treat all apparent partners of the old firm as still being partners of the firm until he has notice of the change.

(2) An advertisement in the *Gazette* shall be sufficient notice as to persons who had dealings with the firm before the date of the dissolution or change so advertised.

(3) The estate of a partner who dies, or who becomes bankrupt, or of a partner who, not having been known to the person dealing with the firm to be a partner, retires from the firm, is not liable for partnership debts contracted after the date of such death, bankruptcy or retirement.

Right of partners to notify dissolution.

39. On the dissolution of a partnership or retirement of a partner any partner may publicly notify the same, and may require the other partner or partners to concur for that purpose in all necessary or proper acts, if any, which cannot be done without his or their concurrence.

Continuing authority of partners for purposes of winding up

40.(1) Subject to subsection (2), after the dissolution of a partnership the authority of each partner to bind the firm, and the other rights and obligations of the partners, continue notwithstanding the dissolution so far as may be necessary to wind up the affairs of the partnership and to complete transactions begun but unfinished at the time of the dissolution, but not otherwise.

(2) The firm is in no case bound by the acts of a partner who has become bankrupt, but this exception does not affect the liability of any person who has after the bankruptcy represented himself or knowingly suffered himself to be represented as a partner of the bankrupt.

Rights of partners as to application of partnership property

41.(1) Subject to subsection (2), on the dissolution of a partnership every partner is entitled, as against the other partners in the firm and all persons claiming through them in respect of their interests as partners, *(a)* to have the property of the partnership applied in payment of the debts and liabilities of the firm; and

(b) to have the surplus assets after such payment applied in payment of what may be due to the partners respectively after deducting what may be due from them as partner to the firm,

and for that purpose any partner or his executors or administrators may on the termination of the partnership apply to the court to wind up the business and affairs of the firm.

(2) Where the dissolution of a partnership is caused by a wrongful act of a partner in contravention of the partnership agreement such partner shall be entitled only to the value of his interest in the partnership at the dissolution less any damages payable by him to the other partners for his breach of the partnership agreement.

Apportionment of premium where partnership prematurely dissolved

42. Where one partner has paid a premium to another on entering into a partnership for a fixed term, and the partnership is dissolved before the expiration of that term otherwise than by the death of a partner, the court may order the repayment of the premium, or of such part thereof as it thinks just, having regard to the terms of the partnership contract and to the length of time during which the partnership has continued, unless

(a) the dissolution is, in the judgment of the court, wholly or chiefly due to the misconduct of the partner who paid the premium; or

(b) the partnership has been dissolved by an agreement containing no provision for a return of any part of the premium.

Rights where partnership dissolved for fraud or misrepresentation.

43. Where a partnership contract is rescinded on the grounds of the fraud or misrepresentation of one of the parties thereto, the party entitled to rescind is, without prejudice to any other right, entitled

(a) to a lien on, or right of retention of, the surplus of the partnership assets, after satisfying the partnership liabilities, for any sum of money paid by him for the purchase of a share in the partnership and for any capital contributed by him;

(b) to stand in the place of the creditors of the firm for any payments made by him in respect of the partnership liabilities; and

(c) to be indemnified by the person guilty of the fraud or making the representation against all the debts and liabilities of the firm.

Right of outgoing partner in certain cases to share profits made after dissolution

44.(1) Where any partner of a firm has died or otherwise ceased to be a partner, and the surviving or continuing partners carry on the business of the firm with its capital or assets without any final settlement of accounts as between the firm and the outgoing partner or his estate, then, in the absence of any agreement to the contrary, the outgoing partner or his estate is entitled at the option of himself or his executors or administrators to such share of the profits made since the dissolution as the court may find to be attributable to the use of his share of the partnership assets, or to interest at such rate as may be determined by the court.

(2) Notwithstanding the provisions of subsection (1), where by the partnership contract an option is given to surviving or continuing partners to purchase the interest of a deceased or outgoing partner, and that option is duly exercised, the estate of the deceased partner or the outgoing partner or his estate, as the case may be, is not entitled to any further share of profits; but if any partner assuming to act in exercise of the option does not in all material respects comply with the terms thereof, he is liable to account under the foregoing provisions of subsection (1).

Retiring or deceased partner's share to be a debt

45. Subject to any agreement between the partners, the amount due from surviving or continuing partners to an outgoing partner or the executors or administrators of a deceased partner in respect of the outgoing or deceased partner's share is a debt accruing at the date of the dissolution or death.

Rule for distribution of assets on final settlement of accounts

46. In settling accounts between the partners after a dissolution of partnership, the following rules shall, subject to any agreement, be observed -

(a) losses, including losses and deficiencies of capital, shall be paid first out of profits, next out of capital, and lastly if necessary, by the partners individually in the proportion in which they were entitled to share profits; and

(b) the assets of the firm including the sum, if any, contributed by the partners to make up losses or deficiencies of capital, shall be applied in the following manner and order -

(i) in paying the debts and liabilities of the firm to persons who are not partners therein,

(ii) in paying to each partner rateably what is due from the firm to him for advances as distinguished from capital,

(iii) in paying to each partner rateably what is due from the firm to him in respect of capital, and

(iv) the ultimate residue, if any, shall be divided among the partners in the proportion in which profits are divisible.

PART VI - Limited Partnerships

Limited partnerships

47.(1) A limited partnership is a partnership formed by two or more persons under this Part which has one or more general partners and one or more limited partners, and a limited partnership may be either a local limited partnership or an international limited partnership.

(2) A body corporate, with or without limited liability, or a partnership may be a general partner or a limited partner of a limited partnership.

(3) Subject to sections 47 to 108, sections 1 to 46 shall apply to a limited partnership.

Local limited partnership

48. A local limited partnership may be established under this Act for any object or purpose not prohibited under this Act or any law for the time being in force in the Territory and subject to

(a) the conditions, limitations, restrictions and liabilities in its memorandum and articles; and

(b) subsection (1) of section 50.

International limited partnership

49. An international limited partnership may be established under this Act for any object or purpose not prohibited under this Act or under any law for the time being in force in the Territory and subject to

(a) the conditions, limitations, restrictions and liabilities in its memorandum and articles; and

(b) subsections (1) and (2) of section 50.

Restrictions on limited partnership

50.(1) A limited partnership shall not carry on

(a) banking business;

(b) trust business;

(c) the business of insurance, reinsurance, insurance agent, insurance adjuster or insurance broker or any other kind of insurance business; or

(d) the business of company management unless it is licensed or is exempt from being licensed under the Company Management Act.

(2) An international limited partnership shall not

(a) carry on business with persons resident in the Territory;

(b) own an interest in real property situate in the Territory other than a lease referred to in paragraph (e) of subsection (3).

(3) For the purposes of paragraph (a) of subsection (2), an international limited partnership shall not be treated as carrying on business with persons resident in the Territory by reason only that

(a) it transacts banking business in the Territory with or through a bank licensed under the Banks and Trust Companies Act;

(b) it makes or maintains professional contact with solicitors, barristers, accountants, bookkeepers, trust companies, administration companies, investment advisers or other similar persons carrying on business within the Territory;

(c) it prepares or maintains books and records within the Territory;

(d) it holds, within the Territory, meetings of its partners;

(e) it holds a lease of property for use as an office from which to communicate with partners or where books and records of the partnership are prepared or maintained;

(f) it holds shares, debt obligations or other securities in a company incorporated under the International Business Companies Act; or

(g) any person resident in the Territory or any company registered under the Companies Act or incorporated under the International Business Companies Act is one of its partners.

(4) Notwithstanding anything to the contrary in this Act and in the Company Management Act, an international limited partnership

(a) may serve as a general partner of another international limited partnership;

(b) may hold, within the Territory, meetings of its partners, managers or advisers; and

(c) shall not be required to hold a licence under the provisions of the Company Management Act for the purposes mentioned in paragraphs (a) and (b).

Effect of failure to satisfy the requirements of section 50

51.(1) Where an international limited partnership is formed under this Act without having satisfied the requirements prescribed for an international limited partnership by section 49, or if having satisfied the requirements it subsequently ceases to satisfy the requirements for a continuous period of thirty days, the international limited partnership shall, upon the expiration of the period notify the Registrar of that fact.

(2) A general partner of an international limited partnership that contravenes subsection (1) commits an offence and shall be liable on summary conviction to a fine of $100 for each day or part thereof during which the contravention continues.

Registrar

52. The Registrar of Companies appointed under the Companies Act and any other officer so appointed who acts under the delegated authority of the Registrar pursuant to section 207(6) of the Companies Act shall be the Registrar of Limited Partnerships.

Procedure for forming a limited partnership

53.(1) Two or more persons desiring to form a limited partnership shall execute articles and shall submit them to the registered agent named in the articles and shall cause a memorandum to be submitted to the Registrar.

(2) The memorandum shall include

(a) the firm-name;

(b) the objects and purposes for which the partnership is established;

(c) the address of the registered office of the partnership in the Territory;

(d) the name and address of registered agent of the partnership in the Territory;

(e) the full name of each of the general partners and their respective addresses;

(f) the term, if any, for which the partnership is to exist;

(g) a statement that the partnership is limited;

(h) a statement that every partner not named as a general partner in the memorandum is a limited partner;

(i) in the case of an international limited partnership, a statement that the limited partnership may not carry on the activities set forth in subsections (1) and (2)

of section 50 which statement shall set forth verbatim the activities described in that subsection; and

(j) such other information, if any, as the registered agent shall be instructed to include in the memorandum by the provisions of the articles.

(3) The memorandum shall be subscribed by the registered agent named in the memorandum in the presence of another person who shall sign his name as a witness.

Establishment of register

54.(1) The Registrar shall establish and maintain in such form as he shall determine, a register of limited partnerships in which shall be registered each memorandum submitted pursuant to sections 53 and 57 and all certificates and advertisements required by this Act.

(2) The register shall be open, during office hours, to the inspection of all persons desiring to view the register.

(3) A certificate of the Registrar certifying that anything required by this Act to be registered by him has been so registered shall be received in all courts and in all proceedings whatsoever as evidence of the matter to which the certificate relates.

Certificate of limited partnership

55.(1) Upon payment of the prescribed fee, the Registrar shall register each memorandum of partnership submitted pursuant to section 53 and shall issue a certificate of limited partnership under his hand and seal certifying that the partnership is formed in the Territory as a local limited partnership or an international limited partnership, as the case may be.

(2) Upon the issue by the Registrar of a certificate of limited partnership, the partnership is, from the date shown on the certificate of limited partnership, a limited partnership under the name contained in the memorandum.

(3) A certificate of limited partnership of a limited partnership formed under this Act issued by the Registrar is *prima facie* evidence of compliance with all requirements of this Act with respect to the formation of a limited partnership.

Effect of failure to register

56. A limited partnership shall be registered as such in accordance with section 53 and in default thereof it shall be deemed to be a general partnership and every partner thereof shall be deemed to be a general partner.

Amendment of the memorandum and articles of partnership

57.(1) The memorandum and articles may be amended in such manner as may be set forth in the articles.

(2) Where a change is made or a change occurs in or with respect to any of the details set forth in the memorandum registered with the Registrar the limited partnership shall cause a supplementary memorandum to be submitted to the Registrar.

(3) The supplementary memorandum referred to in subsection (2) shall be subscribed by the registered agent named therein in the presence of another person who shall sign his name as a witness.

(4) The Registrar shall upon payment of the prescribed fee register in the register each supplementary memorandum submitted pursuant to this section and shall issue a certificate of amendment which shall set forth particulars of the amendment.

Contribution

58. The contribution of a limited partner may be cash, property or services.

Name

59.(1) The name of each limited partnership formed under this Act shall have at its end the words "Limited Partnership" or the abbreviation "L.P."

(2) The name of a limited partner shall not appear in the name of a limited partnership, unless

(a) it is also the name of a general partner; or

(b) prior to the time when the limited partner became a limited partner the business had been carried on under a name in which the name of the limited partner appeared.

(3) A limited partner whose name appears in the name of a limited partnership contrary to the provisions of subsection (2) is liable as a general partner to partnership creditors who extend credit to the partnership without actual knowledge that he is not a general partner.

(4) No limited partnership shall be formed under this Act under a name that

(a) is identical with that under which a limited partnership in existence under this Act is formed or a company is incorporated under the International Business Companies Act or registered under the Companies Act, the Limited Life Companies Act or the Business Names Registration Act or so nearly resembles the name as to be calculated to deceive, except where the partnership or company in existence gives its consent; or

(b) contains the words "Assurance", "Bank", "Chartered", "Cooperative", "Imperial", "Insurance", "Municipal", "Royal", "Trust", "Trustee" or a word or abbreviation conveying a similar meaning, or any other word or abbreviation that, in the opinion of the Registrar, suggests or is calculated to suggest

(i) the patronage of Her Majesty or that of a member of the Royal Family;

(ii) a connection with Her Majesty' s Government or a department thereof; or

(iii) a connection with a municipality or other local authority or with a society or body incorporated by Royal Charter, except with the approval of the Registrar in writing.

(5) A limited partnership may amend its memorandum to change its name.

(6) If a limited partnership formed under a name that

(a) is identical with a name under which a limited partnership in existence under this Act is formed or under which a company in existence was incorporated under the International Business Companies Act or registered under the Companies Act, or

(b) so nearly resembles the name as to be calculated to deceive,

the Registrar may, without the consent of the limited partnership in existence, give notice to the last registered limited partnership to change its name and if it fails to do so within 60 days from the date of the notice, the Registrar shall amend the memorandum to change its name to such name as the Registrar deems appropriate, and the Registrar shall publish notice of the change in the *Gazette*.

(7) Subject to subsections (4) and (6) where a limited partnership changes its name, the Registrar shall enter the new name on the register and, upon payment of the prescribed Fee, shall issue a certificate of amendment which shall set forth particulars of the amendment.

(8) A change of name does not affect any right or obligation of a limited partnership, or render defective any legal proceedings by or against a limited partnership, and all legal proceedings that have been commenced against a limited partnership in its former name may be continued against it in i

Reservation of name

60.(1) Subject to subsection (4) of section 59 the Registrar may upon the application of any person and upon payment of the prescribed fee, reserve for a period of ninety days a name for future adoption by a limited partnership under this Act.

(2) Once having reserved a name under subsection (1), the same applicant may, upon payment of the prescribed fee, again reserve the same name for successive ninety day periods.

(3) The right to the exclusive use of a reserved name may be transferred to any other person by paying the prescribed fee and by filing with the Registrar a notice of the transfer executed by the applicant for whom the name was reserved specifying the name to be transferred and the name and address of the transferee.

Liability for false statements in Memorandum.

61. If a memorandum contains a false statement, one who suffers loss by reliance on such statement may hold liable the general partners and the registered agent who made the statement and who knew or should have known the statement to be false

(a) at the time the registered agent signed the memorandum; or

(b) after the memorandum was signed, but within a sufficient time before the statement was relied upon to allow the filing of a supplementary memorandum with the necessary changes.

Liability of limited partner to third parties

62.(1) A limited partner is not liable for the obligations of a limited partnership unless he is also a general partner or, in addition to the exercise of his rights and powers as a limited partner, he participates in the control of the partnership business and, if the limited partner participates in the control of partnership business, he is liable only to persons who transact business with the limited partnership reasonably believing, based upon the limited partner's conduct, that the limited partner is a general partner.

(2) A limited partner shall not be deemed to participate in the control of the partnership business within the meaning of subsection (1) by virtue of his possessing or, regardless of whether or not the limited partner has the rights or powers, or exercising or attempting to exercise one or more of the following rights or powers having or, regardless of whether or not the limited partner has the rights or powers, acting or attempting to act in one or more of the following capacities:

(a) to be an independent contractor for or to transact business with, including being a contractor for, or to be an agent or employee of, the limited partnership or a general partner, or to be a limited partner of a partnership that is a general partner of the limited partnership, or to be a trustee, administrator, executor, custodian or other fiduciary or beneficiary of an estate or trust which is a general partner, or to be a trustee, officer, advisor, stockholder or beneficiary of a business trust which is a general partner or to be a member, manager agent or employee of a limited liability company which is a general partner;

(b) to consult with or advise a general partner with respect to any matter, including the business of the limited partnership;

(c) to act as surety, guarantor or endorser for the limited partnership or a general partner, to guarantee or assume one or more obligations of the limited partnership or a general partner, to borrow money from the limited partnership or a general partner, to lend money to the limited partnership or a general partner, or to provide collateral for the limited partnership or a general partner;

(d) to call, request, or attend or participate at a meeting of the partners or the limited partners;

(e) to wind up a limited partnership pursuant to this Act;

(f) to take any action required or permitted by law to bring, pursue or settle or otherwise terminate a derivative action in the right of the limited partnership;

(g) to serve on a committee of the limited partnership or the limited partners or to appoint, elect or otherwise participate in the choice of a representative or another person to serve on any such committee, and to act as a member of any such committee directly or by or through any such representative or other person;

(h) to act or cause the taking or refraining from the taking of any action, including by proposing, approving, consenting or disapproving by voting or otherwise, with respect to one or more of the following matters:

(i) the dissolution and winding up of the limited partnership or an election to continue the limited partnership or an election to continue the business of the limited partnership;

(ii) the sale, exchange, lease, mortgage, assignment, pledge or other transfer of, or granting of a security interest in, any asset or assets of the limited partnership;

(iii) the incurrence, renewal, refinancing or payment or other discharge of indebtedness by the limited partnership;

(iv) a change in the nature of the business;

(v) the admission, removal or retention of a general partner;

(vi) the admission, removal or retention of a limited partner;

(vii) a transaction or other matter involving an actual or potential conflict of interest;

(viii) an amendment to the memorandum or articles of partnership;

(ix) the merger or consolidation of a limited partnership;

(x) the making of or calling for or the making of other determinations in connection with contributions;

(xi) the indemnification of any partner or other person; or

(xii) such other matters as are stated in the memorandum of partnership or in any written agreement;

(i) to serve on the board of directors or a committee of, to consult with or advise, to be an officer, director, stockholder, partner (other than a general partner of a general partner of the limited partnership), member, manager, trustee, agent or employee of, or to be a fiduciary or contractor for, any person in which the limited partnership has an interest or any person providing management, consulting, advisory, custody or other services or products for, to or on behalf of, or otherwise having a business or other relationship with, the limited partnership or a general partner of the limited partnership; or

(j) any right or power granted or permitted to limited partners under this Act and not specifically enumerated in this subsection.

(3) The list of powers and capacities set forth in subsection (2) shall not be construed as exclusive or as indicating that any other powers possessed or exercised or any other capacities held or acted in by a limited partner shall be sufficient to cause the limited partner to be deemed to take part in the control of the partnership business within the meaning of subsection (1).

(4) This section does not create rights or powers of limited partners, such rights and powers may be created only by the memorandum and articles, a partnership agreement or any other agreement or in writing, or by other sections of this Act.

(5) A limited partner shall not be deemed to participate in the control of the partnership business within the meaning of subsection (1) by

(a) his possessing any one or more of the rights or powers set forth in subsection (2) regardless of the nature, extent, scope, or frequency of his possession of the rights or powers; or

(b) his exercising or attempting to exercise one or more of the rights or powers set forth in subsection (2) regardless of whether he possesses the rights or powers; or

(c) his holding or acting or attempting to act in one or more of the capacities set forth in subsection (2) regardless of whether he has the right or power to hold or act in those capacities.

Admission of additional limited partners

63. After the formation of a limited partnership, additional limited partners may be admitted upon making an amendment to the articles.

Rights, powers and liabilities of a general partner

64. A general partner shall have all the rights and powers and be subject to all the restrictions and liabilities of a partner in a partnership without limited partners, except that without the written consent or ratification of the specific act by all the limited partners, a general partner or all the general partners have no authority to do any one or more of the following:

(a) do any act in contravention of the articles;

(b) do any act which would make it impossible to carry on the ordinary business of the partnership;

(c) enter a judgment against the partnership;

(d) possess partnership property, or assign their rights in specific partnership property, for other than a partnership purpose;

(e) admit a person as a general partner, unless the right so to do is given in the articles;

(f) admit a person as a limited partner, unless the right so to do is given in the articles; or

(g) continue the business with partnership property on the death, retirement, bankruptcy or incapacity of a general partner, unless the right so to do is given in the articles.

Rights of a Limited Partner

65.(1) A limited partner shall have the same rights as a general partner to

(a) inspect at all times and to copy any of the partnership books;

(b) receive on demand

(i) true and full information of all things affecting the partnership, and

(ii) a formal account of partnership affairs whenever circumstances render it just and reasonable; and

(c) subject to any limitation set forth in the articles apply to the court for an order that the partnership be dissolved and wound up.

(2) A limited partner shall have the right to receive a share of the profits or other compensation by way of income, and to the return of his contribution as provided in sections 71 and 78.

Status of person erroneously believing himself to be a limited partner

66. A person who has contributed to the capital of a business conducted by a person or partnership erroneously believing that he has become a limited partner in a limited partnership is not, by reason of his exercise of the rights of a limited partner, a general partner with the person or in the partnership carrying on the business or bound by the obligations of such person or partnership if on ascertaining the mistake he promptly renounces his interest in the profits of the business or other compensation by way of income.

One person both general and limited partner

67.(1) A person may be a general partner and a limited partner in the same partnership at the same time.

(2) A person who is a general partner, and also at the same time a limited partner, shall have all the rights and powers and be subject to all the restrictions of a general partner, except that in respect to his contribution he shall have the rights against the other partners which he would have had if he were not also a general partner.

Loans and other business transactions with limited partner

68.(1) A limited partner may loan money to and transact other business with the partnership, and, unless he is also a general partner, receive on account of resulting claims against the partnership, with general creditors, a pro rata share of the assets.

(2) No limited partner shall in respect to any such claim

(a) receive or hold as collateral security any partnership property; or

(b) receive from a general partner or the partnership any payment, conveyance or release from liability, if at the time the assets of the partnership are not sufficient to discharge partnership liabilities to persons not claiming as general partners or limited partners.

(3) The receiving of collateral security, payment, conveyance or release in violation of subsection (2) is a fraud on the creditors of the partnership.

Relation of limited partners *inter se*

69.(1) Where there are several limited partners, the partners may agree that one or more of the limited partners shall have a priority over other limited partners as to

(a) the return of their contributions;

(b) their compensation by way of income; or

(c) any other matter.

(2) If such an agreement is made, it shall be stated in the articles, and in the absence of such a statement all the limited partners shall stand upon equal footing in proportion to their respective contributions actually made to the partnership.

Compensation of limited partner

70. A limited partner may receive from the partnership the share of the profits or the compensation by way of income stipulated in the articles, provided that after the payment is made, whether from the property of the partnership or that of a general partner, the partnership assets are in excess of all liabilities of the partnership except liabilities to limited partners on account of their contributions and to general partners.

Withdrawal or reduction of limited partner's contribution

71.(1) A limited partner shall not receive from a general partner or out of partnership property any part of his contribution until

(a) all liabilities of the partnership, except liabilities to general partners and to limited partners on account of their contributions, have been paid or there remains property of the partnership sufficient to pay them;

(b) the consent of all partners is given, unless the return of the contribution may be rightfully demanded under subsection (2); and

(c) the articles are amended as to set forth the withdrawal or reduction provided that no amendment is required where the withdrawal or reduction occurs in accordance with the articles.

(2) Subject to the provisions of subsection (1), a limited partner may rightfully demand the return of his contribution

(a) upon the dissolution of the partnership unless its business is continued pursuant to the exercise by other partners of a right or power set forth in the articles; or

(b) when the time specified in the articles for its return has arrived or the events set forth in the articles on the happening of which its return shall be made has occurred; or

(c) after he has given six months' notice in writing to all other partners if no time is specified in the articles either for the return of the contribution or for the dissolution of the partnership and no events are set forth in the articles on the happening of which the return of the contribution shall occur.

(3) In the absence of any statement in the articles to the contrary or the consent of all partners, a limited partner, irrespective of the nature of his contribution, has only the right to demand and receive cash in return for his contribution.

(4) A limited partner may have the partnership dissolved and its affairs wound up when

(a) he rightfully but unsuccessfully demands the return of his contribution; or

(b) the other liabilities of the partnership have not been paid or the partnership property is insufficient for their payment as required by paragraph (a) of subsection (1) and the limited partner would otherwise be entitled to the return of his contribution.

Liability of limited partner to partnership

72.(1) A limited partner is liable to the partnership

(a) for the difference between his contribution as actually made and that stated in the articles as having been made; and

(b) for any unpaid contribution which he agreed in the articles to make in the future at the time and on the conditions stated in the articles.

(2) A limited partner holds as trustee for the partnership

(a) specific property stated in the articles as contributed by him but which was not contributed or which has been wrongfully returned; and

(b) money or other property wrongfully paid or conveyed to him on account of his contribution.

(3) The liabilities of a limited partner as set forth in this section can be waived or compromised only by the consent of all partners, but a waiver or compromise shall not affect the right of a creditor of a partnership who extended credit or whose claim arose before an amendment of the articles to enforce such liabilities.

(4) A limited partner who receives any part of his contribution in violation of subsection (1) of section 71 and who knew at the time of the receipt that the withdrawal or reduction of this contribution violated subsection (1) of section 71 shall be liable to the limited partnership for the amount of the withdrawal or reduction and a limited partner who receives any part of his contribution in violation of subsection (1) of section 71 and who did not know at the time of the receipt that the withdrawal or reduction violated subsection (1) of section 71 shall not be liable for the amount of the distribution.

(5) Subject to subsection (6), subsection (4) shall not affect any obligation or liability of a limited partner under a partnership agreement or other applicable law for the amount of the withdrawal or deduction received.

(6) Unless otherwise agreed, a limited partner who receives any part of his contribution from a limited partnership shall have no liability under this Act or other applicable law for the amount received after the expiration of three years from the date of receipt.

Assignment of limited partner's interest

73.(1) Unless otherwise provided in the articles, a limited partner's interest is assignable.

(2) The successor in interest of a limited partner who has died shall have all the rights of an assignee of that limited partner's interest until the successor in interest is admitted as a substituted limited partner.

Admission as a substituted limited partner

74.(1) An assignee has the right to become a substituted limited partner if

(a) all the partners, except the assignor, consent thereto;

(b) the assignor, being empowered by the articles gives the assignee that right; or

(c) the articles condition the admission of the assignee on the prior approval of one or more partners other than the assignor, and such approval is obtained.

(2) An assignee becomes a substituted limited partner upon the execution of the necessary amendment to the articles reflecting such admission or such later date as is set forth in the amendment, provided that where the assignor's identity is set forth in the memorandum such admission shall not become effective until the memorandum shall have been amended in accordance with section 57.

(3) A substituted limited partner has all the rights and powers which were possessed by the assignor and, subject to subsection (4), is subject to all the restrictions and liabilities to which the assignor was subject regardless of whether the substituted limited partner had knowledge of those restrictions and liabilities at the time he became a substituted limited partner and regardless of whether those restrictions and liabilities were ascertainable from the articles.

(4) The substitution of an assignee as a limited partner does not release the assignor from liability to the partnership under section 72.

(5) An assignee who does not become a substituted limited partner has no right to require any information or account of the partnership transactions or to inspect the partnership books but is only entitled to receive the share of the profits or other compensation by way of income, or the return of contribution to which the assignor would otherwise be entitled.

Effect of retirement, death, incapacity or bankruptcy of a general partner

75. The retirement, death, incapacity, or bankruptcy or insolvency of a general partner dissolves the partnership, unless the business is continued by the remaining general partners *(a)* under a right so to do stated in the articles; or

(b) with the consent of all partners,

Death of limited partner

76.(1) On the death of a limited partner his executor or administrator shall have all the rights of a limited partner for the purpose of settling his estate and such power as the deceased had to constitute his assignee a substituted limited partner.

(2) The estate of a deceased limited partner shall be liable for all his liabilities as a limited partner.

Rights of creditors of limited partner

77.(1) On due application to a court of competent jurisdiction by any judgment creditor of a limited partner, the court may

(a) charge the partnership interest of the indebted limited partner with payment of the unsatisfied amount of the judgment debt;

(b) appoint a receiver of the limited partner's interest in the partnership; and

(c) make all other orders, directions and inquiries which the circumstances of the case may require.

(2) The interest to be charged pursuant to paragraph (a) of subsection (1) may be redeemed with the separate property of any general partner but may not be redeemed with partnership property.

(3) The remedies conferred by subsection (1) shall not be deemed exclusive of others which may exist.

Distribution of assets

78.(1) In settling accounts after dissolution the liabilities of the partnership shall be entitled to payment in the following order:

(a) those to creditors, in the order of priority as provided by law, except those to limited partners on account of their contributions, and to general partners;

(b) except as otherwise provided in the articles -

(i) those to limited partners in respect of their share of the profits and other compensation by way of income on their contributions;

(ii) those to limited partners in respect of the capital of their contributions;

(iii) those to general partners other than for capital and profits;

(iv) those to general partners in respect of profits; and

(v) those to general partners in respect of capital.

(2) Subject to any provision in the articles, limited partners share in the partnership assets in respect of their claims for capital, and in respect of their claims for profits or for compensation by way of income on their contributions, respectively, in proportion to the amounts of such claims.

Service of notice on partners

79.(1) Any notice, information or written statement required under this Act to be given by a limited partnership formed under this Act to partners must be served

(a) in the manner prescribed in the articles;

(b) in the absence of a provision in the articles, by personal service or by mail addressed to each partner at the address shown in the articles.

Service of process, etc., on limited partnership

80.(1) Any summons, notice, order, document, process, information or written statement to be served on a limited partnership formed under this Act may be served by leaving it, or by sending it by registered mail addressed to the limited partnership, at its registered office, or by leaving it with, or by sending it by registered mail to, the registered agent of the limited partnership.

(2) Service of any summons, notice, order, document, process, information or written statement to be erved on a limited partnership formed under this Act may be proved by showing that the summons, notice, order, document, process, information or written statement

(a) was mailed in such time as to admit its being delivered in the normal course of delivery, within the period prescribed for service; and

(b) was correctly addressed and the postage was prepaid.

Books and records

81. A limited partnership formed under this Act shall keep such accounts and records as the partners consider necessary or desirable in order to reflect the financial position of the limited partnership.

Registered office

82. A limited partnership shall at all times have a registered office in the Territory which shall be maintained by the limited partnership or its registered agent.

Register of limited partnership interests

83.(1) Notwithstanding section 81, the general partners of a limited partnership shall maintain or cause to be maintained at the registered office of the limited partnership a register in which shall be recorded the name and address, amount and dates of contributions of each partner and the amount and date of any payment representing a return of any part of any partner's contribution.

(2) The register referred to in subsection (1) shall

(a) be updated within 21 business days of any change in the particulars required to be entered therein; and

(b) constitute *prima face* evidence of the matters which by subsection (1) are directed to be entered therein.

Registered agent

84.(1) A limited partnership shall at all times have a registered agent in the Territory.

(2) No person shall be a registered agent of a limited partnership unless he is so registered pursuant to the Company Management Act, 1990 or under the Banks and Trust Companies Act except that the registered agent of a local limited partnership may be one of its general partners.

Penalty for contravention of Sections 82, 83 and 84.

85. A general partner of a limited partnership that wilfully contravenes section 82, 83 or 84(1) commits an offence and is liable on summary conviction to a penalty of $100.00, and is liable to the same penalty for each day or part thereof during which the contravention continues.

Registered agent desiring to resign

86.(1) Where the registered agent of a limited partnership desires to cease to act as registered agent and is unable to reach an agreement with the limited partnership for which he is registered agent concerning his replacement, the following provisions apply:

(a) the registered agent shall give not less than ninety days written notice to any partner of the limited partnership of which he is the registered agent at the partner's last known address specifying his wish to resign as registered agent;

(b) the registered agent shall submit to the Registrar a copy of the notice;

(c) if, at the time of expiry of the notice, the limited partnership has not caused to be registered a supplementary memorandum to change its registered agent, the registered agent shall inform the Registrar in writing that the limited partnership has not changed its registered agent whereupon the Registrar shall publish a notice in the *Gazette* that the name of the limited partnership

will be struck off the register, unless within thirty days from the date of the publication of the notice in the *Gazette*, there is registered with the Registrar a supplementary memorandum to change its registered agent; and

(d) if within thirty days from the date of the publication of the notice referred to in paragraph (c) there has not been registered with the Registrar a supplementary memorandum to change the registered agent, the Registrar shall strike the name of the limited partnership off the register and shall publish in the *Gazette* a notice that the name of the limited partnership has been struck off.

(2) Where the licence of a registered agent under the Company Management Act or the Banks and Trust Companies Act has been revoked has not been renewed or has expired due to the death of the registered agent,

(a) the Inspector of Company Managers or the Inspector of Banks and Trust Companies, as the case may be, shall notify the Registrar forthwith; and

(b) the Registrar shall forthwith send a notice, by registered mail to any partner of the limited partnership whose registered agent's licence has been revoked, has not been renewed or has expired by reason of the death of the registered agent, specifying that unless within ninety days of the date of the notice there is filed with him a supplementary memorandum to change its registered agent, the name of the limited partnership shall be struck off the register; and

(c) if, at the expiry of the ninety days specified in paragraph (b) there shall not have been filed a supplementary memorandum to change its registered agent, the Registrar shall strike the name of the limited partnership off the register and shall publish a notice in the *Gazette* to that effect.

(3) A limited partnership that has been struck off the register under this section remains liable for all claims, debts, liabilities and obligations of the limited partnership, and the striking-off does not affect the liability of any of its partners.

Licence Fees.

87. A limited partnership the name of which is on the register shall pay to the Registrar the annual licence fee prescribed in Part I of the Schedule and, in default of payment of the fee, it is liable to the penalties prescribed therein.

Limited partnership struck off liable for fees, etc.

88. A limited partnership formed under this Act continues to be liable for all fees, licence fees and penalties payable under this Act notwithstanding that the name of the limited partnership has been struck off the Register and all those fees, licence fees and penalties have priority to all other claims against the assets of the limited partnership.

Fees

89.(1) There shall be paid to the Registrar the fees specified in Part II of the Schedule.

(2) Parts I and II of the Schedule may be amended by the Governor in Council by Order published in the *Gazette*.

Recovery of penalties

90. Any fee payable under this Act which remains unpaid for thirty days following the date on which demand for payment is made by the Registrar is recoverable before a magistrate in civil proceedings by the Registrar as a debt due.

Fees, etc. to be paid into Consolidated Fund

91. All fees, licence fees and penalties paid to the Registrar under this Act shall be paid by the Registrar into the Consolidated Fund.

Fees payable to Registrar

92. The Registrar may refuse to take any action required of him under this Act for which a fee is prescribed until all requisite fees have been paid.

Exemptions from tax, etc.

93.(1) Notwithstanding any provision of the Income Tax Ordinance,

(a) an international limited partnership formed under this Act,

(b) all payments made by an international limited partnership to persons who are not resident in the Territory, and

(c) capital gains realized with respect to any interest in an international limited partnership by persons who are not resident in the Territory,

are exempt from all provisions of the Income Tax Ordinance.

(2) No estate, inheritance, succession or gift tax, rate, duty, levy or other charge is payable by persons who are not resident in the Territory with respect to any interest in an international limited partnership.

(3) Notwithstanding any provision of the Stamp Act,

(a) all instruments relating to transfers of property to or by an international limited partnership,

(b) all instruments relating to transactions in respect of the interests of an international limited partnership, and

(*c*) all instruments relating to other transactions relating to the business of an international limited partnership,

are exempt from the payment of stamp duty.

Regulations

94. The Governor in Council may make Regulations

(*a*) with respect to the duties to be performed by the Registrar under this Act;

(*b*) prescribing the place where the office for the registration of limited partnerships is located;

(*c*) providing for the conduct and regulation of the registration of limited partnerships under this Act;

(*d*) prescribing the fees to be paid in respect of matters arising under or provided for or authorised by this Act;

(*e*) prescribing the forms to be used in respect of matters arising under or provided for or authorised by this Act;

(*f*) with respect to the conduct, duties and responsibilities of registered agents; and

(*g*) providing for the restoration of a limited partnership, the name of which has been struck off the register, to the register and the fees applicable thereto;

(*h*) providing for such matters as are contemplated by or necessary for giving full effect to the provisions of this Act and for its due administration.

Form of Certificate

95. Any certificate or other document required to be issued by the Registrar under this Act shall be in such form as the Governor in Council may approve.

Certificate of good standing

96.(1) The Registrar shall, upon request by any person, and payment of the prescribed fee, issue a certificate of good standing under his hand and seal certifying that a limited partnership formed under this Act is of good standing if the Registrar is satisfied that

(*a*) the name of the limited partnership is on the register; and

(*b*) the limited partnership has paid all fees, licence fees and penalties due and payable.

(2) The Registrar shall state on the certificate of good standing issued under subsection (1) whether any proceedings to strike the name of the limited partnership off the register have been instituted.

(3) The certificate of good standing is *prima facie* evidence of the matters contained therein.

Inspection and copies of documents

97.(1) Any person may, on payment of the prescribed fee,

(a) inspect the documents kept by the Registrar pursuant to this Act; and

(b) require that the Registrar issue

(i) a certified copy of the certificate of limited partnership of a limited partnership; or

(ii) a certified copy of or extract from any document filed with the Registrar pursuant to this Act.

(2) A certificate of limited partnership or extract from any document filed with the Registrar pursuant to this Act if certified as a true copy under the hand and official seal of the Registrar shall in all legal proceedings, civil or criminal, and in all cases whatsoever, be receivable in evidence in proof of the matters which it states.

Appointment and duties of inspector

98.(1) The Minister, on the application of a limited partnership or of the partners together holding not less than a one fourth interest therein, may appoint one or more inspectors to investigate the affairs of a limited partnership and to report thereon in such manner as the Minister may direct.

(2) The application referred to in subsection (1) shall be supported by such evidence as the Minister may require for the purpose of showing that the applicant has good reason for requiring the investigation, and the expenses of and incidental to such investigation shall be defrayed by the limited partnership unless the Minister otherwise directs.

(3) A partner or a registered agent of a limited partnership shall produce to an inspector such books or documents as the inspector may require for the purposes of his investigation.

(4) A partner or a registered agent of a limited partnership who, in the course of an investigation of the affairs of the limited partnership

(a) refuses to produce any book or document required by the inspector to be produced, or

(b) refuses to answer any question relating to the affairs of the limited partnership, commits an offence and shall be liable on summary conviction to a fine of five thousand dollars.

(5) An inspector may take evidence upon oath in investigating the affairs of a limited partnership and for that purpose may administer an oath.

(6) An investigation under this section shall be held in private unless the limited partnership requests that it be held in public.

(7) An inspector investigating the affairs of a limited partnership may from time to time report to the Minister and shall, on completion of the investigation submit a written report to the Minister.

(8) The Minister may, if he thinks fit,

(a) forward a copy of the report to the registered office of the limited partnership;

(b) furnish a copy or request and upon payment of the prescribed fee to

(i) any partner of the limited partnership;

(ii) any person whose conduct is referred to in the report;

(iii) any other person whose financial interests appear to the Minister to be affected by the matters dealt with in the report;

(c) cause the report to be printed and published.

(9) If the Minister, after examining a report considers that a limited partnership, a partner, the registered agent or any officer, agent or employee of the limited partnership

(a) has knowingly and wilfully done anything in contravention of this Act, the Minister may petition the Court for the dissolution of the limited partnership; or

(b) is carrying on its affairs in a manner that is detrimental to its creditors or the public interest, the Minister may require the limited partnership to take such measures as he considers necessary in relation to its affairs.

(10) A copy of the petition referred to in subsection (9) shall be served on the limited partnership at least seven clear days before the day set by the Court for the hearing thereof.

(11) If the Court, on the hearing of the petition referred to in subsection (9) is satisfied that the limited partnership, or any officer, agent or employee of the limited partnership has done anything in contravention of the provisions of this Act, the Court may

(a) make an order for the dissolution of the limited partnership;

(b) impose a fine not exceeding five thousand dollars on the limited partnership;

(c) impose a like fine on any partner or resident agent or any officer, agent or employee of the limited partnership who knowingly and wilfully authorised or submitted the contravention; or

(d) make an order under paragraph (a) and impose a fine under paragraph (b) and (c).

(12) Any proceedings in connection with the holding of an investigation by an inspector in pursuance of the provisions of this section shall, for the purposes of the Perjury Act be deemed to be an enquiry held before a commissioner.

Minister's power to require production of documents

99.(1) The Minister may, at any time, if he thinks there is good reason to do so, require a limited partnership, a partner or the registered agent of a limited partnership to produce at the time and place as may be specified in the directions, to the officer of the Minister specified in the directions, the books and documents as may be so specified.

(2) The Minister or the officer of the Minister specified in the directions referred to in subsection (1) may take copies of any books and papers produced and require any past or present, partner, registered agent, officer or agent of a limited partnership to provide an explanation of any of them or make a statement in relation to any of them.

(3) A partner, registered agent, officer or agent of a limited partnership who refuses to produce books or papers as required under subsection (1) commits an offence and shall be liable on summary conviction to a fine of five thousand dollars.

(4) A past or present partner, registered agent, officer or agent of a limited partnership who refuses to provide an explanation or make a statement as required by subsection (2) commits an offence and shall be liable on summary conviction to a fine of five thousand dollars.

(5) If the requirement to produce books or papers is not complied with, a magistrate may, if satisfied on information on oath laid under the authority of the Minister that there are reasonable grounds for suspecting that there are any books or papers of which production has been required under subsection (1), issue a warrant authorising any member of the Royal Virgin Islands Police Force together with any other persons named in the warrant to enter the premises specified in the warrant, using such force as is reasonably necessary for the purpose, and to search the premises and take possession of any books or papers appearing to be the books or papers, the production of which have been required under subsection (1) and to take any other steps which may appear necessary for preserving them or preventing interference with them.

(6) A warrant issued under subsection (5) continues in force until the end of one month after the date on which it is issued.

(7) A person who

(a) obstructs the exercise of a right of entry or search conferred by a warrant issued under this section, or

(b) obstructs the exercise of a right conferred by a warrant issued under this section to take possession of any books or papers,

commits an offence and shall be liable on summary conviction to a fine of five thousand dollars.

(8) Any books or papers of which possession is taken under this section may be retained for a period not exceeding three months unless within that period there are commenced criminal proceedings to which the books or papers are relevant, in which case, they may be retained until the conclusion of those proceedings.

Privileged information

100. Nothing in sections 98 and 99

(a) compels the production by any person of any book or document which he would, in an action in the High Court, be entitled to refuse to produce on grounds of legal professional privilege;

(b) authorises the taking of possession of any such book or document which is in the person's possession; or

(c) requires the disclosure by any person to the Minister or to an inspector appointed by the Minister of information which in an action in the High Court that person would be entitled to refuse to disclose on grounds of legal professional privilege except, if he is a lawyer, the name and address of his client.

Provision for security of information obtained

101.(1) Subject to subsections (2) and (3), no information or document which has been obtained under section 97 and which relates to any person shall, without the previous consent in writing of that person, be published or disclosed unless the publication or disclosure is required

(a) with a view to the institution of or otherwise for the purpose of criminal proceedings;

(b) for the purpose of the examination of any person by inspectors appointed under section 98 in the course of their investigation;

(c) for the purposes of proceedings under subsections (3), (4) and (7) of section 99;

(d) for the purpose of enabling or assisting an official receiver to discharge his functions under enactments relating to insolvency or for the purpose of enabling or assisting a body which is for the time being a recognised professional body for the purposes of any insolvency enactment to discharge its functions as such;

(e) with a view to the institution of, or otherwise for the purpose of, any disciplinary proceedings relating to the exercise by a lawyer, auditor, accountant, valuer or actuary of his professional duties; or

(f) for the purpose of enabling or assisting an authority in a country or territory outside the Territory to exercise functions corresponding to those of the Inspector of Banks and Trust Companies, the Inspector of Company Managers, the Insurance Supervisor appointed respectively under the provisions of the Banks and Trust Companies Act, the Company Management Act and the Insurance Act or any Act amending or substituted for those Acts.

(2) Any information or document obtained under section 99 may without the consent of the person to whom it relates, be published or disclosed to

(a) the Minister;

(b) an inspector appointed by the Minister under section 100;

(c) the Attorney General;

(d) the Inspector of Banks and Trust Companies;

(e) the Inspector of Company Managers;

(f) the Insurance Supervisor;

(g) any authority designated for the purpose under subsection (3).

(3) The Minister may by order published in the *Gazette* designate any public or other authority to be an authority to which information obtained under section 99 may be published or disclosed subject to such conditions and restrictions as he may deem appropriate and such order shall be subject to annulment pursuant to a resolution of the Legislative Council.

(4) The Minister may, if he thinks fit, disclose any information obtained under sections 98 and 99 to the persons listed at paragraphs (b) to (g) of subsection (2) in any circumstances in which or for any purpose for which the preceding subsections of this section do not preclude disclosure.

Powers of general partners in the event of dissolution

102. Subject to sections 35 (1) and 108, in the event of a dissolution under this Act the general partners may only

(a) authorise a liquidator, who shall not be a body corporate, to carry on the business of the limited partnership if the liquidator determines that to do so would be necessary or in the best interests of the limited partnership or its creditors; and

(b) determine to rescind the articles of dissolution as permitted under section 106.

Duties of liquidator

103.(1) A liquidator shall, upon his appointment by a limited partnership and upon the commencement of a winding-up proceed

(a) to identify all assets of the limited partnership;

(b) to identify all creditors of and claimants against the limited partnership;

(c) to pay or provide for the payment of, or to discharge, all claims, debts, liabilities and obligations of the limited partnership;

(d) to distribute any surplus assets of the limited partnership to the partners in accordance with the actions and transactions of the liquidator;

(e) to prepare or cause to be prepared a statement of account in respect of the actions and transactions of the liquidator; and

(f) to send a copy of the statement of account to all partners if so required by the plan of dissolution required by section 105.

Powers of liquidator

104. In order to perform the duties imposed on him under section 105, a liquidator has all powers of the general partners including, but not limited to, the power

(a) to take custody of the assets of the limited partnership and in connection therewith, to register any property of the limited partnership in the name of the liquidator or that of his nominee;

(b) to sell any assets of the limited partnership at public auction or by private sale without any notice;

(c) to collect the debts and assets due or belonging to the limited partnership;

(d) to borrow money from any person for any purpose that will facilitate the winding-up and dissolution of the limited partnership and to pledge or mortgage any property of the limited partnership as security for any such borrowing;

(e) to negotiate, compromise and settle any claim, debt, liability or obligation of the limited partnership;

(f) to prosecute and defend, in the name of the limited partnership or in the name of the liquidator or otherwise, any action or other legal proceedings;

(g) to retain solicitors, accountants and other advisers and appoint agents;

(h) to carry on the business of the limited partnership, if the liquidator has received authorisation to do so in the plan of liquidation or by the general partners as permitted under section 102, as the liquidator may determine to be necessary or to be in the best interests of the creditors or the partners;

(i) to execute any contract, agreement or other instrument in the name of the limited partnership or in the name of the liquidator; and

(j) to make any distribution in money or in other property or partly in each, and if in other property, to allot the property, or an undivided interest therein, in equal or unequal proportions.

(2) Notwithstanding paragraph (h) of subsection (1), a liquidator shall not, without the permission of the court, carry on for a period in excess of 2 years the business of a limited partnership that is being wound up and dissolved under this Act.

Procedure on winding-up and dissolution

105.(1) The general partners of a limited partnership required or proposing under this Act to wind up and dissolve shall approve a plan of dissolution containing

(a) a statement of the reason for the winding-up and dissolution;

(b) a statement that the limited partnership is, and will continue to be, able to discharge or pay or provide for the payment of all claims, debts, liabilities and obligations in full;

(c) a statement that the winding up will commence on the date when articles of dissolution are submitted to the Registrar or on such date subsequent thereto, not exceeding thirty days, as is stated in the articles of dissolution;

(*d*) a statement of the estimated time required to wind up and dissolve the limited partnership;

(*e*) a statement as to whether the liquidator is authorised to carry on the business of the limited partnership if the liquidator determines that to do so would be necessary or in the best interests of the limited partnership or creditors;

(*f*) a statement of the name and address of each person to be appointed a liquidator and the remuneration proposed to be paid to each liquidator; and

(*g*) a statement as to whether the liquidator is required to send to all partners a statement of account prepared or caused to be prepared by the liquidator in respect of his actions or transactions.

(2) After approval of the plan of dissolution, articles of dissolution shall be executed by the limited partnership and shall contain

(*a*) the plan of dissolution; and

(*b*) the manner in which the plan of dissolution was authorised.

(3) The general partners of a limited partnership shall submit articles of dissolution to the Registrar who shall retain and register them and within thirty days immediately following the date on which the articles of dissolution are submitted to the Registrar, the general partners of the limited partnership shall cause to be published, in the *Gazette*, and in a publication of general circulation in the Territory, a notice stating

(*a*) that the limited partnership is in dissolution;

(*b*) the date of commencement of the dissolution; and

(*c*) the names and addresses of the liquidators.

(4) A winding-up and dissolution commences on the date the articles of dissolution are registered by the Registrar or on such date subsequent thereto, not exceeding thirty days, as is stated in the articles of dissolution.

(5) A liquidator shall, upon completion of a winding-up and dissolution, submit to the Registrar a statement that the winding-up and dissolution has been completed in accordance with this Act and upon receiving the notice, the Registrar shall

(*a*) strike the limited partnership off the register; and

(*b*) issue a certificate of dissolution under his hand and seal certifying that the limited partnership has been dissolved.

(6) Where the Registrar issues a certificate of dissolution under his hand and seal certifying that the limited partnership has been dissolved,

(a) the certificate is *prima facie* evidence of compliance with all requirements of this Act in respect of dissolution; and

(b) the dissolution of the limited partnership is effective from the date of issue of the certificate.

(7) Immediately following the issue by the Registrar of a certificate of dissolution under subsection (5), the liquidator shall cause to be published, in the Gazette, and in a publication of general circulation in the Territory, a notice that the limited partnership has been dissolved and has been struck off the register.

(8) A general partner of a limited partnership that contravenes subsection (3) commits an offence and shall be liable on summary conviction to a penalty of $100.00 and shall be liable to the same penalty for each day or part thereof during which the contravention continues.

Rescission of dissolution

106.(1) A limited partnership may, prior to submitting to the Registrar the articles of dissolution specified in subsection (3) of section 105, rescind the articles of dissolution by notice in writing to the Registrar.

(2) A copy of the notice referred to in subsection (1) shall be submitted to the Registrar who shall retain and register it in the register.

(3) Within 30 days immediately following the date on which the notice referred to in subsection (1) has been submitted to the Registrar, the limited partnership shall cause a notice stating that the limited partnership has rescinded its intention to wind up and dissolve to be published in the *Gazette*, and in a publication of general circulation in the Territory.

Winding-up and dissolution of limited partnership unable to pay claims, etc.

107.(1) Where, in the event of a dissolution other than a dissolution by the Court,

(a) the general partners of a limited partnership have reason to believe that the limited partnership will not be able to pay or provide for the payment of or discharge all claims, debts, liabilities and obligations of the limited partnership in full, or

(b) the liquidator after his appointment has reason so to believe,

then, the general partners or the liquidator, as the case may be, shall immediately give notice of the fact to the Registrar.

(2) Where notice has been given to the Registrar under subsection (1) , all winding-up and dissolution proceedings after the notice has been given shall be in accordance with the provisions of the Companies Act relating to winding-up and dissolution and those provisions shall apply *mutatis mutandis* to the winding-up and dissolution of the limited partnership.

Winding-up where dissolution ordered by the court

108. Where dissolution of a limited partnership is ordered by the Court under section 37, the Court may make such orders and give such directions for the winding-up of the limited partnership as it deems just and equitable in the circumstances.

PART VII - Miscellaneous.

Declaration by the court

109.(1) A general partner of a limited partnership formed under this Act may, without the necessity of joining any other party, apply to the Court, by summons supported by any affidavit, for a declaration on any question of interpretation of this Act or of the memorandum or the articles of a limited partnership.

(2) A person acting in accordance with a declaration made by the court as a result of an application under subsection (1) shall be deemed, in so far as regards the discharge of any fiduciary or professional duty, to have properly discharged his duties in the subject matter of the application.

Application of Part VIII of Cap. 291

110. Part VIII of the International Business Companies Act applies, *mutatis mutandis*, to this Act.

Judge in Chambers

111. A judge of the High Court may exercise in Chambers any jurisdiction that is vested in the court by this Act and in exercise of that jurisdiction, may award such costs as may be just.

Time for prosecution

112. A prosecution for an offence under this Act or any Regulations made thereunder may be commenced within five years from the date of the commission of the offence but not thereafter.

General penalty

113. Any person who contravenes any provision of this Act or any Regulation made thereunder commits an offence, and, unless otherwise provided in the Act or the Regulations, is liable on summary conviction to a fine of $5,000.00.

Repeals

114.(1) The Partnership Act, 1888 is repealed.

(2) Section 3 of the Companies Act is repealed.

SCHEDULE

(Section 87)

PART I - Licence Fees

(a) A limited partnership the name of which is on the Register on the 31st December in a year shall, before 30th April of the following year, pay to the Registrar an annual licence fee of $500.

(b) If a limited partnership fails to pay the annual licence fee under paragraph (a) by the date specified therein, the licence fee increases by 10 percent of that amount.

(c) If a limited partnership fails to pay the amount due as an increased licence fee under paragraph (b) by 31st July, then the licence fee increases by 25 percent of the licence fee specified in paragraph (a).

(d) If a limited partnership fails to pay the amount due as an increased licence fee under paragraph (c) by 31st October, then the licence fee increases by 50 percent of the licence fee specified in paragraph (a).

PART II

(Section 89(1))

There shall be paid to the Registrar fees as follows:

(a) $500 for the registration of the memorandum of a limited partnership;

(b) for the registration of an amendment to the memorandum of a limited partnership,

(i) if the registration is within 30 days immediately following the amendment of the Articles;

(ii) $50 if the registration is within 60 days immediately following the amendment of the Articles;

(iii) $75 if the registration is within 90 days immediately following the amendment of the Articles; and

(iv) $100 if the registration is later than 90 days following the amendment of the Articles;

(c) $25 for the issue of a certificate of limited partnership or good standing, other than at the time of the registration of a limited partnership;

(d) $25 for the issue of a copy or extract of a document or a part of a document;

(e) $10 for the inspection of the documents kept by the Registrar pursuant to this Act;

(f) $25 for the reservation of a name as provided for in section 60;

(g) $10 for an inspection of each entry in the Register of Limited Partnerships;

(h) $25 to conduct a search of a file kept by the Registrar; and

(i) $15 for any other service provided by the Registrar for which no fee is prescribed.

BANKS AND TRUST COMPANIES ACT, 1990

ARRANGEMENT OF SECTIONS

Short title.

1. This Act may be cited as the Banks and Trust Companies Act, 1990.

PART I - Preliminary

Interpretation

2.(1) In this Act,

"auditor" means a person who

(a) is qualified as an accountant by examination conducted by one of the institutes of Chartered Accountants or Certified Accounts in England and Wales, Ireland or Scotland, the Canadian Institute of Chartered Accountants or the American Institute of Certified Public Accountants and is a current member in good standing of one of those institutes; or

(b) possesses such other qualification in accountancy as the Governor in Council, by order, approves and is in good standing with respect to such qualification;

"authorized agent" means a person designated an authorized agent by a bank or trust company under paragraph (b) of subsection (1) of section 9;

"bank" means a person carrying on banking business;

"banking business" means the business of receiving (other than from a bank or trust company) and holding on current, savings, deposit or similar account money that is repayable by cheque or order and is capable of being invested by way of advances to customers or otherwise but does not include the receiving on savings, deposit or similar account money which is paid by one company to another at a time when

(a) one is the subsidiary of the other; or

(b) both are subsidiaries of another company;

"financial year" means, in relation to a licensee under this Act,

(a) the period not exceeding 53 weeks at the end of which the balance of the licensee's account is struck; or

(b) if no such balance is struck, or if a period in excess of 53 weeks is used, then, a calendar year;

"Governor" means the Governor in Council;

"Inspector" means the Inspector of Banks and Trust Companies appointed under subsection (1) of section 15;

"licence" means a licence granted under subsection (3) of section 4;

"licensee" means a company holding a licence under this Act;

"Registrar" means the Registrar of the High Court;

"trust company" means a company carrying on trust business;

"trust" means the legal relationship created inter vivos or on death by a person, known as a settlor or grantor, when assets have been placed under the control of a person, known as a trustee, for the benefit of a person, known as a beneficiary, or for a specified purpose or when a person declares that he holds assets as trustee for the benefit of a beneficiary or a specified purpose and

(a) the assets constitute a separate trust fund and are not part of the trustee's own estate;

(b) title to the trust assets stand in the name of the trustee or in the name of another person on behalf of the trustee; and

(c) the trustee has the power and the duty, in respect of which he is accountable, to manage, employ or dispose of the assets in accordance with the terms of the trust and the special duties imposed on him by law;

"trust business" means the business of

(a) acting as a professional trustee, protector or administrator of a trust or settlement;

(b) managing or administering any trust or settlement; and

(c) company management as defined by the Company Management Act, 1990.

(2) For the purposes of this Act and subject to subsection (5), a company is deemed to be a subsidiary of another if

(a) that other either

(i) is a member of it and controls the composition of its board of directors, or

(ii) holds more than half in nominal value of its equity share capital; or

(b) the first-mentioned company is a subsidiary of any company that is the other's subsidiary.

(3) For the purposes of subsection (2), the composition of a company's board of directors is deemed to be controlled by another company if that other company by the exercise of some power exercisable by it without the consent or concurrence of any other person can appoint or remove the holders of all or a majority of the directorships.

(4) For purposes of subsection (3), the other company is deemed to have power to appoint to a directorship with respect to which any of the following conditions is satisfied:

(a) that a person can not be appointed to it without the exercise in his favour by the other company of such a power as is mentioned in subsection (3);

(b) that a person's appointment to the directorship follows necessarily from his appointment as a director of the company; or

(c) that the directorship is held by the other company itself or by a subsidiary of it.

(5) In determining whether one company is a subsidiary of another

(a) any shares held or power exercisable by the other in a fiduciary capacity are to be treated as not held or exercisable by it;

(b) subject to paragraphs (c) and (d), any shares held or power exercisable

(i) by any person as nominee for the other except where the other is concerned only in a fiduciary capacity, or

(ii) by, or by a nominee for, a subsidiary of the other not being a subsidiary which is concerned only in a fiduciary capacity,

are to be treated as held or exercisable by the other;

(c) any shares held or power exercisable by any person by virtue of the provisions of any debentures of the first-mentioned company or of a trust deed securing any issue of such debentures are to be disregarded; and

(d) any shares held or power exercisable by, or by a nominee for, the other or its subsidiary, not being held or exercisable as mentioned in paragraph (c), are to be treated as not held or exercisable by the other if the ordinary business of the other or its subsidiary, as the case may be, includes the lending of money and the shares are held or the power is exercisable as above-mentioned by way of security only for the purposes of a transaction entered into the ordinary course of that business.

(6) For purposes of this Act,

(a) a company is deemed to be another's holding company if the other is its subsidiary; and

(b) a body corporate is deemed the wholly-owned subsidiary of another if it has no members except that other and that other's wholly-owned subsidiaries and its or their nominees.

PART II - Licences

Requirement For Licence

3.(1) No person shall carry on banking business, and no trust company shall carry on trust business, from within the Virgin Islands, whether or not such business is carried on within or outside the Virgin Islands, unless the person or the trust company, as the case may be, has obtained a licence under this Act for the purpose.

(2) No company incorporated in the Virgin Islands shall carry on banking business or trust business within or outside the Virgin Islands unless the company has obtained a licence under this Act for the purpose.

Application for licence

4.(1) A licence is obtainable by making application therefor to the Governor in the prescribed form.

(2) An application under subsection (1) shall contain the particulars set out in the First Schedule and shall be accompanied by the fee prescribed in Part I of the Second Schedule.

(3) The Second Schedule may be amended by an order made by the Governor and an order made under this subsection shall be subject to affirmative resolution.

(4) If the Governor is satisfied that an application to carry on banking business or trust business is not against the public interest and that the applicant is a person qualified to carry on banking business or trust business, he may grant the application and issue to the applicant a licence subject to such terms and conditions as the Governor thinks fit.

(5) A decision to refuse to grant a licence, other than a licence in respect of a business in existence at the date of the commencement of this Act, is final and is not subject to any appeal.

(6) The Governor shall cause notice of the grant of a licence under this Act to be published in the Gazette.

(7) A licence is issued under this Act shall be prominently displayed on the premises where the business is carried on.

Duration of licence

5. A licence issued under this Act is valid until 31st December of the year in which it is issued and is renewable during the month of January in the following year upon payment of the fee prescribed in Part II of the Second Schedule.

Exemptions

6.(1) A person who is licensed under this Act is not required to be licensed under the Business Professions and Trade Licences Act, 1989 to carry on banking business or trust business.

(2) This Act does not apply to a person licensed under the Company Management Act, 1990.

Existing businesses

7. A person who at the commencement of this Act is carrying on banking business or trust business has a period of 3 months to comply with the provisions of this Act.

Notification of change in particulars of licensee

8. Where a change occurs in the particulars of a licensee as set out in the application for the particulars licence, the licensee shall, as soon as possible thereafter, inform the Governor of the change.

Principal office and authorized agent

9.(1) A licence shall not be granted to any person unless the person designates, and notifies the Governor,

(a) a principal office in the Virgin Islands; and

(b) by name, two individuals, approved by the Governor and the Inspector, to be that person's authorized agents in the Virgin Islands.

(2) The functions of an authorized agent are to act as an intermediary between the licensee and, as the case may be, the Governor or the Inspector, except that in the absence or inability of one authorized agent may carry out the functions of both authorized agents under this subsection.

(3) It shall be a condition of every licence granted that the licensee shall forthwith notify the Governor in writing of any change of

(a) its principal office in the Virgin Islands; or

(b) any of the persons designated as an authorized agent pursuant to paragraph (b) of subsection (1).

(4) Where the Governor has approved a person under paragraph (b) of subsection (1) as an authorized agent, he may in writing revoke the approval.

Types of licences

10.(1) A licence issued under this Act must be in one of the following categories:

(a) a general banking licence, for the purposes of carrying on banking business within and outside the jurisdiction of the Virgin Islands without any restrictions on that business;

(b) a restricted Class I banking licence, for the purpose of carrying on banking business with the restrictions on that business set forth in section 11;

(c) a restricted Class II banking licence, for the purpose of carrying on banking

business with the restrictions on that business set forth in section 11 with the further restriction that the licensee shall not receive or solicit funds by way of trade or business from persons other than those listed in any undertaking accompanying the application for the licence;

(d) a general trust licence, for the purpose of carrying on trust business without any restrictions; and

(e) a restricted trust licence, for the purpose of carrying on trust business with the restriction that the licensee shall not undertake trust business for persons other than those listed in any undertaking accompanying the application for the licence.

(2) There may be listed in a schedule to the application for a general trust licence the name of any company engaging in trust business being a subsidiary of the company applying for a general trust licence together with a description of the particular type of trust business being carried on or to be carried on by the subsidiary and the Governor may, upon granting the general trust licence to the applicant company, include in the licence the name of each subsidiary to be included in the licence together with the terms and conditions, if any, subject to which the licence is extended to include each subsidiary.

Limitations on restricted banking licences.

11. The holder of a restricted Class I banking licence shall not

(a) take banking deposits from any person resident in the Virgin Islands other than another licensee or a company incorporated under the International Business Companies Act, 1984;

(b) invest in any asset that represents a claim on any person resident in the Virgin Islands except a claim resulting from

(i) a transaction with another licensee, or

(ii) the purchase of bonds or other securities issued by the Government, a statutory corporation or a company in which the Government is the sole or majority beneficial owner; or

(c) without the written approval of the Governor, carry on any business in the Virgin Islands other than the business for which the restricted Class I banking licence has been obtained.

Capital requirements

12.(1) No general banking licence shall be granted to a company unless the company

(a) has a fully paid up capital of not less than $2,000,000 or its equivalent in foreign currencies, or such greater sum as the Governor, by order, determines; and

(b) has deposited or invested the sum of $500,000 in such manner as the Governor, by order, prescribes.

(2) No restricted Class I banking licence or restricted Class II banking licence shall be granted to any company unless the company

(a) has a fully paid-up capital of not less than $1,000,000, or its equivalent in foreign currencies, or such greater sum as the Governor, by order, determines; and

(b) has deposited or invested a sum of $500,000 in such manner as the Governor, by order, prescribes.

(3) No general trust licence shall be granted to any trust company unless the trust company

(a) has a fully paid-up capital of not less than $250,000, or its equivalent in foreign currencies, or such greater sum as the Governor, by order, determines; and

(b) has deposited or invested a sum of money as may be specified by the Governor but not to exceed $100,000, in such manner as the Governor, by order, prescribes.

(4) The Governor may, on the recommendation of the Inspector, require a licensee to increase its fully paid-up capital to such greater amount as the Governor may determine for the nature of the banking business or trust business being, or sought to be, undertaken.

Surrender of licence

13.(1) A licensee that has ceased to carry on the business in respect of which its licence was granted may apply to the Governor to surrender its licence if the licensee

(a) produces evidence that it has repaid all deposits and has transferred all trust assets held or administered by it; or

(b) being a company, is being wound up voluntarily and produces evidence that it is solvent and is able on demand to repay all its other deposits held by it and all its other creditors and has transferred all trust assets held or administered by it, and the Governor may thereupon approve the surrender.

(2) In the case of an application under paragraph (b) of subsection (1) the Attorney General may apply to the court for an order that the licensee be wound up, either by the court, or subject to the supervision of the court, and where the court so orders the provisions of the Companies Act relating to the winding up of a company by or subject to the supervision of the court, mutatis mutandis, apply.

PART III - Transferability Of Shares And Beneficial Interests

Shares not to be issued or transferred without approval.

14. No shares or other interests, whether legal or equitable, in a bank or trust company shall be issue, transferred or otherwise disposed of without the prior written approval of the Governor, except that the Governor may exempt any bank or trust company from the provisions of this section, subject to such terms and conditions as the Governor considers necessary.

PART IV - Administration

Inspector of Banks and Trust Companies

15.(1) The Governor shall appoint a public officer to be known as the Inspector of Banks and Trust Companies for the purpose of ensuring the proper administration of this Act.

(2) The functions of the Inspector are

(a) to maintain a general review of banking and trust company practice in the Virgin Islands;

(b) where he thinks fit or when required by the Governor, to examine by way of the receipt of regular returns or in such other manner as he thinks fit the affairs or business of any licensee carrying on business within or outside the Virgin Islands for the purpose of satisfying himself that all provisions of this Act are being complied with and that the licensee is in a sound financial position and is carrying on its business in a satisfying manner, and to report to the Governor the results of such examination;

(c) to assist in the investigation of any contravention of the laws of the Virgin Islands that he has reasonable grounds to believe has or may have been committed by a licensee or by any of its directors or officers;

(d) to examine accounts and audited annual accounts forwarded to him under section 17 and to report his findings to the Governor; and

(e) to examine, and make recommendations to the Governor with respect to, applications for licenses.

(3) In the performance of his functions under this Act and subject to the provisions of section 24, the Inspector may at all reasonable times

(a) have access to the books, records, vouchers, documents, cash and securities of any licensee;

(b) request any information, matter or thing from any person whom he has reasonable grounds to believe is carrying on banking business or trust business in the Virgin Islands in contravention of section 3; and

(c) demand of the authorized agent of the licensee any reasonable information or explanation for the purpose of enabling the Inspector to perform his functions under the Act.

(4) For the purposes of subsection (3), the Inspector shall have access to the name or title of an account of a depositor of a licensee or to the settlor, name or title of a trust, only under the authority of any order of the court made on the ground that there is no other way of obtaining the information required by him.

(5) The Inspector, with the written approval of the Governor, may authorize in writing any other person to assist him in the performance of his functions under this Act.

(6) The Inspector may, if it appears to him that there is reasonable ground for suspecting that there is a contravention of this Act or that a contravention is likely, apply to the court for an order authorizing him to take such action as he considers necessary in the interests of the depositors, the beneficiaries of any trust, or other creditors and to preserve any assets of the bank or trust company that is the subject of the order.

Use of word "bank", etc.

16.(1) No person, other than a licensee, shall except with the approval of the Governor,

(a) use or continue to use the words "bank", "savings", "savings and loan", "trust", "trustee", "trust company" or "trust corporation", or any of their derivatives, either in English or in any other language, in the name, description or title under which that person is carrying on business from within the Virgin Islands, whether or not the business is carried on within or outside the Virgin Islands;

(b) make or continue to make any representation in any advertisement, billhead, circular, letter, letterhead, notice, paper or in any other manner that that person is carrying on banking business or trust business; or

(c) in any manner solicit or receive deposits from the public.

(2) No company incorporated in the Virgin Islands shall, except with the approval of the Governor, be registered, or continue to be registered, by a name which contains the words "bank", "savings", savings and loan", "trust", "trustee", "trust company" or "trust corporation" or any of their derivatives, either in English or in any other language, in the description or title under which the company is carrying on business within or outside the Virgin Islands.

(3) The Governor may, before giving his approval under subsection (1) or (2), require the production of such references and such information and particulars as may be prescribed.

(4) The Governor may withdraw any approval given under subsection (1) where he considers it to be in the public interest.

(5) The Governor may refuse to grant a licence to a bank or trust company or, if the bank or trust company is already in possession of a licence, he may revoke the licence if, in his opinion, the bank or trust company is carrying on or appears likely to be carrying on banking business or trust business, as the case may be, under a name that is *(a)* identical with that of any other person whether within or outside the Virgin Islands, or which so nearly resembles that name as to be calculated to deceive;

(b) calculated to suggest falsely the patronage of or connection with some person, whether within or outside the Virgin Islands; or

(c) calculated to suggest falsely that the person

(i) has special status in relation to or derived from the Government,

(ii) has the official approval of or acts on behalf of the Government or of any department, branch, agency or organ of Government, or any officer thereof, or

(iii) is recognized in the Virgin Islands as a national or central bank or trust company.

Accounts.

17.(1) Every licensee shall have its accounts audited by an auditor annually or at such other periods as the Governor or the Inspector may require.

(2) The audited accounts shall be forwarded to the Inspector within 3 months from the end of the financial year of the licensee, unless prior written approval for an extension has been granted by the Inspector.

(3) Where a licensee changes its auditor, the Inspector may require the former auditor to explain the circumstances that gave rise to the change.

Certain approvals required.

18. A licensee shall not change its name or operate outside the Virgin Islands any subsidiary, branch, agency or representative office without the prior written approval of the Governor.

Number and approval of directors

19.(1) A licensee shall at no time have less than 2 directors.

(2) A licensee shall, before the appointment of a director or other senior officer, apply to the Governor for his written approval of the appointment.

(3) Notwithstanding subsection (2), the Governor may exempt a licensee from the requirements specified in that subsection if such an exemption

(a) ipso facto lapses if the director or senior officer becomes bankrupt, makes an

arrangement or composition with his creditors or is convicted of an offence involving dishonesty; and

(b) may be revoked by the Governor.

Specific powers of Governor.

20.(1) Where the Governor is satisfied that a licensee

(a) has ceased to carry on banking business or trust business;

(b) has gone into liquidation or is wound up or is otherwise dissolved;

(c) has made any arrangement or composition with its creditors;

(d) is unable or appears likely to become unable to meet its obligations as they fall due;

(e) is carrying on business in a manner detrimental to the public interest, the interests of its depositors or of the beneficiaries of any trust, or to the interests of other creditors;

(f) has contravened any provision of this Act; or

(g) has failed to comply with a condition of its licence,

he may take any of the actions set forth in subsection (2).

(2) The actions that the Governor may take in pursuance of subsection (1) re:

(a) revocation of the licence;

(b) imposition of new or additional conditions upon the licensee;

(c) the substitution of any director or officer of the licensee;

(d) the appointment, at the expense of the licensee, of a person to advise the licensee on the proper conduct of its affairs and to report to the Inspector thereon within 3 months of such appointment;

(e) the appointment, at the expense of the licensee, of a person to assume control of the licensee's affairs who shall mutatis mutandis have all the powers of a person appointed as a receiver or manager of a business appointed under the Bankruptcy Act; or

(f) the requiring of the taking of such action by the licensee as the Governor thinks fit.

(3) Notwithstanding subsection (1) of section 26, a licensee may within 7 days from the date of a decision taken under subsection (2) apply to the Governor for a reconsideration of his decision if that decision involves the revocation of a licence.

(4) A person appointed under paragraph (d) or (e) of subsection (2) or whose appointment has been extended under paragraph (b) of subsection (5) may at his discretion and in any case within 3 months from the date of his appointment or of the extension of his appointment, as the case may be, prepare and furnish a report to the Governor and the Inspector of the affairs of the licensee and may make recommendations thereon.

(5) The Governor may, on receipt of a report under subsection (4),

(a) revoke the appointment of the person appointed under paragraph (d) or (e) of subsection (2);

(b) extend the period of appointment of the person appointed under paragraph (d) or (e) of subsection (2);

(c) subject to such conditions as the Governor may impose, allow the licensee to reorganize its affairs in such manner as the Governor approves; or

(d) revoke the licence and instruct the Attorney General to apply to the court for an order that the licensee be forthwith wound up by the court; in which case, the provisions of the Companies Act relating to the winding up of a company by the court apply mutatis mutandis for the purpose of giving the necessary effect to this provision.

(6) Whenever the Governor revokes a licence under paragraph (a) of subsection (2) or paragraph (d) of subsection (5) or under subsection (5) of section 16, he shall cause notice of the revocation to be published in the Gazette and may also cause to be published, whether within the Virgin Islands or elsewhere, in such newspaper or other publication as he may think fit in the circumstances.

Attorney General may apply to court

21. The Attorney General may, upon being instructed by the Inspector in any case in which a licensee or a person who has at any time been a licensee is being wound up voluntarily, apply to the court for leave to intervene on behalf of any interested party if he considers that the winding up is not being conducted in the best interests of its depositors, the beneficiaries of any trust, or other creditors, and the court may make such order as it shall consider appropriate.

Power of search

22.(1) If a Judge or Magistrate is satisfied by information on oath, whether oral or written, given by the Inspector or a person authorized by the Inspector that *(a)* there is reasonable ground for suspecting that an offence against this Act has been or is being committed and that evidence of the commission of the offence is to be found at any premises, or in any vehicle, vessel or aircraft specified in the information; or

(b) that any documents, cash, or securities that ought to have been produced under subsection (3) of section 15 and have not been produced are to be found at any premises, vehicle, vessel or aircraft specified in the information,

he may issue a search warrant authorizing the Inspector, together with any other person named in the warrant, to enter the premises specified in the information or, as the case may be, any premises upon which the vehicle, vessel, or aircraft so specified may be, at any time within one month from the date of the warrant, and to search the premises or the vehicle, vessel or aircraft.

(2) The Inspector or any other person authorized by a warrant to search any premises or any vehicle, vessel or aircraft may search every person who is found in or who he has reasonable grounds to believe to have recently left or to be about to enter those premises, or that vehicle, vessel or aircraft, and may seize any document, cash or securities found in the premises or in the vehicle, vessel or aircraft which he has reasonable grounds for believing ought to have been produced under subsection (3) of section 15, except that no female shall, in pursuance of any warrant issued under this section, be searched except by a female.

(3) Where by virtue of this section a person has any power to enter any premises, or a vehicle, vessel or aircraft, he may use such force as is reasonably necessary for the purpose of exercising that power.

PART V - Miscellaneous

Power of Inspector to require insurance

23. The Inspector may require a licensee to effect a policy of insurance with a reputable insurance company against

(a) losses arising out of claims by negligence or breach of duty by the licensee or any employee;

(b) the dishonesty of employees or of the licensee;

(c) loss of documents; and

(d) such other risks as the Inspector may from time to time stipulate, in such amount and of such a nature as the Inspector may determine to be fit and proper, having due regard to the nature and type of business carried on by the licensee; and in the event that the insurance is withdrawn, cancelled or not renewed, the licensee shall immediately notify the Inspector and shall cease to carry on its business until the insurance has been reinstated or replaced.

Preservation of secrecy

24.(1) Except for the purpose of the performance or exercise of his duties or functions under this Act or when lawfully required to do so by the court or under the provisions of any other law, neither the Inspector nor any person acting under his authority shall disclose any information relating to any application under the provisions of this Act, or to the affairs of a licensee or of a company managed by a licensee, which he has acquired in the performance or exercise of such duties or functions.

(2) Subsection (1) does not apply to the disclosure by the Inspector or any person acting under his authority, with the consent of the licensee, to a banking supervisory authority outside the Virgin Islands of general information about the licensee.

(3) Any person who contravenes subsection (1) is guilty of an offence and is liable on summary conviction to a fine not exceeding $2,500 or to imprisonment for a term not exceeding one year or both.

Offences.

25.(1) A licensee or any director or officer of a licensee who knowingly or wilfully supplies false or misleading information to the Governor or the Inspector is guilty of an offence and liable on summary conviction to a fine not exceeding $50,000 or to imprisonment for a term not exceeding 2 years or both.

(2) Any person who operates a banking business or a trust business in contravention of section

16 is guilty of an offence and is liable on summary conviction to a fine not exceeding $10,000 or to a term of imprisonment not exceeding one year or both, and in the case of a continuing offence to a fine not exceeding $1,000 for each day during which the offence continues.

(3) Any licensee who advertises inviting either directly or indirectly other parties to commit breaches of the laws of the country in which the advertisement appears or to which such advertisement is directed is guilty of an offence and is liable on summary conviction to a fine not exceeding $1,000 or to imprisonment for a term not exceeding 6 months or both.

(4) Where a limited liability company is convicted of an offence against subsection (3), every director and every officer concerned with the management of the company is liable to be convicted for that offence unless he satisfies the court that the offence was committed without his knowledge or consent and that he took all reasonable steps to prevent the commission of the offence.

(5) Any person who

(a) fails to comply with a request made of him by the Inspector or by any other person acting under this Act;

(b) assaults or obstructs the Inspector or other person in the performance of his functions under this Act;

(c) uses any insulting language to the Inspector or other person in the performance of his functions under this Act;

(d) by the offer of any gratuity, bribe or any other inducement prevents or attempts to prevent the Inspector or other person from performing his functions under this Act; and

(e) contravenes any provision of this Act for which no punishment is specifically provided,

is guilty of an offence and is liable on summary conviction to a fine not exceeding $1,000 or to imprisonment for a term not exceeding 12 months or both.

Appeals.

26.(1) An appeal lies to the High Court from any decision of the Governor

(a) revoking a licence under subsection (5) of section 16 or under paragraph (a) of subsection (2) or paragraph (d) of subsection (5) of section 20;

(b) withdrawing any approval under subsection (4) of section 16; or

(c) requiring a licensee to take certain steps which the Governor may specify under section 20.

(2) An appeal against the decision of the Governor shall be by motion.

(3) The following procedure applies to appeals from the Governor;

(a) the appellant within 21 days after the day on which the Governor has given his decision shall serve a notice in writing, signed by the appellant or his solicitor, on the Attorney General of his intention to appeal and of the general grounds of his appeal except that any person aggrieved by a decision of the Governor may upon serving notice on the Attorney General apply to the court within 14 days after the day on which the Governor has given his decision for leave to extend the time within which notice of appeal prescribed by this section may be served, and the court upon hearing of the application may extend the time prescribed by this section as it deems fit;

(b) the Attorney General shall, within 21 days of receiving the notice of appeal, obtain a copy of the Governor's decision and transmit to the Registrar without delay a copy thereof together with all papers relating to the appeal, except that the Governor is not compelled to disclose any information if he considers that the public interest would suffer by such disclosure and a certificate given by the Governor under the Public Seal is conclusive that disclosure is not in the public interest;

(c) the Registrar shall set down the appeal for hearing on such day as is convenient, and shall cause notice of the hearing to be published, in such manner, as the court may direct; and

(d) the court may adjourn the hearing of any appeal and may, upon the hearing thereof, confirm, reverse, vary or modify the decision of the Governor or remit the matter with the opinion of the court thereon to the Governor.

(8) An appeal against a decision of the Governor shall not operate as a suspension of the decision of the Governor.

Immunity.

27. No liability attaches to the Governor, the Inspector or any person acting under the authority of the Governor or the Inspector for an act done in good faith in the discharge or purported discharge of his functions under this Act.

Regulations.

28. The Governor may make regulations generally for carrying the purpose and provisions of this Act into effect, and specifically, for the following purposes:

(a) prescribing anything by this Act authorised or required to be prescribed;

(b) controlling the form of advertising by licensees; and

(c) exempting any person or business, or class of person or business from any provision of this Act.

Directions.

29. Without limiting or affecting section 28 the Inspector may, from time to time, issue by publication in the Gazette, directions with relation to such matters as he may think fit and appropriate and failure by any licensee to comply with such directions shall be taken into consideration when any action is proposed to be taken under section 20.

Repeal.

30. The Banking Act, 1972 is repealed.

Commencement.

31. This Act comes into operation on such date as the Governor by proclamation published in the Gazette appoints.

First Schedule

(Section 4(2))

Particulars To Be Specified In Applications

Every company applying for a licence under this Act shall furnish in writing to the Governor the following particulars which shall accompany the application:

(1) Name of applicant.

(2) Address in the Virgin Islands of principal office of applicant and, in the case of a company incorporated in the Virgin Islands, its registered office.

(3) The names and addresses of all directors.

(4) The names and addresses of all shareholders.

(5) The names and addresses of all officers and managers.

(6) Names and addresses of solicitors, if any, to the applicant, together with a letter from the solicitors confirming that they act for the applicant.

(7) Names and addresses of auditors of the applicant, together with a letter from the auditors confirming that they act for the applicant.

(8) Evidence of the proper incorporation of the company in the Virgin Islands or in the country of incorporation, as the case may be.

(9) Evidence in writing that the applicant itself or some person directly or indirectly connected with the applicant is possessed of solid and practical experience in banking business or trust business, as the case may be.

(10) The following:

(a) an undertaking in writing to provide and set apart a fully paid up capital before or at the time it commences business, such as the Governor may in his absolute discretion determine, or by a guarantee under seal of such sum given by a holding or parent or other company approved by the Governor; and

(b) the guarantee referred to in subparagraph (a) shall expressly provide that its formal validity, its essential validity, its interpretation and effect and the rights and obligations of the parties to it are governed exclusively by the law of the Virgin Islands and that the court of the Virgin Islands only shall be the forum for these purposes.

(11) Character references in writing, together with such other evidence as the Governor may require, that neither the applicant nor any director or officer of the applicant has a criminal record either in the Virgin Islands or elsewhere.

(12) Annual accounts of its holding company, if any, for the preceding 3 years and thereafter annually duly audited and certified by an independent auditor.

(13) Names of all subsidiary companies of the applicant with addresses of their registered offices.

(14) A copy of the act, charter, certificate of incorporation or memorandum of association and articles of association, as may be appropriate, verified by an affidavit sworn by a director, secretary and duly authenticated as follows:

(a) in the case of a company incorporated in the Virgin Islands, notarised; and

(b) in the case of a foreign company, certified and authenticated under the public seal of the country, city or place under the laws of which such country has been incorporated.

(15) References, including one from a bank or trust company.

(16) Statement of assets and liabilities at the end of the month prior to the submission of the application certified by a director or senior officer.

(17) Statement of capital of any other company held, directly or through a subsidiary, as an asset of the applicant.

Second Schedule

Part I (Section 4(2))

Fees For The Grant Of A Licence

(1) If a licence is granted on or before the 30th day of June in any year:

(a)	a general banking licence	$10,000
(b)	a restricted Class I banking licence	$ 8,000
(c)	a restricted Class II banking licence	$ 6,000
(d)	a general trust licence	$ 4,000
(e)	a restricted trust licence	$ 100

(2) If a licence is granted on or after the 1st day of July in any year:

(a)	a general banking licence	$ 5,000
(b)	a restricted Class I banking licence	$ 4,000
(c)	a restricted Class II banking licence	$ 3,000
(d)	a general trust licence	$ 2,000
(e)	a restricted trust licence	$ 50

Part II (Section 5)

Fees For The Renewal Of A Licence

(a)	a general banking licence	$10,000
(b)	a restricted Class I banking licence	$ 8,000
(c)	a restricted Class II banking licence	$ 6,000
(d)	a general trust licence	$ 4,000
(e)	a restricted trust licence	$ 100

BRITISH VIRGIN ISLANDS

TRUSTEE ORDINANCE

(as amended)

Important

This is an unofficial consolidation of the Trustee Ordinance and the amendments thereto. whilst every effort has been made to ensure correctness, no responsibility is assumed for any errors which may appear.

Note: Whilst the Interpretation Act (Cap. 136) provides that all statutes will henceforth be called Acts, the recent law revision continued the use of the word "Ordinance" for existing Ordinances and therefore this consolidation refers to "Ordinance" but where amended to "Act".

Harney, Westwood & Riegels

ARRANGEMENT OF SECTIONS

Part I - Preliminary

Part II - Investments

Part III - General Powers Of Trustees And Personal Representatives

General Powers

Indemnities

Maintenance, advancement and protective trusts

Part IV- Appointment And Discharge Of Trustees

Part V - Powers of The Court

Appointment of new trustees

Vesting orders

Payment into Court

Part VI - General Provisions

Part VII - Perpetuities and Accumulations

PART I - Preliminary

Short title

1. This Ordinance may be cited as the Trustee Ordinance.

Interpretation

2.(1) In this Ordinance-

"authorised investments" mean investments authorised by the instrument, if any, creating the trust for the investment of money subject to the trust, or by law;

"contingent right," as applied to land includes a contingent or executory interest, a possibility coupled with an interest, whether the object of the gift or limitation of the interest, or possibility is or is not ascertained, also a right of entry, whether immediate or future, and whether vested or contingent;

"convey" and "conveyance" as applied to any person include the execution by that person of every necessary or suitable assurance (including an assent) for conveying, assigning, appointing, surrendering, or otherwise transferring or disposing of land whereof he is seised or possessed, or wherein he is entitled to a contingent right, either for his whole estate or for any less estate, together with the performance of all formalities required by law for the validity of the conveyance;

"Court" means the High Court or a Judge thereof;

"income" includes rents and profits;

"land" includes land of any tenure, houses and other buildings, mines and minerals, and other corporeal hereditaments; also a rent and other incorporeal hereditaments, and an easement, right, privilege, or benefit in, over, or derived from land, and also an undivided share in land; and in this definition "mines and minerals" include any strata or seam of minerals or substances in or under any land, and powers of working and winning the same; and hereditaments mean real property which under an intestacy devolve on the next of kin;

"mortgage" and "mortgagee" include a charge or chargee by way of mortgage and relate to every estate and interest regarded in equity as merely a security for money, and every person deriving title under the original mortgagee, and also include and relate to an encumbrance under the Title by Registration Act;

"pay" and "payment" as applied in relation to stocks and securities and in connexion with the expression "into court" include the deposit or transfer of the same in or into court;

"personal representative" means the executor or administrator for the time being of a deceased person;

"person resident in the Territory" means a person who ordinarily resides within the Territory or carries on business from an office or other fixed place of business within the Territory but does not include a company incorporated under the International Business Companies Act;

"possession" includes receipt of rents and profits or the right to receive the same, if any; and "possessed" applies to receipt of income of and to any vested estate less than a life interest in possession or in expectancy in any land;

"property" includes real and personal property, and any estate, share and interest in any property, real or personal, and any debt, and any thing in action, and any other right or interest, whether in possession or not;

"rights" include estates and interests;

"sale" includes an exchange;

"securities" include stocks, funds, and shares; and so far as relate to payments into court have the same meaning as in the enactments relating to funds in the Court; and "securities payable to bearer" include securities transferable by delivery or by delivery and endorsement;

"settlor" includes a person who transfers property by way of gift or who makes a testamentary disposition on trust or to a trust;

"stock" includes fully paid up shares, and so far as relates to vesting orders made by the Court under this Ordinance, includes any fund, annuity, or security transferable in books kept by any company or society, or by instrument of transfer either alone or accompanied by other formalities, and any share or interest therein;

"transfer" in relation to stock or securities, includes the performance and execution of every deed, power of attorney, act, and thing on the part of the transferor to effect and complete the title in the transferee;

"trust for sale" in relation to land means an immediate binding trust for sale, whether or not exercisable at the request or with the consent of any person, and with or without power at discretion to postpone the sale;

"trustees for sale" means the persons (including a personal representative) holding land on trust for sale.

(2) For the purposes of this Act the term "trust" refers to the legal relationship created, either inter vivos or on death, by a settlor when assets have been placed under the control of a trustee for the benefit of a beneficiary or for a special purpose.

(3) A trust has the following characteristics:

(a) the assets constitute a separate fund and are not part of the trustee's own estate;

(b) title to the trust assets stands in the name of the trustee or in the name of another person on behalf of the trustee; and

(c) the trustee has the power and the duty in respect of which he is accountable to manage, employ or dispose of the assets in accordance with the terms of the trust and the special duties imposed on him by law.

(4) The reservation by the settlor of certain rights and powers, and the fact that the trustee may himself have rights as a beneficiary, are not necessarily inconsistent with the existence of a trust.

(5) A trust does not include the duties incident to an estate conveyed by way of mortgage but it does extend to

(a) implied trusts;

(b) constructive trusts; and

(c) the duties incident to the office of a personal representative.

PART II - Investments

Authorized investments.

3. Subject to any provision contained in the instrument creating the trust, a trustee may at any time invest any portion of the trust funds in any kind of investment

(*a*) wherever the investment is situate; and

(*b*) whether or not at the time the funds are already in a state of investment; and he may vary the investment or retain it in its original state as long as he exercises the diligence and prudence that a reasonable person would be expected to exercise in making an investment as if it were his own money.

Investment in bearer securities.

4.(1) A trustee may, unless expressly prohibited by the instrument creating the trust, retain or invest in securities payable to bearer, which, if not so payable, would have been an authorized investment, except that securities to bearer retained or taken as an investment by a trustee shall, until sold, be retained in safe custody.

(1A) A direction that investments be retained or made in the name of a trustee shall not, for the purposes of subsection (1), be deemed to be an express prohibition.

(2) A trustee shall not be responsible for any loss incurred by reason of such deposit, and any sum payable in respect of such deposit and collection shall be paid out of the income of the trust property.

Discretion of trustees.

5. Every power conferred by the preceding sections shall be exercised according to the discretion of the trustee, but subject to any consent or direction required by the instrument, if any, creating the trust with respect to the investment of the trust funds.

Power to retain investment which has ceased to be authorised.

6. A trustee shall not be liable for breach of trust by reason only of his continuing to hold an investment which has ceased to be an investment authorised by the trust instrument or by the general law.

Loans and investments by trustees not chargeable as breaches of trust.

7.(1) A trustee lending money on the security of any property on which he can properly lend shall not be chargeable with breach of trust by reason only of the proportion borne by the amount of the loan to the value of the property at the time when the loan was made, if it appears to the Court -

(*a*) that in making the loan the trustee was acting upon a report as to the value of the property made by a person whom he reasonably believed to be an able practical surveyor or valuer instructed and employed independently of any owner of the property, whether such surveyor or valuer carried on business in the locality where the property is situate or elsewhere; and

(b) that the amount of the loan does not exceed two-third parts of the value of the property as stated in the report; and

(c) that the loan was made under the advice of the surveyor or valuer expressed in the report.

(2) A trustee shall not be chargeable with breach of trust only upon the ground that in effecting the purchase, or in lending money upon the security, of any property he has accepted a shorter title than the title which a purchaser is, in the absence of a special contract, entitled to require if in the opinion of the Court the title accepted be such as a person acting with prudence and caution would have accepted.

(3) This section applies to transfers of existing securities as well as to new securities and to investments made before as well as after the commencement of this Ordinance.

Liability for loss by reason of improper investment.

8.(1) Where a trustee improperly advances trust money on a mortgage security which would at the time of the investment be a proper investment in all respects for a smaller sum than is actually advanced thereon, the security shall be deemed an authorised investment for the smaller sum, and the trustee shall only be liable to make good the sum advanced in excess thereof with interest.

(2) This section applies to investments made before as well as after the commencement of this Ordinance.

Powers supplementary of powers of investment.

9.(1) Trustees lending money on the security of any property on which they can lawfully lend may contract that such money shall not be called in during any period not exceeding seven years from the time when the loan was made, provided interest be paid within a specified time not exceeding thirty days after it becomes due, and provided there be no breach of any covenant by the mortgagor contained in the instrument of mortgage or charge for the maintenance and protection of the property.

(2) On a sale of land for an estate in fee simple, trustees may, where the proceeds are liable to be invested, contract that the payment of any part, not exceeding two-thirds, of the purchase money shall be secured by a charge by way of first mortgage of the land sold, with or without the security of any other property, such charge or mortgage, if any buildings are comprised in the mortgage, to contain a covenant by the mortgagor to keep them insured against loss or damage by fire to the full value thereof.

The trustees shall not be bound to obtain any report as to the value of the land or other property to be comprised in such charge or mortgage, or any advice as to the making of the loan, and shall not be liable for any loss which may be incurred by reason only of the security being insufficient at the date of the charge or mortgage.

(3) Where any securities of a company are subject to a trust, the trustees may concur in any scheme or arrangement-

(a) for the reconstruction of the company,

(b) for the sale of all or any part of the property and undertaking of the company to another company,

(c) for the amalgamation of the company with another company, or

(d) for the release , modification, or variation of any rights, privileges or liabilities attached to the securities or any of them, in like manner as if they were entitled to such securities beneficially, with power to accept any securities of any denomination or description of the reconstructed or purchasing or new company in lieu of or in exchange for all or any of the first-mentioned securities; and the trustees shall not be responsible for any loss occasioned by any act or thing so done in good faith, and may retain any securities so accepted as aforesaid for any period for which they could have properly retained the original securities.

(4) If any conditional or preferential right to subscribe for any securities in any company is offered to trustees in respect of any holding in such company, they may as to all or any of such securities, either exercise such right and apply capital money subject to the trust in payment of the consideration, or renounce such right, or assign for the best consideration that can be reasonably obtained the benefit of such right or the title thereto to any person, including any beneficiary under the trust, without being responsible for any loss occasioned by any act or thing so done by them in good faith:

Provided that the consideration for any such assignment shall be held as capital money of the trust.

(5) The powers conferred by this section shall be exercisable subject to the consent of any person whose consent to a change of investment is required by law or by the instrument, if any, creating the trust.

(6) Where the loan referred to in subsection (1), or the sale referred to in subsection (2), is made under the order of the Court, the powers conferred by those subsections respectively shall apply only if and as far as the Court may by order direct.

Power to deposit money at bank and to pay calls.

10.(1) Trustees may, pending the negotiation and preparation of any mortgage or charge, or during any other time while an investment is being sought for, pay any trust money into a bank to a deposit or other account, and all interest, if any, payable in respect thereof shall be applied as income.

(2) Trustees may apply capital money subject to a trust in payment of the calls on any shares subject to the same trust.

PART III - General Powers of Trustees and Personal Representatives

General Powers

Power of trustees for sale to sell by auction or private contract

11.(1) Where a trust for sale or a power of sale of property is vested in a trustee, he may sell or concur with any other person in selling all or any part of the property, either subject to prior charges or not, and either together or in lots, by public auction or by private contract, subject to any such conditions respecting title or evidence of title or other matter as the trustee thinks fit, with power to vary any contract for sale, and to buy in at any auction, or to rescind any contract for sale and to re-sell, without being answerable for any loss.

(2) A trust or power to sell or dispose of land includes a trust or power to sell or dispose of part thereof, whether the division is horizontal, vertical, or made in any other way.

Power to postpone sale.

12.(1) A power to postpone sale shall, in the case of every trust for sale of land, be implied unless a contrary intention appears.

(2) Where there is a power to postpone the sale then (subject to any express direction to the contrary in the instrument, if any, creating the trust for sale) the trustees for sale shall not be liable in any way for postponing the sale, in the exercise of their discretion, for any indefinite period; nor shall a purchaser of a legal estate be concerned in any case with any directions respecting the postponement of a sale.

(3) The foregoing provisions of this section apply whether the trust for sale is created before or after the commencement of this Ordinance.

(4) Where a disposition or settlement coming into operation after the commencement of this Ordinance contains a trust either to retain or sell land the same shall be construed as a trust to sell the land with power to postpone the sale.

Trust for sale of mortgaged property where right of redemption is barred.

13.(1) Where any property, vested in trustees by way of security, becomes, by virtue of any enactment relating to the limitation of actions, or of an order for foreclosure or otherwise, discharged from the right of redemption, it shall be held by them on trust for sale.

(2) The net proceeds of sale, after payment of costs and expenses, shall be applied in like manner as the mortgage debt, if received, would have been applicable, and the income of the property until sale shall be applied in like manner as the interest, if received, would have been applicable; but this subsection operates without: prejudice to any rule of law relating to the apportionment of capital and income between tenant for life and remainderman.

(3) This section does not affect the right of any person to require that, instead of a sale, the property shall be conveyed to him or in accordance with his directions.

Power to sell subject to depreciatory conditions

14.(1) No sale made by a trustee shall be impeached by any beneficiary upon the ground that any of the conditions subject to which the sale was made may have been unnecessarily depreciatory, unless it also appears that the consideration for the sale was thereby rendered inadequate.

(2) No sale made by a trustee shall, after the execution of the conveyance, be impeached as against the purchaser upon the ground that any of the conditions subject to which the sale was made may have been unnecessarily depreciatory, unless it appears that the purchaser was acting in collusion with the trustee at the time when the contract for sale was made.

(3) No purchaser, upon any sale made by a trustee, shall be at liberty to make any objection against the title upon any of the grounds aforesaid.

(4) This section applies to sales made before or after the commencement of this Ordinance.

Power of trustees to give receipts

15.(1) The receipt in writing of a trustee for any money, securities, or other personal property or effects payable, transferable, or deliverable to him under any trust or power shall be a sufficient discharge to the person paying, transferring, or delivering the same and shall effectually exonerate him from seeing to the application or being answerable for any loss or misapplication thereof.

(2) This section applies notwithstanding anything to the contrary in the instrument, if any, creating the trust.

Power to compound liabilities

16. A personal representative, or two or more trustees acting together. may, if and as he or they think fit -

(a) accept any property, real or personal, before the time at which it is made transferable or payable; or

(b) sever and apportion any blended trust funds or property; or

(c) pay or allow any debt or claim on any evidence that he or they think sufficient; or

(d) accept any composition or any security, real or personal, for any debt or for any property, real or personal, claimed; or

(e) allow any time of payment of any debt; or

(f) compromise, compound, abandon, submit to arbitration, or otherwise settle any debt, account, claim, or thing whatever relating to the testator's or intestate's estate or to the trust;

and for any of those purposes may enter into, give, execute, and do such agreements, instruments of composition or arrangement, releases, and other things as to him or them seem expedient, without being responsible for any loss occasioned by any act or thing so done by him or them in good faith.

Power to raise money by sale, mortgage, or otherwise

17.(1) Where trustees are authorised by the instrument, if any, creating the trust or by law to pay or apply capital money subject to the trust for any purpose or in any manner, they shall have and shall be deemed always to have had power to raise the money required by sale, conversion, calling in, or mortgage of all or any part of the trust property for the time being in possession.

(2) This section applies notwithstanding anything to the contrary contained in the instrument, if any, creating the trust.

Protection to purchasers and mortgagees dealing with trustees

18. No purchaser or mortgagee, paying or advancing money on a sale or mortgage purporting to be made under any trust or power vested in trustees, shall be concerned to see that such money is wanted, or that no more than is wanted is raised, or otherwise as to the application thereof.

Devolution of powers or trusts

19.(1) Where a power or trust is given to or imposed on two or more trustees jointly, the same may be exercised or performed by the survivors or survivor of them for the time being.

(2) Until the appointment of new trustees, the personal representatives or representative for the time being of a sole trustee, or, where there were two or more trustees, of the last surviving or continuing trustee, shall be capable of exercising or performing any power or trust which was given to, or capable of being exercised by, the sole or last surviving or continuing trustee, or other the trustees or trustee for the time being of the trust.

(3) In this section "personal representative" does not include an executor who has renounced or has not proved.

Power to insure

20.(1) A trustee may insure against loss or damage by fire any buildings or other insurable property to any amount, including the amount of any insurance already on foot, not exceeding the value of the building or property, and pay the premiums for such insurance out of the income thereof or out of the income of any other property subject to the same trusts without obtaining the consent of any person who may be entitled wholly or partly to such income.

(2) This section does not apply to any building or property which a trustee is bound forthwith to convey absolutely to any beneficiary upon being requested to do so.

Application of insurance money where policy kept up under any trust, power or obligation

21.(1) Money receivable by trustees or any beneficiary under a policy of insurance against the loss or damage of any property subject to a trust or to a settlement whether by fire or otherwise, shall, where the policy has been kept up under any trust in that behalf or under any power statutory or otherwise, or in performance of any covenant or of any obligation statutory or otherwise, or by a tenant for life impeachable for waste, be capital money for the purposes of the trust or settlement, as the case may be.

(2) If any such money is receivable by any person, other than the trustees of the trust or settlement, that person shall use his best endeavours to recover and receive the money and shall pay the net residue thereof, after discharging any costs of recovering and receiving in, to the trustees of the trust or settlement, or, if there are not trustees capable of giving a discharge therefor, into Court.

(3) Any such money-

(a) if it was receivable in respect of property held upon trust for sale, shall be held upon the trusts and subject to the powers and provisions applicable to money arising by a sale under such trust;

(b) in any other case, shall be held upon trusts corresponding as nearly as may be with the trusts affecting the property in respect of which it was payable.

(4) Such money, or any part thereof, may also be applied by the trustees, or, if in Court, under the direction of the Court, in rebuilding, reinstating, replacing, or repairing the property lost or damaged, but any such application by the trustees shall be subject to the consent of any person whose consent is required by the instrument, if any, creating the trust to the investment of money subject to the trust.

(5) Nothing contained in this section shall prejudice or affect the right of any person to require any such money or any part thereof to be applied in rebuilding, reinstating, or repairing the property lost or damaged, or the rights of any mortgagee, lessor, or lessee, whether under any law or otherwise.

(6) This section applies to policies effected either before or after the commencement of this Ordinance, but only to money received after such commencement.

Deposit of documents for safe custody

22. Trustees may deposit any documents held by them relating to the trust, or to trust property, with any banker or banking company or any other company whose business includes the undertaking of the safe custody of documents, and any sum payable in respect of such deposit shall be paid out of the income of the trust property.

Reversionary interests, valuations, and audit

23.(1) Where trust property includes any share or interest in property not vested in the trustees, or the proceeds of the sale of any such property, or any other thing in action, the trustees on the same falling into possession or becoming payable or transferable may-

(a) agree or ascertain the value thereof or any part thereof in such manner as they may think fit;

(b) accept in or towards satisfaction thereof, at the market or current value, or upon any valuation or estimate or value which they may think fit, any authorised investments;

(c) allow any deductions for duties, costs, charges and expenses which they think proper or reasonable;

(d) execute any release in respect of the premises so as effectually to discharge all accountable parties from all liability in respect of any matters coming within the scope of such release, without being responsible in any such case for any loss occasioned by any act or thing so done by them in good faith

.

(2) The trustees shall not be under any obligation and shall not be chargeable with any breach of trust by reason of any omission-

(a) to place any distringas notice or apply for any stop or other like order upon any securities or other property out of or in which such share or interest or other thing in action as aforesaid is derived, payable or charged; or

(b) to take any proceedings on account of any act, default, or neglect on the part of the persons in whom such securities or other property or any of them or any part thereof are for the time being, or had at any time been, vested, unless and until required in writing so to do by some person, or the guardian of some person, beneficially interested under the trust, and unless also due provision is made to their satisfaction for payment of the costs of any proceedings required to be taken:

Provided that nothing in this subsection shall relieve the trustees of the obligation to get in and obtain payment or transfer of such share or interest or other thing in action on the same falling into possession.

(3) Trustees may, for the purpose of giving effect to the trust, or any of the provisions of the instrument, if any, creating the trust or of any law, from time to time (by duly qualified agents) ascertain and fix the value of any trust property in such manner as they think proper, and any valuation so made in good faith shall be binding upon all persons interested under the trust.

(4) Trustees may, in their absolute discretion, from time to time, but not more than once in every three years unless the nature of the trust or any special dealings with the trust property make a more frequent exercise of the right reasonable, cause the accounts of the trust property to be examined or audited by an independent accountant, and shall, for that purpose, produce such vouchers and give such information to him as he may require; and the costs of such examination or audit including the fee of the auditor, shall be paid out of the capital or income of the trust property, or partly in one way and partly in the other, as the trustees, in their absolute discretion, think fit, but, in default of any direction by the trustees to the contrary in any special case, costs, attributable to capital shall be borne by capital and those attributable to income by income.

Powers to employ agents

24.(1) Trustees or personal representatives may, instead of acting personally, employ and pay an agent, whether a solicitor, banker, stockbroker, or other person, to transact any business or do any act required to be transacted or done in the execution of the trust, or the administration of the testator's or intestate's estate, including the receipt and payment of money, and shall be entitled to be allowed and paid all charges and expenses so incurred, and shall not be responsible for the default of any such agent if employed in good faith.

(2) Trustees or personal representatives may appoint any person to act as their agent or attorney for the purpose of selling, converting, collecting, getting in, and executing and perfecting assurances of, or managing or cultivating, or otherwise administering, any property subject to the trust or forming part of the testator's or intestate's estate in any place outside the Territory, or executing or exercising any discretion or trust or power vested in them in relation to any such property, with such ancillary powers, and with and subject to such provisions and restrictions as they may think fit, including a power to appoint substitutes, and shall not, by reason only of their having made such appointment, be responsible for any loss arising thereby.

(3) Without prejudice to such general power of appointing agents as aforesaid-

(a) a trustee may appoint a solicitor to be his agent to receive and give a discharge for any money or valuable consideration or property receivable by the trustee under the trust, by permitting the solicitor to have the custody of, and to produce a deed having in the body thereof or endorsed thereon a receipt for such money or valuable consideration or property, the deed being executed, or the endorsed receipt being signed, by the person entitled to give a receipt for that consideration;

(b) a trustee shall not be chargeable with breach of trust by reason only of his having made or concurred in making any such appointment; and the production of any such deed by the solicitor shall have the same statutory validity and effect as if the person appointing the solicitor had not been a trustee;

(*c*) a trustee may appoint a banker or solicitor to be his agent to receive and give a discharge for any money payable to the trustee under or by virtue of a policy of insurance, by permitting the banker or solicitor to have the custody of and to produce the policy of insurance with a receipt signed by the trustee, and a trustee shall not be chargeable with a breach of trust by reason only of his having made or concurred in making such appointment:

Provided that nothing in this subsection shall exempt a trustee from any liability which he would have incurred if this Ordinance had not been passed, in case he permits any such money, valuable consideration, or property to remain in the hands or under the control of the banker or solicitor for a period longer than is reasonably necessary to enable the banker or solicitor, as the case may be, to pay or transfer the same to the trustee.

This subsection applies whether the money or valuable consideration or property was or is received before or after the commencement of this Ordinance.

Power to concur with others

25. Where an undivided share in the proceeds of sale of land directed to be sold, or in any other property, is subject to a trust, or forms part of the estate of a testator or intestate, the trustees or personal representative may (without prejudice to the trust for sale affecting the entirety of the land and the powers of the trustees for sale in reference thereto) execute or exercise any trust or power vested in them in relation to such share in conjunction with the persons entitled to or having power in that behalf over the other share or shares, and notwithstanding that any one or more of the trustees or personal representatives may be entitled to or interested in any such other share, either in his or their own right or in a fiduciary capacity.

Power to delegate trusts during absence abroad

26.(1) A trustee may, notwithstanding any rule of law or equity to the contrary, by power of attorney delegate to any person the execution or exercise of all or any trusts, powers and discretions vested in him as such trustee, either alone or jointly with any other person.

(2) The donor of a power of attorney given under this section shall be liable for the acts or defaults of the donee in the same manner as if they were the acts or defaults of the donor.

(4) In favour of any person dealing with the donee, any act done or instrument executed by the donee shall, notwithstanding that the power has never come into operation or has become revoked by the act of the donor or by his death or otherwise, be as valid and effectual as if the donor were alive and of full capacity, and had himself done such act or executed such instrument, unless such person had actual notice that the power had never come into operation or of the revocation of the power before such act was done or instrument executed.

(5) For the purpose of executing or exercising the trusts or powers delegated to him, the donee may exercise any of the powers conferred on the donor as trustee by law or by the instrument creating the trust, including power, for the purpose of the transfer of any inscribed stock, himself to delegate to an attorney power of transfer but not including the power to delegation conferred by this section.

(6) The fact that it appears from any power of attorney given under this section that in dealing with any stock the donee of the power is acting in the execution of a trust shall not be deemed for any purpose to affect any person in whose books the stock is inscribed or registered with any notice of the trust.

Indemnities.

Protection against liability in respect of rents and covenants

27.(1) Where a personal representative or trustee liable as such for-

(a) any rent, covenant, or agreement reserved by or contained in any lease; or

(b) any rent, covenant or agreement payable under or contained in any grant made in consideration or a rent-charge; or

(c) any indemnity given in respect of any rent, covenant or agreement referred to in either of the foregoing paragraphs,

satisfies all liabilities under the lease or grant which may have accrued, or been claimed, up to the date of the conveyance hereinafter mentioned, and, where necessary, sets apart a sufficient fund to answer any future claim that may be made in respect of any fixed and ascertained sum which the lessee or grantee agreed to lay out on the property demised or granted, although the period for laying out the same may not have arrived, then and in any such case the personal representative or trustee may convey the property demised or granted to a purchaser, legatee, devisee, or other person entitled to call for a conveyance thereof, and thereafter-

(i) he may distribute the residuary real and personal estate of the deceased testator or intestate, or, as the case may be, the trust estate (other than the fund, if any, set apart as aforesaid) to or amongst the persons entitled thereto, without appropriating any part, or any further part, as the case may be, of the estate of the deceased or of the trust estate to meet any future liability under the said lease or grant;

(ii) notwithstanding such distribution, he shall not be personally liable in respect of any subsequent claim under the said lease or grant.

(2) This section operates without prejudice to the right, of the lessor or grantor, or the persons deriving title under the lessor or grantor, to follow the assets of the deceased or the trust property into the hands of the persons amongst whom the same may have been respectively distributed, and applies notwithstanding anything to the contrary in the will or other instrument, if any, creating the trust.

(3) In this section "lease" includes an underlease and an agreement for a lease or underlease and any instrument giving any such indemnity as aforesaid or varying the liabilities under the lease; "grant" applies to a grant whether the rent is created by limitation, grant, reservation, or otherwise, and includes an agreement for a grant and any instrument giving any such indemnity as aforesaid or varying the liabilities under the grant; "lessee" and "grantee" include persons respectively deriving title under them.

Protection by means of advertisement

28.(1) With a view to the conveyance to or distribution among the persons entitled to any real or personal property, the trustees of a settlement or of a disposition on trust for sale, or personal representatives, may give notice by advertisement in the Gazette, and in a local newspaper, and such other like notices, including notices elsewhere than in the Territory, as would, in any special case, have been directed by the Court in an action for administration, of their intention to make such conveyance or distribution as aforesaid, and requiring any person interested to send to the trustees or personal representatives within the time, not being less than twenty-eight days, fixed in the notice, or, where more than one notice is given, in the last of the notices, particulars of his claim in respect of the property or any part thereof to which the notice relates.

(2) At the expiration of the time fixed by the notice the trustees or personal representatives may convey or distribute the property or any part thereof to which the notice relates, to or among the persons entitled thereto, having regard only to the claims, whether formal or not, of which the trustees or personal representatives then had notice and shall not, as respects the property so conveyed or distributed, be liable to any person of whose claim the trustees or personal representatives have not had notice at the time of conveyance or distribution; but nothing in this section prejudices the right of any person to follow the property, or any property representing the same, into the hands of any person who may have received it.

(3) This section applies notwithstanding anything to the contrary in the will or other instrument, if any, creating the trust.

Protection in regard to notice

29. A trustee or personal representative acting for the purposes of more than one trust or estate shall not, in the absence of fraud, be affected by notice of any instrument, matter, fact or thing in relation to any particular trust, or estate if he has obtained notice thereof merely by reason of his acting or having acted for the purposes of another trust or estate.

Exoneration of trustees in respect of certain powers of attorney

30. A trustee acting or paying money in good faith under or in pursuance of any power of attorney shall not be liable for any such act or payment by reason of the fact that at the time of the act or payment the person who gave the power of attorney was subject to any disability, or bankrupt, or dead, or had done or suffered some act or thing to avoid the power, if this fact was not known to the trustee at the time of his so acting or paying:

Provided that-

(a) nothing in this section shall affect the right of any person entitled to the money against the person to whom the payment is made;

(b) the person so entitled shall have the same remedy against the person to whom the payment is made as he would have had against the trustee.

Implied indemnity of trustees

31.(1) A trustee shall be chargeable only for money and securities actually received by him notwithstanding his signing any receipt for the sake of conformity, and shall be answerable and accountable only for his own acts, receipts, neglects, or defaults, and not for those of any other trustee, nor for any banker, broker, or other person with whom any trust money or securities may be deposited, nor for any other loss, unless the same happens through his own wilful default.

(2) A trustee may reimburse himself or pay or discharge out of the trust premises all expenses incurred in or about the execution of the trusts or powers.

Maintenance, advancement and protective trusts

Power to apply income for maintenance and to accumulate surplus income during a minority

32.(1) Where any property is held by trustees in trust for any person for any interest whatsoever, whether vested or contingent, then, subject to any prior interests or charges affecting that property -

(a) during the infancy of any such person, if his interest so long continues, the trustees may, at their sole discretion, pay to his parent or guardian, if any, or otherwise apply for or towards his maintenance, education, or benefit, the whole or such part, if any, of the income of that property as may, in all the circumstances, be reasonable, whether or not there is-

(i) any other fund applicable to the same purpose, or

(ii) any person bound by law to provide for his maintenance or education; and

(b) if such person on attaining the age of twenty-one years has not a vested interest in such income, the trustees shall thenceforth pay the income of that property and of any accretion thereto under subsection (2) to him, until he either attains a vested interest therein or dies, or until failure of his interest:

Provided that in deciding whether the whole or any part of the income of the property is during a minority to be paid or applied for the purposes aforesaid, the trustees shall have regard to the age of the infant and his requirements and generally to the circumstances of the case, and in particular to what other income, if any, is applicable for the same purposes; and where trustees have notice that the income of more than one fund is applicable for this purpose, then so far as practicable, unless the entire income of the funds is paid or applied as aforesaid or the Court otherwise directs, a proportionate part only of the income of each fund shall be so paid or applied.

(2) During the infancy of any such person, if his interest so long continues, the trustees shall accumulate all the residue of that income in the way of compound interest by investing the same and the resulting income thereof from time to time in authorised investments, and shall hold those accumulations as follows-

(a) if any such person-

(i) attains the age of twenty-one years, or marries under that age, and his interest in such income during his infancy or until his marriage is a vested interest, or

(ii) on attaining the age of twenty-one years or on marriage under that age becomes entitled to the property from which such income arose in fee simple, absolute or determinablc, or absolutely, or for an entailed interest,

the trustees shall hold the accumulations in trust for such person absolutely, and so that the receipt of such person after marriage, and though still an infant, shall be a good discharge; and

(b) in any other case the trustees shall, notwithstanding that such person had a vested interest in such income, hold the accumulations as an accretion to the capital of the property from which such accumulations arose, and as one fund with such capital for all purposes, and so that, if such property is settled land, such accumulations shall be held upon the same trusts as if the same were capital money arising therefrom;

but the trustees may, at any time during the infancy of such person, if his interest so long continues, apply those accumulations, or any part thereof, as if they were income arising in the then current year.

(3) This section applies in the case of a contingent interest only if the limitation or trust carries the intermediate income of the property, but it applies to a future or contingent legacy by the parent of, or a person standing in loco parentis to, the legatee, if and for such period as, under the general law, the legacy carries interest for the maintenance of the legatee, and in any such case as last aforesaid the rate of interest shall (if the income available is sufficient, and subject to any rules of court to the contrary) be five per cent per annum.

(4) This section applies to a vested annuity in like manner as if the annuity were the income of property held by trustees in trust to pay the income thereof to the annuitant for the same period for which the annuity is payable, save that in any case accumulations made during the infancy of the annuitant shall be held in trust for the annuitant or his personal representatives absolutely.

Power of advancement

33.(1) Trustees may at any time or times pay or apply any capital money subject to a trust, for the advancement or benefit in such manner as they may, in their absolute discretion, think fit, of any person entitled to the capital of the trust property or of any share thereof, whether absolutely or contingently on his attaining any specified age or on the occurrence of any other event, or subject to a gift over on his death under any specified age or on the occurrence of any other event, and whether in possession or in remainder or reversion, and such payment or application may be made notwithstanding that the interest of such person is liable to be defeated by the exercise of a power of appointment or revocation, or to be diminished by the increase of the class to which he belongs:

Provided that-

(a) the money so paid or applied for the advancement or benefit of any person shall not exceed altogether in amount one-half of the presumptive or vested share or interest of that person in the trust property; and

(b) if that person is or becomes absolutely and indefensibly entitled to a share in the trust property the money so paid or applied shall be brought into account as part of such share; and

(c) no such payment or application shall be made so as to prejudice any person entitled to any prior life or other interest whether vested or contingent, in the money paid or applied unless such person is in existence and of full age and consents in writing to such payment or application.

(2) This section applies only where the trust property consists of money or securities or of property held upon trust for sale, calling in and conversion, and such money or securities, or the proceeds of such sale, calling in and conversion are not by law or in equity considered as land.

Protective trusts

34.(1) Where any income, including an annuity or other periodical income payment, is directed to be held on protective trusts for the benefit of any person (in this section called "the principal beneficiary") for the period of his life or for any less period, then, during that period (in this section called the "trust period") the said income shall, without prejudice to any prior interest, be held on the following trusts, namely-

(a) upon trust for the principal beneficiary during the trust period or until he, whether before or after the termination of any prior interest, does or attempts to do or suffers any act or thing, or until any event happens, other than an advance under any statutory or express power, whereby, if the said income were payable during the trust period to the principal beneficiary absolutely during that period, he would be deprived of the right to receive the same or any part thereof, in any of which cases, as well as on the termination of the

trust period, whichever first happens, this trust of the said income shall fail or determine;

(b) if the trust aforesaid fails or determines during the subsistence of the trust period, then, during the residue of that period, the said income shall be held upon trust for the application thereof for the maintenance or support, or otherwise for the benefit, of all or any one or more exclusively of the other or others of the following persons (that is to say)-

(i) the principal beneficiary and his or her wife or husband, if any, and his or her children or more remote issue, if any, or

(ii) if there is no wife or husband or issue of the principal beneficiary in existence, the principal beneficiary and the persons who would, if he were actually dead, be entitled to the trust property or the income thereof or to the annuity fund, if any, or arrears of the annuity, as the case may be,

as the trustees in their absolute discretion, without being liable to account for the exercise of such discretion, think fit.

(2) This section does not apply to trusts coming into operation before the commencement of this Ordinance, and has effect subject to any variation of the implied trusts aforesaid contained in the instrument creating the trust.

(3) Nothing in this section operates to validate any trusts which would, if contained in the instrument creating the trust, be liable to be set aside.

PART IV - Appointment and Discharge of Trustees

Limitation of the number of trustees

35.(1) Where, at the commencement of this Ordinance, there are more than four trustees of a settlement of land, or more than four trustees holding land on trust for sale, no new trustees shall (except where as a result of the appointment the number is reduced to four or less) be capable of being appointed until the number is reduced to less than four, and thereafter the number shall not be increased beyond four.

(2) In the case of settlements and dispositions on trust for sale of land made or coming into operation after the commencement of this Ordinance-

(a) the number of trustees thereof shall not in any, case exceed four, and where more than four persons are named as such trustees, the four first named (who are able and willing to act) shall alone be the trustees, and the other persons named shall not be trustees unless appointed on the occurrence of a vacancy;
(b) the number of the trustees shall not be increased beyond four.

(3) This section only applies to settlements and dispositions of land, and the restrictions imposed on the number of trustees do not apply -

(a) in the case of land vested in trustees for charitable, ecclesiastical, or public purposes; or

(b) where the net proceeds of the sale of the land are held for like purposes.

Power of appointing new or additional trustees

36.(1) Where a trustee, either original or substituted, and whether appointed by the Court or otherwise is dead, or remains out of the Territory for more than twelve months, or desires to be discharged from all or any of the trusts or powers reposed in or conferred on him, or refuses or is unfit to act therein, or is incapable of acting therein, or is an infant, then, subject to the restrictions imposed by this Ordinance on the number of trustees-

(a) the person or persons nominated for the purpose of appointing new trustees by the instrument, if any, creating the trust, or

(b) if there is no such person, or no such person able and willing to act, then the surviving or continuing trustee or trustees for the time being, or the personal representatives of the last surviving or continuing trustee, may, by deed, appoint one or more other persons (whether or not being the persons exercising the power) to be a trustee or trustees in the place of the trustee so deceased, remaining out of the Territory, desiring to be discharged, refusing, or being unfit or being incapable, or being an infant, as aforesaid.

(2) Where a trustee has been removed under a power contained in the instrument creating the trust, a new trustee, or new trustees, may be appointed in the place of the trustee who is removed, as if he were dead, or, in the case of a corporation, as if the corporation desired to be discharged from the trust, and the provisions of this section shall apply accordingly, but subject to the restrictions imposed by this Ordinance on the number of trustees.

(3) Where a corporation being a trustee is or has been dissolved, either before or after the commencement of this Ordinance, then, for the purposes of this section, the corporation shall be deemed to be and to have been from the date of the dissolution incapable of acting in the trusts or powers reposed in or conferred on the corporation.

(4) The power of appointment given by subsection (1) or any similar previous enactment to the personal representatives of a last surviving or continuing trustee shall be and shall be deemed always to have been exercisable by the executors for the time being (whether original or by representation) of such surviving or continuing trustee, who have proved the will of their testator or by the administrators for the time being of such trustee without the concurrence of any executor who has renounced or has not proved.

(5) Where a sole trustee is or has been originally appointed to act in a trust, or where, in the case of any trust, there are not more than three trustees either original or substituted and whether appointed by the Court or otherwise, then and in such case-

(a) the person or persons nominated for the purpose of appointing new trustees by the instrument, if any, creating the trust, or

(b) if there is no such person, or no such person able and willing to act, then the trustee or trustees for the time being, ay, by deed, appoint another person or other persons to be an additional trustee or additional trustees, but it shall not be obligatory to appoint any additional trustee, unless the instrument, if any, creating the trust provides to the contrary, nor shall the number of trustees be increased beyond four by virtue of any such appointment.

(6) Every new trustee appointed under this section as well before as after all the trust property becomes by law, or by assurance, or otherwise, vested in him, shall have the same powers, authorities, and discretions, and may in all respects act as if he had been originally appointed a trustee by the instrument, if any, creating the trust.

(7) The provisions of this section relating to a trustee who is dead include the case of a person nominated trustee in a will but dying before the testator, and those relative to a continuing trustee include a refusing or retiring trustee, if willing to act in the execution of the provisions of this section.

(8) Where a person of unsound mind, being a trustee, is also entitled in possession to some beneficial interest in the trust property, no appointment of a new trustee in his place shall be made by the continuing trustees or trustee, under this section, unless leave has been given by the Court to make the appointment.

Power to appoint trustees of property belonging to infants or to persons out of the Territory

37.(1) Where an infant or a person out of the Territory is absolutely entitled under the will or on the intestacy of a person dying before or after the commencement of this Ordinance (in this subsection called "the deceased") to a devise or legacy, or to the residue of the estate of the deceased, or any share therein, and such devise, legacy, residue or share is not under the will, if any, of the deceased, devised or bequeathed to trustees for the infant or the person out of the Territory, the personal representatives of the deceased may by writing appoint two or more persons not exceeding four (whether or not including the personal representatives or one or more of the personal representatives), to be the trustee or trustees of such devise, legacy, residue or share for the infant or the person out of the Territory, and may execute or do any assurance or thing requisite for vesting such devise, legacy, residue or share in the trustee or trustees so appointed.

On such appointment the personal representatives, as such, shall be discharged from all further liability in respect of such devise, legacy, residue or share, and the same may be retained in its existing condition or state of investment, or may be converted into money, and such money may be invested in any investment authorised by this Ordinance.

(2) Where a personal representative has before the commencement of this Ordinance retained or sold any such devise, legacy, residue or share, and invested the same or the proceeds thereof in any investments in which he was authorised to invest money subject to the trust, then, subject to any order of the Court made before such commencement, he shall not be deemed to have incurred any liability on that account, or by reason of not having paid or transferred the money or property into Court.

Supplemental provisions as to appointment of trustees

38. On the appointment of a trustee for the whole or any part of trust property-

(a) the number of trustees may, subject to the restrictions imposed by this Ordinance on the number of trustees, be increased; and

(b) a separate set of trustees, not exceeding four, may be appointed for any part of the trust property held on trusts distinct from those relating to any other part or parts of the trust property, notwithstanding that no new trustees or trustee are or is to be appointed for other parts of the trust property, and any existing trustee may be appointed or remain one of such separate set of trustees or, if only one trustee was originally appointed, then save as hereinafter provided, one separate trustee may be so appointed; and

(c) it shall not be obligatory to appoint more than one new trustee where only one trustee was originally appointed, or to fill up the original number of trustees where more than two trustees were originally appointed; and

(d) any assurance or thing requisite for vesting the trust property, or any part

thereof, in a sole trustee, or jointly in the persons who are the trustees, shall be executed or done.

Evidence as to a vacancy in a trust

39.(1) A statement, contained in any instrument coming into operation after the commencement of this Ordinance by which a new trustee is appointed for any purpose connected with land, to the effect that a trustee has remained out of the Territory for more than twelve months or refuses or is unfit to act, or is incapable of acting, or that he is not entitled to a beneficial interest in the trust property in possession, shall, in favour of a purchaser of a legal estate, be conclusive evidence of the matter stated.

(2) In favour of such purchaser any appointment of a new trustee depending on that statement, and any vesting declaration, express or implied, consequent on the appointment, shall be valid.

Retirement of trustee without a new appointment

40.(1) Where a trustee is desirous of being discharged from the trust then, if such trustee as aforesaid by deed declares that he is desirous of being discharged from the trust, and if his co-trustees and such other person, if any, as is empowered to appoint trustees, by deed consent to the discharge of the trustee, and to the vesting in the co-trustees alone of the trust property, the trustee desirous of being discharged shall be deemed to have retired from the trust, and shall, by the deed, be discharged therefrom under this Ordinance, without any new trustee being appointed in his place.

(2) Any assurance or thing requisite for vesting the trust property in the continuing trustees alone shall be executed or done.

Vesting of trust property in new or continuing trustees

41.(1) Where by a deed a new trustee is appointed to perform any trust, then-

(a) if the deed contains a declaration by the appointer to the effect that any estate or interest in any land subject to the trust, or in any chattel so subject, or the right to recover or receive any debt or other thing in action so subject, shall vest in the persons who by virtue of the deed become or are the trustees for performing the trust, the deed shall operate, without any conveyance or assignment, to vest in those persons as joint tenants and for the purposes of the trust the estate, interest or right to which the declaration relates; and

(b) if the deed is made after the commencement of this Ordinance and does not contain such a declaration, the deed shall, subject to any express provisions to the contrary therein contained, operate as if it had contained such a declaration by the appointer extending to all the estates, interests and rights with respect to which a declaration could have been made.

(2) Where by a deed a retiring trustee is discharged under the statutory power without a new trustee being appointed, then-

(a) if the deed contains such a declaration as aforesaid by the retiring and continuing trustees, and by the other person, if any, empowered to appoint trustees, the deed shall, without any conveyance or assignment, operate to vest in the continuing trustees alone, as joint tenants, and for the purposes of the trust, the estate, interest or right to which the declaration relates; and

(b) if the deed is made after the commencement of this Ordinance and does not contain such a declaration, the deed shall, subject to any express provision to the contrary therein contained, operate as if it had contained such a declaration by such persons as aforesaid extending to all the estates, interest and rights with respect to which a declaration could have been made.

(3) An express vesting declaration whether made before or after the commencement of this Ordinance, shall, notwithstanding that the estate, interest and right to be vested is not expressly referred to, and provided that the other statutory requirements were or are complied with, operate and be deemed always to have operated (but without prejudice to any express provisions to the contrary contained in the deed of appointment or discharge) to vest in the persons respectively referred to in subsections (1) and (2), as the case may require, such estates, interest and rights as are capable of being and ought to be vested in those persons.

(4) This section does not extend-

(a) to land conveyed by way of mortgage for securing money subject to the trust, except land conveyed on trust for securing debentures or debenture stock;

(b) to land held under a lease which contains any covenant, condition or agreement against assignment or disposing of the land without licence or consent, unless, prior to the execution of the deed containing expressly or impliedly the vesting declaration, the requisite licence or consent has been obtained, or unless, by virtue of any law, the vesting declaration, express or implied, would not operate as a breach of covenant or give rise to a forfeiture;

(c) to any share, stock, annuity or property which is only transferable in books kept by a company or other body, or in manner directed by or under an Act.

In this subsection "lease" includes an underlease and an agreement for a lease or underlease

PART V - Powers of The Court

Appointment of new trustees.

Power of Court to appoint new trustees

42.(1) The Court may, whenever it is expedient to appoint a new trustee or new trustees, and it is found inexpedient, difficult or impracticable so to do without the assistance of the Court, make an order appointing a new trustee or new trustees either in substitution for or in addition to any existing trustee or trustees, or although there is no existing trustee.

In particular and without prejudice to the generality of the foregoing provision, the Court may make an order appointing a new trustee in substitution for a trustee who is convicted of a felony, or is a person of unsound mind, or is a bankrupt, or is a corporation which is in liquidation or has been dissolved.

(2) An order under this section, and any consequential vesting order or conveyance, shall not operate further or otherwise as a discharge to any former or continuing trustee than an appointment of new trustees under any power for that purpose contained in any instrument would have operated.

(3) Nothing in this section gives power to appoint an executor or administrator.

Power to authorise remuneration

43. Where the Court appoints a corporation to be a trustee either solely or jointly with another person, the Court may authorise the corporation to charge such remuneration for its services as trustee as the Court may think fit.

Powers of new trustee appointed by the Court

44. Every trustee appointed by the Court shall, as well as before as after the trust property becomes by law, or by assurance, or otherwise, vested in him, have the same powers, authorities, and discretions, and may in all respects act as if he had been originally appointed a trustee by the instrument, if any, creating the trust.

Vesting orders

Vesting orders of land

45. In any of the following cases namely-

(a) where the Court appoints or has appointed a trustee, or where a trustee has been appointed out of court under any statutory or express power;

(b) where a trustee entitled to or possessed of any land or interest therein, whether by way of mortgage or otherwise, or entitled to a contingent right therein, either solely or jointly with any other person-

(i) is under disability, or

(ii) is out of the jurisdiction of the Court, or

(iii) cannot be found, or being a corporation, has been dissolved;

(c) where it is uncertain who was the survivor of two or more trustees jointly entitled to or possessed of any interest in land;

(d) where it is uncertain whether the last trustee known to have been entitled to or possessed of any interest in land is living or dead;

(e) where there is no personal representative of a deceased trustee who was entitled to or possessed of any interest in land, or where it is uncertain who is the personal representative of a deceased trustee who was entitled to or possessed of any interest in land;

(f) where a trustee jointly or solely entitled to or possessed of any interest in land, or entitled to a contingent right therein, has been required, by or on behalf of a person entitled to require a conveyance of the land or interest or a release of the right, and has wilfully refused or neglected to convey the land or interest or release the right for twenty-eight days after the date of the requirement;

(g) where land or any interest therein is vested in a trustee whether by way of mortgage or otherwise, and it appears to the Court to be expedient, the Court may make an order (in this Ordinance called a vesting order) vesting the land or interest therein in any such person in any such manner and for any such estate or interest as the Court may direct, or releasing or disposing of the contingent right to such person as the Court may direct:

Provided that-

(i) where the order is consequential on the appointment of a trustee the land or interest therein shall be vested for such estate as the Court may direct in the persons who on the appointment are the trustees; and

(ii) where the order relates to a trustee entitled or formerly entitled jointly with another person, and such trustee is under disability or out of the jurisdiction of the Court or cannot be found, or being a corporation has been dissolved, the land interest or right shall be vested in such other person who remains entitled, either alone or with any other person the Court may appoint.

Orders as to contingent rights or unborn persons

46. Where any interest in land is subject to a contingent right in an unborn person or class of unborn persons who, on coming into existence would, in respect thereof, become entitled to or possessed of that interest on any trust, the Court may make an order releasing the land or interest therein from the contingent right, or may make an order vesting in any person the estate or interest to or of which the unborn person or class of unborn persons would, on coming into existence, be entitled or possessed in the land.

Vesting order in place of conveyance by infant mortgagee

47. Where any person entitled to or possessed of any interest in land, or entitled to a contingent right in land, by way of security for money, is an infant, the Court may make an order vesting or releasing or disposing of the interest in the land or the right in like manner as in the case of a trustee under disability.

Vesting order consequential an order for sale or mortgage of land

48. Where the Court gives a judgment or makes an order directing the sale or mortgage of any land, every person who is entitled to or possessed of any interest in the land, or entitled to a contingent right therein, and is a party to the action or proceeding in which the judgment or order is given or made or is otherwise bound by the judgment or order, shall be deemed to be so entitled or possessed, as the case may be, as a trustee for the purposes of this Ordinance, and the Court may, if it thinks expedient, make an order vesting the land or any part thereof for such estate or interest as the Court thinks fit in the purchaser or mortgagee or in any other person.

Vesting order consequential on judgement for specific performance, etc

49. Where a judgment is given for the specific performance of a contract concerning any interest in land or for sale or exchange of any interest in land, or generally where any judgment is given for the conveyance of any interest in land either in cases arising out of the doctrine of election or otherwise, the Court may declare-

(a) that any of the parties to the action are trustees of any interest in the land or any part thereof within the meaning of this Ordinance, or

(b) that the interests of unborn persons who might claim under any party to the action, or under the will or voluntary settlement of any deceased person who was during his lifetime a party to the contract or transaction concerning which the judgment is given, are the interests of persons who, on coming into existence, would be trustees within the meaning of this Ordinance, and thereupon the Court may make a vesting order relating to the rights of those persons, born and unborn, as if they had been trustees.

Effect of vesting order

50. A vesting order under any of the foregoing provisions shall in the case of a vesting order consequential on the appointment of a trustee, have the same effect-

(a) as if the persons who before the appointment were the trustees, if any, had duly executed all proper conveyances of the land for such estate or interest as the Court directs; or

(b) if there is no such person, or no such person of full capacity, as if such person had existed and been of full capacity and had duly executed all proper conveyances of the land for such estate or interest as the Court directs;

and shall in every other case have the same effect as if the trustee or other person or description or class of persons to whose rights or supposed rights the said provisions respectively relate had been an ascertained and existing person of full capacity, and had executed a conveyance or release to the effect intended by the order.

Power to appoint person to convey

51. In all cases where a vesting order can be made under any of the foregoing provisions, the Court may, if it is more convenient, appoint a person to convey the land or any interest therein or release the contingent right, and a conveyance or release by that person in conformity with the order shall have the same effect as an order under the appropriate provision.

Vesting orders as to stocks and things in action

52.(1) In any of the following cases, namely-

(a) where the Court appoints or has appointed a trustee, or where a trustee has been appointed out of court under any statutory or express power;

(b) where a trustee entitled, whether by way of mortgage or otherwise, alone or jointly with another person, to stock or to a thing in action-

(i) is under disability, or

(ii) is out of the jurisdiction of the Court, or

(iii) cannot be found, or being a corporation, has been dissolved, or

(iv) neglects or refuses to transfer stock or receive the dividends or income thereof, or to sue for or recover a thing in action, according to the direction of the person absolutely entitled thereto for twenty-eight days next after a request in writing has been served on him; or

(v) neglects or refuses to transfer stock or receive the dividends or income

53. thereof, or to sue for or recover a thing in action, for twenty-eight days next after an order of the Court for that purpose has been served on him;

(c) where it is uncertain whether a trustee entitled alone or jointly with another person to stock or to a thing in action is alive or dead;

(d) where stock is standing in the name of a deceased person whose personal representative is under disability;

(e) where stock or a thing in action is vested in a trustee whether by way of mortgage or otherwise and it appears to the Court to be expedient, the Court may make an order vesting the right to transfer or call for a transfer of stock, or to receive the dividends or income thereof, or to sue for or recover the thing in action, in any such person as the Court may appoint:

Provided that-

(i) where the order is consequential on the appointment of a trustee, the right shall be vested in the persons who, on the appointment, are the trustees; and

(ii) where the person whose right is dealt with by the order was entitled jointly with another person, the right shall be vested in the last-mentioned person either alone or jointly with any other person whom the Court may appoint.

(2) In all cases where a vesting order can be made under this section, the Court may, if it is more convenient, appoint some proper person to make or join in making the transfer.

(3) The person in whom the right to transfer or call for the transfer of any stock is vested by an order of the Court under this Ordinance, may transfer the stock to himself or any other person, according to the order, and all companies shall obey every order under this section according to its tenor.

(4) After notice in writing of an order under this section it shall not be lawful for any company to transfer any stock to which the order relates or to pay any dividends thereon except in accordance with the order.

(5) The Court may make declarations and give directions concerning the manner in which the right to transfer any stock or thing in action vested under the provisions of this Ordinance is to be exercised.

(6) The provisions of this Ordinance as to vesting orders shall apply to shares in ships registered under the Acts of Parliament or other law relating to merchant shipping as if they were stock.

Vesting orders of charity property

53. The powers conferred by this Ordinance as to vesting orders may be exercised for vesting any interest in land, stock, or thing in action in any trustee of a charity or society over which the Court would have jurisdiction upon action duly instituted, whether the appointment of the trustee was made by instrument under a power or by the Court under its general or statutory jurisdiction.

Vesting orders in relation to infant's beneficial interests

54. Where an infant is beneficially entitled to any property the Court may, with a view to the application of the capital or income thereof for the maintenance, education, or benefit of the infant, make an order-

(a) appointing a person to convey such property; or

(b) in the case of stock, or a thing in action, vesting in any person the right to transfer or call for a transfer of such stock, or to receive the dividends or income thereof, or to sue for and recover such thing in action, upon such terms as the Court may think fit.

Orders made upon certain allegations to be conclusive evidence

55. Where a vesting order is made as to any land under this Ordinance founded on an allegation of any of the following matters namely-

(a) the personal incapacity of a trustee or mortgagee; or

(b) that a trustee or mortgagee or the personal representative of or other person deriving title under a trustee or mortgagee is out of the jurisdiction of the Court or cannot be found, or being a corporation has been dissolved; or

(c) that it is uncertain which of two or more trustees, or which of two or more persons interested in a mortgage, was the survivor; or

(d) that it is uncertain whether the last trustee or the personal representative of or other person deriving title under a trustee or mortgagee, or the last surviving person interested in a mortgage is living or dead; or

(e) that any trustee or mortgagee has died intestate without leaving a person beneficially interested under the intestacy or has died and it is not known who is his personal representative or the person interested, the fact that the order has been so made shall be conclusive evidence of the matter so alleged in any court upon any question as to the validity of the order; but this section does not prevent the Court from directing a reconveyance or surrender or the payment of costs occasioned by any such order if improperly obtained.

Orders of Court to be registered

56. In all cases where the Court shall, under the provisions of this Ordinance, make a vesting order, or any order having the effect of a conveyance or assignment of any land or any interest therein, or having the effect of a release or disposition of the contingent right of any unborn person, or class of unborn persons, in any land, an office copy of such order shall be registered in the office of the Registrar of Deeds, and such order shall take effect upon and from the time of the registration of such office copy:

Provided that where the land or any interest therein is subject to the provisions of the Title by Registration Act, the Registrar of Deeds shall, on production of an office copy of the order and on payment of the prescribed fees, duly register such order and cause a note thereof to be endorsed on the grant or certificate of title in respect of such land, and thereupon the person in whom the land is vested by the order shall be the registered proprietor thereof without the production of any instrument of transfer.

Registration of vesting order made by Court in England

57.(1) Where the court in England has made a vesting order under the Trustee Act, 1925, in respect of land or personal estate in the Territory, and the vesting order so made is produced to the Registrar of Deeds for registration, such vesting order shall, on payment of a fee of five dollars be registered in the office of the Registrar of Deeds.

(2) For the purposes of this section, a duplicate of a vesting order sealed with the seal of the court making the same, or a copy thereof certified as correct by the officer having the custody of the original order, shall have the same effect as the original.

(3) In this section "court" has the same meaning as the court referred to in section 67 of the Trustee Act, 1925.

Jurisdiction of Court to vary trusts

58.(1) Where property, whether real or personal, is held on trusts arising whether before or after the passing of this Ordinance, under any will, settlement or other disposition, the Court may if it thinks fit by order approve on behalf of -

(a) any person having, directly or indirectly, an interest, whether vested or contingent, under the trusts who by reason of infancy or other incapacity is incapable of assenting; or

(b) any person (whether ascertained or not) who may have become entitled, directly or indirectly, to an interest under the trusts as being at a future date or on the happening of a future event a person of any specified description or a member of any specified class of persons, so however that this paragraph shall not include any person who would be of that description or a member of that class, as the case may be, if the said date had fallen or the said event had happened at the date of the application to the Court; or

(c) any unborn person; or

(d) any person in respect of any discretionary interest of his under protective trusts where the interest of the principal beneficiary has not failed or determined;

any arrangement (by whomsoever proposed, and whether or not there is any other person beneficially interested who is capable of assenting thereto) varying or revoking all or any of the trusts or enlarging the powers of the trustees of managing or administering any of the property subject to the trusts:

Provided that except by virtue of paragraph (d) the Court shall not approve an arrangement on behalf of any person unless the carrying out thereof would be for the benefit of that person.

(2) In the foregoing subsection "protective trusts" means an interest specified in paragraphs (a) and (b) of subsection (1) of section 34 or any like trusts, "the principal beneficiary" has the same meaning as in the said subsection (1); and "discretionary interest" means an interest arising under the trust specified in paragraph (a) of the said subsection.

(3) Nothing in the foregoing provisions of this section shall apply to trusts affecting property settled by any law of the Territory.

(4) Nothing in this section shall be taken to limit the powers conferred by section 59 or by section 6 of the West Indies Associated States Supreme Court (Virgin Islands) Ordinance.

Power of Court to authorise dealings with trust property

59.(1) Where in the management or administration of any property vested in trustees, any sale, lease, mortgage, surrender, release, or other disposition, or any purchase, investment, acquisition, expenditure, or other transaction, is in the opinion of the Court expedient, but the same cannot be effected by reason of the absence of any power for that purpose vested in the trustees by the trust instrument, if any, or by law, the Court may by order confer upon the trustees, either generally or in any particular instance, the necessary power for that purpose, on such terms, and subject to such provisions and conditions, if any, as the Court may think fit and may direct in what manner any money authorised to be expended, and the costs of any transaction, are to be paid or borne as between capital and income.

(2) The Court may, from time to time, rescind or vary any order made under this section, or may make any new or further order.

(3) An application to the Court under this section may be made by the trustees, or by any of them, or by any person beneficially interested under the trust.

Persons entitled to apply for orders

60.(1) An order under this Ordinance for the appointment of a new trustee or concerning any interest in land, stock, or thing in action subject to a trust, may be made on the application of any person beneficially interested in the land, stock, or thing in action, whether under disability or not, or on the application of any person duly appointed trustee thereof.

(2) An order under this Ordinance concerning any interest in land, stock, or thing in action subject to a mortgage may be made on the application of any person beneficially interested in the equity of redemption, whether under disability or not, or of any person interested in the money secured by the mortgage.

Power to give judgement in absence of a trustee

61. Where in any action the Court is satisfied that diligent search has been made for any person who, in the character of trustee, is made a defendant in an action, to serve him with a process of the Court, and that he cannot be found, the Court may hear and determine the action and give judgment therein against that person in his character of a trustee as if he had been duly served, or had entered an appearance in the action, and had also appeared by his counsel and solicitor at the hearing, but without prejudice to any interest he may have in the matters in question in the action in any other character.

Power to charge costs on trust estate

62. The Court may order the costs and expenses of and incident to any application for an order appointing a new trustee, or for a vesting order, or of an incident to any such order, or any conveyance or transfer in pursuance thereof, to be raised and paid out of the property in respect whereof the same is made, or out of the income thereof, or to be borne and paid in such manner and by such persons as to the Court may seem just.

Power to relieve trustee from personal liability

63. If it appears to the Court that a trustee, whether appointed by the Court or otherwise, is or may be personally liable for any breach of trust, whether the transaction alleged to be a breach of trust occurred before or after the commencement of this Ordinance, but has acted honestly and reasonably, and ought fairly to be excused for the breach of trust and for omitting to obtain the directions of the Court in the matter in which he committed such breach, then the Court may relieve him either wholly or partly from personal liability for the same.

Power to make beneficiary indemnify for breach of trust

64.(1) Where a trustee commits a breach of trust at the instigation or request or with the consent in writing of a beneficiary, the Court may, if it thinks fit, and notwithstanding that the beneficiary may be a married woman restrained from anticipation, make such order as to the Court seems just, for impounding all or any part of the interest of the beneficiary in the trust estate by way of indemnity to the trustee or persons claiming through him.

(2) This section applies to breaches of trust committed as well before as after the commencement of this Ordinance.

Payment into Court by trustees

65.(1) Trustees, or the majority of trustees, having in their hands or under their control money or securities belonging to a trust, may pay the same into Court; and the same shall, subject to rules of court, be dealt with according to the orders of the Court.

(2) The receipt or certificate of the proper officer shall be a sufficient discharge to trustees for the money or securities so paid into Court.

(3) Where money or securities are vested in any persons as trustees, and the majority are desirous of paying the same into Court, but the concurrence of the other or others cannot be obtained, the Court may order the payment into Court to be made by the majority without the concurrence of the other or others.

(4) Where any such money or securities are deposited with any banker, broker, or other depositary, the Court may order payment or delivery of the money or securities to the majority of the trustees for the purpose of payment into Court.

(5) Every transfer payment and delivery made in pursuance of any such order shall be valid and take effect as if the same had been made on the authority or by the act of all the persons entitled to the money and securities so transferred, paid or delivered.

PART VI - General Provisions

Application of Ordinance

66.(1) This Ordinance, except where otherwise expressly provided, applies to trusts including, so far as this Ordinance applies thereto, executorships and administratorships constituted or created either before or after the commencement of this Ordinance.

(2) The powers conferred by this Ordinance on trustees are in addition to the powers conferred by the instrument, if any, creating the trust, but those powers, unless otherwise stated, apply if and so far only as a contrary intention is not expressed in the instrument, if any, creating the trust, and have effect subject to the terms of that instrument.

(3) This Ordinance does not affect the legality or validity of any thing done before the commencement of this Ordinance, except as otherwise hereinbefore expressly provided.

Indemnity

67. This Ordinance, and every order purporting to be made under this Ordinance, shall be a complete indemnity to all persons for any acts done pursuant thereto, and it shall not be necessary for any person to inquire concerning the propriety of the order, or whether the Court by which the order was made had jurisdiction to make it.

PART VII - Perpetuities and Accumulations

Power to specify perpetuity period

68.(1) Subject to subsection (2) and subsection (3) of section 76, where the instrument by which any disposition is made so provides, the perpetuity period applicable to the disposition under the rule against perpetuities, instead of being of any other duration, shall be of a duration equal to such number of years not exceeding 100 as is specified in that behalf in the instrument.

(2) Subsection (1) shall not have effect where the disposition is made in exercise of a special power of appointment, but where a period is specified under that subsection in the instrument creating such a power the period shall apply in relation to any disposition under the power as it applies in relation to the power itself.

Presumptions and evidence as to future parenthood

69.(1) Where in any proceedings there arises on the rule against perpetuities a question which turns on the ability of a person to have a child at some future time, then, subject to subsection (2), it shall be presumed that a male can have a child at the age of 14 years or over, but not under that age, and that a female can have a child at the age of 12 years or over, but not under that age or over the age of 55 years.

(2) In the case of a living person evidence may be given to show that he or she will or will not be able to have a child at the time in question.

(3) Where any such question is decided by treating a person as unable to have a child at a particular time, and he or she does so, the Court may make such order as it thinks fit for placing the persons interested in the property comprised in the disposition, so far as may be just, in the position they would have held if the question had not been so decided.

(4) Subject to subsection (3) above, where any such question is decided in relation to a disposition by treating a person as able or unable to have a child at a particular time, then he or she shall be so treated for the purpose of any question which may arise on the rule against perpetuities in relation to the same disposition in any subsequent proceedings.

(5) In the foregoing provisions of this section references to having a child are references to begetting or giving birth to a child, but those provisions, except subsection (2), shall apply in relation to the possibility that a person will at any time have a child by adoption, legitimation or other means as they apply to his or her ability at that time to beget or give birth to a child.

Uncertainty as to remoteness

70.(1) Where, apart from the provisions of this section and sections 71 and 72 ("the said provisions") a disposition would be void on the ground that the interest disposed of might not become vested until too remote a time, the disposition shall be treated, until such time, if any, as it becomes established that the vesting must occur, if at all, after the end of the perpetuity period, as if the disposition were not subject to the rule against perpetuities; and its becoming so established shall not affect the validity of anything previously done in relation to the interest disposed of by way of advancement, application of intermediate income or otherwise.

(2) Where, apart from the said provisions, a disposition consisting of the conferring of a general power of appointment would be void on the ground that the power might not become exercisable until too remote a time, the disposition shall be treated, until such time, if any, as it becomes established that the power will not be exercisable within the perpetuity period, as if the disposition were not subject to the rule against perpetuities.

(3) Where, apart from the said provisions, a disposition consisting of the conferring of any power, option or other right would be void on the ground that the right might be exercised at too remote a time, the disposition shall be treated as regards any exercise of the right within the perpetuity period as if it were not subject to the rule against perpetuities and, subject to the said provisions, shall be treated as void for remoteness only if, and so far as, the right is not fully exercised within that period.

(4) Where this section applies to a disposition and the duration of the perpetuity period is not determined by virtue of section 68 or subsection (3) of section 76, it shall be determined as follows:

(a) where any persons falling within subsection (5) are individuals in being and ascertainable at the commencement of the perpetuity period the duration of the period shall be determined by reference to their lives and no others, but so that the lives of any description of persons falling within paragraph (b) or (c) of that subsection shall be disregarded if the number of persons of that description is such as to render it impracticable to ascertain the date of death of the survivor; and

(b) where there are no lives in being within the meaning of paragraph (a) the period shall be 21 years.

(5) The said persons are as follows:-

(a) the person by whom the disposition was made;

(b) a person to whom or in whose favour the disposition was made, that is to say,

(i) in the case of a disposition to a class of persons, any member or potential member of the class,

(ii) in the case of an individual disposition to a person taking only on certain conditions being satisfied, any person as to whom some of the conditions are satisfied and the remainder may in time be satisfied,

(iii) in the case of a special power of appointment exercisable in favour of members of a class, any member or potential member of the class,

(iv) in the case of a special power of appointment exercisable in favour of one person only, that person or, where the object of the power is ascertainable only on certain conditions being satisfied, any person as to whom some of the conditions are satisfied and the remainder may in time be satisfied,

(v) in the case of any power, option or other right, the person on whom the right is conferred;

(c) a person having a child or grandchild within sub-paragraphs (i) to (iv) of paragraph (b), or any of whose children or grandchildren, if subsequently born, would by virtue of his or her descent fall within those sub-paragraphs; and

(d) any person on the failure or determination of whose prior interest the disposition is limited to take effect.

(6) The provisions of this section shall be deemed to apply to any trust created on or after 16th July, 1964 with an express perpetuity period not exceeding 80 years, and where a disposition made on or after 16th July, 1964 would have been void *ab initio* but for this provision the disposition shall be deemed to be valid if the trustees of the trust declare in writing that the provisions of this subsection shall apply to the disposition.

Reduction of age and exclusion of class members to avoid remoteness

71.(1) Where a disposition is limited by reference to the attainment by any person or persons of a specified age exceeding 21 years, and it is apparent at the time the disposition is made or becomes apparent at a subsequent time that the disposition would, apart from this section, be void for remoteness, but that it would not be so void if the specified age had been 21 years, the disposition shall be treated for all purposes as if, instead of being limited by reference to the age in fact specified, it had been limited by reference to the age nearest to that age which would, if specified instead, have prevented the disposition from being so void.

(2) Where in the case of any disposition different ages exceeding 21 years are specified in relation to different persons

(a) the reference in subsection (1) to the specified age shall be construed as a reference to all the specified ages; and

(b) subsection (1) shall operate to reduce each such age so far as is necessary to save the disposition from being void for remoteness.

(3) Where the inclusion of any persons, being potential members of a class or unborn persons who at birth would become members or potential members of the class, prevents the foregoing provisions of this section from operating to save a disposition from being void for remoteness, those persons shall thenceforth be deemed for all the purposes of the disposition to be excluded from the class, and the said provisions shall thereupon have effect accordingly.

(4) Where , in the case of a disposition to which subsection (3) does not apply, it is apparent at the time the disposition is made or becomes apparent at a subsequent time that, apart from this subsection, the inclusion of any persons, being potential members of a class or unborn persons who at birth would become members or potential members of the class, would cause the disposition to be treated as void for remoteness, those persons shall, unless their exclusion would exhaust the class, thenceforth be deemed for all the purposes of the disposition to be excluded from the class.

(5) Where this section has effect in relation to a disposition to which section 70 above applies, the operation of this section shall not affect the validity of anything previously done in relation to the interest disposed of by way of advancement, application of intermediate income or otherwise.

Condition relating to death of surviving spouse

72. Where a disposition is limited by reference to the time of death of the survivor of a person in being at the commencement of the perpetuity period and any spouse of that person, and that time has not arrived at the end of the perpetuity period, the disposition shall be treated for all purposes, where to do so would save it from being void for remoteness, as if it had instead been limited by reference to the time immediately before the end of that period.

Saving and acceleration of expectant interests

73. A disposition shall not treated as void for remoteness by reason only that the interest disposed of is ulterior to and dependent upon an interest under a disposition which is so void, and the vesting of an interest shall not be prevented from being accelerated on the failure of a prior interest by reason only that the failure arises because of remoteness.

Powers of appointment

74. For the purposes of the rule against perpetuities, a power of appointment shall be treated as a special power unless

(a) in the instrument creating the power it is expressed to be exercisable by one person only; and

(b) it could, at all times during its currency when that person is of full age and capacity, be exercised by him so as immediately to transfer to himself the whole of the interest governed by the power without the consent of any other person or compliance with any other condition, not being a formal condition relating only to the mode of exercise of the power, except that for the purpose of determining whether a disposition made under a power of appointment exerciseable by will only is void for remoteness, the power shall be treated as a general power where it would have fallen to be so treated if exercisable by deed.

Administrative powers of trustees

75.(1) The rule against perpetuities shall not operate to invalidate a power conferred on trustees or other persons to sell, lease, exchange or otherwise dispose of any property for full consideration, or to do any other act in the administration (as opposed to the distribution) of any property, and shall not prevent the payment to trustees or other persons of reasonable remuneration for their services.

(2) Subsection (1) shall apply for the purpose of enabling a power to be exercised at any time after the commencement of this Part notwithstanding that the power is conferred by an instrument which took effect before that commencement.

Options relating to land

76.(1) The rule against perpetuities shall not apply to a disposition consisting of the conferring of an option to acquire for valuable consideration an interest reversionary, whether directly or indirectly, on the term of a lease if

(a) the option is exercisable only by the lessee or his successors in title; and

(b) it ceases to be exercisable at or before the expiration of one year following the determination of the lease.

(2) Subsection (1) shall apply in relation to an agreement for a lease as it applies in relation to a lease, and "lessee" shall be construed accordingly.

(3) Except as provided in subsection (1), in the case of a disposition consisting of the conferring of an option to acquire for valuable consideration any interest in land, the perpetuity period under the rule against perpetuities shall be 21 years, and section 68 shall not apply.

(4) Subsection (3) shall not apply to a right of pre-emption conferred on any governmental or public authority in respect of land used or to be used for religious purposes where the right becomes exercisable only if the land ceases to be used for such purposes.

Possibilities of reverter conditions subsequent exceptions and reservations

77.(1) In the case of

(a) a possibility of reverter on the determination of a determinable fee simple; or

(b) a possibility of a resulting trust on the determination of any other determinable interest in property, the rule against perpetuities shall apply in relation to the provision causing the interest to be determinable as it would apply if that provision were expressed in the form of a condition subsequent giving rise, on breach thereof, to a right of re-entry or an equivalent right in the case of property other than land, and where the provision falls to be treated as void for remoteness the determinable interest shall become an absolute interest.

Accumulation of income

78. Subject to any term of a trust prohibiting the accumulation of income or directing or authorizing the accumulation of income for a period shorter than the period of the trust, income may be accumulated for the duration of the period of the trust.

Interpretation and extent of Part VII

79.(1) In this Part

(a) "disposition", includes the conferring of a power of appointment and any other disposition of an interest in or right over property, and references to the interest disposed of shall be construed accordingly;

(b) "in being" means living or *en ventre sa mere*;

(c) "power of appointment" includes any discretionary power to transfer a beneficial interest in property without the furnishing of valuable consideration; and

(d) "will" includes a codicil.

(2) For the purposes of this Part a disposition contained in a will shall be deemed to be made at the death of the testator.

(3) For the purposes of this Part a person shall be treated as a member of a class if in his case all the conditions identifying a member of the class are satisfied, and shall be treated as a potential member if in his case some only of those conditions are satisfied but there is a possibility that the remainder will in time be satisfied.

(4) Nothing in this Part shall affect the operation of the rule of law rendering void for remoteness certain dispositions under which property is limited to be applied for purposes other than the benefit of any person or class of persons in cases where the property may be so applied after the end of the perpetuity period.

(5) This Part shall apply in relation to a disposition made otherwise than by an instrument as if the disposition had been contained in an instrument taking effect when the disposition was made.

(6) This Part shall apply, except as provided in subsection (6) of section 70, and subsection (2) of section 75, only in relation to instruments taking effect after the commencement of this Part, and in the case of an instrument made in the exercise of a special power of appointment shall apply only where the instrument creating the power takes effect after that commencement except that section 74 shall apply in all cases for construing the foregoing reference to a special power of appointment.

PART VIII - Special Provisions

Determination of proper law of trust

80.(1) The proper law of a trust or a particular aspect of a trust is

(a) the law of the jurisdiction expressly designated by the terms of the trust as being the law that is to govern the trust or the particular aspect of the trust, as the case may be;

(b) if the terms of the trust do not expressly designate the governing law for the trust or the particular aspect of the trust, then the law of the jurisdiction that may reasonably be inferred from the terms of the trust as being the law that is to govern the trust or the particular aspect of the trust, as the case may be; or

(c) if the terms of the trust do not expressly designate the governing law for the trust or the particular aspect of the trust and no reasonable inference may be drawn from the terms of the trust as to the governing law, then the law of the jurisdiction with which the trust at the time it was created had the closest connection.

(2) For the purposes of paragraph (c) of subsection (1) in ascertaining the law with which a trust is most closely connected at the time it was created reference shall be made in particular to

(a) the place of administration of the trust designated by the settlor;

(b) the situs of the assets of the trust;

(c) the place of residence or business of the trustee; and

(d) the objects of the trust and the places where they are to be fulfilled.

Change of proper law

81.(1) If the terms of the instrument creating a trust so provide, the proper law of the trust may be changed from the law of the Territory to the law of another jurisdiction, or from the law of another jurisdiction to the law of the Territory, provided that in the case of a change from the law of the Territory the new proper law would recognize the validity of the trust and the respective interests of the beneficiaries.

(2) A change in proper law shall not affect the legality or validity of, or render any person liable for, anything done before the change.

(3) Without limiting or affecting subsection (2), the instrument creating a trust may provide that

(a) the proper law be changed to that of any other jurisdiction specified in the trust; or *(b)* the trust assets be transferred to a trustee in that other jurisdiction,

upon the occurrence of an event specified in the trust instrument.

Jurisdiction of court

82. The court has jurisdiction where

(a) the proper law of a trust or a particular aspect of a trust is the law of the Territory;

(b) the trustee of any trust is resident in the Territory;

(c) in the case of a corporate trustee of any trust, it is incorporated or registered to do business in the Territory;

(d) any trust property is situate in the Territory but only in respect of property so situate;

(e) the administration of any trust is carried on in the Territory; or

(f) the court thinks it appropriate.

Proper law to determine disposition of personal property

83.(1) If a person transfers or disposes of personal property to the trustee of a trust

(a) he shall be deemed to have had capacity to do so if he is at the time of such transfer or disposition of full age and of sound mind under the law of his domicile; and

(b) no rule relating to inheritance or succession of the law of his domicile shall affect any such transfer or disposition or otherwise affect the validity of such trust.

(2) For the avoidance of doubt it is declared that the provisions of this section shall apply notwithstanding any other provisions of this Part and shall apply only to transfers or dispositions of property made to a trustee of a trust after the commencement of this Part, but this declaration shall be without prejudice to the validity or otherwise of transfers or dispositions made before that time.

Purpose trusts

84.(1) For the purpose of this section

(a) "designated person" means

(i) a barrister or solicitor practising in the Territory,

(ii) an accountant practising in the Territory who qualifies as an "auditor" for purposes of the Banks and Trust Companies Act, 1990,

(iii) a licensee under the Banks and Trust Companies Act, 1990, or

(iv) such other person as the Minister of Finance may by order designate; and

(b) "trust for any purpose" means a trust other than a trust

(i) that is for the benefit of particular persons whether or not immediately ascertainable, or

(ii) that is for the benefit of some aggregate of persons ascertained by reference to some personal relationship.

(2) A person may create a valid trust for any purpose, whether charitable or not, if

(a) the purpose is specific, reasonable and possible;

(b) the purpose is not immoral, contrary to public policy or unlawful;

(c) at least one trustee of the trust is a designated person;

(d) the trust instrument appoints a person, who may be a protector, to enforce the trust and provides for the appointment of a successor to such person;

(e) the person appointed to enforce the trust is a party to the trust instrument or consents in writing, addressed to the trustee who is a designated person, to enforce the trust; and

(f) the trust instrument specifies the event upon the happening of which the trust terminates and provides for the disposition of surplus assets of the trust upon its termination.

(3) The rule against perpetuities and remoteness of vesting shall not apply to a trust to which subsection (2) applies.

(4) Nothing in this section shall affect the existing law with respect to trusts established for charitable purposes.

(5) Where a trustee who is a designated person has reason to believe that a person who is appointed to enforce the trust is dead, is unwilling, refuses or is unfit to act or is incapable of acting, then that trustee shall as soon as practicable inform the Attorney General in writing of the fact and send him a copy of the instrument creating the trust.

(6) The Attorney General on being informed under subsection (5) shall within 90 days apply for the appointment of a person to enforce the trust and the court may, unless it feels that the person is not fit, by order declare that person to be the person to enforce the trust.

(7) The order of the court under subsection (6) is conclusive evidence of the appointment of the person to enforce the trust and the appointment takes effect as from the date of the order.

(8) Where any costs are incurred by the Attorney General in connection with any application under subsection (6), the court may make such order as it considers just as to the payment of those costs out of the assets of the trust.

(9) Where a designated person fails to comply with subsection (5), then, subject to subsection (10), the designated person is guilty of an offence and is liable on summary conviction to a fine of not more than $5,000.

(10) It shall be a defence to a charge of committing an offence under subsection (9) to prove that the designated person took all reasonable steps and exercised all due diligence to avoid committing the offence.

(11) The person appointed pursuant to paragraph (d) of subsection (1) shall be entitled, in addition to any documents, information or other rights specifically provided for in the trust instrument, to

(a) annual accounts of the trust;

(b) copies of the trust instrument and deeds and other written instruments executed pursuant to the trust instrument; and

(c) counsels' opinions and legal advice received by the trustees.

Trustees to act by majority

85.(1) Subject to any provision contained in the instrument creating the trust,

(a) every decision made, resolution passed or power or discretion exercised by trustees is valid if made, passed or exercised by a majority of the trustees if there are more than 2 of them; and

(b) any deed or other instrument executed pursuant to such a decision, resolution or exercise of power or discretion is likewise valid as if it had been executed by all the trustees.

(2) This section shall not apply to trusts in existence at the time the section comes into effect.

Protector of trusts

86.(1) An instrument creating a trust may contain provisions by virtue of which the exercise by the trustees of any of their powers and discretions shall be subject to the previous consent of the settlor or some other person, whether named as protector, nominator, committee or any other name; and if so provided in the instrument creating the trust the trustees shall not be liable for any loss caused by their actions if the previous consent was given.

(2) There may be conferred on the settlor or some other person, whether named as protector, nominator, committee or by any other name, by the instrument creating the trust, any powers, and without limitation to the foregoing power may be conferred on that person to do any one or more of the following:

(a) determine the law of which jurisdiction shall be the proper law of the trust;

(b) change the forum of administration of the trust;

(c) remove trustees;

(d) appoint new or additional trustees;

(e) exclude any beneficiary as a beneficiary of the trust;

(f) include any person as a beneficiary of the trust in substitution for or in addition to any existing beneficiary of the trust; and

(g) withhold consent from specified actions of the trustees either conditionally or unconditionally.

(3) A person exercising any of the powers set forth in paragraphs (a) to (d) and (g) of subsection (2) shall not by virtue only of the exercise of the power be deemed to be a trustee; and unless otherwise provided in the instrument creating the trust, is not liable to the beneficiaries for the bona fide exercise of the power.

Managing trustee

87. A trust instrument may contain provisions by virtue of which the exercise of any of the trustee's powers may be reserved to a managing trustee, and no other trustee is liable for any of the decisions, acts or transactions of the managing trustee in so far as they amount to exercise of powers reserved by the trust instrument to the managing trustee.

Successor trustee

88. In the absence of any contrary provisions in the trust instrument, a successor trustee may exercise all powers and discretions granted to the original trustee including, without limitation, any power to select from a class of beneficiaries those persons entitled to income or principal of the trust fund.

Power to revoke or amend trust

89. A trust may be revoked or amended only to the extent and in the manner expressly stated in the trust instrument or as provided by section 58.

Exemption from income tax, etc

90.(1) Notwithstanding any provisions of the Income Tax Act, the income of any trust in the hands of a trustee is exempt from income tax and the beneficiaries of any trust who are not persons resident in the Territory shall likewise be exempt from payment of income tax in respect of any moneys received by them from the trustee of any trust.

(2) No estate tax, inheritance tax, succession tax, gift tax, rate, duty, levy or other charge is payable by beneficiaries who are not resident in the Territory in respect of any distribution to them by the trustee of any trust.

(3) Notwithstanding any provision of the Stamp Act, any trust that does not have as beneficiaries persons resident in the Territory shall be exempt from the payment of stamp duty with respect to

(a) the deed or other written instrument creating the trust;

(b) all deeds and other written instruments of appointment made pursuant to the trust;

(c) all deeds and other instruments by which assets are transferred to or from the trustee of a trust; and

(d) all instruments relating to the transfer of beneficial interests in a trust.

(4) The exemptions in this section do not apply to any trust which

(a) has as an underlying asset land in the Territory; or

(b) carries on a business or trade in the Territory.

(5) The provisions of this section apply to all trusts in existence at the time of the coming into operation of this Act.

Exemption from registration

91.(1) Notwithstanding any provisions of the Registration and Records Act,

(a) any deed creating a trust;

(b) all deeds of appointment made pursuant to the terms of a trust; and

(c) all other deeds executed by the trustees, settlors, beneficiaries or protectors of a trust pursuant to the powers and discretions specified in the instrument creating the trust,

are exempt from registration under the provisions of the Registration and Records Act.

(2) The exemption granted by subsection (1) applies to all deeds referred to therein executed prior to the time when this provision becomes effective.

Trust duty

92.(1) Every trust instrument of which the proper law is the law of the Virgin Islands and which does not create a bare trust shall be liable to a duty called "the trust duty" in the sum of $50.00.

(2) The payment of the trust duty shall be denoted or expressed by the affixing of a revenue stamp to the trust instrument.

(3) A trust instrument shall be deemed to be duly stamped only when the person executing the trust instrument cancels the revenue stamp by writing on or across the stamp the name or initials of the trustee or the person acting on behalf of a corporation trustee as well as the date on which the name or initials of the person is affixed.

(4) A trust instrument not cancelled in accordance with the provisions of subsection (3) above shall not be admissible in civil proceedings, provided that a trust instrument may in the discretion of the Court be admissible in proceedings on proof of the payment in the manner prescribed by the Governor in Council of the trust duty together with a penalty in the sum of $100.00 for each calendar year from the execution of the trust instrument.

(5) The provisions of this section shall apply only to trusts created after the coming into effect of this section.

(6) Any trust instrument that is liable to trust duty shall not be produced to the Treasury, Post Office or any other public body for purposes of payment of trust duty.

(7) No trust instrument of which the proper law is the law of the Territory and of which a designated person is a trustee shall, except in criminal proceedings, be pleaded or given in evidence, or admitted to be good, useful or available in law or equity, unless it is duly stamped with trust duty in accordance with the law in force at the time when it was first executed.

(8) Any unstamped or insufficiently stamped trust instrument that is liable to be stamped pursuant to the provisions of this section may be pleaded or given in evidence or admitted to be good, useful or available in law or equity upon payment of the trust duty together with a penalty in the sum of $100.00 for each complete calendar year from execution of the instrument.

(9) The penalty referred to in subsection (8) shall be paid in such manner as the Governor in Council may by order direct.

(10) This section applies only to trust instruments created after the section comes into effect.

(11) This section comes into operation on such date as the Governor may appoint by proclamation published in the Gazette.

PART IX - Incorporation of Administrative Powers by Reference

Incorporation by reference

93.(1) Any instrument creating any trust may incorporate by reference any of the provisions set out in the Schedule, in which case the following expressions appearing in the provisions have, unless a contrary intention appears, the meanings respectively assigned to them:

"the Trustees" means the trustees for the time being of the trust;

"the Trust Fund" means -

(a) the property in respect of which trusts are declared;

(b) all property paid or transferred to or otherwise vested in and accepted by the Trustees;

(c) all income which, in accordance with the provisions of the trust, is accumulated by the Trustees and added to the capital thereof; and

(d) all money, investments and other property from time to time representing all property and income mentioned in paragraphs (a), (b) and (c) and any part of the said property or income.

(2) A memorandum signed by the Trustees as to property paid or transferred to or otherwise vested in or accepted by the Trustees is conclusive evidence of the payment, transfer or other vesting.

SCHEDULE

Trust for sale

1.(1) The Trustees shall stand possessed of any real property from time to time comprised in the Trust Fund Upon Trust to sell the same with power to postpone the sale thereof or of any part thereof for such period as they shall in their absolute discretion think fit and shall stand possessed of all other investments comprised in the Trust Fund Upon Trust at such discretion either to retain the same in the existing state thereof for such period as they shall think fit or at any time or times to sell the same or any part thereof.

(2) The Trustees shall hold the net proceeds of any sale of investments comprised in the Trust Fund and all other monies held or received by them as capital monies Upon Trust to invest the same at their discretion in or upon any of the investments by this instrument authorised with power to vary or transpose such investments for or into any others of a like nature.

Powers of Investment

2. TRUST moneys to be invested under the trusts of this instrument may be applied or invested in any currency and in any part of the world in the purchase of or upon the security of such common or preferred stocks shares mutual fund shares unit trust units or other securities or commodities (including precious metals) bonds notes debentures certificates of deposit or time deposits land or other investments or property of whatever nature (and whether or not income-producing or paying dividends or interest) and whether involving liabilities or not or upon such personal credit with or without security as the Trustees in their absolute discretion think fit without being restricted to trustee investments prescribed under the proper law governing this instrument and to the intent that the Trustees shall have the same powers in all respects as if they were absolute owners beneficially entitled And in addition (but without prejudice to the generality of the foregoing) the Trustees may invest the Trust Fund in the shares or debentures of any company whatsoever and wheresoever incorporated without the need for diversification and without being liable for any loss occasioned thereby.

Power with regard to mode of application of capital and income

3. ANY power by this instrument or by law conferred on the Trustees to pay transfer appropriate or apply the Trust Fund or any income therefore for the benefit of any beneficiary may at the discretion of the Trustees be validly exercised (without prejudice to the generality of such power or to any other mode of application) -

(a) by paying or transferring the same to the trustees of any settlement (whether or not such trustees are resident in the British Virgin Islands and whether or not the proper law of such settlement is the law of the British Virgin Islands) the provisions of which are in the opinion of the Trustees for the benefit of such beneficiary notwithstanding that such settlement may also contain trusts

powers or provisions (discretionary or otherwise) in favour of other persons or objects Provided however that no such payment or transfer shall be made so as to infringe the rule against perpetuities as applicable to the trusts created by this instrument; or

(b) (in the case of any such person who is a minor) by paying or transferring the same to such minor's parent or guardian or some other person for the time being having the care or custody of such minor upon the recipient undertaking to apply the same for the benefit of the minor;

And the Trustees shall not thereafter be under any obligation to see to the further application of the capital or income so paid or transferred and the receipt of such trustees parent guardian or other person shall be a full sufficient and complete discharge to the Trustees.

Additional Powers

4. THE Trustees shall have the following powers in addition to those conferred by law:

(a) power to receive any property from any person as an addition to the Trust Fund either by gift inter vivos or by will or under the provisions of any other settlement or trust or otherwise;

(b) power to borrow on the security of the Trust Fund and for such purpose to make any outlay out of the Trust Fund or the income thereof and to enter into such contracts mortgages charges or undertakings relating thereto as the Trustees may in their absolute discretion think fit;

(c) power to lend any part of the Trust Fund to any person (whether or not a beneficiary) upon such terms (if any) as to security repayment rate of interest and otherwise as the Trustee in their absolute discretion may determine;

(d) with respect to any property comprised in the Trust Fund power to exercise all powers relating thereto as if beneficially entitled thereto and without being restricted in any way by the office of trustee including (without prejudice to the generality of the foregoing power) -

(i) power to vote upon or in respect of any shares securities bonds notes or other evidence of interest in or obligations of any corporation trust association or concern whether or not the exercise of such power affects the security or the apparent security of the Trust Fund or the purchase or sale or lease of the assets of any such corporation trust association or concern,

(ii) power to deposit any such shares securities or property in any voting trust or with any depository designated thereby,

(iii) power to give proxies or powers of attorney with or without power of substitution for voting or acting on behalf of the Trustees as the owners of any such property, and

(iv) power to omit to register bonds or securities;

(e) power (at the expense of the Trust Fund) to incorporate or register or to procure the incorporation or registration of any company (with limited or unlimited liability) in any part of the world for any purpose including the acquisition of the Trust Fund or any part thereof and so that (if thought fit) the consideration on the sale of the Trust Fund to any such company may consist wholly or partly of fully paid shares debentures debenture stock or other securities of the company credited as fully paid which shall be allotted to or otherwise vested in the Trustees and be capital moneys in the Trustees' hands;

(f) power at any time to apply any part of the Trust Fund of the income thereof in effecting or joining in effecting or otherwise acquiring any policy of assurance on the life of any beneficiary or of any other person or any endowment or other policy and to maintain surrender exchange exercise any option thereunder or otherwise deal with such policies as if the Trustees were absolutely entitled thereto;

(g) power to pay out at any time any part of the Trust Fund in purchasing or acquiring or making improvements in or repairs to or on any land or building (whether freehold leasehold or of any other tenure or interest and of whatsoever description and situate in any part of the world) in the occupation of or intended for occupation by any beneficiary And power to permit any beneficiary to occupy until sale any land or building purchased or acquired as aforesaid or otherwise comprised in the Trust Fund upon such terms (as to payment or non-payment of rent outgoings repairs or otherwise) as the Trustees may think fit;

(h) power at any time or times to lay out any part of the Trust Fund in the purchase or other acquisition of any yachts boats motor vehicles works of art household furniture plate linen china cutlery other articles of household use ornament or equipment and other chattels for the use of any beneficiary whether occupying a building purchased or acquired as aforesaid or otherwise And power to hand over to any such beneficiary for his use any property so purchased or acquired by the Trustees as aforesaid or otherwise forming part of the Trust Fund upon and subject to such terms and conditions (if any) as to insurance preservation maintaining inventories and otherwise as the Trustees think fit;

(i) power to grant options for such consideration and exercisable at such time or times or within such period as the Trustees think fit for the purchase of any property subject to the trusts of this instrument or the acquisition of any interest therein;

(j) power to keep the Trust Fund either in or out of the British Virgin Islands and if the Trustees think fit to hold in any part of the world all or any securities or other property in bearer form or registered in the name of the Trustees or nominees without disclosing the fiduciary relationship;

(k) in the event of any duties fees or taxes whatsoever becoming payable in any part of the world in respect of the Trust Fund or any part thereof in any circumstances whatsoever power to pay all such duties fees or taxes out of the Trust Fund or the income thereof with discretion as to the time and manner in which the said duties fees or taxes shall be paid and the Trustees may pay such duties fees or taxes notwithstanding that the same shall not be recoverable from the Trustees or from any persons interested under the trusts of this instrument or that the payment shall not be to the advantage of such persons;

(l) power to make such reserves out of the Trust Fund or the income thereof as the Trustees deem proper for expenses taxes and other liabilities and to pay from capital or income or to apportion between capital and income any expenses of making or changing investments and selling exchanging or leasing (including brokers commissions and charges) and generally to determine what part of the expenses of administering the trusts of this instrument shall be charged to capital and what part to income;

(m) power to make execute and deliver deeds assignments transfers leases mortgages instruments of pledge creating liens contracts and other instruments sealed and unsealed;

(n) power to institute prosecute and defend any suits or actions or other proceedings affecting the Trustees or the Trust Fund and to compromise any matter of difference or to submit such matter for arbitration and to compromise or compound any debt owing to the Trustees or any other claims and to adjust any disputes in relation to debts or claims against them as trustees upon evidence that the Trustees shall deem sufficient and to make partition upon such terms (including if thought fit the payment or receipt of equality money) as the Trustees shall deem desirable with co-owners or joint tenants besides the Trustees having any interest in any property in which the Trustees are interested and to make partition either by sale or by set-off or by agreement or otherwise;

(o) power to make any distribution of the Trust Fund pursuant to the trusts of this instrument in cash or in kind or partly in cash and partly in kind and in

the case of a distribution to more than one person not strictly rateably but on the basis of equal or other proportionate value (as the case may require) according to the judgment of the Trustees which shall be binding on all persons interested under this instrument;

(p) power to take at the expense of the Trust Fund or the income thereof the opinion of legal counsel concerning any question arising under this instrument or on any matter in any way relating to the Trust Fund or the duties of the Trustees in connection with this instrument And the Trustees shall not be liable for any action taken in good faith pursuant to or otherwise in accordance with the opinion or advice of such counsel;

(q) power -

(i) to engage the services of such investment counsel adviser or manager ("the Investment Adviser") as the Trustees may from time to time think fit (including the settlor or any trustee of this instrument or any corporate trustee or any parent subsidiary or affiliate of such corporate trustee) in order to obtain advice on the investment and reinvestment of the Trust Fund AND to delegate to the Investment Adviser without being liable for any consequential loss discretion to manage the portfolio or any part thereof within the limits and for the period stipulated by the Trustees and the Trustees

(aa) shall settle the terms and conditions for the remuneration of the Investment Adviser and the reimbursement of the Investment Adviser's expenses as in their uncontrolled discretion they deem proper and such remuneration and expenses may be paid by the Trustees from and out of the Trust Fund, and

(bb) shall not be liable for any action taken in good faith pursuant to or otherwise in accordance with the advice of the Investment Adviser,

(ii) to employ and pay at the expense of the capital or income of the Trust Fund any agent or agents in any part of the world whether solicitors bankers accountants stockbrokers managers or other persons (including the settlor or any trustee of this instrument or any corporate trustee or any parent subsidiary or affiliate of such corporate trustee) to transact any business or to do any act requiring to be transacted or done in execution of the trusts of this instrument including the receipt and payment of money and the execution of documents and in any such event the trustee, the corporate trustee or the parent subsidiary or the affiliate of such corporate trustee is entitled to charge and be paid and to retain for his or its own account all usual professional and other fees and commissions normally paid for such services including fees and commissions shared with other agents;

(r) power for all or any of the Trustees

(i) to exercise or join or concur in exercising all or any of the powers and discretions by this instrument or by law given to the Trustees notwithstanding that such trustee may have a personal interest in the mode or result of exercising any such power or discretion or may be interested therein in some other fiduciary capacity but any trustee may abstain from acting except as a merely formal party in any matter in which he may be so interested as aforesaid and may allow his co-trustees to act alone in the exercise of such powers and discretions in relation to such matter, and

(ii) to purchase or sell any property notwithstanding that the vendor or purchaser is the same as or includes the Trustees or any of them provided that the price payable on any such purchase or sale is certified as fair and reasonable by an independent valuer employed for the purpose by the Trustees;

(s) power to effect any transaction concerning or affecting the Trust Fund or any other property whatsoever and to do all other acts and things which the Trustees may in their absolute discretion think expedient in the interests of the Trust Fund or any beneficiary and for the purpose of this sub-paragraph "transaction" includes any sale exchange assurance conveyance grant lease surrender reconveyance release reservation or other disposition and any purchase or other acquisition and any covenant contract licence option right or pre-emption and any compromise or partition and any company reconstruction or amalgamation and any other dealing or arrangement And "effect" has the meaning appropriate to the particular transaction and references to property include references to restrictions and burdens affecting the property;

(t) all the powers of sale (by public auction or private contract) exchange mortgaging leasing or other disposition management repair building and improvement and all other powers of an absolute beneficial owner in respect of any property for the time being comprised in the Trust Fund including (without prejudice to the generality of the foregoing) the power of borrowing on the security of the Trust Fund and for such purpose to make any outlay out of the income or capital of the Trust Fund and to make such contracts and to enter into such undertakings relating thereto as the Trustees in their absolute discretion shall think fit;

(*u*) power at any time in the Trustees' discretion and on such terms as they deem fit to appropriate or to apply the capital or income of the Trust Fund or any part thereof in order to secure the payment of money owed by any beneficiary or the performance of any obligations of any beneficiary and to give any guarantee or to become surety for any beneficiary and for such purposes to mortgage or charge any investments or property for the time being forming part of the Trust Fund or to deposit or transfer any such investments or property with or to any person by way of security; and

(*v*) power from time to time by deed revocable or irrevocable wholly or partially to release extinguish or restrict any power by this instrument or by law conferred on the Trustees notwithstanding the fiduciary nature of any such power (but not so as to invalidate any prior exercise thereof).

Exclusion of appointments

5. UNLESS the Trustees in their absolute discretion shall otherwise determine all dividends and other income received shall be treated for all purposes as income accruing at the due date of payment whether or not such dividends or income may have been earned and accrued wholly or partially in respect of a period prior to such date.

Protection of third parties in dealings with trustees

6.(1) NO person or corporation dealing with the Trustees and no purchaser on any sale made by the Trustees shall be concerned to enquire into the propriety or validity of any act of the Trustees or to see to the application of any money paid or property transferred to or upon the order of the Trustees.

(2) NO firm association or corporation any of whose securities are comprised in the Trust Fund and no purchaser or person dealing with any trustee purporting to act under any delegation of authority from any other trustee shall be required to ascertain or enquire whether a case exists in which such delegation is permitted or whether such delegated authority is still subsisting.

(3) WHEN anything is dependent upon the value of any property or the existence of any fact a certificate of the Trustees as to such value or fact shall be conclusive in favour of anyone thereon in good faith.

Power in relation to underlying company

7. ANY trustee of this instrument and director officer or employee of a corporate trustee or of a parent subsidiary or affiliate of such corporate trustee may act as a director officer manager or employee of any company whose shares or debentures may be comprised in the Trust Fund or as a director officer manager or employee of any subsidiary or holding company of any such company and may retain for himself or itself any remuneration which he or it may receive as such director officer manager or employee notwithstanding that any votes or other rights attaching to such shares or debentures may have been instrumental either alone or in conjunction with other matters or by reason of their non-exercise in procuring or continuing for him or it his or its position as such director officer manager or employee or that his or its qualifications for any such position may be constituted in part or in whole by any such shares or debenture.

Trustees not bound to interfere with company management

8. THE Trustees shall not be bound or required to interfere in the management or conduct of the affairs or business of any company in which the Trust Fund may be invested (and whether or not the Trustees have the control of such company) And so long as no trustee of this instrument has notice of any wilful negligence wilful default or fraud or dishonesty on the part of the directors having the management of such company they may leave the same (including the payment or non-payment of dividends) wholly to such directors And no beneficiary is entitled as such beneficiary in any way to compel control or forbid the exercise (including in any particular manner) of any voting or other rights at any time vested in the Trustees with regard to such company including without prejudice to the generality of the foregoing any powers the Trustees may have (even if also directors of such company) of compelling such company to distribute any dividend.

BRITISH VIRGIN ISLANDS

INCOME TAX ACT (as amended)

ARRANGEMENT OF SECTIONS

Temporary Residents

Rate Of Tax

Trustees, Agents, Etc.

Returns: By Whom To Be Made

Partnerships

Pay As You Earn

Assessment And Assessment Lists

Additional Assessments

49 Omissions and undercharges may be rectified.

Appeals

49A Board of Referees.
49B Appeals to the Board.
49C Appeals to a Judge.
50 Miscellaneous re: Appeals.

Errors In Assessments And Notices

51 Assessments, etc. not void by reason of errors therein in names and descriptions.

Repayment Of Tax

52 Circumstances under which repayment may be made.

Relief In Cases Of Double Taxation

54 Unilateral relief.
55 Double taxation arrangements.
56 Tax credits.

General Powers Of Commissioner

58 Powers of Commissioner to require returns and particulars.

Collection And Recovery Of Tax

59 Payment of tax.
60 Penalty for non-payment of tax.
61 Recovery of tax.
62 Provost Marshal to levy on goods, etc.
63 Sale to be public auction.
64 Application of proceeds of sale.
65 Commission to Provost Marshal.
65 Power to declare.
66. Recovery of tax in certain cases.

Notices

67 Signature of notices.
68 Service of notices.

General

Tax in the British Virgins Islands is basically similar to that imposed in the United Kingdom before 1965 - that is, there is a single income tax imposed on companies (other than IBCs) as well as on individuals and the BVI has no capital gains tax. There is no kind of death duty or inheritance tax. There are some differences between the two systems: the Acts here are very much shorter than the Acts of Parliament of the UK, and are relatively free of anti-avoidance provisions. But the basic concepts are sufficiently similar - the phraseology of the Income Tax Act of 1946 having clear antecedents in the UK's Income Tax Act 1918 - for the cases decided in the United Kingdom to be useful in interpreting the Law of the Virgin Islands, and in practice - the Territory having no body of case law of its own - both the Commissioner and taxpayers treat the UK cases (so far as relevant) as persuasive - if not actually binding - here.

Short Title.

1. This Act may be cited as the Income Tax Act.

Interpretation.

2. In this Act

"Board" means the Board of Referees appointed under section 49A;

"body of persons" means any body, politic, corporate or collegiate and any company, fraternity, fellowship, or society of persons whether corporate or not corporate;

"cent'" and c'" mean in the currency of the United States of America;

"chargeable income" means the aggregate amount of the income of any person from the sources specified in section 5 remaining after allowing the appropriate deductions and exemptions under this Act;

"Collector" includes a Commissioner appointed under section 3 and an officer acting in that capacity or any other person deputed by him for any purpose under this Act;

"Commissioner" means the Commissioner appointed under section 3;

"company" means any company incorporated or registered under any law for the time being in force in the Virgin Islands and any company which, though incorporated or registered outside the Virgin Islands, carries on business or has an office or place of business therein;

"dollar" and '$" mean dollar in the currency of the United States of America;

"earned income" means any income arising in respect of any gains or profits immediately derived by the individual from any trade, business, profession, employment or vocation carried on or exercised by him either as an individual or in the case of a partnership, as a partner personally acting therein, or in respect of any person, superannuation or other allowance given in respect of past services of the individual or the husband or parent of the individual or given to the individual in respect of the past services of any deceased person whether the individual or husband or parent of the individual shall have contributed to such pension, superannuation or other allowance or not after deducting the expenses referred to in sections 11 and 14, but before allowing thc other deductions to be made in arriving at the chargeable income;

"employee" includes a director of a company;

"Government employee" means an individual who is in the employment of the Crown in the right of its Government of the Virgin Islands and is subject to the General Orders for the Public Service;

"Off-shore trading company" means a company that is resident in the Virgin Islands and has satisfied the Commissioner that

(a) it carries on a trade or business the gains or profits of which are chargeable to tax under the provision of section 5(a); and

(b) at least 90 per cent of the gains or profits of the trade or business so chargeable arise from trading or business transactions carried on wholly and exclusively outside the Virgin Islands;

"Office of employment" includes a directorship of a Company;

"Inspector" means an inspector assigned as such under 44B;

"Investment income" means dividends arising from stocks, shares or interest arising from Government Securities, bank deposits, loans or other income of a similar nature;

"prescribed" means prescribed by rule under this Act;

"real estate holding company" means any company incorporated outside the Virgin Islands where more than 50 per centum of the market value of its assets in the Virgin Islands comprise real estate;

"resident" in relation to an individual means an individual resident in the Territory, and in relation to a body of persons means that the control and management of affairs of that body of persons was exercised in the Territory in the year of income, and without limitation to the foregoing definition, the control and management shall be deemed to be so exercised whenever on or after the 1st January, 1978 more than half the members of the board of directors (as defined by the memorandum and articles of association of the company in the case of a company incorporated under the Companies Act) or other controlling persons (in the case of a body of persons other than a company) are resident in the Territory; A company is resident if "control and management of affairs of that body of persons was exercised in the Territory in the year of income". Students of tax treaties will find the definition not unexpected - though it should be noted that the test is to be applied in the "year of income" (which is in general the 12 month period preceding the year of assessment) and not - as is the case with individuals - in the year of assessment itself. The deeming provision was added in 1977 to make it easier for a company whose business is in fact managed and controlled outside the Territory to take advantage of the exemptions and reliefs afforded by tax treaties.

"tax" means the income tax imposed by this Act;

"year of assessment" means the period of twelve months commencing on the first day of January in each year;

"year of income" or "income year" means the period of 12 months immediately preceding the commencement of the year of assessment except in cases specified in paragraphs (a), (b) and (c) of section 6(2) where "year of income" or "income year" means the year of assessment itself.

Administration

Appointment

3.(1) The Governor may appoint a Commissioner and such other officers as may be necessary for the due administration of this Act.

(2) Every officer serving in the Income Tax Department immediately before this Act comes into effect shall be deemed to have been appointed under this section.

(3) Where under this Act any power is conferred or any duty imposed on the Commissioner, then such power may be exercised or such duty performed by any officer appointed under this section who is authorized in writing by the Commissioner so to do.

(4) Notwithstanding anything contained in this section, the Commissioner is subject to such policy directives as may be issued to him by the Minister.

4.(1) Every person having any official duty or being employed in the administration of this Act shall regard and deal with all documents, information, returns, assessment lists, and copies of such lists relating to the income or items of income of any person, as secret and confidential, and shall make and subscribe a declaration to that effect before a Magistrate.

(2) Every person having possession of or control over any documents, information, returns or assessment lists or copies of such lists relating to the income or items of income of any person who at any time communicates or attempts to communicate such information or anything contained in such documents, returns, lists or copies to any person

(a) other than a person to whom he is authorized by the Governor to communicate it;

(b) otherwise than for the purposes of this Act, shall be guilty of an offence against this Act.

(3) Where, under any law in force in any part of the Commonwealth, provision is made for the allowance of relief from income tax in respect of the payment of income tax in the Virgin Islands, the obligation as to secrecy imposed by this section shall not prevent the disclosure to the authorized officers of the Government in that part of the Commonwealth of such facts as may be necessary to enable the proper relief to be given in cases where relief if claimed from income tax in the Virgin Islands or from income tax in that part aforesaid.

Imposition Of Income Tax

5. Income tax shall, subject to the provisions of this Act, be payable at the rate or rates specified hereafter for the year of assessment commencing on the 1st day of January, 1946, and for each subsequent, upon the income of any person accruing in or derived from the Virgin Islands or elsewhere, and whether received in the Virgin Islands or not in respect of:-

(a) gains or profits from any trade, business, profession, or vocation, for whatever period of time such trade, business, profession or vocation may have been carried on or exercised;

It is considered that the effect of the reference to "period of time" extends the ambit of this paragraph to cover an isolated transaction - some degree of continuity being otherwise indicated by "trade" etc., so that a single purchase and sale, for example, or the giving of a single piece of professional advice may give rise to taxable income. But this should not blur the distinction between capital and income: an isolated transaction may well not be of a trading (etc.) nature at all, and if it is not, the resulting profit is not taxable under this paragraph.

Members of a mutual insurance association do not trade with each other: their insurance surpluses (though not the income from investing their reserves) are free of tax.

The use of the word "business" extends the tax charge to profits of farming and market gardening, which are not "trades", but does not appear to have any more far reaching effect. The words "profession" and "vocation" together cover most of the rest of those who are generally called "self-employed".

Non-residents will be liable to tax under this paragraph if the income from their trade etc., has its source in the Virgin Islands. Here we come to the well-known distinction between trading "in" and trading "with" a country. Only if the non-resident is trading in the Territory will he be liable to tax here under the paragraph (and even then he may be exempted under a tax treaty). In determining whether a trade is carried on in the Territory, one primarily looks to see whether the contracts are made here, but that test should not be applied mechanically.

(b) gains or profits from any office or employment;

(d) dividends, interest or discounts;

But see paragraphs (q) and (r) and the second proviso to s.8(1).

(e) any charge of annuity;

The reference to "charge" is obscure. As regards annuities, there is no machinery for separating the capital element in any kind of annuity and the whole amount is to be treated as income.

(f) rents, royalties, premiums and any other profits arising from property;

The expression "profits" here must be taken as referring to profits of an income nature and not to the profit arising on disposal of a property - which would only be taxed if it were a profit of a trade or business. And it is submitted that a similar restriction is to be placed on the meaning of "premiums" in this paragraph.

(g) any gains from the sale of shares of any real estate holding company by a non-resident corporate majority shareholder, only that part of the gains which is attributable to such real estate in the Virgin Islands.

(h) any annual gains or profits not falling under any of the foregoing heads.

The adjective "annual" does not require the gains or profits to occur in more than one year, but the category of items under this head is not limitless. It does not charge amounts which are not income at all - e.g. are capital gains, or have no source (like gifts). What it essentially covers are profits of a casual nature - payments made to a taxpayer who provided his life story to a newspaper, and payments to a professional person for services outside the scope of his professional activities, may be taxed under this head.

Provided that in the case of income arising outside the Virgin Islands which is earned income of an individual or which accrues to any person who is not ordinarily resident, or who is not domiciled, in the Virgin Islands, tax shall be payable on the amount received in the Virgin Islands.

This proviso may be particularly relevant to the vacation home owner who will not be ordinarily resident even though he could be regarded as resident here. The effect of the proviso on individuals not ordinarily resident here is to limit the extent to which tax is levied on their income arising outside the Territory: tax on foreign income is payable only on the amount received in the Territory.

The same favourable treatment is accorded to the foreign income of persons not domiciled here. The concept of "domiciled" comes from English law. Putting the matter very shortly, an individual is domiciled here if he truly belongs here. An infant has his father's domicil - or his mother's if he is illegitimate - during his infancy, and retains that domicil on attaining his majority. This is his "domicil of origin". By going to live elsewhere with the intention of making it his permanent home, he can acquire a "domicil of choice" in some other country, state or province, and a woman during marriage takes the domicil of her husband as a "dependent" domicil. An individual cannot be without a domicil; if circumstances giving rise to such domicil of choice or dependent domicil cease, new circumstances may create a new domicil of choicc or dependent domicil, but if they do not, the individual's domicil of origin revives. It is inherent in the concept of domicil that an individual may live a long time in a place without becoming domiciled there. Suppose for example, a man born and brought up in Scotland comes to run a business in Road Town; he likes living on Tortola, and spends many years here, but he never intends to end his days here, planning (let us say) to return to the Outer Hebrides when he retires. He would be a typical example of an individual resident and ordinarily resident, but not domiciled here.

The proviso to section 5 affords the same treatment to foreign earned income of resident individuals. Earned income is defined in section 2 to include income from any trade, business, profession, employment, or vocation; it extends to partnership income, if the individual acts personally in the partnership, and to certain pensions. Whether such income has its source abroad is not always easy to say. The old UK cases indicate that the test for an employment is where payment can be claimed and is made, but this is not in line with current UK enactments and it is submitted that the test here ought to be where the services in substance are performed.

Locating the source of business or professional income can also be difficult: it seems that all - absolutely all - the profit-earning activities must take place abroad if the income is to have a foreign source; even mere passive oversight from within the Virgin Islands causes the income to arise in the Territory.

Basis Of Assessment

6.(1) Tax shall, in respect of each year of assessment, be charged, levied and collected upon the chargeable income of any person for the year immediately preceding the year of assessment, except that in cases specified in subsection (2) the tax shall be assessed, charged, levied and collected on the chargeable income of a person for the year of assessment itself.

(2) The exceptions referred to in subsection (1) are as follows: -

(a) gains or profits arising after 31st December 1981, from any office or employment and chargeable to tax under paragraph (b) of section 5;

(b) subject to subsection (3), gains or profits arising after the 31st December 1986 from any trade, profession or vocation or chargeable to tax under paragraph (a) of section 5; and

(c) any other income arising after 31st December 1986 and chargeable to tax under paragraph (d), (e), (f), (g) or (h) of section 5.

(3) For the purposes of paragraph (b) of subsection (2), where

(a) the accounts of a trade, business, profession or vocation are usually made up to an accounting date other than the 31st December of any year; and

(b) the year ending on the accounting date has been used as a special period of assessment under the provisions of section 7;

then, the accounting date so used that immediately precedes the 31st December 1986 shall be substituted for the 31st December 1987.

Special periods of assessment.

7.(1) The Commissioner may, where he is satisfied that a person usually makes up the accounts of this trade or business on some day other than the last day of the year of income, permit the gains or profits of that trade or business to be computed for the purposes of this Act upon the income of the year terminating on that day in the year of income on which the accounts of the trade or business are usually made up.

(2) Notwithstanding subsection (1), where permission has been granted by the Commissioner under that subsection in respect of any year or assessment, tax shall be assessed, charged, levied and collected for each subsequent year upon the gains or profits for the full year terminating on the like date in the year of income, subject to any adjustment as the Commissioner considers reasonable.

Exemptions

Exemptions.

8.(1) There shall be exempt from the tax:-

(a) the official emoluments received by the Governor;

(b) the estimated annual value of any quarters, board or residence provided for a Government employee;

(c) any pension payable

(i) by the Government in respect of service rendered to the Government; or

(ii) from a source other than the Government for past services rendered in any office or employment, the gains or profits from which were chargeable to tax under paragraph (b) of section 5, exemption shall be given under this section only in so far as the amount of the pension payable is such as the Commissioner considers just and reasonable, having regard to the nature and duration of the past services rendered in that office or employment;

(d) the income of any ecclesiastical charitable educational institution of a public character in so far as such income is not derived from a trade or business carried on by such institution;

(e) the emoluments payable to members of the permanent consular services of foreign countries in respect of their offices or in respect of services rendered by them in their official capacity;

(f) the emoluments payable from Imperial funds to members of Her Majesty's Forces and to persons in the permanent service of the Imperial Government in the Virgin Islands in respect of their offices under the Imperial Government;

(g) wound and disability pensions granted to members of Her Majesty's Forces;

(h) gratuities granted to members of Her Majesty's Forces in respect of services rendered during war;

(i) interest earned by an individual resident in the Territory on any deposit in any Bank to which the Banking Act 1972 (No. 17 of 1972) applies;

(j) the incomes of Ministers of Religion derived from their occupation as such;

(k) income arising from the business of shipping or airline services carried on by a person not resident in the Virgin Islands, if the Governor is satisfied that a reciprocal exemption from income tax is granted by the country or place where the person is resident to persons resident in the Virgin Islands;

(l) gratuities due and paid on or after the 1st January, 1962, to "non-pensionable" public officers under contracts of service entered into between the Government of the Virgin Islands and such officers; The expression "non-pensionable" herein means not eligible for or not in receipt of a pension under the Pension Act, 1947;

(m) education allowances paid to public officers under the Overseas Service (Virgin Islands) Agreement, 1961, ratified and confirmed by the Overseas Service Act, 1961; This exemption applies even if the emoluments are remitted to the Territory.

(n) any earned income arising from sources in the United States Virgin Islands and Puerto Rico accruing to an individual who is resident in the Virgin Islands;

(o) the income of a pension fund approved by the Commissioner;

(p) the emoluments payable to any person arriving in the Virgin Islands for the purpose of rendering any technical assistance under arrangements between the Virgin Islands' Government and another Government or between the Virgin Islands' Government and the United Nations or an International Agency;

(q) dividends paid by any company which is registered in the Territory under the provisions of the Companies Act;

(r) interest arising in the Territory which accrues to any person who is not ordinarily resident in the Territory;

(s) emoluments received by persons engaged solely in domestic duties in private households.

Provided that nothing in this section shall be construed to exempt in the hands of the recipients any dividends, interest, bonuses, salaries or wages paid wholly or in part out of the income so exempted.

And provided further that where it appears to the Commissioner that the rate of dividend or interest paid to a person as described in paragraph (q) or (r) ante is by reason by the commercial or financial relationship between such person and the payer higher than the rate which but for such relationship would have been paid, he may direct that the dividend or excess interest paid by reason of such higher rate shall not be treated as exempt from tax.

(2) For the purposes of paragraph (k) of subsection (1)(a) "business of shipping or airline services" means the business carried on by an owner of ships or aircraft and for the purposes of this definition, "owner" includes a charterer.

(3) A company shall be deemed to be resident in the country or place where it has the central management and control of its business.

Power to exempt licensed broadcasting station from tax.

9. The Governor may by order in council published exempt "Gazette" provide that the income of any licensed broadcasting station shall be exempted from the tax for such period not exceeding five years as he shall deem fit; and such income shall from that shall from that date and to the extent specified in the order be exempt accordingly.

Government Loans.

10. The Governor may by order in council published in the "Gazette" provide that the interest payable on any loan charged on the public revenue of the Virgin Islands shall be exempted from the tax, either generally or only in respect of interest payable to persons not resident in the Virgin Islands; and such interest shall as from the date and to the extent specified in the order be exempt accordingly.

Ascertainment Of Chargeable Income

The profits of trade, business, profession or vocation taxed under paragraph (a) of section 5 (and, in appropriate cases, casual profits taxable under paragraph (g) of that section) are to be ascertained on ordinary accounting principles - except insofar as those principles are modified by provisions of the Act. The Act proceeds by permitting certain deductions (in this section) and prohibiting others (in section 13). These provisions modify ordinary accounting principles very little, and most deductions in computing trading profits are made by authority of accounting principles - the statutory provisions simply not, so to speak, interfering with their deduction. But as regards other kinds of income, any deductions require to be authorised by this section and not forbidden by section 13.

Deductions Allowed.

11.(1) For the purpose of ascertaining the chargeable income of any person for any year of income, there shall be deducted all outgoings and expenses wholly and exclusively incurred during that year of income by that person in the production of the income, including:

(a) sums paid by such person by way of interest upon any money borrowed by him, where the Commissioner is satisfied that the interest was paid on capital employed in acquiring the income.

(b) rent paid by any tenant of land or buildings occupied by him for the purpose of acquiring the income;

(c) any sum expended for repair of premises, plant and machinery employed in acquiring the income, or for the renewal, repair or alteration of any implement, utensil or article so employed;

(d) bad debts incurred in any trade, business, profession or vocation, proved to the satisfaction of the Commissioner to have become bad during the year immediately preceding the year of assessment, and doubtful debts to the extent that they are respectively estimated to the satisfaction of the Commissioner to have become bad during the said year notwithstanding that such bad or doubtful debts were due and payable prior to the commencement of the said year:

Provided that all sums recovered during the said year on account of amounts previously written off or allowed in respect of bad or doubtful debts shall for the purposes of this Act be treated as receipts of the trade, business, profession or vocation for that year;

(f) such other deductions (not being deductions of the kind disallowed by section 13) as may be prescribed by any rule made under this Act.

(2) The Governor in Council may by rules provide for the method of calculating or estimating the deductions allowed under this section.

Relief to hotel proprietors from income tax.

12.(1) Where

(a) a licence has been granted to a person under the provisions of section 3 of the of the Hotel Aid Act, 1977, for the construction of a new hotel or for the extension of an existing hotel; and

(b) the person to whom that licence was granted has incurred capital expenditure in respect of the construction or extension then, the deductions allowable to that person in respect of the capital expenditure under section 14(1) shall, for all purposes of this Act, be treated as increased by 20 per centum and the increased deductions so allowed are not recoverable under the provisions of section 14 in the event of a subsequent sale or disposal of the hotel.

(2) In this section "capital expenditure" means such sum as the Commissioner is satisfied has been expended on the purchase of building materials or of articles of hotel equipment for the construction or extension of the hotel and upon effecting such construction or extension and upon the installation of such equipment, but does not include any sum paid in respect of the purchase price of any land or of any existing hotel or in respect of goodwill.

Deductions not to be allowed.

13. For the purpose of ascertaining the chargeable income of any person no deduction shall be allowed in respect of:

(a) domestic or private expenses;

(b) any disbursements or expenses not being money wholly and exclusively laid out or expended for the purpose of acquiring the income;

It has been said that "wholly" refers to the amount, and "exclusively" to the motive or object of the expenditure. At all events, the test is a strict one - particularly, in practice, when it comes to expenses (like travelling and entertaining) which may be a pleasure to incur.

(c) any capital withdrawn or any sum employed or intended to be employed as capital;

Since capital receipts are not included in income, it is in principle logical that no deduction should be permitted for capital outgoings or expenditure. This provision prevents any deduction for depreciation - which general accounting principles on their own might permit, but allowances are provided by s.14.

(d) any capital employed in improvements;

(e) any sum recoverable under an insurance or contract of indemnity;

(f) rent of or cost of repairs to any premises or part of premises not paid or incurred for the purpose of producing the income;

Anything disallowed here would in any case be disallowed under head (b) above.

(g) any licence fee payable under the Companies Act for which a tax credit has been allowed under section 26(3).

Allowance for wear and tear

14.(1) In ascertaining the chargeable income of any person engaged in a trade, business, profession or vocation, there shall be allowed as a deduction a reasonable amount for the exhaustion, wear and tear of property owned by him, including plant and machinery, plant and machinery, arising out of the use or employment of such property in the trade, business, profession or vocation during the year of income.

The allowances extend beyond the categories of plant and machinery, to all kinds of "property" subject to "exhaustion" - which would presumably extend to incorporeal assets of limited life - like know-how, patents and copyrights. No scale of allowances is provided by the Act: they are to be "such as the Commissioner may consider just and reasonable".

(2) The deductions to be allowed under this section for exhaustion, wear and tear shall be such as the Commissioner may consider just and reasonable.

(3) The deductions to be allowed under this section shall in total be equal to, but not greater than, the excess of the original cost of the property, by reference to which the deductions due under this section have been calculated, over the sales price or the proceeds of disposal or the market value of the property when it is sold or disposed of or otherwise ceases to be used or employed in the trade, business, profession or vocation.

(4) Where there is an excess of the original cost of the property over:

(a) the sales price;

(b) the proceeds of disposal; or

(c) the market value, as the case may be, as described in subsection (3), the adjustment needed to ensure that the deductions allowed under this section are in total equal to but not greater than that excess shall be made by way of an addition to, or a deduction from, the chargeable income of the year in which the property is sold or disposed of or otherwise ceases to be used or employed in the trade, business, profession or vocation.

(5) Where there is no excess of the original cost of the property over

(a) the sales price;

(b) the proceeds of disposal; or

(c) the market value, as the case may be, as described in subsection (3), no deductions shall be due under this section, and any deductions previously allowed shall be recovered by way of an addition to the chargeable income of the year in which the property is sold or disposed of or otherwise ceases to be used or employed in the trade, profession or vocation.

(6) For the purposes of this section, any amount recovered under a policy of insurance in respect of the loss or destruction of any property in respect of which deductions have been allowed under this section shall, as the case may be, treated as the sales price or the proceeds of disposal or the market value of the property.

Allowance of trade losses.

15.(1) Where, in any year of income, a person incurs a loss in a trade, business, profession or vocation, the gains or profits of which are chargeable to tax under paragraph (a) of section 5, that person may, for the purposes of this Act, make a claim to the Commissioner to have the amount of that loss set off against all his other income of any description whatsoever that arises in that same year of income and is chargeable to tax under this Act.

(2) No set-off for a loss incurred in any trade, business, profession or vocation shall be allowed under subsection (1) unless the trade, business, profession or vocation is bona fide and carried on with the intention of making a profit and there is a reasonable expectation that a profit will be made.

(3) Where, in any year of income,

(a) a claim for the set-off of a loss has been allowed by the Commissioner under subsection (1), but the amount of the loss incurred in the trade, business, profession or vocation exceeds the amount of all the other income; and

(b) the amount of the loss incurred can not for that reason be wholly set off against the other income arising in that year of income, an application may be made to the Commissioner to have the excess amount of the loss not so set off carried forward to the next year of Income and to have it set off for the purposes of this Act, against the gains or profits arising from the same trade, business, profession or vocation in the next successive years of income, until the amount of the loss has been completely set off.

(4) For the purposes of this section, the amount of the loss incurred in any trade, business, profession or vocation shall be computed in the same way as the amount of the gains or profits arising from that trade, business, profession or vocation would have been computed.

(5) The application for the set-off of losses under this section must be made to the Commissioner not later than two years immediately following the end of the year of assessment to which the application relates.

Insurance And Shipping Companies

Special provisions as to certain companies, etc.

23. Notwithstanding anything to the contrary contained in this Act, it is hereby provided

Insurance companies other than life insurance companies.

(a) in the case of an insurance company (other than a life insurance company) where the gains accrue in part outside the Territory, the gains or profits on which tax is payable shall be ascertained by taking the gross premiums and interest and other income received or receivable in the Virgin Islands (less any premiums returned to the insured and premiums paid on re-insurances) and deducting from the balance so arrived at deducting the actual losses (less the amount recovered in respect thereof under re-insurance), the agency expenses in the Virgin Islands and a fair proportion of the expenses of the Head Office of the company.

Life insurance companies.

(b) in the case of a life insurance company, whether mutual or proprietary, the gains or profits on which tax is payable shall be the investment income less the management expenses (including commission):

Provided that where such a company received premiums outside the Virgin Islands, the gains or profits shall be the same proportion of the total investment income of the company as the premiums received or annuities paid in the Virgin Islands bore to the total premiums received or annuities paid after deducting from the amount so arrived at the agency expenses in the Virgin Islands and a fair proportion of the expenses of the

Temporary Residents

Temporary residents

24. Tax shall not be payable in respect of any income arising outside the Virgin Islands and accruing to any income arising outside the Virgin Islands and accruing to any person who is in the Virgin Islands for some temporary purpose only and not with any intent to establish his residence there in and who has not actually resided in the Virgin Islands at one or more times for a period equal in the whole to six months in the year of income.

Income tax is, in general terms, imposed on the worldwide income of residents and on the income of non-residents to the extent that it has its source here. This simple statement of the position is not to be found anywhere in the Act and requires to be extracted from the general scheme of this enactment. The draftsman of this section clearly did not envisage that a person who never set foot in the Virgin Islands should be in a worse position than a temporary resident; his purpose, rather, was to give to a temporary resident the advantages enjoyed by a true non-resident. That a non-resident is within the charge to tax on such of his income as arises in the Territory is clear from subsection (1) of section 31.

How does the section affect the individual resident elsewhere who buys a holiday home (or otherwise has a place of abode available for his use) here, and visits it in the year of assessment in question. At first sight he would appear to be able to take advantage of the provisions of section 24, but the UK cases indicate that such a person must be treated as resident in any year in which he visits his holiday home. It is submitted, however, that even regular visits for vacations would not make him "ordinarily" resident - and, although no authority can be found for that proposition, it is understood that in practice no attempt is made to apply this rule to owners of vacation homes. See also the proviso to s.5.

Rate Of Tax

Rate of Tax.

25. Subject to the provisions of section 26 and 27, the tax payable under the provisions of section 5 shall be charged at the following rates:

On every dollar of the first $2,500.00, 3c in the dollar;

On every dollar of the next $5,000.00, viz from $2,501.00 to $7,500.00, 6c in the dollar;

On every dollar of the next $10,000.00, viz from $15,001 to $25,000.00, 15c in the dollar;

On every dollar beyond $25,000.00, 20c in the dollar.

Rate of tax on companies.

26.(1) Subject to this section, the tax payable on the chargeable income of the company shall be charged at the rate of 15 per centum.

(2) Where

(a) the chargeable income of a company exceeds $100,000.00 and not less than 90 per centum of that income consists of profits or gains arising within the Virgin Islands from contracts of exchange of currencies; and

(b) an amount representing not less than 8 per centum of those profits or gains is paid

(i) without demand therefore, and

(ii) as an advance of tax by the company on or before the 31st January in the year of assessment; the tax on the chargeable income shall be charged at the rate of 10 per centum.

(3) All gains and profits of an off-shore trading company that are chargeable to tax under paragraph (a) of section 5 are chargeable to tax at the rate of 1 per centum.

(4) Where part or all of the income of a company consists of investment Income which arises outside of the Territory and is exempt from tax in the jurisdiction where it arises other than by reason of any arrangement made in accordance with the provisions of subsection (1) of section 55 of this Act, such proportion of the chargeable income as is represented by the investment income shall be chargeable to tax at the rate of 1 per centum.

(5) All gains from the sale of shares of a real estate holding company which are chargeable to tax under paragraph (g) of section 5 are chargeable to tax at the rate of 15 per centum.

There are two classes of entity which come within the charge to tax but for which the Act omits to fix any rate. The first class is the body of persons which is not a company. An example of this is the mutual insurance society: although its operating surplus would be free of tax on "mutuality" principles, its investment income would be taxable. The omission of section 26 to fix a rate produces the anomalous result that such income though taxable, cannot be taxed, since no rate of tax is prescribed for it.

The other class of taxable entity for which the section falls to provide a rate of tax is the company incorporated outside the Virgin Islands which carries on no business in the Territory, has no office or place of business there and is not registered under the Companies Act. A person may have a source of income in the Territory without "carrying on business" here.

Such a company could be liable for tax in the Virgin Islands for either of two reasons - because it is resident or deemed to be resident here (see p.6) or because it has a source of income here. Again, the effect of the omission of section 26 is that such a company is taxable but not taxed.

Tax on service charges.

27.(1) Where an amount is collected by way of a service charge, howsoever described, on each bill tendered to a customer by a proprietor of an establishment to which the Hotel Accommodation (Taxation) Act, 1969 (No. 7 of 1969) applies, tax at the rate of seven per centum shall be payable by the proprietor on the amount collected for each month.

(2) The tax payable under subsection (1) shall be remitted by the proprietor to the Commissioner not later than fifteen days after the month for which the tax is due, and every such remittance shall be accompanied with a statement setting out:

(a) the month to which the remittance relates;

(b) the total amount of the charges collected during that month; and

(c) such other particulars as the Commissioner may require.

(3) Where an amount of the service charge referred to in subsection (1) is distributed amongst all or any of the employees of the proprietor, the amount received by each employee shall not be considered as remuneration of such employee for the purposes of this Act.

Trustees, Agents, Etc.

Chargeability of trustees, etc.

30. A receiver, trustee, guardian, curator, or committee, having the direction, control or management of any property or concern on behalf of any person, shall be chargeable to tax in respect of the income derived from such property or concern in like manner and to the like amount as such person would be chargeable if he had received such income, and every such receiver, trustee, guardian, curator or committee shall be answerable for doing all matters and things required to be done under this Act for the purpose of assessment and payment of tax:

Provided that nothing in this section shall affect the liability of any person represented by any such receiver, trustee, guardian, curator or committee to be himself charged to tax in his own name.

Chargeability of agent of person residing out of the Virgin Islands

31.(1) A person not resident in the Virgin Islands (hereinafter in this section referred to as a non-resident person) whether a British subject or not, shall be assessable and chargeable in the name of his trustee, guardian, curator or committee, or of any attorney, factor, agent, receiver, branch or manager, whether such attorney, factor, agent, receiver, branch or manager has the receipt of the income or not, in like manner and to the like amount as such non-resident person would be assessed and charged if he were resident in the Virgin Islands and in the actual receipt of such income; provided that in the case of any individual who is not resident in the Virgin Islands, and who is not a British subject, no deduction shall be allowed in respect of earned income or in respect of wife or child or in respect of life insurance.

A non-resident person shall be assessable and chargeable in respect of any income arising, whether directly or indirectly, through or from any attorneyship, factorship, agency, receivership, branch or management, and shall be so assessable and chargeable in the name of the attorney, factor, agent, receiver, branch or manager.

(2) Where a non-resident person carries on business with a resident person, and it appears to the Commissioner that owing to the close connection between the resident person and the non-resident person, and to the substantial control exercised by the non-resident person over the resident person, the course of business between those persons can be so arranged and is so arranged that the business done by the resident person in pursuance of his connection with the non-resident person produces to the resident person either no profits or less than the ordinary profits which might be expected to arise from that business, the non resident person shall be assessable and chargeable to tax in the name of the resident person as if the resident person were an agent of the non-resident person.

(3) Where it appears to the Commissioner by whom the assessment is made, or to the Board or Judge by whom an appeal is heard, that the true amount of the gains or profits of any non-resident person chargeable with tax in the name of a resident person can not in any case be readily ascertained, the Commissioner, Board of Judge may, if he thinks fit, assess and charge the non-resident person on a fair and reasonable percentage of the turnover of the business done by the non-resident person through or with the resident person in whose name he is chargeable as aforesaid, and in such case the provisions of this Act relating to the delivery of returns or particulars by persons acting on behalf of others shall extend so as to require returns or particulars to be furnished by the resident person of the business so done by the non-resident person through or with the resident person in the same manner as returns or particulars of income to be charged are to be delivered by persons acting for non-resident persons:

Provided that the amount of the percentage shall in such case be determined having regard to the nature of the business, and shall, when determined by the Commissioner be subject to an appeal to the Board and thereafter to a Judge as provided by section 50.

(4) Nothing in this section shall render a non-resident person chargeable in the name of a broker or general commission agent, or other agent when such broker, general commission agent, or agent is not an authorized person carrying on the regular agency of the non-resident person or a person chargeable as if he were an agent in pursuance of sub-sections (2) and (3), in respect of gains or profits arising from sales or transactions carried out through such a broker or agent.

(5) The fact that a non-resident person executes sales or carries out transactions with other non-residents in circumstances which would make him chargeable in pursuance of sub-sections (2) and (3) in the name of a resident person shall not of itself make him chargeable in respect of gains or profits arising from those sales or transactions.

(6) Where a non-resident person is chargeable to tax in the name of any attorney, factor, agent, receiver, branch, or manager, in respect of any gains or profits arising from the sale of goods or produce manufactured or produced out of the Virgin Islands by the non-resident person, the person in whose name the non-resident person is so chargeable may, if he thinks fit, apply to the Commissioner or, in the case of an appeal, to the Board and thereafter to the Judge, to have the assessment to tax in respect of those gains or profits made or amended on the basis of the profits which might reasonably be expected to have been earned by a merchant, or where the goods are retailed by or on behalf of the manufacturer or producer, by retailer of the goods sold, who had bought from the manufacturer or producer direct, and on proof to the satisfaction of the Commissioner, Board or Judge of the amount of the profits on the basis aforesaid, the assessment shall be made or amended accordingly.

Acts, etc. to be done by trustees, etc.

32. The person who is chargeable to tax under sections 30 and 31 shall be answerable all matters required to be done by virtue of this Act for the assessment Act for the assessment of the income of any person for whom he acts and for the payment of the tax chargeable thereon.

Income derived from property transferred to minors.

33. Where a person transfers property to a minor, either directly or indirectly, or through the intervention of a trust or by any other means whatsoever, such person shall, nevertheless, during the period of the minority of the transferee, be liable to be taxed on the income derived from such property, or from property substituted therefore, as if such transfer had not been made, and subsequent to such period of minority, the transferor shall continue to be taxed in respect of the income derived from such property, or from property substituted therefore, as if such transfer had not been made unless the Commissioner is satisfied that such transfer was not made for the purpose of evading the taxes imposed by this Act.

Income of property transferred in trust to be income of transferor in certain cases

34. Where a person transfers property in trust and provides that the corpus of the trust shall revert either to the transferor or to such person as he may determine at a future date, or where a trust provides that during the lifetime of the transferor no disposition or other dealing with the trust property shall be made without the consent, written or otherwise of the transferor, such person shall nevertheless be liable to be taxed on the income derived from the property transferred in trust, or from property substituted therefore, as if such transfer had not been made.

In this section "disposition" includes any trust, grant, covenant, agreement or arrangement.

Lists to be prepared by representative or agent.

35.(1) Every person who, in whatever capacity, is in receipt of any money or value being income arising from any of the sources mentioned in this Act of or belonging to any other person who is chargeable in respect thereof, or would be so chargeable if he were resident in the Virgin Islands, shall, whenever required to do so by any notice from the Commissioner, prepare and deliver within the period mentioned in such notice a list in a form approved by the Commissioner, signed by him, containing -

(a) a true and correct statement of all such income;

(b) the name and address of every person to whom the same shall belong.

(2) Every person who refuses, fails or neglects to comply with the provision of this section shall be guilty of an offence against this Act.

Manager of corporate bodies of persons.

36. The Manager or other principal officer of every corporate body of persons shall be answerable for doing all such acts, matters and things as are required to be done by virtue of this Act for the assessment of such body and for payment of the tax.

Agents, etc. of non-residents to be assessed.

37. Any resident agent, trustee, mortgagor, or other person who transmits rent, interest, or income derived income derived from any other source within the Virgin Islands to a non-resident person shall be deemed to be the agent of such non-resident person and shall be assessed and shall pay the tax accordingly.

Indemnification of representative.

38. Every person answerable under this Act for the payment of tax on behalf of another person may retain out of any money coming to his hands on behalf of such other person so much thereof as shall be sufficient to pay such tax, and shall be and is hereby indemnified against any person whatsoever for all payments made by him in pursuance and virtue on this Act.

Deduction of and accounting for tax on rent, annuities, or other annual payments.

39.(1) Where any person pays to any other person not resident in the Virgin Islands any rent, annuity or any other annual payment which the payor is entitled to deduct under section 11(1) in arriving at his chargeable income, the payor shall upon paying such rent, annuity or other annual payment payments deducted therefrom payment deducted therefrom tax at the rate of fourteen cents on every dollar or such rent, annuity or other annual payment payable to such person or at the rate set out on Section 26 in the case of payment as aforesaid to a company and the payor shall forthwith render an account to the Commissioner of the amount so deducted and every such amount shall be recoverable in the like manner as is provided in section 61.

Provided that the Commissioner may by notice in writing require such person to deduct tax at a lower rate.

(2) In the case of a company, the account aforesaid shall be rendered by the manager or other principal officer of the company.

(3) Any person who neglects to render account under this section shall be guilty of an offence against this Act.

Deceased persons.

40. When any person dies during the year preceding the year of assessment, and such person would, but for his death have been chargeable to tax for the year of assessment, or when any person dies during the year of assessment or within two years after the expiration thereof, and no assessment has been made upon him for that year, the personal representative of such person shall be liable and charged with the payment of the tax with which such person would have been chargeable, and shall be answerable for doing all such acts, matters and things as such person, if he were alive, would be liable to do under this Act:

Provided that in the case of a person dying during the year preceding the assessment, if his personal representative distributes his estate before the commencement of the year of assessment, such personal representative shall pay the tax at the rate or rates in force at the date of distribution of the estate, if the rate of tax for the year of assessment has not been fixed at that date.

Returns: By Whom To Be Made

Return of income and notice of chargeability.

41.(1) The Commissioner may, by notice in writing, require any person to furnish him within a reasonable time, being not less than thirty days from the date of the notice, with a true and correct return of his income from every source whatsoever for any year of income and if absent from the Virgin Islands to give the name and address of an agent residing in the Virgin Islands.

(2) Every person chargeable with tax for any year of assessment who has not been required by the 31st March in that year of assessment or in the cases specified in paragraphs (a), (b) and (c) of subsection (2) of section 6 by the 31st day of March in the year following the year of assessment to make a return for that year in accordance with the provisions of sub-section (1) of this section, shall within thirty days after the 31st day of March, give notice to the Commissioner that he is so chargeable and if that person is a company shall give in the notice an address for service in Road Town, Tortola, and shall thereafter, whether chargeable to tax or not give notice to the Commissioner of all subsequent changes of such address as and when such changes occur.

Official information and official secrecy.

42.(1) The Commissioner may require any officer in the employment of the Government or any municipality or other public body to supply such particulars as may be required for the purposes of this Act and which may be in the possession of such officer, provided that no such officer shall by virtue of this section be obliged to disclose any particulars as to which he is under any statutory obligation to observe secrecy.

(2) The Commissioner may by notice in writing require any employer to furnish him within reasonable time with a return for any year containing

(a) the names and places of residence of all persons employed by him: and

(b) the payments and allowances made to those persons in respect of that employment, except persons who are not employed in any other employment and whose remuneration in the employment for the year does not exceed three hundred dollars.

The expression "remuneration" in this sub-section shall be deemed to include not only moneys paid as salary, wages, overtime or bonus, but also the annual value of any residence, quarters, board and lodging, or other allowances in kind received by an employee in respect of his services.

(3) Where the employer is a body of persons, the officer shall be deemed to be the employer for the purposes of this section, and any director of a company, person engaged in the management of a company, shall be deemed to be a person employed.

(4) Returns required under the provisions of this section shall be in the form approved by the Commissioner.

(5) Any person who refuses or neglects to deliver any return required under the provisions of this section shall be guilty of an offence against this Act.

(6) Any person who, after being required by the Commissioner to make a return, neglects to do so within the time specification shall, whether or not any liability to tax is involved, be guilty of an offence against this Act.

43.(1) The Commissioner may, by notice, require any person, or the attorney of any person, or the secretary, attorney, manager, agent, or other principal officer of a company residing in the Virgin Islands, to make returns under this Act within the time specified in such notice.

Partnerships

Partnerships.

44. Where a trade, business, profession or vocation is carried on by two or more persons jointly

(1) The income of any partner from the partnership shall be deemed to be the share to which he was entitled during the year of income in the income of the partnership (such income being ascertained in accordance with the provisions of this Act) and shall be included in the return of income to be made by such partner under the provisions of this Act.

(2) *(a)* The precedent partner, that is to say the partner who of the partners resident in the Virgin Islands

(i) is first named in the agreement of partnership, or

(ii) if there be no agreement, is named singly or with precedence to the other partners in the usual name of the firm; or

(iii) is the precedent acting partner, if the partner named with precedence is not an acting partner,

shall, when required by the Commissioner, make and deliver a return of the income of the partnership for any year, such income being ascertained in accordance with the provisions of this Act, and declare there the names and addresses of the other partners in the firm together with the amount of the share of the said income to which each partner was entitled for that year;

(b) Where no partner is resident in the Virgin Islands, the return shall be made and delivered by the attorney, agent, manager, or factor of the firm resident in the Virgin Islands.

(3) Any person who refuses, fails or neglects to deliver any return required under the provisions of this section shall be guilty of an offence against this Act.

Pay As You Earn

Imposition of tax on emoluments at time of payment.

44A.(1) Notwithstanding anything to the contrary contained in this Act or any other law for the time being in force in the Territory, upon making payment of remuneration payable in respect of an office or employment, there shall be deducted from that remuneration, pursuant to paragraph (b) of section 5, tax as prescribed by this Act, unless the remuneration is exempt from taxation.

(2) For the purpose of ascertaining and determining the tax to be levied and deducted by the employers under subsection (1) the Commissioner shall issue to each registered employer Tax Tables bearing his official seal, hereinafter referred to as P.A.Y.E. - Tax Tables.

(3) Any person aggrieved by a determination and levy of tax under the aforesaid provisions of this section, may appeal in conformity with the provisions of this Act relating to appeals, and in such appeals, shall be construed as if they were appeals from assessment under those provisions, and the necessary modifications and adaptations of the provisions shall be made accordingly.

(4) The Governor in Council may make rules in connection with all matters for which rules are required to be made in respect of income tax payable on income under sub-section (b) of section 5 of this Act and generally to give effect to the principles and provisions of this Act, inter alia -

(a) for the registration of employers;

(b) P.A.Y.E. - Tax Tables and for matters connected therewith.

(c) remittances of tax deductions to the Commissioner;

(d) the Forms and Certificates to be used in the administration of this Act.

(5) The provisions of subsection (2) of section 72 of this Act shall apply to rules made under subsection (4), as if such rules were made under section 72 of this Act.

(6) Where, for any year of assessment, tax has been levied and deducted on the payment of remuneration as provided in this section and in the Income Tax (Employment) Rules, 1981 the levy or deduction shall be deemed to be an assessment on that remuneration for the purposes of section 45(1).

Inspectors appointment and functions.

44B.(1) For the purpose of the effective enforcement of section 44A, the Commissioner may assign as Inspectors such number of public officers employed in the Inland Revenue Department as he considers necessary.

(2) An Inspector may

(a) enter at all reasonable times any premises or place where persons are employed and in respect of whose emoluments tax is deductible under section 44A;

(b) make inquiry for ascertaining whether tax is being deducted from the emoluments of the employees as required by section 44A; and

(c) examine either alone or in the presence of any other person any records kept on those premises in that place for the purposes of an inquiry referred to in paragraph (b).

(3) Every inspector assigned under this section must be supplied with a certificate of his assignment or other form of identification signed by the Commissioner and upon entering any premises or place shall produce the certificate or other form of identification on demand.

(4) Where an Inspector enters premises or a place for the purposes of subsection (2), the proprietor or other person for the time being in charge of the premises or place shall furnish him with the information he requires except that no person shall be required to answer any question the answer to which is likely to incriminate himself.

Assessment And Assessment Lists

Commissioner to make assessments.

45.(1) The Commissioner shall proceed to assess every person chargeable with the tax as soon as may be after the date prescribed for delivering the returns.

(2) Where a person has delivered a return, the Commissioner may -

(a) accept the return and make an assessment accordingly; or

(b) refuse to accept the return and, to the best of his judgment, determine the amount of the chargeable income of the person and assess him accordingly.

(3) Where any transaction which reduces or would reduce the amount of tax payable by any person is artificial or fictitious, or where effect has not, in fact been given to any disposition, the Commissioner may disregard any such transaction or disposition, and the persons concerned shall be assessable accordingly.

In this section "disposition" includes any trust, grant, covenant, agreement or arrangement.

(4) Where a person has not delivered a return and the Commissioner is of the opinion that such person is liable to pay tax he may, according to the best of his judgment, determine the amount of the chargeable income of such person and assess him accordingly, but such assessment shall not affect any liability otherwise incurred by such person by reason of his failure to neglect to deliver a return.

Lists of persons assessed.

47.(1) After completing his assessments, the Commissioner shall prepare lists of persons assessed to tax.

(2) Such lists (herein called the assessment lists) shall contain the names and addresses of the persons assessed to tax, the amount of the chargeable income of each person, the amount of the tax payable by him, and such other particulars as may be prescribed.

Notices to be served on persons assessed.

48.(1) The Commissioner shall cause to be served personally on or sent through the post to each person whose name appears on the assessment lists a notice addressed to him at his usual place of abode or business stating the amount of his chargeable income and the amount of tax payable by him, and informing him of his rights under the next subsection.

(2) If any person disputes the assessment he may apply to the Commissioner, by notice of objection in writing, to review and revise the assessment made upon him. Such application shall state precisely the grounds of his objections to the assessment and shall be made within thirty days from the date of the service of the notice of assessment:

Provided that the Commissioner upon being satisfied that owing to absence from the Virgin Islands, sickness or other reasonable cause, the person disputing the assessment was prevented from making application within such period, shall extend the period as may be reasonable in the circumstances.

(3) On receipt of the notice of objection referred to in sub-section (2), the Commissioner may require the person giving the notice of objection to furnish such particulars as the Commissioner may deem necessary with respect to the income of the person assessed and to produce all books or other documents in his custody or under his control relating to such income and may summon any person who he thinks is unable to give evidence respecting the assessment, to attend before him and may examine such person (except the clerk, agent, servant or other person confidentially employed in the affairs of the person to be charged) on oath or otherwise.

(4) In the event of any person assessed, who has objected to an assessment made upon him, agreeing with the Commissioner as to the amount at which he is liable to be assessed, the amount so agreed shall be the amount at which such person shall stand assessed, and the assessment shall be confirmed or amended accordingly;

Provided always, that in the event of any person who under subsection (2), has applied to the Commissioner for a revision of the assessment made upon him failing to agree with the Commissioner as to the amount at which he is liable to be assessed, his right of appeal to the Board and thereafter to a Judge under the provisions of this Act, against the assessment made upon him, shall remain unimpaired.

Additional Assessments

Omissions and undercharges may be rectified.

49. Where it appears to the Commissioner that any person liable to tax has not been assessed or has been assessed at a less amount that which ought to have been charged, the Commissioner may, within the year of assessment or within six years after the expiration thereof, assess such person at amount or additional amount as according to his judgment ought to have been charged, and the provisions of this Act as to notice of assessment, appeal, and other proceedings under this Act shall apply to such assessment or additional assessment and to the tax charged thereunder.

Provided that no assessment shall be made for any year of assessment prior to the year 1970, except that where any fraud or wilful neglect has been committed by any person in relation to tax for any year of assessment after 1967, an assessment in relation to that year of assessment may be made at any time.

Appeals

Board of Referees.

49A.(1) The Governor shall appoint a Board of Referees, and a Clerk to the Board, for the purpose of hearing appeals in the first instance against assessments to income tax made under this Act.

(2) The Board shall consist of not more than five members one of whom shall be nominated by the Governor to be Chairman.

(3) At any meeting of the Board convened under this Act the Board may act by any three of its members, and may so act notwithstanding any vacancy in the number of members constituting the Board.

(4) The Governor may appoint a person to act in the place of the Chairman or any other member of the Board in the case of his absence or inability to act as such Chairman or other member.

Appeals to the Board.

49B.(1) Any person who, being aggrieved by an assessment made upon him, has failed to agree with the Commissioner in the manner provided in sub-section (4) of section 48 may appeal to writing to the Commissioner and to the Clerk to the Board. Such notice must state precisely the grounds of appeal and the date of the refusal of the Commissioner to amend the assessment as desired, and must be delivered within thirty days from the date of that refusal:

Provided that the Board may allow also any notice of appeal delivered after the lapse of such period of thirty days if the Board if satisfied that by his absence from the Virgin Islands, sickness or other reasonable cause the aggrieved person was prevented from giving notice of appeal within such period and that there has been no unreasonable delay on his part.

(2) The appeal may be heard on only the grounds stated in the notice of appeal, and in concluding the proceedings the Board shall determine the assessments by either confirming the amount of the assessment as it stands or, if satisfied that the person assessed was thereby overcharged, or undercharged, by reducing or increasing the assessment accordingly by the amount of the overcharge or undercharge as the case may warrant.

(3) Any party to an appeal shall be entitled to adduce any lawful evidence, and the Board may require the appellant to furnish the Board with such particulars as the Board may deem necessary respecting the income of the person assessed and may summon any person (other than the appellant), who may be able to give evidence in that respect to attend before the Board and may examine such person on oath or otherwise:

Provided that any agent or servant of the appellant, and any other person confidentially employed in the affairs of the appellant may, without incurring any penalty under this Act therefore, refuse to be sworn or to answer any question to which he objects.

(4) Subject to further proceeding on appeal in respect of the same assessment being brought before a Judge under the provisions of section 49C, the decision of the Board shall be final.

Appeals to a Judge.

49C.(1) Any person, including the Commissioner, aggrieved by any act, decision or omission of the Board on appeal under the provisions of section 49B may appeal from the Board to a Judge upon giving notice of appeal in writing to the Registrar of the High Court. Such notice must state precisely the grounds of appeal and must be delivered within thirty days from the day on which the assessment was determined by the Board.

Provided that a Judge may allow also any notice of appeal delivered after the lapse of such period of thirty days if he is satisfied that the absence from the Virgin Islands of the aggrieved person, sickness or other reasonable cause prevented the notice of appeal being given within such period and that there has been no unreasonable delay on the part of that person.

(2) The Judge may hear the appeal on the grounds stated in the notice of appeal to the Court and may confirm the amount of the assessment as determined by the Board, or if he is satisfied that the person assessed was thereby overcharged or undercharged, he may accordingly determine the assessment by reducing, or increasing the assessment accordingly by the amount of the overcharge or undercharge as the case may warrant.

(3) Notwithstanding anything contained in subsection (2) of section 59, if the Judge is satisfied that tax in accordance with his decision upon the appeal may not be recovered, the Judge may require the appellant forthwith to furnish such security for payment of the tax, if any, which may become payable by the appellant as may seem to the Judge to be proper. If such security is not given the tax assessed shall become payable forthwith and shall be recoverable forthwith by suit by the Collector in his official name as well as in the manner provided by section 61.

(4) The costs of an appeal to a Judge shall be in the discretion of the Judge hearing the appeal and shall be a sum fixed by the Judge.

(5) The decision of the Judge hearing the appeal shall be final:

Provided that the Judge hearing such appeal may, if he so desires, and shall on the application of the appellant or the Commissioner state a case on a question of law for the opinion of the Court of Appeal.

(6) The Chief Justice may make rules governing appeals to a Judge and providing for the method of tendering evidence and appointing places for the hearing of such appeals and prescribing the procedure to be followed on a case being stated.

Miscellaneous re: Appeals.

50.(1) Seven clear days notice shall, unless rules made hereunder otherwise provide, be given to the Commissioner and to the appellant, of the place and date fixed for the hearing of the appeal.

(2) Every person appealing shall attend before the Board, or the Judge, as the case may be on the day and at the time fixed for the hearing of his appeal:

Provided always that if it be proved to the satisfaction of the Board or the Judge, as the case may be, that owing to absence from the Virgin Islands, sickness or other reasonable cause, any person is prevented from attending in person at the hearing of his appeal on the date and at the time fixed for that purpose, the Board or the Judge, as the case may be, may postpone the hearing of the appeal for such reasonable time as it or he thinks necessary for the attendance of the appellant, or may admit the appeal to be made by any agent, clerk or servant of the appellants on his behalf.

(3) All appeals shall be heard in camera unless the Board or the Judge, as the case may be, shall, on the application of the appellant, otherwise direct.

(4) Either party to an appeal may be represented by counsel or solicitor at the hearing of such appeal.

(5) In every appeal the onus of proving that the assessment complained of is excessive shall be on the appellant.

(6) In any appeal to a Judge the onus of proving that the act, decision or omission of the Board complained of was against the provisions of this Act shall be on the appellant.

(7) Notice of the amount of tax payable under the assessment as determined by the Board or the Judge as the case may be, shall be served by the Commissioner upon the appellant.

Errors In Assessments And Notices.

Assessments, etc. not void by reason of errors therein in names and descriptions

51.(1) No assessment, warrant or other proceedings purporting to be made in accordance with the provisions of this Act, shall be quashed, or deemed to be void or voidable, for want of form, or be affected by reason of therein in names mistake, defect or omission therein, if the same is in substance and effect in conformity with or according to the intent and meaning of this Act or any Act amending the same, and if the person assessed or intended to be assessed or affected thereby is designated therein according to common intent and understanding.

(2) An assessment shall not be impeached or affected -

(a) by reason of a mistake therein as to-

(i) the name or surname of a person liable; or

(ii) the description of any income; or

(iii) the amount of tax charged;

(iv) by reason of any variance between the assessment and the notice thereof:

Provided that in cases of assessment the notice thereof shall be duly served on the person intended to be charged, and such notice shall contain, in substance and effect, the particulars on which the assessment is made.

Repayment Of Tax.

Circumstances under which repayment may be made.

52.(1) If it is proved to the satisfaction of the Commissioner that any person for any year of assessment has paid tax, by deduction or otherwise, in excess of the amount with which he is properly chargeable, such person shall be entitled to have the amount so paid in excess refunded. Every claim for repayment under this section shall be within two years from the end of the year of assessment to which the claim relates. The Commissioner shall give a certificate of the amount to be repaid and upon the receipt of the certificate the Treasurer shall cause repayment to be made in conformity therewith.

(2) Except as regards sums repayable on an objection or appeal, no repayment shall be made to any person in respect of any year of assessment as regards which that person has failed or neglected to deliver a return or has been assessed in a sum in excess of the amount contained in his return:

Provided that he has received notice of the assessment made upon him for that year, unless it is proved to the satisfaction of the Commissioner that such failure or neglect to deliver a true and correct return did not proceed from any fraud or wilful act or omission on the part of that person.

Relief In Cases Of Double Taxation.

Unilateral relief.

54.(1) To the extent appearing from the following provisions of this section, relief from income tax shall be given to persons in respect of tax payable under the law of any Territory outside the Virgin Islands by allowing the last mentioned tax as a credit against income tax payable for the year of assessment commencing 1st January 1972, and each subsequent year of assessment notwithstanding that there are not for the time being in force any arrangements under section 55 below providing for such relief.

(2) The said relief (hereinafter referred to as "Unilateral relief") shall be such relief as would fall to be given to persons under section 56 below if arrangements with the Government of the territory in question containing the provisions specified in sub-section (3) and (4) below were in force by virtue of the said section 55; and any expression in the said section 56 which imports a reference to relief under arrangements for the time being having effect by virtue of the said section 55 shall be deemed to import also a reference to unilateral relief.

(3) Credit for tax paid under the law of the territory outside the Virgin Islands and computed by reference to income arising in that territory shall be allowed against any income tax charged by this Act computed by reference to that income (profits from, or remuneration for, personal or professional services performed in that territory being deemed for this purpose to be income arising in that territory):

Provided that-

(a) where arrangements made with the Government of the Territory by virtue of section 55 below provide for relief from double taxation of any income (whether by credit or otherwise), credit for tax paid under the law of the Territory in respect of the income shall not be allowed by virtue of this sub-section except to the extent that the arrangements so provide;

(b) credit shall not be allowed by virtue of this sub-section for overseas tax on a dividend or a royalty paid by a company resident in the territory unless the overseas tax is directly charged on the dividend, or royalty whether by charge to tax, deduction of tax at source or otherwise, and the whole of it represents tax which neither the company nor the recipient would have borne if the dividend or the royalty had not been paid.

(4) In this section and in section 56 below in its application to unilateral relief, references to tax payable or paid under the law of a territory outside the Virgin Islands include only references to taxes which are charged on income and correspond to income tax in the Virgin Islands, but, for this purpose tax under the law of any such territory shall not be treated as not corresponding to income tax by reason only that it is payable under the law of a province, state or other part of a country, or is levied by or on behalf of a municipality or other local body.

Double taxation arrangements.

55.(1) If the Governor in Council by Order declares that arrangements specified in the Order have been made with the Government of any territory outside the Virgin Islands with a view to affording relief from double taxation in relation to income tax and any tax of a similar character imposed by the laws of that territory, and that it is expedient that those arrangements shall have effect in relation to income tax notwithstanding anything to the contrary contained in any enactment.

The Virgin Islands is a dependent territory of the United Kingdom; it has its own tax system - quit separate from that of the United Kingdom, but the government of the Territory does not itself conclude double tax treaties with other governments. What happens is that the treaties made by the United Kingdom are, in certain cases, extended - either in whole or in part - to particular territories.

Treaties with Denmark, Japan, Norway, Sweden and Switzerland have been extended to the Virgin Islands. Several of these have been superseded by new tax treaties between the UK and the other countries concerned, but the old treaty remains applicable to the Virgins.

The effect of the treaties presently in force is summarised in the table at the end of this enactment.

(2) On the making of an Order under this section with respect to arrangements relating to any territory outside the Virgin Islands section 54 shall cease to have effect as respects that territory except in so far as the arrangements otherwise provide.

(3) Any Order made under this section may be revoked by a subsequent Order.

(4) Where any arrangements have effect by virtue of this section the obligation as to secrecy imposed by section 4 shall not prevent the disclosure to any authorized officer of the Government with which the arrangements are made of such information as is required to be disclosed under the arrangements.

(5) The Governor in Council may make rules for carrying out the provisions of any arrangements having effect under this section.

Tax credits.

56.(1) The provisions of this section shall have effect where, under arrangements having effect under section 55, tax payable in respect of any income in the territory with the Government of which the arrangements are made is to be allowed as a credit against tax payable in respect of that income in the Virgin Islands, and in this section and in section 27 the expression "foreign tax" means any tax payable in that territory which under the arrangements is to be so allowed, and the expression "income tax" means tax chargeable under this Act.

(2) The amount of the income tax chargeable in respect of the income shall be reduced by the amount of the credit which subject to the provisions of sub-sections (3) to (10) inclusive shall be deemed to include such tax as would be allowed as a credit against United Kingdom tax in accordance with the provisions of the laws of the United Kingdom in force at the date hereof.

Provided that credit shall not be allowed against income tax for any year of assessment unless the person entitled to the income is resident in the Virgin Islands for that year.

(3) The credit shall not exceed the amount which would be produced by computing the amount of the income in accordance with the provisions of this Act and then charging it to income tax at a rate ascertained by dividing the income tax chargeable (before allowance of credit under any arrangements having effect under section 55) on the total income of the person entitled to the income by the amount of his total income.

(4) Without prejudice to the provisions of the preceding sub-section, the total credit to be allowed for a person for any year of assessment for foreign tax under all arrangements having effect under section 55 shall not exceed the total income tax payable by him for that year of assessment, less any tax payable by him under the provisions of section 39.

(5) In computing the amount of the income -

(a) no deduction shall be allowed in respect of foreign tax (whether in respect of the same or any other income);

(b) wherein the income tax chargeable depends on the amount received in the Virgin Islands, the said amount shall be increased by the appropriate amount of the foreign tax in respect of the income;

(c) where the income includes a dividend and under the arrangements foreign tax not chargeable directly or by deduction in respect of the dividend is to be taken into account in considering whether any, and if so what, credit is to be given against income tax in respect of the dividend the amount of the foreign tax not so chargeable which falls to be taken into account in computing the amount of the credit; but notwithstanding anything in the preceding provision of this sub-section a deduction shall be allowed of any amount by which the foreign tax in respect of the income exceeds the credit therefore.

(6) Paragraphs (a) and (b) of the preceding sub-section (but not the remainder thereof) shall apply to the computation of total income for the purposes of determining the rate mentioned in sub-section (3) and shall apply thereto in relation to all income in the case of which credit falls to be given for foreign tax under arrangements for the time being in force under section 55.

(7) Where

(a) the arrangements provide, in relation to dividends of some classes, but not in relation to dividends of other classes, that foreign tax not chargeable directly or by deduction in respect of dividends is to be taken into account considering whether any, and if so what, credit is to be given against income tax in respect of the dividends; and

(b) a dividend is paid which is not of a class in relation to which the arrangements so provided, then, if the dividend is paid to a company which controls directly or indirectly, not less than one-half of the voting power in the company paying the dividend, credit shall be allowed as if the dividend were a dividend of a class in relation to which the arrangements so provide.

(8) Credit shall not be allowed under the arrangements against income tax chargeable in respect of the income of any person for any year of assessment if he elects that credit shall not be allowed in the case of his income for that year.

(9) Any claim for an allowance by way of credit shall be made not later than two years after the end of the year of assessment; and, in the event of any dispute as the amount allowable, the claim shall be subject to objection and appeal in like manner as an assessment.

(10) Where the amount of any credit given under the arrangements is rendered excessive or insufficient by reason of any adjustment of the amount of any tax payable either in the Virgin Islands or elsewhere, nothing in this Act limiting the time for the making of assessments or claims for relief shall apply to any assessment or claim to which the adjustment gives rise, being an assessment or claim made not later than two years from the time when all such assessments, adjustments and other determinations have been made, whether in the Virgin Islands or elsewhere, as are material in determining any, and if so, what credit fails to be given.

General Powers Of Commissioner

Powers of Commissioner to require returns and particulars.

58.(1) The Commissioner may, by notice in writing, writing, require any person to furnish him within a specified time with a return and such particulars as he may require for the purposes of this Act with respect to the income of such person.

(2) Any person who neglects duly to furnish such return or particulars shall be guilty of an offenc against this Act.

(3) The Commissioner may, by not less than fourteen days' notice in writing, require any person to attend before him and give evidence with respect to his income, and to produce all books or other documents in his custody or under his control relating to such income.

(4) Any person who, without lawful excuse, refuses or neglects to attend or give evidence in pursuance of such notice or to produce such books or other documents or who refuses to answer any lawful question touching the matters under consideration or knowingly or wilfully, gives any false evidence under this section, shall be guilty of an offence against this Act.

Collection And Recovery Of Tax.

Payment of tax.

59.(1) Subject to the provisions of this Act, the tax charged in an assessment made on any person shall be payable -

(a) where such tax does not exceed the sum of fifty dollars, in one sum within thirty days of the date of the assessment; or

(b) where such tax exceeds the sum of fifty dollars, in two equal instalments; the first instalment within thirty days of the date of the assessment, and the second instalment within ninety days of the date of the assessment:

(2) In a case where notice of an objection or an appeal has been given against an assessment, the tax charged on that assessment is payable as follows:

(a) if the tax charged in the assessment is not in dispute by reason of the notice of objection or appeal, the tax charged is payable in accordance with the provisions of subsection (1); and

(b) if the tax charged in the assessment is in dispute by reason of the notice of objection or appeal, the tax charged is payable not later than the expiration of 30 days immediately following the day on which the objection or appeal is determined.

(3) For the purposes of subsection (2), the amount of tax that is not in dispute and the amount of tax that is in dispute are the amounts agreed with the Commissioner; but if no amounts are so agreed, then, they shall be the amounts fixed by the Board of Referees.

Penalty for non-payment of tax.

60.(1) Where any tax payable by any person is not paid within a period of thirty days from the prescribed date, such person shall pay in addition to such tax a sum equal to five per centum of such tax.

(2) Where the tax in arrears payable by any person under subsection (1) is not paid within the period of three months from the prescribed date, such person shall pay a further sum equal to one and one half per centum of the amount of tax in arrears for each month such tax remains unpaid.

(3) The sums added to the tax under subsections (1) or (2) shall not aggregate exceed thirty per centum of the tax which was due on the prescribed date.

(4) The provisions of this Act relating to the collection and recovery of tax shall apply to the collection and recovery of any sum payable under subsections (1) or (2) of this section.

(5) Where the total amount of tax in arrears is recovered, the Commissioner may for reasons which appear to him sufficient, remit in whole or in part any additional sum payable under this section.

Recovery of tax.

61. In the event of any tax or any portion thereof not being paid on or before the date fixed by the last preceding section it shall be lawful for the Collector in his official name to sue for and recover the tax or such portion thereof as a civil debt to be recoverable summarily or to issue a warrant under his hand directed to the Provost Marshal of the Virgin Islands setting out in the same or in a schedule thereto the several sums due on account of the tax from the persons against whom the warrant is directed.

Provost Marshal to levy on goods, etc.

62. Immediately on receipt of the warrant the Provost Marshal shall proceed to levy upon the goods and chattels of the persons against whom the warrant is directed and immediately thereafter give notice in the "Gazette" and also in such other manner and form as the Governor may from time to time direct of his intention to sell the same.

Sale to be public auction.

63. Every sale under this Act shall be by public auction held at such time and as the Provost Marshal shall direct, and notice sale shall be exhibited at the Court House in the Virgin Islands for two consecutive weeks before the day of sale.

Application of proceeds of sale.

64. The proceeds of the sale shall be applied to the payment of the tax due and the expenses of levy and sale and the surplus, if any, shall be paid on application to the person entitled thereto.

Commission to Provost Marshal.

65.(1) There shall be paid to the Provost Marshal in respect of the duties performed by him under this under this Act a commission at the rate of two and a half per centum over and above the other expenses of the levy and sale on the net proceeds of any sale under this Act.

(2) All sums of money received or recovered by the Provost Marshal as commission shall be paid into the Treasury.

65A.(1) The Commissioner may at his discretion by notice in writing to any person declare him to be the agent of any other person for the purposes of the collection and recovery of tax due by such other person; and the person so declared agent shall pay any tax so due and specified in such notice from any monies, including pensions, salary, wages or any other remuneration which may, at any time within twelve months from the date of such notice, be held by him for, or due by him to, such other person.

(2) For the purposes of this section the Commissioner may by notice in writing, at any time require any person to furnish him within a reasonable time, not being less than thirty days from the date of such notice, with a return showing any monies which may have been held for him for, or due by him to, any other person from whom tax is due.

(3) Where any person declared as agent under sub-section (1) of this section fails to pay to the Commissioner within thirty days of the date of the notice referred to in that sub-section or of the date on which any monies referred to in that sub-section are held by him for, or due by him to, the person of whom he is so declared to be agent, whichever is the later, any amount which he is required to pay under that sub-section, then the provisions of this Act relating to the collection and recovery of tax shall apply to the collection and recovery of such amount as if it were tax the due date for payment of which was the date upon which such person should have paid such amount to the Commissioner under this sub-section.

(4) Every person responsible under this Act for the payment of tax on behalf of another person may retain out of any money coming into his hands on behalf of such other person so much thereof as is sufficient to pay such tax; and such person shall be and is hereby indemnified against any person whatsoever for payments so made by him under the provisions of this Act.

Recovery of tax in certain cases.

66.(1) If in any particular case the Commissioner has reason to believe that a person who has been assessed to tax may leave the Virgin Islands before such tax becomes payable without having paid such tax, he may by notice in writing to such person demand payment of such tax within the time to be limited in such notice. Such tax shall thereupon be payable at the expiration of the time so limited and shall, in default of payment, unless security for payment thereof be given to the satisfaction of the Commissioner, be recoverable forthwith in the manner provided by section 61.

(2) If in any particular case the Commissioner has reason to believe that tax upon any chargeable income may not be recovered, he may at any time and as the case may require -

(a) forthwith by notice in writing require any person to make a return and to furnish particulars of any such income within the time to be specified in such notice; and

(b) make an assessment upon such person in the amount of income returned, or if default is made in making such return or the Commissioner is dissatisfied with such return, in such amount as the Commissioner may think reasonable; and may by notice in writing to the person assessed require that the tax be paid forthwith or that security for the payment of tax assessed be forthwith given to his satisfaction.

(3) Notwithstanding any of the provisions of this Act if in any particular case the Commissioner has reason to believe that tax upon any income chargeable to such tax may not be recovered, he may at any time -

(a) by notice in writing to the person by whom the tax would be payable determine a period for which tax shall be charged and require such person to render within the time specified therein returns and particulars of such income for that period;

(b) make an assessment upon such person in the amount of the income returned, or if default is made in making a return, or the Commissioner is dissatisfied with such return, in such amount as the Commissioner may think reasonable.

(4) Notice of assessment made in accordance with the provisions of sub-sections (2) and (3) of this section shall be given to the person assessed and any tax so assessed (in accordance with the provisions of sub-sections (2) and (3) of this section) shall be payable on demand made in writing under the hand of the Commissioner, and shall in default of payment, unless security for the payment thereof be given to the satisfaction of the Commissioner, be recoverable forthwith.

(5) Any person who has paid the tax in accordance with a demand made by the Commissioner or who has given security for such payment under sub-sections (2) and (3) shall have the rights of objection and appeal conferred by sections 48 and 50, and the amount paid by him shall be adjusted in accordance with the result of any such objection or appeal.

(6) The provisions of sub-sections (2) and (3) shall not affect the powers conferred upon the Commissioner by section 49.

Notices

Signature of notices.

67.(1) Every notice to be given by the Commissioner under this Act shall be signed by the Commissioner or by some person or persons from time to time appointed by him for that purpose, and every such notice shall be valid if the signature of the Commissioner or of such person or persons is duly printed or written thereon:

Provided that any notice in writing under this Act to any person requiring him to furnish particulars to the Commissioner or any notice under this Act requiring the attendance of any person or witness before the Commissioner shall be personally signed by the Commissioner or by any person duly authorized by him.

(2) A signature attached to any notice and purporting to be the signature of any person so appointed shall be taken to be the signature of that person until the contrary be shown.

Service of notices.

68. Notice may be served on a person either personally or by being sent through the post to his last known business or private address, and shall in the latter case be deemed to have been served, in the case of persons resident in the Virgin Islands, not later than two days succeeding the day when posted, and in the case of persons not so resident, one month succeeding the day on which the notice would have been received in the ordinary course of the post, and in providing such service it shall be sufficient to prove that the letter containing the notice was properly addressed and posted.

General

False statements and returns.

69.(1) Any person who, for the purpose of obtaining any deduction, rebate, reduction or repayment in respect of tax for himself or for any other person, or who in any return, account, or particulars made or furnished with reference to tax, knowingly makes any false statement or false representations; and

(2) Any person who aids, abets, assists, counsels, incites or induces another reason -

(a) to make or deliver any false return or statement under this Act, or

(b) to keep or prepare any false accounts or particulars concerning any income on which tax is payable under this Act, shall be guilty of an offence and shall be liable on summary conviction to a fine not exceeding one thousand five hundred dollars or to imprisonment, with or without hard labour, for a term not exceeding six months.

Failure to perform required duty.

70. Any person who refuses or neglects to perform any duty required to be performed under this Act shall be guilty of an offence against this Act.

Saving for criminal proceedings.

71. The provisions of this Act shall not effect any criminal proceedings under any other Act or law.

Rules.

72.(1) The Governor in Council may make rules generally for carrying out the provisions of this Act, and may, in particular, by those rules provide -

(a) for the form of returns, claim statements and notices under this Act;

(b) for the deduction and payment of tax at the source in respect of emoluments and pensions payable out of the revenue of the Virgin Islands;

(c) for any such matters as are authorized by this Act to be prescribed; and

(d) for any other matter or thing, whether similar or not to those above mentioned, in respect of which is may be expedient to make rules for the purpose of carrying this Act into execution.

(2) All rules purporting to be made in pursuance of this section shall be published in the "Gazette" and shall come into operation on such publication or at such other time as may be named in such rules.

(3) If any person fails to comply with or contravenes the provisions of any rules under this Act he shall be guilty of an offence against this Act.

Penalties for offences.

73.(1) Any person guilty of an offence against this Act shall, unless some other penalty is specifically provided for such offence, be liable on summary conviction to a penalty not exceeding three hundred dollars, and in default of payment to imprisonment with or without hard labour, for a term not exceeding six months.

(2) Any person who -

(a) hinders, assaults, obstructs or wilfully delays an Inspector in the performance of his functions;

(b) uses any indecent, abusive or insulting language to an Inspector in the performance of his functions;

(c) subject to subsection (4) of section 44B, refuses or neglects to answer a question or to furnish information required by an Inspector in the performance of his functions; or

(d) by the offer of any gratuity, bribe or other inducement attempts to prevent an Inspector from performing his functions under this Act, is guilty of an offence and is liable on summary conviction to a fine of $500.00 or to imprisonment for a term of six months or both.

VIRGIN ISLANDS

MUTUAL FUNDS ACT, 1996

(as amended, 1997)

ARRANGEMENT OF SECTIONS

Preliminary

Part I - Administration

Part II - Public Funds

Part III - Private and Professional Funds

20. Power to grant recognition.
21. Recognition procedure.

Part IV - Managers and Administrators

22. Licensing.
23. Application for a licence.
24. Power to grant licences.
25. Licensing procedure.
25A. Code of Practice

Part V - General

26. Notices to accompany applications.
27. Form and conditions of certificates and licences.
28. Annual fees,
29. Cancellation of certificates or licences.
30. Cancellation procedure.
31. Appeal of cancellations.
32. Appeal by existing entities.
33. Appeal procedure.
34. Grant or cancellation to be published.
35. Power to grant exemptions.
35A. Restriction on the use of the words "fund" or "mutual fund".
36. Access to information and records.
37. Immunity and actions by the Registrar-
38. Confidentiality.
39. Exemption from certain enactments.
40. Offences and penalties
41. Power of the Minister to vary the Schedule.
42. Regulations.
43. Transitional

SCHEDULE 1
SCHEDULE 2

The Mutual Funds Act, 1996

(as amended, 1997)

An Act to provide for the regulation, authorisation and Control of mutual funds and their managers and administrators carrying on business in or from within the Virgin Islands and for related matters.

ENACTED by the Legislature of the Virgin Islands as follows:

Preliminary

Short title and Commencement

1.This Act may be cited as the Mutual Funds Act, 1996 and shall come into force on such date as the Governor may appoint by proclamation published in the Gazette.

Interpretation

2. (1) In this Act, unless the context otherwise requires,

"administrator" means a person who,

(a) for valuable consideration provides a mutual fund with administrative services alone or together with accounting services; or

(b) is entitled to provide to mutual funds (by whatever name called) such services and facilities as provided in paragraph (a) under the laws of a recognised Country or Jurisdiction;

"auditor" means a person who is entitled to practice as public accountant and to perform audits under the Laws of the Territory or of a recognised Country or Jurisdiction;

"company" means a body corporate, wherever incorporated or constituted;

"constitutional documents" means,

(a) in the case of a company, the memorandum and articles of association or other instrument of incorporation;

(b) in the case of a partnership, the agreement or other instrument by which the partnership is formed and governed;

(c) in the case of a unit trust, the trust deed or other instrument by which the unit trust is organised or governed;

"custodian" means the person who holds the property of the mutual fund in safe keeping;

"existing entity" means

(a) a public fund

(b) a private fund, or

(c) a manager or administrator,

which was carrying its business or, in the case of a public, private or professional fund, was managing or administering its affairs in or from within the Territory immediately before the coming into force of this Act;

"financial year" means the period not exceeding twelve months at the end of which the balance of the accounts is struck, and may be up to eighteen months in the case of the first or last period or when the period is changed;

"Governor" means the Governor in Council;

"investor" means a person who owns or holds shares (as herein defined) issued by a mutual fund;

"manager" means a person, not being an officer of an employee of a person licensed under this Act or a mutual fund which has delegated management functions to a person licensed under this Act who,

(a) for valuable consideration, provides a mutual fund with management services alone or together with investment advice or administrative services; or

(b) is entitled to provide to mutual funds (by whatever name called), such services or advice as provided in paragraph (a) under the laws of a recognised country or jurisdiction;

"Minister" means the minister responsible for the administration of this Act;

"mutual fund" or fund" means a company incorporated, a partnership formed, a unit trust organised or other similar body formed or organised under the laws of the Territory or of any other country or jurisdiction which

(a) collects and pools investor funds for the purpose of collective investment, and

(b) issues shares (as herein defined) that entitle the holder to receive on demand or within a specified period after demand an amount computed by reference to the value of a proportionate interest in the whole or in a part of the net

assets of the company, the partnership, the unit trust or other similar body, as the case may be,

and includes

(i) an umbrella fund whose shares are split into a number of different class funds or sub- funds, and

(ii) a fund which has a single investor which is a mutual fund not registered or recognised under this Act,

but excludes any arrangements which are designated by regulations as not being mutual funds;

"officer" includes

(a) a director, alternate director, the president, a vice-president, and any other person designated as an officer of a company by by-law, by resolution of the directors or by any other instrument;

(b) a general partner of a partnership; and

(c) a trustee of a unit trust;

"partnership" means a contractual relation which subsists between persons carrying on a business in common with a view of profit and includes a partnership formed under the laws of the Territory or of any other country or jurisdiction notwithstanding any statutory definition thereof to the contrary;

"person" includes an individual natural person, a mutual fund, any company, partnership, unit trust or trustee;

"private fund" means a mutual fund

(a) the constitutional documents of which specify that it will have no more than fifty investors;

(b) the constitutional documents of which specify that the making of an invitation to subscribe for or purchase shares issued by the mutual fund is to be made on a private basis; or

(c) which is designated as a private fund by regulations;

"professional fund" means a mutual fund

(a) the shares of which are made available only to professional investors and the initial investment in which, in respect of the majority of each of such investors,

is not less than one hundred thousand dollars in the United States currency or its equivalent in any other currency; or

(b) is designated as a professional fund by regulations;

"professional investor" means a person

(a) whose ordinary business involves, whether for its own account or the accounts of others, the acquisition or disposal of property of the same kind as the property, or a substantial part of the property, of the fund; or

(b) who has signed a declaration that he, whether individually or jointly with his spouse, has net worth in excess of one million dollars in the United States currency or its equivalent in any other currency and that he consents to being treated as a professional investor;

"promoter" means a person acting alone or in conjunction with others directly or indirectly who takes the initiative in forming or organising the business of a mutual fund, but does not include an underwriter who receives underwriting commission without taking any part in the founding or organising of the mutual fund business;

"prospectus" means any prospectus or similar document the purpose of which is to make an invitation to the public or any section thereof to subscribe for or purchase shares issued by a public fund;

"public fund" means a mutual fund which is not a private fund or a professional fund;

"recognised Country or Jurisdiction" means any Country or Jurisdiction recognised by the Minister under subsection (3);

"Registrar" means the Registrar of Mutual Funds appointed under this Act or such other person as may be performing the duties of the Registrar under this Act;

"regulations or the regulations" means regulations made under this Act;

"security" means any document or instrument constituting evidence of title to or interest in the capital assets, property, profits, earnings or royalties of any person, as herein defined, and includes

(a) bonds, debentures, notes, mortgages and other evidence of indebtedness;

(b) any share, stock, document or instrument commonly known as a security; and

(c) any document or instrument constituting evidence of an option, subscription or other interest in a security or constituting evidence of an interest in an association of legatees or heirs;

"share" means share in the share capital of a mutual fund company and includes an interest in a mutual fund partnership and a unit in a mutual fund unit trust;

"underwriter" means a person who,

(a) as principal, agrees to purchase shares issued by mutual funds with a view to offering them to the public; or

(b) as agent for a mutual fund, offers for sale or sells to the public shares issued by the mutual fund;

"unit trust" means an arrangement creating a trust under the laws of the Territory or of any other country or jurisdiction in which unit holders participating in the arrangement are the beneficiaries of the trust.

(1A) For the purpose of

(a) paragraph (b) of the definition of "private fund", an invitation to subscribe for or purchase shares issued by a mutual fund on a private basis includes an invitation which is made

(i) to specified persons (however described) and is not calculated to result in shares becoming available to other persons or to a large number of investors; or

(ii) by reason of a private or business connection between the person making the invitation and the investor; and

(b) paragraph (a) of the definition of "professional fund", the minimum investment limit referred to in that paragraph shall not apply in respect of an investment made by the manager, administrator, promoter or underwriter of the professional fund.

(2) In this Act,

(a) every company incorporated and every partnership formed or unit trust organised under the laws of the Territory for the purpose of carrying on business as a mutual fund, a manager or administrator shall, if carrying on business anywhere outside the Territory, be deemed to be carrying on business from within the Territory;

(b) the expression "carrying on business from within the Territory" includes carrying on business outside the Territory from a place of business or a registered office within the Territory; and

(c) a mutual fund which is not incorporated, formed or organised or carrying on its business in or from within the Territory shall be deemed to be carrying on business in the Territory if it solicits an individual within the Territory to purchase its shares, except where the purchase is a result of an approach made by the individual without any solicitation being made.

(3) The Minister may recognise any Country or Jurisdiction for the purposes of this Act and shall cause a notice of such recognition to be published in the Gazette.

PART I - Administration

Appointments.

3.(1) There shall be appointed

(a) a Registrar of Mutual Funds who shall be public officers; and

(b) any other public officers as may be necessary to administer this Act.

(2) The Registrar has

(a) the duty to supervise mutual funds and managers and administrators in accordance with this Act;

(b) in and for the discharge of that duty, the powers conferred upon him by this Act; and

(c) the power to prescribe such forms as he considers necessary for the purposes of this Act or the regulations; and

(d) the authority to issue directives and policy guidelines for the purposes of this Act or the regulations.

(3) The Registrar may, upon request by any person to whom this Act applies and the payment of the fee set out in Part I of Schedule 2 or such other amount as may be prescribed by regulations, issue to such person a certificate of compliance in such form as the Registrar thinks fit.

(4) The Registrar or any employee of the office of the Registrar shall not, knowingly, have any financial interest in any person registered, recognised or licensed under this Act.

Delegation of Power

4. (1) The Governor and the Minister may in writing delegate any of their respective powers conferred upon them by this Act to the Registrar or any other person and thereupon this Act shall be read as if those powers were originally conferred upon the Registrar or that other person.

(2) The Registrar may delegate any of his powers or duties under this Act to another public officer and thereupon this Act shall be read as if those powers or duties were originally conferred or imposed upon that officer.

Annual Report

5.(1) The Registrar shall, on or before the 30th day of April in each year, prepare and deliver to the Minister a report consisting of

(a) a summary of the nature and number of

(i) filings made under this Act;

(ii) registrations, recognitions and licences granted under this Act;

(iii) enforcement proceedings or disciplinary measures taken under this Act; and

(b) a general commentary on the law relating to the mutual funds industry and on the practice and development of that law.

(2) On receiving the report delivered to him pursuant to subsection (1), the Minister shall lay the report before the Legislative Council.

Records of the Registrar

6.(1) The Registrar shall keep separate registers for all

(a) registered public funds;

(b) recognised private or professional funds; and

(c) licensed managers and administrators.

(2) The registers required under subsection (1) shall show

(a) the information required under section 26 (a), (b) and (c) with respect to each registered public fund, recognised private or professional fund and licensed manager or administrator;

(b) the date of registration, recognition or licence, as the case may be; and

(c) the status of such registration, recognition or licence if cancelled and the date thereof.

(3) Registers kept by the Registrar shall be in such form as he may determine and, subject to section 38, shall be open to public inspection during ordinary office hours on payment of an inspection fee of five dollars or such other amount as may be prescribed by regulations.

Mutual Funds Advisory Committee

7.(1) There shall be a Committee called the Mutual Funds Advisory Committee which shall consist of not more than five persons appointed by the Minister from among members of the private sector who are known to him to have adequate knowledge of and experience in the mutual funds industry.

(2) The Minister shall appoint a senior public officer who shall be the Chairman of the Mutual Funds Advisory Committee and the Registrar of Mutual Funds shall be an ex officio member thereof.

(3) The Mutual Funds Advisory Committee shall

(a) advise the Minister on any matter referred to it by him relating to the mutual funds industry;

(b) on its own motion report and make recommendations to the Minister on any matter relating to mutual funds as it sees fit; and

(c) have power to establish

(i) its own working rules and procedures; and

(ii) as many sub-committees as it thinks necessary.

PART II - Public Funds

Registration.

8. No public fund shall carry on its business or manage or administer its affairs in or from within the Territory unless it is registered under this Act.

Application for registration.

9.(1) A public fund may apply to the Governor for registration to carry on in or from within the Territory.

(2) An application shall be

(a) made in the form and contain the information as set out in Schedule 1; and

(b) accompanied by

(i) a statement setting out the nature and scope of the business to be carried on by the applicant in or from within the Territory, including the name of any other country or jurisdiction where the applicant is carrying on or intends to carry on business;

(ii) the application fee set out in Part II of Schedule 2 or such other amount as may be prescribed by regulations;

(iii) the instrument by which the applicant is constituted or such other proof as may be satisfactory to the Governor that the applicant is lawfully constituted under the laws of the Territory or of any other country or jurisdiction;

(iv) the notices required under section 26; and

(v) such other documents or information as the Governor may reasonably require for the purpose of determining the application.

Application for consent to be registered.

10.(1) The promoters of a public fund that is proposed to be formed, may apply to the Governor for his consent to register such proposed public fund upon being lawfully constituted under the laws of the Territory or of any other country or jurisdiction and upon complying with the requirements of this Act.

(2) An application for consent under subsection (1) shall be

(a) in the form of a letter setting out the particulars of the proposed public fund; and

(b) accompanied by the application fee set out in Part II of Schedule 2 or such other amount as may be prescribed by regulations.

(3) The consent of the Governor shall be

(a) in such form as the Governor may direct; and

(b) valid for a period of three months from the date it is granted subject to there being no change, that the Governor considers material, in any of the particulars contained in the application for consent.

(4) The promoters of a proposed public fund may, upon the expiry of the three months period referred to in subsection (3) (b), apply for the renewal of the Governor's consent subject to

(a) supplying such documents or information as the Governor may require; and

(b) the payment of the application fee required under subsection (2) (b).

Power to grant registration or consent.

11.(1) The Governor may, in his discretion, grant or refuse to grant

(a) registration under section 9; or

(b) his consent under section 10.

(2) Notwithstanding subsection (1), the Governor shall refuse to grant registration or his consent, as the case may be, if

(a) the public fund has a name which is undesirable or misleading;

(b) the public fund does not have a custodian who is functionally independent of the manager or administrator; or

(c) he determines that it is not in the public interest that such registration or consent should be granted.

(3) Except as provided in section 32, where the Governor, in the exercise of his powers under subsection (1) (a) or (b), makes a decision refusing to grant registration or consent he shall not be bound to assign any reasons for his decision which shall not be subject to appeal or review in any court.

Registration procedure

12.(1) Where the Governor grants registration pursuant to section 9 he shall direct the Registrar accordingly and the Registrar shall *(a)* register the public fund in the register maintained by him for the purpose under section 6; and

(b) issue a certificate to the registered public fund as directed by the Governor showing the date of registration.

(2) Where the Governor grants his consent under section 10, the promoters of the proposed public fund shall, within the three months period referred to in section 10 (3) (b) from the date of granting such consent or the renewal thereof, deliver to the Registrar

(a) the consent of the Governor;

(b) satisfactory proof that the proposed public fund is lawfully constituted in the Territory or elsewhere;

(c) the application fee required under section 9 (2) (b) (ii); and
(d) the notices referred to in section 9 (2) (b) (iv).

(3) If the Registrar is satisfied that the proposed public fund has complied with the requirements of subsection (2), he shall register the public fund and issue to it a certificate of registration in accordance with the procedure set out in subsection (1).

(4) The Registrar shall refuse to register the proposed public fund if he determines that

(a) its registration has not received the consent of the Governor pursuant to section 10; or

(b) it has not complied with any of the requirements of subsection (2).

(5) Any person aggrieved by a decision of the Registrar under subsection (4) may appeal to the Governor whose decision shall be final.

Accounting records and financial statements

13.(1) Every registered public fund shall

(a) maintain adequate accounting records and prepare financial statements in respect of each financial year in accordance with generally accepted accounting principles; and

(b) keep such accounting records and financial statements available for examination by the Registrar or any person authorised under his hand at

(i) its place of business or registered office in the Territory; or

(ii) such other place as its officers may see fit, provided that copies of such records and statements or such other documents or information as the Registrar may consider adequate are kept at its place of business or registered office in the Territory.

(2) The financial statements required under subsection (1) shall be

(a) audited by an auditor acceptable to the Registrar (in this Act called "the approved auditor") in accordance with generally accepted auditing standards;

(b) accompanied by the report of the approved auditor thereon which shall include a statement of the accounting principles under which statements have been prepared and a statement of the auditing standards which have been applied in the audit of such statements; and

(c) provided to or made available for examination by all investors of the registered public fund.

Duty to publish and file a prospectus

14.(1) No registered public fund shall in or outside the Territory make an invitation to the public or any section thereof to purchase its shares unless prior to such invitation it publishes in writing a prospectus signed by or on behalf of the board of directors (by whatever name called) or, in the case of a partnership, unit trust or other similar body, the equivalent governing body of the fund which approved the contents of the prospectus or authorised its publishing, and files a copy thereof with the Registrar.

(2) Every prospectus shall

(a) provide full and accurate disclosure of all such information as investors would reasonably require and expect to find for the purpose of making an informed investment decision;

(b) contain a summary statement of investors' rights as provided in section 16; and

(c) be accompanied by or contain reference to the availability of the financial statements for the last financial year of the fund and the auditor's report thereon if the fund has completed a financial year in operation.

(3) Repealed.

(4) f all or any part of the prospectus is not in the English language, the Registrar may require that an English translation of the prospectus or that part of the prospectus, verified in a manner satisfactory to him, be filed along with the prospectus.

(5) Where in a prospectus any of the disclosures required under subsection (2) (a) ceases to be accurate in a material particular, the registered public fund shall, within fourteen days of the change occurring, publish an amendment thereto giving accurate disclosures and provide a copy thereof to each of its investors and to the Registrar.

Certificate of compliance

15.(1) Every registered public fund, wherever it is constituted, which carries on business outside the Territory under the laws of another country or jurisdiction, shall every year, within three months of the end of its financial year, file with the Registrar a certificate of compliance from the competent authority that is responsible for the regulation and supervision of the conduct of its business in that other country or jurisdiction.

(2) A registered public fund to which subsection (1) applies is deemed to have complied with that subsection if it is proven to the satisfaction of the Registrar that the required certificate could not be obtained for reasons beyond the control of the fund.

(3) Where a registered public fund which carries on business outside the Territory carries on business in more than one country or jurisdiction other than the Territory, the certificate required to be filed under subsection (1) shall be from the competent authority in the country or jurisdiction in or from which it carries on its principal business.

Investors' rights.

16.(1) If a registered public fund publishes a prospectus or any amendment thereto that contains misrepresentation relating to any of the disclosures required under section 14 (2) (a), a person who purchased any shares pursuant to such prospectus or amendment thereto is deemed to have relied upon the misrepresentation and shall have the rights provided in subsection (2).

(2) A person referred to in subsection (1) may elect to exercise a right of action

(a) for the rescission of the purchase, or

(b) for damages,

jointly and severally against the fund, and every member of the board of directors (by whatever name called) or, in the case of a partnership, unit trust or other similar body, every member or the equivalent governing body who, while aware of the misrepresentation, or would have been aware of the misrepresentation had he made reasonable investigations consistent with his duties, authorised the signing of or approved the prospectus or amendment thereto and consented to its publication and filing or caused it to be signed or published and filed.

(3) For the purposes of this section, "misrepresentation" means

(a) an untrue or misleading statement of any of the disclosures required under section l4 (2) (a) ; or

(b) an omission to disclose any of such disclosures.

(4) No person is liable under this section if he proves that the purchaser purchased the shares offered by the prospectus or amendment thereto with knowledge of the misrepresentation.

(5) The right of action for rescission or for damages conferred by subsection (2) is in addition to and without derogation from any other right the plaintiff may have at law.

Limitation of action and amount recoverable

17.(1) Notwithstanding any provision of law to the contrary, any action pursuant to section 16 (2) may not be commenced after

(a) one hundred and eighty days from the day that the plaintiff first had knowledge of the misrepresentation, or

(b) one year from the date of the purchase transaction that gave rise to the cause of action,

whichever is earlier.

(2) In any action under section 16(2), the amount recoverable shall not exceed the amount at which the shares were purchased or subscribed, including any fees or other charges paid by the plaintiff.

PART III - Private and Professional Funds

Recognition.

18.(1) Subject to subsection (2), no private or professional fund shall carry on its business or manage or administer its affairs in or from within the Territory unless it is recognised under this Act.

(2) A professional fund may carry on its business or manage or administer its affairs in or from within the Territory for a period of up to fourteen days without being recognised under this Act.

Application for recognition

19.(1) A private or professional fund that is constituted under the laws of the Territory is entitled to be recognised under this Act if it provides

(a) proof satisfactory to the Minister that it

(i) is a private or professional fund within the meaning of this Act; and

(ii) is lawfully constituted under the laws of the Territory; and

(b) the notices required under section 26;

(2) A private or professional fund that is constituted outside the Territory may apply for recognition under this Act by sending to the Minister a letter setting out the nature and scope of its business which shall be accompanied by

(a) the application fee set out in Part II of Schedule 2 or such other amount as may be prescribed by regulations;

(b) the notices required under section 26; and

(c) proof satisfactory to the Minister that the applicant is

(i) a private or professional fund within the meaning of this Act; and

(ii) lawfully constituted under the laws of another country or jurisdiction.

(3) In the case of a professional fund, the matters required by subsections (1) and (2) shall be provided within fourteen days of commencement of its business.

Power to grant recognition.

20.(1) The Minister may, in his discretion, grant or refuse to grant recognition under section 19(2).

(2) Where the Minister refuses to grant recognition under section 19 (2), the provisions of section 11(3) shall apply mutatis mutandis.

(3) The Minister shall not refuse to grant recognition under section 19 (1) unless the applicant fails to comply with the requirements of that section.

(4) Where the Minister refuses to grant recognition under section 19 (1), he shall give the applicant notice in writing of his decision and the reasons therefor and the applicant may appeal such decision pursuant to section 33.

Recognition Procedure

21. Where the Minister grants recognition to a private or professional fund, he shall direct the Registrar accordingly and the Registrar shall

(a) enter the particulars relating to the private or professional fund in the register maintained by him for the purpose under section 6; and

(b) issue a certificate of recognition to the private or professional fund as directed by the Minister showing the date of recognition.

PART IV - Managers and Administrators

Licensing.

22.(1) No person shall, in or from within the Territory, carry on or hold himself out as carrying on business as manager or administrator of mutual funds unless that person is licensed for the purpose under this Act.

(2) Subsection (1) does not apply to a person who

(a) is not ordinarily resident or domiciled in the Territory;

(b) is a manager or administrator of mutual funds (by whatever name called) under the laws of a recognised Country or Jurisdiction; and

(c) has received written permission from the Minister to carry on business as manager or administrator of mutual funds in or from within the Territory.

Application for a licence.

23.(1) A person who wishes to do so may make an application to the Minister to carry on business in or from within the Territory as

(a) manager;

(b) administrator; or

(c) both manager and administrator of mutual funds.

(2) An application shall be accompanied by

(a) the application fee set out in Part II of Schedule 2 or such other amount as may be prescribed by regulations;

(b) a statement of the financial and human resources and administrative facilities available to the applicant for the competent and efficient conduct of its business; and

(c) such other documents or information as the Minister may reasonably require for the purpose of considering the application.

Power to grant licences.

24.(1) The Minister may, in his discretion, grant or refuse to grant a licence to any applicant.

(2) The Minister shall not grant a licence unless he is satisfied that the applicant *(a)* is a fit and proper person to be engaged in the business proposed; and

(b) has or has available to him adequate knowledge, expertise, resources and facilities necessary for the nature and scope of the business proposed: and

(c) has appointed an auditor satisfying such conditions as may be prescribed by the Minister.

(3) Notwithstanding subsections (1) and (2), the Minister shall refuse to grant a licence if he determines that it is not in the public interest that a licence should be granted.

(4) Where the Minister refuses to grant a licence to an applicant, the provisions of section 11(3) shall apply mutatis mutandis.

Licensing procedure.

25. Where the Minister grants a licence to an applicant, he shall direct the Registrar accordingly and the Registrar shall

(a) enter the particulars of the applicant in the register maintained by him for the purpose under section 6; and

(b) issue a licence to the applicant as directed by the Minister showing the date on which the licence is granted.

Code of Practice.

25A.(1) The Minister may by Order prescribe a Code of Practice directing the holder of a licence under section 24 to comply with the requirements of the Code which may include matters relating to

(a) conduct of business;

(b) financial resources;

(c) the giving of notice of specified events;

(d) advertising;

(e) clients' money and custody of investments; and

(f) accounting records and audit requirements.

(2) A Code of Practice prescribed under subsection (1) may provide for such enforcement mechanisms as the Minister may consider necessary to ensure compliance with the provisions of the Code.

PART V - General

Notices to accompany applications.

26.(1) In addition to any other requirement under this Act, every application for registration, recognition or a licence made under this Act shall be accompanied by a notice of

(a) the address of the applicant's place of business and its address for service in the Territory;

(b) the name and address of a person resident in the Territory who is authorised to represent the applicant and to accept service on its behalf; and

(c) the address of any place or places of business that the applicant may have outside the Territory.

(2) If any information contained in any of the notices required to accompany the application pursuant to subsection (1) is altered at any time thereafter, the applicant, upon being a registered public fund, a recognised private or professional fund or a licensed manager or administrator, as the case may be, shall give in writing to the Registrar particulars of the alteration within twenty-one days after the alteration is made.

Form and conditions of certificates and licences.

27.(1) A certificate or a licence may be granted subject to terms, conditions, restrictions or limitations as the Governor or the Minister, as the case may be, sees fit to specify therein.

(2) A certificate or a licence shall

(a) be in such form as may be directed by the Governor or the Minister, as the case may be;

(b) be admitted in all courts as prima facie evidence of the facts stated therein; and

(c) remain in force until it is cancelled.

Annual Fees.

28.(1) Where

(a) a public fund is granted registration,

(b) a private or professional fund is granted recognition, or

(c) a person is granted a licence, there shall be payable for the year in which such registration, recognition or licence is granted the fee set out in paragraph

(A) of Part III of Schedule 2, or such other amounts as may prescribed by regulations.

(2) On or before the 31st day of March every year following the year in which registration, recognition or licence is granted there shall be payable the annual fee set out in paragraph (B) of Part III of Schedule 2 or such other amounts as may prescribed by regulations.

(3) An unpaid annual fee may be sued for by the Government by action as a civil debt and the Government may require, and the court may order, the payment of a penalty in an amount equal to the amount of the fee for late payment of the fee.

Cancellation etc. of certificates or licences.

29. The Governor, in the case of a registered public fund, and the Minister, in the case of a recognised private or professional fund or a licensed manager or administrator, may, subject to sections 30 and 31, cancel a certificate or a licence, as the case may be, or impose new or additional conditions, restrictions or limitations in respect of such certificate or licence

(a) at the request of the holder thereof; or

(b) where the holder thereof

(i) has ceased to carry on business in or from within the Territory;

(ii) has contravened any provision of this Act, the regulations or the Code of Practice prescribed under section 25A or any term, condition, restriction or limitation attached to the holder's certificate or licence, as the case may be;

(iii) has been convicted of an offence under this Act or of a criminal offence in any country or jurisdiction;

(iv) has knowingly and wilfully supplied false, misleading or inaccurate information or failed to disclose information required for the purposes of any provision of this Act or the regulations;

(v) is carrying on business in a manner detrimental to the interests of mutual funds investors or to the public interest; or

(vi) is declared bankrupt or is being wound-up or otherwise dissolved.

Cancellation procedure.

30.(1) Before cancelling a certificate or a licence under paragraph (b) of section 29, the Governor or the Minister, as the case may be, shall *(a)* give the holder thereof notice in writing of the grounds on which he intends to do so;

(b) afford the holder an opportunity to make written representations to him within a period of thirty days after receipt of the notice; and

(c) take any such representations into consideration.

(2) Where in the exercise of his powers under section 29 (b)

(a) the Governor decides to cancel a certificate, or

(b) the Minister decides to cancel a certificate or a licence, as the case may be, he shall give notice in writing to the holder thereof of such cancellation and the reasons therefor.

Appeal of cancellations.

31. The holder of a certificate or a licence aggrieved by the decision cancelling such certificate or licence may appeal such decision in accordance with section 33.

Appeal by existing entities.

32. Notwithstanding any provision in this Act, where

(a) the Governor, in the exercise of his powers under section 11 (1) (a), refuses to grant registration, or

(b) the Minister, in the exercise of his powers

(i) under section 20 (1) refuses to grant recognition, or

(ii) under section 24 (1) refuses to grant a licence, to an existing entity, he shall give such existing entity a notice in writing of his decision and the reasons therefor and the existing entity may appeal such decision in accordance with section 33.

Appeal Procedure

33.(1) An appeal under sections 20 (4), 31 or 32 shall be by

(a) way of summons to a Judge in Chambers; and

(b) serving the Governor or the Minister, as the case may be, with a notice of appeal within twenty-one days or such longer period as the judge may allow,

after receipt of the notice required under sections 20 (4), 30 (2) or 32, as the case may be.

(2) The bringing of an appeal under section 31 suspends the decision appealed against pending the determination or abandonment of the appeal.

Grant or cancellation to be published

34. The Registrar shall publish in the ***Gazette***, in such form as he thinks fit, notice of every grant or cancellation of a certificate or a licence under this Act.

Power to grant exemptions.

35.(1) Upon the recommendation of the Registrar, the Governor may, if he is satisfied that to do so would not be prejudicial to the public interest, direct that all or any of the provisions of this Act or the regulations shall

(a) not apply, or

(b) apply subject to such modifications as he may specify in the direction, to any person or any class of persons.

(2) A direction under this section may be

(a) subject to any conditions as the Governor may see fit to specify therein; and

(b) revoked at any time at the discretion of the Governor.

(3) Repealed.

Restriction on the use of the words "fund" or "mutual fund".

35A. Except where a person is a mutual fund within the meaning of this Act, or with the written consent of the Registrar, no person shall

(a) use or continue to use the words "fund" of "mutual fund", either in English or in any other language, in the name, description or title under which that person is carrying on business in or from within the Territory; and

(b) make or continue to make any representation in any advertisement, billhead, circular, letter, letterhead, notice, paper or in any other manner that that person is carrying on business as a fund or mutual fund.

Access to information and records.

36. For the purpose of discharging his duties under this Act and the regulations and subject to section 38, the Registrar or any person acting under his authority, may, at all reasonable times, in writing, direct any person to whom this Act applies to

(a) furnish information, or

(b) provide access to any records, books, or other documents,

relating to the business of that person being carried on under this Act which, in the opinion of the Registrar, are necessary to enable him to ascertain compliance with the provisions of this Act or the regulations.

Immunity and actions by the Registrar.

37.(1) No liability shall be incurred by and no suit, action or proceeding shall be brought against the Crown, any agent thereof, the Registrar or any person acting under his authority for any act done or omitted to be done in good faith

(a) in the performance or intended performance of any function or duty, or

(b) in the exercise or intended exercise of any power, under this Act or the regulations.

(2) The Registrar may bring actions and institute proceedings in his name of office for the enforcement of any provision of this Act or the regulations, or for the recovery of fees or other sums of money payable under this Act or the regulations.

Confidentiality

38. Notwithstanding section 6,

(a) any information, material or document furnished to or filed with the Registrar by any recognised private or professional fund is privileged and shall not be disclosed to any person except

(i) the Governor, the Minister, the Attorney General or a public officer authorised by the Governor or the Minister; or

(ii) on the order of a court of competent jurisdiction for the purpose of criminal proceedings;

(b) the Governor may direct that any specified information, material or document furnished to or filed with the Registrar by any registered public fund shall be held in confidence and shall not be disclosed to any person so long as the Governor is of the opinion that to do so is in the public interest.

Exemption from certain enactments.

39.(1) Notwithstanding any statutory provision or rule of law to the contrary

(a) a public fund that is registered or a private or professional fund that is recognised under this Act, and

(b) an investor in any such registered public fund or recognised private or professional fund who is not ordinarily resident or domiciled in the Territory,

are in all respects exempt from any and all of the provisions of the Income Tax Act, the Stamps Act, and the Registration and Records Act.

(2) Notwithstanding the provisions of Part IX (section 235A) of the Companies Act, a company that is incorporated outside the Territory which establishes a place of business within the Territory to carry on business in accordance with the provisions of this Act as

(a) a registered public fund,

(b) a recognised private or professional fund, or

(c) a licensed manager or administrator, is exempt from the provisions of that Part IX (section 235A) of the Companies Act.

Offences and penalties

40.(1) A person who,

(a) wilfully makes a misrepresentation in any document required to be filed, furnished or delivered under this Act or the regulations,

(b) wilfully makes any statement or gives any information required for the purposes of this Act or the regulations that he knows to be false or misleading,

(c) knowingly fails to disclose any fact or information required to be disclosed for the purposes of this Act or the regulations, or

(d) being in charge of or having possession of or control over any information, records, books or other documents referred to in section 36, refuses or wilfully neglects to comply with any lawful direction given under that section,

commits an offence under this Act and is liable on summary conviction to a fine of not less than five thousand dollars and not more than fifty thousand dollars or to imprisonment for a period not exceeding two years or both such fine and imprisonment.

(2) Any person who, without reasonable cause, contravenes a provision of this Act or the regulations for which no penalty is provided commits an offence against this Act or the regulations, as the case may be, and is liable on summary conviction,

(a) in the case of a body corporate or unincorporated, a fine of not more than fifty thousand dollars; and

(b) in the case of an individual, to a fine of not more than five thousand dollars or to imprisonment for a period not exceeding one month or to both such fine and imprisonment.

(3) A prosecution for an offence under this Act may be commenced within five years from the date of the commission of the offence but not thereafter.

Power to the Minister to vary the Schedule.

41. The Minister may by Notice published in the *Gazette,*

(a) vary the form of Schedule 1 provided such variation does not, in any material respect, change the substance of the Schedule; or

(b) subject to the affirmative resolution procedure of the Legislative Council modify, delete, repeal or replace any Schedule to this Act in whole or in part.

Regulations.

42. The Governor may make regulations

(a) prescribing fees payable under this Act;

(b) repealed;

(c) repealed;

(d) designating arrangements which are not mutual funds;

(e) designating mutual funds or a class or classes thereof as private or professional mutual funds;

(ea) designating a class or sub-classes of a public fund;

(f) authorising the Registrar to require that any document, statement, report, certificate, release, agreement, or other information be filed with, furnished or delivered to him;

(g) defining, for the purposes of this Act, terms or expressions used in this Act that are not defined in this Act;

(h) prescribing any matter required to be or which may be prescribed under this Act;

(i) relating to

(i) the constitution, powers and duties of the manager, administrator and custodian;

(ii) the issue and redemption of shares;

(iii) the appointment, removal and powers and duties of auditors;

(iv) the restriction or regulation of investment and borrowing powers;

(v) the preparation of periodical reports;

(vi) the rights of investors; and

(vii) the contents of constitutional documents, in respect of a public fund or a sub-class of such fund;

(ia) relating to the matters which should be contained in a prospectus of a public fund or a sub-class of such fund; and

(j) generally for the better administration of this Act and for carrying the intent and purpose of its provisions into effect.

Transitional

43.(1) Any person performing the functions of a manager or an administrator who, on the date of the coming into force of this Act, is carrying on any business or engaged in any activity in relation to which he is required to be licensed under this Act shall, within three months of the coming into force of this Act, comply with the requirements of this Act.

(2) Any person who, on the date of the coming into force of this Act, is carrying on any business or engaged in any activity as a mutual fund shall, within nine months from that date, comply with the provisions of this Act.

(3) Where a person fails to comply with subsection (2), it shall pay a non-compliance penalty of five thousand dollars for each month or part thereof during which it fails to comply with that subsection up to a period of twelve months.

(4) If after the period of twelve months prescribed under subsection (3) a person fails to comply with subsection (2), he commits an offence and may be proceeded against under section 40(2).

(5) Where a person is proceeded against under section 40(2), it shall, in addition to any penalty imposed on it, pay the non-compliance penalty to which it is liable under subsection (3).

SCHEDULE 1 (Section 9 (2) (a))

APPLICATION FOR REGISTRATION OF A PUBLIC FUND

1. Applicant:

state name and address of the fund

2. Constitution:

*(a)*state the legal form of the fund

(i) company

(ii) partnership

(iii) unit trust

(b) state the name of the country or Jurisdiction where the fund is constituted

(c) state the title of the law under which the fund is constituted

3. Officers:

(a) state name, address, place of birth and citizenship of each of the following officers of the fund:

(i) directors;

(ii) general partners; or

(iii) trustees

(b) state educational and professional qualifications of each of the officers in sub-paragraph (a)

(c) give details of business, occupation or employment of each of the officers mentioned in sub-paragraph (a)

4. References:

give two personal references, a bank reference and where it is the practice to make one available in the relevant jurisdiction, a police clearance certificate for each of the officers mentioned in paragraph 3(a)

5. Functionaries:

state names, addresses and business activities of each of the fund's

(a) managers;

(b) administrators;

(c) investment advisers; and

(d) custodians.

6. Prior Registration:

state if the fund is now or has been registered, licensed, recognised or authorised under any law or regulations relating to mutual funds, collective investment schemes/funds or securities in any country or jurisdiction.

7. Refusal or Disciplinary Measure:

Has the fund, any of its officers mentioned in paragraph 3(a), managers, administrators, investment advisers or custodians been the subject of

(a) refusal of an application for registration, licensing, recognition or authorisation, or

(b) suspension, cancellation or revocation of registration, licence, recognition or authorisation by any authority in any country or jurisdiction?

give details and reasons

8. Civil Proceedings:

Has a judgement been rendered or any suit, action or proceedings pending against any of the officers mentioned in paragraph 3(a) or of any of the functionaries listed in question 5 above, in civil proceedings in any court or tribunal in any country or jurisdiction which has been or is based in whole or in part on fraud, theft, deceit, misrepresentation or similar conduct?

give details

9. Offences:

Has any of the officers mentioned in paragraph 3(a) or of any of the functionaries listed in question 5 above been or is being charged, indicted or convicted in any country or jurisdiction for any offence in any criminal or civil proceedings relating to fraud or theft arising out of dealing in mutual funds, collective investment schemes/funds or securities?

10. Bankruptcy:

Has any of the officers mentioned in paragraph 3(a) or of any of the functionaries listed in question 5 above been

(a) declared bankrupt or been party to bankruptcy or insolvency proceedings,

(b) subject to proceedings relating to winding-up, dissolution or creditors' arrangement, or

(c) subject to proceedings relating to receivership or Creditors, compromise, in any country or jurisdiction?

AFFIDAVIT

I, ...of...........................(address), in my capacity as director/general partner/ trustee,* acting for and on behalf of ...., the applicant public mutual fund herein, do depose and say that I have read and understood the questions in the application submitted herewith and hereby certify under oath that the answers and statements provided in respect of the application are true, correct and complete to the best of my knowledge, information and belief.

Sworn before me   Name and Signature

SCHEDULE 2

FEES

PART I

(Sections 3 (3))

Fee for issuing a Certificate of Compliance

The fee for issuing a Certificate of Compliance pursuant to section 3 (3) is $25.00

PART II

Application Fees

(Sections) 9(2) (b) (ii)

10(2) (b) 19(2) (a)

23(2) (a))

The fee for

(a) an application for registration under section 9 (2) (b) (ii) is $ 500.00

(b) an application for consent to be registered under section 10 (2) (b) is $ 100.00

(c) an application for recognition under section 19 (2) (a) is $ 350.00

(d) an application for a licence under section 23 (2) (a) is $ 250.00

PART III

Annual Fees

(Section 28 (1) and (2))

(A) Fee payable for the year in which registration, recognition or licence is granted pursuant to section 28 (1):

(1) where registration, recognition or licence is granted on or before the 30th day of June in any year, the fee payable for that year is

(a) by a registered public fund;

(b) $350.00 by a recognised private or professional fund;

(c) $500.00 by a person licensed as manager or administrator; and

(d) $1000.00 by a person licensed as both manager and administrator.

(2) Where registration, recognition or licence is granted on or after the 1st day of July in any year, the fee payable for that year is

(a) by a registered public fund;

(b) $175.00 by a recognised private or professional fund;

(c) $250.00 by a person licensed as manager or administrator; and

(d) $500.00 by a person licensed as both manager and administrator.

(B) The annual fee payable pursuant to section 28 (2) is

(a) by a registered public fund;

(b) $350.00 by a recognised private or professional fund;

(c) $500.00 by a person licensed as manager or administrator; and

(d) $1000.00 by a person licensed as both manager and administrator.

AGREEMENT OF 18TH FEBRUARY, 1981

United States

CONVENTION BETWEEN THE GOVERNMENT OF THE UNITED STATES OF AMERICA AND THE GOVERNMENT OF THE BRITISH VIRGIN ISLANDS FOR THE AVOIDANCE OF DOUBLE TAXATION AND THE PREVENTION OF FISCAL EVASION WITH RESPECT TO TAXES ON INCOME

The Government of the United States of America and the Government of the British Virgin Islands (being duly authorized in that behalf by the Government of the United Kingdom), desiring to conclude a new Convention for the avoidance of double taxation and the prevention of fiscal evasion with respect to taxes on income, have agreed as follows:

Article 1

Personal Scope

1. Except as specially provided herein, this Convention is applicable to persons who are residents of one or both of the Covered Jurisdictions.

2. Notwithstanding any provision of this Convention except paragraph (3), a Covered Jurisdiction may tax its residents (as determined under Article 4 (Fiscal Residence)) and its nationals as if this Convention had not come into effect. For this purpose the term "national" shall include, in the case of the United States, a former citizen whose loss of citizenship had as one of its principal purposes the avoidance of income tax, but only for a period of 10 years following such loss.

3. Nothing in paragraph (2) shall affect the application by a Covered Jurisdiction of:

(a) paragraphs (1)(b) and (4) of Article 18 (Pensions, Annuities, Alimony and Child Support), and Articles 22 (Elimination of Double Taxation), 23 (Non-Discrimination) and 24 (Mutual Agreement Procedure); and

(b) Articles 19 (Government Service) and 20 (Students and Trainees), and paragraph (1) of Article 26 (Miscellaneous), with respect to individuals who are neither nationals of, nor have immigrant status in, that Covered Jurisdiction.

Article 2

Taxes Covered

1. The existing taxes to which this Convention shall apply are:

(a) in the case of the United States, the Federal income taxes imposed by the

Internal Revenue Code (but excluding the accumulated earnings tax and the personal holding company tax); the foregoing taxes covered are hereinafter referred to as "United States tax";

(b) in the case of the Virgin Islands, the taxes imposed on income (but excluding the petroleum income tax); the foregoing taxes covered sere hereinafter referred to as "Virgin Islands tax."

2. This Convention shall also apply to any identical or substantially similar taxes which are imposed by a Covered Jurisdiction after the date of signature of this Convention in addition to, or in place of, the existing taxes. The competent authorities of the Covered Jurisdictions shall notify each other of any significant changes which have been made in their respective taxation laws.

3. For the purpose of Article 23 (Non-Discrimination), this Convention shall also apply to taxes of every kind and description imposed by a Covered Jurisdiction, or by a political subdivision or local authority thereof. For the purpose of Article 25 (Exchange of Information and Administrative Assistance), this Convention shall also apply to taxes of every kind and description imposed by a Covered Jurisdiction.

Article 3

General Definitions

1. In this Convention, unless the context otherwise requires:

(a) **(i)** the term "United States corporation" means a corporation (or any unincorporated entity treated as a corporation for United States tax purposes) which is created under the laws of the United States or any state thereof or the District of Columbia;

(ii) the term "Virgin Islands corporation" means any body corporate which is created under the laws of the Virgin Islands;

(b) the term "person" includes an individual, a corporation, a partnership, an estate, a trust and any other body of persons;

(c) the term "enterprise of a Covered Jurisdiction" means an industrial or commercial undertaking carried on by a resident of a Covered Jurisdiction;

(d) the term "international traffic" means any transport by a ship or aircraft except when the ship or aircraft is operated solely between places within a Covered Jurisdiction;

(e) the term "competent authority" means:

(i) in the case of the United States, the Secretary of the Treasury or his delegate; and

(ii) in the case of the Virgin Islands, the Minister of Finance or his delegate;

(f) **(i)** the term "United States means the United States of America; and

(ii) when used in a geographical sense, means the states thereof and the District of Columbia, but does not include Puerto Rico, the United States Virgin Islands, Guam or any other United States possession or territory;

(g) the term "Virgin Islands" means the islands in the Eastern Caribbean known as the British Virgin Islands;

(h) the term "Covered Jurisdiction" means the United States or the Virgin Islands, as the context requires;

(i) the term "nationals" means:

(i) in relation to the United States, United States citizens;

(ii) in relation to the Virgin Islands, Virgin Islands belongers.

2. As regards the application of this Convention by a Covered Jurisdiction, stay term not otherwise defined shall, unless the context otherwise requires and subject to the provisions of Article 24 (Mutual Agreement Procedure), have the meaning which it has under the laws of that Covered Jurisdiction relating to the taxes which are the subject of this Convention.

Article 4

Fiscal Residence

1. For the purposes of this Convention:

(a) the term "resident of the United States" means:

(i) any person, other than a corporation, resident in the United States for the purposes of United States tax; but in the case of a partnership, estate or trust, only to the extent that the income derived by such partnership, estate or trust is subject to United States tax as the income of a resident, either in its hands or in the hands of its partners or beneficiaries; and

(ii) a United States corporation;

(b) the term "resident of the Virgin Islands" means:

(i) any person, other than a corporation, resident in the Virgin Islands for the purposes of Virgin Islands tax; but in the case of a partnership, estate or trust, only to the extent that the income derived by such partnership, estate or trust is subject to Virgin Islands tax as the income of a resident, either in its hands or in the hands of its partners or beneficiaries; and

(ii) a Virgin Islands corporation resident in the Virgin Islands for the purposes of Virgin Islands tax.

2. Where by reason of the provisions of paragraph (1) an individual is a resident of both Covered Jurisdictions, then the individual's tax status shall be determined as follows:

(a) the individual shall be deemed to be a resident of the Covered Jurisdiction in which he has a permanent home available to him. If the individual has a permanent home available to him in both Covered Jurisdictions, or in neither, he shall be deemed to be a resident of the Covered Jurisdiction with which his personal and economic relations are closer ("center of vital interests");

(b) if the Covered Jurisdiction in which the individual's center of vital interests is located cannot be determined, he shall be deemed to be a resident of the Covered Jurisdiction in which he has an habitual abode;

(c) if the individual has an habitual abode in both Covered Jurisdictions, or in neither, he shall be deemed to be a resident of the Covered Jurisdiction of which he is a national; and

(d) if the individual is a national of both Covered Jurisdictions, or of neither, the competent authorities of the Covered Jurisdictions shall settle the question by mutual agreement.

3. Where by reason of the provisions of paragraph (1) a person other than an individual or a corporation is a resident of both Covered Jurisdictions, the competent authorities of the Covered Jurisdictions shall settle the question of residence by mutual agreement.

Article 5

Permanent Establishment

1. For the purposes of this Convention, the term "permanent establishment" means a fixed place of business through which the business of an enterprise is wholly or partly carried on.

2. The term "permanent establishment" shall include especially:

(a) a branch;

(b) an office;

(c) a factory;

(d) a workshop;

(e) a mine, oil or gas well, quarry or other place of extraction of natural resources;

(f) a building site or construction or installation project, or an installation or drilling rig or ship used for or in connection with the exploration for or exploitation of natural resources, or a supervisory activity connected with any of the foregoing, if, but only if, it exists for more than 24 months; and

(g) a boat which is used in a Covered Jurisdiction for renting or chartering primarily for recreational purposes if, but only if, such use is for more than three months in any 12 month period.

3. Notwithstanding the provisions of paragraphs (1) and (2), the term "permanent establishment" shall be deemed not to include a fixed place of business used solely for one or more of the following activites:

(a) the storage, display or delivery of goods or merchandise belonging to the enterprise;

(b) the maintenance of a stock of goods or merchandise belonging to the enterprise for the purpose of storage, display or delivery;

(c) the maintenance of a stock of goods or merchandise belonging to the enterprise for the purpose of processing by another person;

(d) the maintenance of a fixed place of business for the purpose of purchasing goods or merchandise, or for oollecting information, for the enterprise; or

(e) the maintenance of a fixed place of business for the purpose of advertising, for the supply of information, for scientific research or for similar activities which have a preparatory or auxiliary character, for the enterprise.

4. A person acting in a Covered Jurisdiction on behalf of an enterpries of the other Covered Jurisdiction—other than an agent of an independent status to whom paragraph (5) applies—shall be deemed to be a permanent establishment of the enterprise in the first-mentioned Covered Jurisdiction if, but only if, such person has, and habitually exercises therein, an authority to conclude contracts in the name of the enterprise, unless the contracts are confined to the activities described in paragraph (3).

5. An enterprise (other than an enterprise carrying on the business of insurance) of a Covered Jurisdiction shall not be deemed to have a permanent establishment in the other Covered Jurisdiction merely because it carries on business in that other Covered Jurisdiction through a broker, general commission agent or any other agent of an independent status, where such persons are acting in the ordinary course of their business.

6. The fact that a corporation which is a resident of a Covered Jurisdiction controls or is controlled by a corporation which is a resident of the other Covered Jurisdiction, or which carries on business in that other Covered Jurisdiction (whether through a permanent establishment or otherwise) shall not of itself constitute either corporation a permanent establishment of the other.

Article 6

Income From Real Property

1. Income from real property, including income from agriculture or forestry, may be taxed in the Covered Jurisdiction in which such property is situated.

2. The term "real property" shall be defined in accordance with the laws of the Covered Jurisdiction in which the property in question is situated. The term shall in any case include usufruct of real property and rights to variable or fixed payments as consideration for the working of, or the right to work, mineral deposits, sources and other natural resources.

3. The provisions of paragraph (1) shall apply to income derived from the direct use, letting or use in any other form of real property.

4. A resident of a Covered Jurisdiction who is subject to tax in the other Covered Jurisdiction on income from real property situated in that other Covered Jurisdiction may elect for any taxable year to compute the tax on such income on a net basis as if such income were attributable to a permanent establishemnt in that other Covered Jurisdiction. Any such election shall be binding for the taxable year of the election and all subsequent taxable years unless the competent authority of that other Covered Jurisdiction agrees to a termination of the election.

Article 7

Business Profits

1. The business profits of an enterprise of a Covered Jurisdiction shall be taxable only in that Covered Jurisdiction unless the enterprise carries on business in the other Covered Jurisdiction through a permanent establishment situated therein. If the enterprise carries on business as aforesaid, the business profits of the enterprise may be taxed in that other Covered Jurisdiction, but only so much of them as is attributable to that permanent establishment.

2. Subject to the provisions of paragraph (3), where an enterprise of a Covered Jurisdiction carries on business in the other Covered Jurisdiction through a permanent establishment situated therein, there shall in each Covered Jurisdiction be attributed to that permanent establishment the profits which it might be expected to make if it were a distinct and independent enterprise engaged in the same or similar activities under the same or similar conditions.

3. In the determination of the profits of a permanent establishment, there shall be allowed as deductions those expenses which are incurred for the purposes of the permanent establishment, including a reasonable allocation of executive and general administrative expenses, research and development expenses, interest and other expenses incurred for the purposes of the enterprise as a whole (or the part thereof which includes the permanent establishment), whether incurred in the Covered Jurisdiction in which the permanent establishment is situated or elsewhere.

4. No business profits shall be attributed to a permanent establishment by reason of the mere purchase by that permanent establishment of goods or merchandise for the enterprise.

5. For the purposes of the preceding paragraphs, the profits to be attributed to the permanent establishment shall be determined by the same method year by year unless there is good and sufficient reason to the contrary.

6. Where profits include items of income which are dealt with separately in other Articles of this Convention, then the provisions of those Articles shall not be affected by the provisions of this Article.

7. For the purposes of this Convention, the term "business profits" includes, but is not limited to, income derived from manufacturing, mercantile, banking, insurance, agricultural, fishing or mining activities, the operation of ships or aircraft and the furnishing of services. Such term also includes any other income attributable to a permanent establishment which the recipient, being a resident of a Covered Jurisdiction, has in the other Covered Jurisdiction. Such term does not include the performance of a personal services by an individual either as an employee or in an independent capacity; nor does such term include income from the rental of tangible personal property or the rental or licensing of cinematographic films or films or tapes used for radio or television broadcasting or from copyrights thereof.

Article 8

Shipping And Air Transport

1

1. Profits derived by an enterprise of a Covered Jurisdiction from the operation of ships or aircraft in international traffic or between two places within that Covered Jurisdiction shall be taxable only in that Covered Jurisdiction.

2. For the purpose of this Article, profits derived by an enterprise of a Covered Jurisdiction from the operation of ships or aircraft in international traffic or between two places within that Covered Jurisdiction include profits derived from the rental on a full or bareboat basis of ships or aircraft if operated in international traffic or between two places within that Covered Jurisdiction by the lessee or if such rental profits are incidental to other income described in paragraph (1), but do not include profits attributable to a permanent establishment described in paragraph (2)(g) of Article 5 (Permanent Establishment).

3. Profits derived by an enterprise of a Covered Jurisdiction from the use, maintenance or rental of containers (including trailers, barges and related equipment for the transport of containers) used for the transport of goods or merchandise in international traffic or between two places within that Covered Jurisdiction shall be taxable only in that Covered Jurisdiction.

4. The provisions of this Article shall also apply to profits from the participation in a pool, a joint business or an international operating agency.

5. Gains derived by an enterprise of a Covered Jurisdiction from the alienation of ships, aircraft or containers owned by such enterprise, the income from which is taxable only in that Covered Jurisdiction, shall be taxable only in that Covered Jurisdiction.

Article 9

Associated Enterprises

1. Where

(a) an enterprise of a Covered Jurisdiction participates directly or indirectly in the management, control or capital of an enterprise of the other Covered Jurisdiction, or

(b) the same persons participate directly or indirectly in the management, control or capital of an enterprise of a Covered Jurisdiction and an enterprise of the other Covered Jurisdiction, and in either case conditions are made or imposed between the two enterprises in their commercial or financial relations which differ from those which would have been made between independent enterprises, then any profits which would, but for those conditions, have accrued to one of the enterprises but, by reason of those conditions, have not so accrued, may be included in the profits of that enterprise and taxed accordingly.

2. Where a Covered Jurisdiction includes in the profits of an enterprise of that Covered Jurisdiction and taxes accordingly profits on which an enterprise of the other Covered Jurisdiction has been charged to tax in that other Covered Jurisdiction, and the profits so included are profits which would have accrued to the enterprise of the first-mentioned Covered Jurisdiction if the conditions made between the two enterprises had been these which would have been made between independent enterprises, then that other Covered Jurisdiction shall make an appropriate adjustment to the amount of the tax charged therein on those profits. In determining such adjustment, due regard shall be had to the other provisions of this Convention and the competent authorities of the Covered Jurisdictions shall if necessary consult each other.

3. The provisions of paragraph (1) shall not limit any provisions of the law of either Covered Jurisdiction which permit the distribution, apportionment or allocation of income, deductions, credits or allowances between persons owned or controlled directly or indirectly by the same interests when necessary in order to prevent evasion of taxes or clearly to reflect the income of any such persons.

Article 10

Dividends

1. Dividends paid by a corporation which is a resident of a Covered Jurisdiction to a beneficial owner who is a resident of the other Covered Jurisdiction may be taxed in the first-mentioned Covered Jurisdiction, but the tax imposed shall not exceed 15 percent of the gross amount of the dividends.

2. The term "dividends" for United States tax purposes includes any item which under the law of the United States is treated as a distribution out of earnings and profits and for Virgin Islands tax purposes includes any item which under the law of the Virgin Islands is treated as a distribution.

3. Paragraph (1) shall not apply if the person deriving the dividends, being a resident of a Covered Jurisdiction, carries on business in the other Covered Jurisdiction through a permanent establishment situated therein, or performs in that other Covered Jurisdiction independent personal services from a fixed base situated therein, and the holding in respect of which the dividends are paid is effectively connected with such permanent establishment or fixed base. In such a case the provisions of Article 7 (Business Profits) or 15 (Independent Personal Services), as the case may be, shall apply.

Article 11

Interest

1. Interest arising in a Covered Jurisdiction and paid to a beneficial owner who is a resident of the other Covered Jurisdiction may be taxed in the first-mentioned Covered Jurisdiction, but the tax imposed shall not exceed 15 percent of the gross amount of the interest.

2. The term "interest" means income from Government securities, and income from bonds, debentures or notes, whether or not secured by mortgage and whether or not carrying a right to participate in profits, and other debt-claims of every kind as well as all other income assimilated to income from money lent by the taxation laws of the Covered Jurisdiction in which the income arises but shall not include any income which is treated as a dividend under the provisions of Article 10 (Dividends). Penalty charges for late payment shall not be regarded as interest for the purpose of this Article.

3. The provisions of paragraph (1) shall not apply if the person deriving the interest, being a resident of a Covered Jurisdiction, carries on business in the other Covered Jurisdiction through a permanent establishment situated therein, or performs in that other Covered Jurisdiction independent personal services from a fixed base situated therein, and the debt-claim in respect of which the interest is paid is effectively connected with such permanent establishment or fixed base. In such a case the provisions of Article 7 (Business Profits) or 15 (Independent Personal Services), as the case may be, shall apply.

4. Where, owing to a special relationship between the payer and the person deriving the interest or between both of them and some other person, the amount of the interest paid exceeds for whatever reason the amount which would have been paid in the absence of such relationship, the provisions of this Article shall apply only to the last-mentioned amount. In that case, the excess part of the payments shall remain taxable according to the laws of each Covered Jurisdiction, due regard being had to the other provisions of this Convention.

5. Interest shall be deemed to arise in a Covered Jurisdiction if, under its domestic laws, such interest has its source in that Covered Jurisdiction.

Article 12

Royalties

1. Royalties arising in a Covered Jurisdiction and paid to a beneficial owner who is a resident of the other Covered Jurisdiction may be taxed in the first-mentioned Covered Jurisdiction, but the tax imposed shall not exceed 15 percent of the gross amount of the royalties.

2. The term "royalties" means payments of any kind received as a consideration for the use of, or the right to use, any copyright of literary, artistic or scientific work (including cinematographic films or films or tapes used for radio or television broadcasting), any patent, trade mark, design or model, plan, secret formula or process or other like right or property, any information concerning industrial, commercial or scientific experience or any tangible personal property; the term "royalties" shall also include gains derived from the alienation of any such right or property which are contingent on the productivity, use or disposition thereof.

3. The provisions of paragraph (1) shall not apply if the person deriving the royalties, being a resident of a Covered Jurisdiction, carries on business in the other Covered Jurisdiction in which the royalties arise, through a permanent establishment situated therein, or performs in that other Covered Jurisdiction independent personal services from a fixed base situated therein, and the right or property in respect of which the royalties are paid is effectively connected with such permanent establishment or fixed base. In such a case the provisions of Article 7 (Business Profits) or 15 (Independent Personal Services), as the case may be, shall apply.

4. Where, owing to a special relationship between the payer and the person deriving the royalties or between both of them and some other person, the amount of the royalties paid exceeds for whatever reason the amount which would have been paid in the absence of such relationship, the provisions of this Article shall apply only to the last-mentioned amount. In that case, the excess part of the payments shall remain taxable according to the laws of each Covered Jurisdiction, due regard being had to the other provisions of this Convention.

5. Royalties shall be deemed to arise in a Covered Jurisdiction if they represent payment in consideration for the use of, or the right to use, rights or property in that Covered Jurisdiction.

Article 13

Investment Or Holding Companies

A corporation which is a resident of a Covered Jurisdiction and which receives dividends, interest or royalties arising within the other Covered Jurisdiction may be taxed in that other Jurisdiction without regard to Articles 10 (Dividends), 11 (Interest) and 12 (Royalties) if:

(a) by reason of special measures the tax imposed by the first-mentioned Covered Jurisdiction on such corporation with respect to such dividends, interest or royalties is less than the tax imposed by the first-mentioned Covered Jurisdiction on corporate profits arising in the first-mentioned Covered Jurisdiction; and

(b) twenty-five percent or more of the capital of such corporation is held of record or is otherwise determined to be owned, directly or indirectly, by one or more individuals who are not residents of the first-mentioned Covered Jurisdiction.

Article 14

Capital Gains

Except as provided in Articles 8 (Shipping and Air Transport) and 12 (Royalties), each Covered Jurisdiction may tax capital gains in accordance with the provisions of its domestic law.

Article 15

Independent Personal Services

Income derived by an individual who is a resident of a Covered Jurisdiction from the performance of personal services in an independent capacity may be taxed in the other Covered Jurisdiction if:

(a) the individual is present in that other Covered Jurisdiction for a period or periods exceeding in the aggregate 183 days in the taxable year concerned, but only so much thereof as is attributable to the services performed in that other Covered Jurisdiction; or

(b) the individual has a fixed base regularly available to him in that other Covered Jurisdiction for the purpose of performing his activities, but only so much thereof as is attributable to the services performed in that other Covered Jurisdiction.

Article 16

Dependent Personal Services

1. Subject to the provisions of Articles 18 (Pensions, Annuities, Alimony and Child Support) and 19 (Government Service), salaries, wages and other similar remuneration derived by a resident of a Covered Jurisdiction in respect of an employment shall be taxable only in that Covered Jurisdiction unless the employment is exercised in the other Covered Jurisdiction. If the employment is so exercised, such remuneration as is derived therefrom may be taxed in that other Covered Jurisdiction.

2. Notwithstanding the provisions of paragraph (1), remuneration derived by a resident of a Covered Jurisdiction in respect of an employment exercised in the other Covered Jurisdiction shall be taxable only in the first-mentioned Covered Jurisdiction if:

(a) the recipient is present in that other Covered Jurisdiction for a period or periods not exceeding in the aggregate 183 days in the taxable year concerned;

(b) the remuneration is paid by, or on behalf of, an employer who is not a resident of that other Covered Jurisdiction; and

(c) the remuneration is not borne by a permanent establishment or a fixed base which the employer has in that other Covered Jurisdiction.

3. Notwithstanding the preceding provisions of this Article, remuneration in respect of an employment as a member of the regular complement of a ship or aircraft operated in international traffic or between two places within a Covered Jurisdiction by an enterprise of that Covered Jurisdiction shall be taxable only in that Covered Jurisdiction.

Article 17

Artistes And Athletes

1. Notwithstanding the provisions of Articles 15 (Independent Personal Services) and 16 (Dependent Personal Services), income derived by a resident of a Covered Jurisdiction as an entertainer, such as a theatre, motion picture, radio or television artiste, or a musician, or as an athlete, from his personal activities as such may be taxed in the Covered Jurisdiction in which those activities are exercised, except where the amount of the gross receipts derived by such entertainer or athlete, including expenses reimbursed to him or borne on his behalf, from such activities in that Covered Jurisdiction does not exceed 15,000 United States dollars in the taxable year concerned.

2. Where income in respect of personal activities of an entertainer or athlete accrues not to that entertainer or athlete himself but to another person, that income may, notwithstanding the provisions of Articles 7 (Business Profits), 15 (Independent Personal Services) and 16 (Dependent Personal Services), be taxed in the Covered Jurisdiction in which the activities of the entertainer or athlete are exercised. For the purposes of the preceding sentence, income of an entertainer or athlete shall be deemed not to accrue to another person if it is established that neither the entertainer or athlete, nor persons related thereto, participate directly or indirectly in the profits of such other person in any manner, including the receipt of deferred remuneration, bonuses, fees, dividends, partnership distributions or other distributions.

Article 18

Pensions, Annuities, Alimony And Child Support

1. Subject to the provisions of paragraph (2) of Article 19 (Government Service):

(a) pensions and other similar remuneration beneficially derived by a resident of a Covered Jurisdiction in consideration of past employment shall be taxable only in that Covered Jurisdiction; and

(b) social security payments and other public pensions paid by a Covered Jurisdiction to an individual who is a resident of the other Covered Jurisdiction or a citizen of the United States shall be taxable only in the first-mentioned Covered Jurisdiction.

2. Annuities beneficially derived by a resident of a Covered Jurisdiction shall be taxable only in that Jurisdiction. The term "annuity" as used in this paragraph means a stated sum paid periodically at stated times during life or during a specified number of years, under an obligation to make the payments in return for adequate and full consideration (other than services rendered).

3. Alimony paid to a resident of a Covered Jurisdiction by a resident of the other Covered Jurisdiction shall be exempt from tax in the other Covered Jurisdiction. The term "alimony" as used in this paragraph, means periodic payments made pursuant to a written separation agreement or a decree of divorce, separate maintenance or compulsory support, which payments are taxable to the recipient under the laws of the Covered Jurisdiction of which he is a resident.

4. Periodic payments for the support of a minor child made pursuant to a written separation agreement or a decree of divorce, separate maintenance or compulsory support, paid by a resident of a Covered Jurisdiction to a resident of the other Covered Jurisdiction, shall be exempt from tax in both Covered Jurisdictions.

Article 19

Government Service

1.(a) Remuneration, other than a pension, paid by a Covered Jurisdiction or a political subdivision or a local authority thereof to an individual in respect of services rendered to that Covered Jurisdiction or subdivision or local authority shall be taxable only in that Covered Jurisdiction.

(b) However, such remuneration shall be taxable only in the other Covered Jurisdiction if the services are rendered in that other Covered Jurisdiction and the recipient is a resident and a national of that other Covered Jurisdiction.

2.(a) Any pension paid by a Covered Jurisdiction or a political subdivision or a local authority thereof to an individual in respect of services rendered to that Covered Jurisdiction or subdivision or local authority shall be taxable only in that Covered Jurisdiction.

(b) However, such pension shall be taxable only in the other Covered Jurisdiction if the recipient is a resident and a national of that other Covered Jurisdiction.

3. The provisions of Articles 15 (Independent Personal Services), 16 (Dependent Personal Services), 17 (Artistes and Athletes) and 18 (Pensions, Annuities, Alimony and Child Support), as the case may be, shall apply to remuneration and pensions in respect of services rendered in connection with a business carried on by or on behalf of a Covered Jurisdiction or a political subdivision or a local authority thereof.

Article 20

Students And Trainees

Payments which a student or business apprentice who is or was immediately before visiting a Covered Jurisdiction a resident of the other Covered Jurisdiction, and who is present in the first-mentioned Covered Jurisdiction for the purpose of his full-time education or training, receives for the purpose of his maintenance, education or training shall not be taxed in the first-mentioned Covered Jurisdiction, provided that such payments are made to him from sources outside the first-mentioned Covered Jurisdiction.

Article 21

Other Income

1. Items of income of a resident of a Covered Jurisdiction, wherever arising, not dealt with in the foregoing Articles of this Convention, shall be taxable only in that Covered Jurisdiction.

2. The provisions of paragraph (1) shall not apply if the person deriving the income, being a resident of a Covered Jurisdiction, carries on business in the other Covered Jurisdiction through a permanent establishment situated therein, or performs in that other Covered Jurisdiction independent personal services from a fixed base situated therein, and the right or property in respect of which the income is paid is effectively connected with such permanent establishment or fixed base. In such a case the provisions of Article 7 (Business Profits) or 15 (Independent Personal Services), as the case may be, shall apply.

Article 22

Elimination Of Double Taxation

1. In accordance with the provisions and subject to the limitations of the law of the United States (as it may be amended from time to time without changing the general principle hereof), the United States shall allow to a resident or national of the United States as a credit against the United States tax the appropriate amount of tax paid to the Virgin Islands; and, in the case of a United States corporation owning at least 10 percent of the voting stock of a corporation which is a resident of the Virgin Islands from which it receives dividends in any taxable year, the United States shall allow credit for the appropriate amount of tax paid to the Virgin Islands by that corporation with respect to the profits out of which such dividends are paid. Such appropriate amount shall be based upon the amount of tax paid to the Virgin Islands, but the credit shall not exceed the limitations (for the purpose of limiting the credit to the United States tax on income from sources outside of the United States) provided by United States law for the taxable year. For the purposes of applying the United States credit in relation to tax paid to the Virgin Islands the Virgin Islands tax referred to in paragraphs (1)(b) and (2) of Article 2 (Taxes Covered) shall be considered to be income taxes.

2. In accordance with the provisions and subject to the limitations of the law of the Virgin Islands regarding the allowance as a credit against Virgin Islands tax of tax payable in a territory outside the Virgin Islands (as it may be amended from time to time without changing the general principle hereof):

(a) United States tax payable under the law of the United States and in accordance with this Convention, whether directly or by deduction, on profits or income from sources within the United States (excluding, in the case of a dividend, tax payable in respect of the profits out of which the dividend is paid) shall be allowed as a credit against any Virgin Islands tax computed by reference to the same profits or income by reference to which the United States tax is computed; and

(b) in the case of a dividend paid by a United States corporation to a corporation which is a resident of the Virgin Islands and which owns at least 10 percent of the voting stock of the United States corporation, the credit shall take into account (in addition to any United States tax creditable under subparagraph (a)) the United States tax payable in respect of the profits out of which such dividend is paid.

3. For the purposes of paragraphs (1) and (2), income or profits derived by a resident of a Covered Jurisdiction which may be taxed in the other Covered Jurisdiction in accordance with this Convention shall be deemed to arise from sources within that other Covered Jurisdiction, except that where the United States taxes solely on the basis of citizenship, the Virgin Islands shall not be bound to give credit to a United States national who is a resident of the Virgin Islands on income from sources outside the United States as determined under the laws of the Virgin Islands (including this Convention).

Article 23

Nondiscrimination

1.Nationals of a Covered Jurisdiction shall not be subjected in the other Covered Jurisdiction to any taxation or any requirement connected therewith which is other or more burdensome than the taxation and connected requirements to which nationals of that other Covered Jurisdiction in the same circumstances are or may be subjected. For purposes of the preceding sentence, nationals of the United States who are not residents of the United States are not, with respect to United States taxation, in the same circumstances as nationals of the Virgin Islands who are not residents of the United States.

2. The taxation on a permanent establishment which an enterprise of a Covered Jurisdiction has in the other Covered Jurisdiction shall not be less favorably levied in that other Covered Jurisdiction than the taxation levied on enterprises of that other Covered Jurisdiction carrying on the same activities.

3. Interest, royalties and other disbursements paid by an enterprise of a Covered Jurisdiction to a resident of the other Covered Jurisdiction shall, if reasonable in amount, be deductible for the purpose of determining the taxable profits of such enterprise under the same conditions as if they had been paid to a resident of the first-mentioned Covered Jurisdiction. For the purpose of this paragraph, the term "other disbursements" shall include charges for amounts expended by such a resident for the purposes of such an enterprise, including a reasonable allocation of executive and general administrative expenses (except to the extent representing expenses of a type of activity which is not for the benefit of such enterprise but constitutes "stewardship" or "over-seeing" functions undertaken for such resident's own benefit as an investor in the enterprise), research and development expenses and other expenses incurred by such a resident for the benefit of a group of related enterprises including such an enterprise.

4. Enterprises of a Covered Jurisdiction, the capital of which is wholly or partly owned or controlled, directly or indirectly, by one or more residents of the other Covered Jurisdiction, shall not be subjected in the first-mentioned Covered Jurisdiction to any taxation or any requirement connected therewith which is other or more burdensome than the taxation and connected requirements to which other similar enterprises of the first-mentioned Covered Jurisdiction are or may be subjected.

5. Nothing contained in this Article shall be construed as obliging either Covered Jurisdiction to grant to an individual who is not a resident of that Covered Jurisdiction any of the personal allowances and reliefs which are granted to individuals who are residents of that Covered Jurisdiction.

Article 24

Mutual Agreement Procedure

1. Where a resident or national of a Covered Jurisdiction considers that the actions of one or both of the Covered Jurisdictions result or will result in taxation not in accordance with this Convention, he may, notwithstanding the remedies provided by the domestic laws of those Covered Jurisdictions, present his case to the competent authority of the Covered Jurisdiction of which he is a resident or national. The competent authority shall endeavour, if the objection appears to it to be justified and if it is not itself able to arrive at an appropriate solution, to resolve the case by mutual agreement with the competent authority of the other Covered Jurisdiction, with a view to the avoidance of taxation not in accordance with the Convention. Where an agreement has been reached, a refund as appropriate shall be made to give effect to the agreement. Any agreement reached shall be implemented notwithstanding any time limits or other procedural limitations in the domestic laws of the Covered Jurisdictions.

2. The competent authorities of the Covered Jurisdictions shall endeavour to resolve by mutual agreement any difficulties or doubts arising as to the interpretation or application of the Convention. In particular, the competent authorities of the Covered Jurisdictions may reach agreement on:

(a) the attribution of income, deductions, credits or allowances of an enterprise of a Covered Jurisdiction to its permanent establishment situated in the other Covered Jurisdiction;

(b) the allocation of income, deductions, credits or allowances between persons;

(c) the nature of particular items of income;

(d) a common meaning of a term used in this Convention; and

(e) the place where a particular item of income has its source.

They may also consult together for the elimination of double taxation in cases not provided for in this Convention.

3. The competent authorities of the Covered Jurisdictions may communicate with each other directly for the purpose of reaching agreement as contemplated by this Convention.

Article 25

Exchange Of Information And Administrative Assistance

1. The competent authorities of the Covered Jurisdictions shall exchange such information (being information available under the respective taxation laws of the Covered Jurisdictions) as is necessary for carrying out the provisions of this Convention or for the prevention of fraud or the administration of statutory provisions against legal avoidance in relation to the taxes which are the subject of this Convention. Any information so exchanged shall be treated as secret but may be disclosed to persons (including a court or administrative body) concerned with the assessment, collection, administration, enforcement or prosecution in respect of taxes which are the subject of this Convention. No information shall be exchanged which would disclose any trade, business, industrial or professional secret. Such persons shall use the information only for such purposes. They may disclose the information in public court proceedings or in judicial proceedings. No such information shall be disclosed to any third Jurisdiction for any purpose.

2. If information is requested by a Covered Jurisdiction in accordance with this Article, the other Covered Jurisdiction shall obtain the information to which the request relates in the same manner and to the same extent as if the tax of the first-mentioned Covered Jurisdiction were the tax of that other Covered Jurisdiction and were being imposed by that other Covered Jurisdiction. If specifically requested by the competent authority of a Covered Jurisdiction, the competent authority of the other Covered Jurisdiction shall provide information under this Article in the form of depositions of witnesses and authenticated copies of unedited original documents (including books, papers, statements, records, accounts or writings), to the same extent such depositions and documents can be obtained under the laws and administrative practices of such other Covered Jurisdiction with respect to its own taxes.

3. In no case shall the provisions of paragraphs (1) and (2) be construed so as to impose on a Covered Jurisdiction the obligation to supply information to the other Covered Jurisdiction which would not be obtainable under the laws or in the normal course of the administration of that other Covered Jurisdiction.

4. Each of the Covered Jurisdictions will endeavour to collect on behalf of the other Covered Jurisdiction such amounts as may be necessary to ensure that relief granted by this Convention from taxation imposed by such other Covered Jurisdiction does not enure to the benefit of persons not entitled thereto. This paragraph shall not impose upon either of the Covered Jurisdictions the obligation to carry out administrative measures which are of a different nature from those used in the collection of its own tax, or which would be contrary to its sovereignty, security or public policy.

5. The competent authorities of the Covered Jurisdictions shall consult with each other for the purpose of cooperating and advising in respect of any action to be taken in implementing this Article.

Article 26

Miscellaneous

1. Nothing in this Convention shall affect the fiscal privileges of diplomatic or consular officials under the general rules of international law or under the provisions of special agreements.

2. Nothing in this Convention shall restrict in any manner any exclusion, exemption, deduction, credit or other allowance now or hereafter accorded by the laws of either Covered Jurisdiction.

3. Where under any provision of this Convention income arising in a Covered Jurisdiction is wholly or partly relieved from tax in that Covered Jurisdiction and, under the laws in force in the other Covered Jurisdiction, a person, in respect of such income, is subject to tax by reference to the amount thereof which is remitted to or received in that other Covered Jurisdiction and not by reference to the full amount thereof, then the relief to be allowed under this Convention in the first-mentioned

Covered Jurisdiction shall apply only to so much of such income as is remitted to or received in the other Covered Jurisdiction during the taxable period in which such income arises.

Article 27

Entry Into Force And Transition Rules

1. This Convention shall be ratified and the instruments of ratification shall be exchanged at Washington as soon as possible.

2. This Convention shall enter into force upon the exchange of instruments of ratification and its provisions shall have effect:

(a) in respect of taxes withheld at the source, for amounts paid or credited on or after the first day of the second month next following the date on which this Convention enters into force;

(b) in respect of other taxes, for taxable periods beginning on or after the first day of January next following the date on which this Convention enters into force.

3. Upon the coming into effect of this Convention, the Convention between the United Kingdom of Great Britain and Northern Ireland and the United States of America for the Avoidance of Double Taxation and the Prevention of Fiscal Evasion with respect to Taxes on Income signed at Washington on 16 April 1945, as amended by the Supplementary Protocol signed at Washington on 6 ? the Supplementary Protocol signed at Washington on ? by the Supplementary Protocol signed at Washington on 19 August 1957, and as extended to the Virgin Islands, shall cease to have ? in respect of taxes to which this Convention, in accordance with the provisions of paragraph (2), applies and the 1945 Convention thereafter will terminate.

4. Notwithstanding any other provisions of this Convention, in determining the source of income for purposes of applying United States taxes to dividends or interest paid on or after the date specified in paragraph 2(a) by a Virgin Islands corporation to a person who is not a citizen or resident of the United States, such Virgin Islands corporation shall be deemed to have been created on the date so specified.

5. Notwithstanding any other provision of this Convention, interest paid by a Virgin Islands corporation on any debt obligation which was issued and outstanding on 1 July 1980, shall be exempt from United States tax except where the recipient is a resident or national of the United States. For the purpose of this paragraph, a debt obligation shall be treated as issued and outstanding on such date if it was issued after such date pursuant to an agreement entered into on or before such date.

Article 28

Termination

1. This Convention shall remain in force indefinitely but either of the Covered Jurisdictions may terminate the Convention at any time after five years from the date on which this Convention enters into force by giving to the other Covered Jurisdiction, through diplomatic channels, at least six months' prior notice of termination; in such event, this Convention shall cease to be effective:

(a) in respect of taxes withheld at the source, for amounts paid or credited on or after the first day of January next following the expiration of the six months' period; and

(b) in respect of other taxes, for taxable periods beginning on or after the first day of January next following the expiration of the six months' period.

2. Notwithstanding the provisions of paragraph (1), if a Covered Jurisdiction determines that the other Covered Jurisdiction has amended its law or procedures in a manner which would unreasonably limit the ability of the competent authority of the first-mentioned Covered Jurisdiction to obtain information from the competent authority of that other Covered Jurisdiction under Article 25 (Exchange of Information and Administrative Assistance), the first-mentioned Covered Jurisdiction may terminate this Convention by giving to that other Covered Jurisdiction, through diplomatic channels, at least six months' prior notice of termination. In such event, this Convention shall cease to be effective in accordance with the provisions of subparagraphs (a) and (b) of paragraph (1).

3. A termination of this Convention shall not have the effect of reviving any treaty or arrangement abrogated by this Convention or by any treaty previously concluded between the United States of America and the United Kingdom for the Virgin Islands.

Capital Preservation Through Global Investing

By Adam Starchild

Investing globally is one of the most successful ways to accomplish capital preservation and growth. In books such as *The Complete Guide to Tax Havens* and *The Conservative Wealthbuilder: Capital Preservation Through Global Investing*, Adam Starchild reveals how you can create an ultimate global portfolio of investments to hedge against inflation, taxes, confiscations, market, fluctuations, currency devaluations, economic and political turmoil...

Starchild reveals the little-known investment secrets that he has been giving to his clients for the past few decades. His recommendations are not high-flying investment tips, but rather solid, conservative recommendations that over time will help build a healthy nest-egg for you.

You will learn how to build a secret stash of cash that:

You can access at any time

Is tax-free and seizure proof

Pays competitive dividends and interest

And has no government reporting requirements (even for Americans)

In fact, if you had put $ 10,000 each year into this investment or the last twenty years you would have $590,697 today!

You will also discover:

How to accumulate income tax-free

Why offshore mutual funds should form a vital part of your global portfolio

How to invest in gold, silver and platinum and the investor potential of these precious metals

Why Switzerland should play an essential part in any global nest-egg strategy

How and where to best form an offshore trust in order to provide tax and creditor protection for your investments

How to invest tax-free in the United States

Everything you need to get yourself started on a global path to a secure fortune is in *The Conservative Wealthbuilder*. Starchild's techniques have been used by many of the world's wealthiest people for decades, including presidents, kings, Arab sheiks... And now for the first time they are available to you. They have been tested and proven over time. You will not find a safer, surer path to financial security than that mapped out for you in this unique work!

Just published (ISBN 0894990500), *The Conservative Wealthbuilder* is available through major bookstores and online booksellers. Also recently published (ISBN 1893713105) *The Complete Guide to Tax Havens* provides a wealth of information on forming offshore corporations and trusts.

The following sections are excerpts from *The Conservative Wealthbuilder* and other books by Adam Starchild:

Investing for the Offshore Entity

Investing for the offshore entity is just as important as creating the corporation or trust in the first place. Failure to invest the corpus and reinvest the income is one of the surest ways to squander the benefits that come from creation of an offshore corporation or trust. Astute choices in investment can lead to the realization of personal financial goals and, potentially, financial freedom. A problem often arises when one considers where to invest his money because there are so many options. Selecting the wrong ones can, at best, hinder the achievement of financial goals, and, at the worst, result in financial ruin. It is important to bear in mind that the investing is as important as the creation and structuring of the offshore entity.

Asset Allocation — The Key To Successful Investing

One of the newest forms of investments in America is called asset allocation. Basically what it means is that one investment is "allocated" to a number of different types of investments by a professional investment allocator. The reason for this allocation is that no one type of investment is the best in all investment climates, and no one type of investment is usually appropriate for all of one person's investment money.

By using an asset allocation program, a person can invest a large amount of his principal in one place, gaining ease of tracking the investment, while attaining the advantage of having a number of different investments to serve his different investment objectives.

The asset allocator performs the service for the investor of allocating varying amounts of a total investment into different areas of investing, such as income stocks, growth stocks, small capitalization stocks, etc., and a variety of fixed income securities.

For modest to medium-sized investments, one method of attaining even more diversification of investments, and expertise in the actual details of the investments, is to allocate the investment among various top-rated mutual funds. As is well known, mutual funds can perform a number of important tasks for the investor. Diversification among a large number of stocks is possible for even a relatively small sum of money. Expertise is available on any type of investment at a relatively low price. Last, there is great liquidity with ease of purchasing and selling.

The actual allocation into different mutual funds will depend upon three principal criteria:

(1) What is the risk to reward profile of the individual investor,

(2) What is the need of the investor for predictable current income as opposed to the desire for capital gains, and

(3) What is the state of the economic and investment cycles at the particular moment in time.

The first and most important criteria are clearly the needs of the investor. These outweigh any thoughts of where any market may be going or where an allocator believes that the most money can be made. The first need which needs to be addressed is the risk which the investor is prepared to accept. All investment involves some degree of risk, but that risk can rage from the minor risk of how inflation can impact an investment in the next 90 days, to the risk of a high flying initial public offering in a company which may have no earnings and no prospect for earnings in the foreseeable future.

The amount of risk which is appropriate for an individual investor depends upon both the investors actual economic situation and his psychological attitudes towards risk of loss. Human temperament plays a very large role in determining risk tolerance. For example, if a person remembers a period of his or her past where they did not have enough money to make ends meet, they may be very adverse to taking any risk at all. Their attitude may be, "We worked hard for that money, and we don't want to lose it."

Others may have almost the opposite approach. They may never have known deprivation, and may have earned a good income all their life. Their attitude may be that they can live very well on their current earnings, and so any savings can be used to speculate. If the speculation turns out to be successful, that will be great and they can raise their standard of living even further. But if the speculation doesn't work out, that's OK too because they will simply continue living as they have.

Thus a good investment allocator will first determine what the needs of his clients are with respect to risk. One method is to determine first how much money is needed to maintain the current standard of living of the investor, and if he or she is not yet retired, how much of the investment will be needed when they do retire. Whatever amount is needed for these purposes is then designated as income producing principal and is invested accordingly into low-risk, high-yielding investments.

The balance can then be invested according to the investor's wishes into areas which can offer the promise of large capital gains in the future. This is the risk portion of the principal, and care must be taken so that the allocator and the investor agree on what amount of risk is to be taken.

The third and equally important task of allocating is to attempt to maximize the return to the investor from the changes in the economic cycle. When business has been in a slump and starts to turn up with both interest rates and inflation low, the largest profits are typically made in the stock market. But as the economy continues to expand, interest rates will rise and so will inflation. These factors make the prognosis for the economy less rosy, and the stock market may start to gyrate, and then fall. Perhaps gently at first and then more rapidly. So the stock market is definitely not the place to be.

At the same time that the stock market is suffering from inflation, the price of hard assets such as gold, oil, and real estate could well be rising rapidly. It is in these areas that fortunes are made during inflationary periods in the economy.

And then as the economy finally begins to cool down due to the effect of high interest rates, interest rates will begin to fall nd the big money may be made by investing in long-term non-callable bonds.

Thus a good allocator must keep in mind the needs of the individual investor and the current status of the economy. And of course he must have an intimate familiarity with specific investments which are available to investors. Whether they be stocks, bonds, or fixed income securities, the allocator must know which are appropriate for the investor and which will likely do well in the present stage of the economy.

As with options in the preceeding chapter, the expertise of Max G. Ansbacher is once again quite useful. His credentials in the stock market are equally impressive. The second book he wrote is titled *How to Profit from the Coming Bull Market* and it was published in the summer of 1981 near the bottom of the long bear market which had actually begun in 1973.

This book explained how and why a strong bull market was about to start on Wall Street. At the time it was published the book was largely ignored by a public which had grown cynical about a stock market which seemed to do nothing but go sideways or down, year after year.

But just one year after Mr. Ansbacher's book was published, the market suddenly took off like a rocket in August 1982, igniting one of its greatest bull markets ever and establishing Mr. Ansbacher's reputation as an insightful student of the stock market.

We recently asked Mr. Ansbacher what his philosophy was concerning asset allocation. He replied, "Asset allocation is probably the most important single aspect of any investment program. And yet what is so strange about it is that it is often not even considered by investors. Some people will have most of their money in the stock market most of the time, unaware of the large risks which the market sometimes contains. Others believe in bonds, and continue to invest most or all of their money there, apparently unaware that in the 1970's and early 1980's the bond market was the biggest money loser of any investment. I would say that asset allocation is not just important, it is the key to successful investing."

Mr. Ansbacher went follows a deliberatly planned, carefully crafted strategy when handling an asset allocation account for a client. "The first thing I do is to talk to the client in whatever depth is necessary to determine the proper risk profile for the client. This depends upon his current financial situation and what he foresees for his future situation as well as his psychological feelings towards money and the potential loss of money. The second thing I do is to make an outline of the client's need for current income. This naturally has a great deal of influence on how we can invest the funds."

"Only after this has been done, do I then discuss with the client where I think the financial markets are heading and where the best returns are likely to be made in the future. The first step in actually making the investments are to decide upon the proportion of money going into each class of investments. The second part is to select the actual investments. For a number of reasons, I select from among the thousands of mutual funds which are available in the U.S. They range all the way from bond to preferred stocks, to common stocks of all types. There is usually a time and a place for almost all of them, but we try to pick the best one for that particular client at that particular time in the client's life, and in the life of the markets."

Mr. Ansbacher explained that his minimum investment is $100,000, and that he works with some of the biggest mutual fund organizations in the U.S., including Fidelity, Dreyfus and other mutual fund management firms. He does not bill his clients for a fee or commission for the work he does, because his compensation is paid to him by the mutual funds.

We have always believed that to be a good asset allocator is one of the most difficult tasks in the investment world, because it requires so many different considerations. To see just what kind of factors Mr. Ansbacher considers we asked him how he would go about planning an asset allocation program we asked him about a potential (though fictitious) client: a 50-year-old German married man who earns the equivalent of $200,000 a year and has a well-funded pension plan with his company. He is in good health and plans to retire at about the age of 65. We asked Mr. Ansbacher to assume that this man comes to him with $300,000 to invest. Here is how Mr. Ansbacher went about making his asset allocation process.

Mr. Ansbacher's recommendation? "The first question I have is about the amount of $300,000. Since he has a pension plan with his company, it is obviously not pension money. It is also a rather large amount for a person earning $200,000 to want to invest in the U.S. Is it inherited money? Does his wife earn money? Is this his life savings? Did he make a successful investment? The reason I ask this question is that it is very important to know if the money is replaceable. If it is inherited, will there be more to follow, or is this all? First I would want to know whether there will be more money coming in or not."

"Second, I would want to know more about his potential future obligations. Do he or his wife having living parents or other relatives who may need financial support in the future? How much support, if any, does he expect that his children will need in the future? Does he have disability insurance or a company plan in case he becomes disabled before he retires? Is there some specific financial goal that he has, such as acquiring a vacation home, yacht or other item which will require a substantial amount of ready cash. All these factors related to the amount of risk which I would want to take."

"The next set of considerations center around his financial situation now. Since he lives in Germany, this means that he pays a high tax on income such as dividends and interest, but pays no capital gains tax. Right away that sways me into investments which are likely to have high capital gains. I would want to know whether the $200,000 he earns covers all of his current expenses, or whether his current standard of living is so high that he needs extra income each year."

"Once we have the answers to these questions, we can begin to solve the problem of how best to allocate this investment. If there are no likely financial needs coming up in the future, and if at the time of the investment I decide that the stock market is not over priced or likely to decline for other reasons, I would place most of the money into various stock funds. I am particularly fond of funds which use value investing, which means that they pick stocks based upon how large an amount of earnings one gets for each dollar invested. This is another way of saying that they seek out stocks with high quality and low price/earnings ratios."

"The reason I like value investing is that many studies have shown that low price/earnings stocks outperform other stocks in normal markets. And in down markets heir inherent value keeps them from falling as far as others. The second group of stocks I would pick would be senior growth stocks. This means stocks which grow year after year because they are gaining market share, or because they are in a solid growth industry. Examples of this are some pharmaceutical companies which are constantly creating new and better drugs, or highly efficient national retail chains which are constantly gaining market share over local competitors."

"One advantage which growth stocks have for this particular client is that they usually don't pay a very large dividend, which fits right in which his local tax structure. Depending upon the wishes of the client, we would consider some gold stocks as a hedge against inflation. And we might add some mutual funds which specialize in large capitalization companies, because these are the tried and proven winners among all the competition in the economy, and often outperform other stocks when the economy softens."

"I would also place a portion of the assets into a short or medium term bond fund for three reasons:

(1) This could be a source of money in case an emergency arose which required a withdrawal from the fund,

(2) It is a reserve in case some outstanding bargains come up for investment, and

(3) It is a hedge against a downturn in the stock market."

Of course the actual percentage allocations would be discussed with the client. The actual funds selected would depend upon their performance records at the time of the investment. And in general, much of the allocation would depend upon the state of the economy at the time of the investment."

Good advice. From a man well-qualified to give it.

Investing in Options

Another vehicle to consider investing your money is in options. Specifically, trading options on stocks or on a stock index (such as the Standard & Poor's 500 Index). This is route is particularly appealing to foreigners, since the gain or loss from trading in options is a capital gain, and any profits made by a foreigner from trading in such options are free from any tax imposed by the United States.

But, as many investors already know, options are notoriously speculative and most people who try trading in them wind up losing money. Therefore, in order to take advantage of this tax benefit, it is first imperative to find a method of trading options which has a good probability of actually making money.

Almost any method of trading options which has the chance of making an above average return also carries a commensurate high degree of risk. But some practitioners of the arcane art of options trading do manage to do better than others over the years. One such person who has done very well for his clients is Max G. Ansbacher, Chairman of Ansbacher Investment Management, Inc., located in the prestigious Rockefeller Center complex in New York City.

Mr. Ansbacher has a long and distinguished involvement with options. In fact, he is the author of the first book published on the modern form of options, titled *The New Options Market, Revised and Enlarged Edition,* first published in 1975. Today, he manages accounts for investors in both the U.S. and overseas.

What sets Mr. Ansbacher apart from many others is that he has an excellent record of bringing in above average profits for his clients. Since most people who buy options seem to lose money, we asked Mr. Ansbacher what the key was to his success. He replied, "Yes, I agree that most people who buy options do seem to lose money. But what many people don't realize is that the money which the options buyers lose, doesn't disappear from the face of the earth. Rather it becomes the profits of the options *sellers*. And therefore, I concentrate in *selling* options."

What Mr. Ansbacher was saying is that options trading is actually a zero sum game when one looks at the total overall economic effect. This means that buying and selling options has no overall impact on the economy. It neither creates any money or lose any (except transaction costs). If the sellers make money, the buyers lose money. And if the buyers make money, then the sellers must lose money.

Since the options *buyers* tend to be the ones who lose money, it therefore must be true that the options *sellers* are the ones who make money over the long run. "The options buyers tend to be less sophisticated than the sellers," Mr. Ansbacher explained. "They don't always carefully assess the chances that their stocks will really go up enough to make money when they buy a call. Similarly, if people think a stock or a stock market is going to go down, they often over estimate how much it is going to go down. They will buy a put which is going to lose money unless the stock makes a really unusually large move within a relatively short period of time. These are the options I sell."

Of course there is not an investment program yet invented which makes money on every single trade, and option selling is no exception. Mr. Ansbacher said, "Certainly there are times when we have losses, but we believe that the probability lies with the sellers. And so we usually find that every loss is matched by many more winners."

If you do become involved in selling options, the best advise is: proceed with caution! Never forget that the risk factor is high. How does a veteran like Mr. Ansbacher control this risk? He said that the first defense was to control the number of options which he sells. "I usually sell only about one fifth the number of options which margin rules permit me to do. The second line of defense is that I use stop loss orders, which in most instances will automatically get me out of the options before the losses rise to a point which I consider unacceptable."

He continued, "The most interesting line of defense and the most important from the point of view of making money, is that I sell out-of-the-money options. This means that I sell options which have a strike price which is a distance away from the current price of the underlying security." We should point out that a strike price is the level at which an option becomes effective.

What Mr. Ansbacher means is that if a stock is 100, for example, he will not sell the 100 strike price call, because it is tool likely that the stock will go above 100 and he might lose money. Instead, he might sell the call with a strike price of 120. The stock would have to be above 120 at the option's expiration for the seller of the option to sustain a loss. Obviously it is less likely that a stock will go up 20 points than it will merely go up a few points. So, by selling out-of-the-money options, Mr. Ansbacher is able to shift the probabilities in his favor.

Another major decision which an options trader has to make is whether to be trading calls, which go up in price when a stock goes up, or puts which go up in price when the stock goes down. Mr. Ansbacher said that he makes this decision based upon a number of factors, including his long experience in the field. "One of the factors I rely upon, is my own Ansbacher Index. This Index tells me whether the puts or the calls are higher priced. Since I am selling these options, I will generally choose to sell the ones which are higher priced. I believe the Index also gives an indication of which way the stock market is likely to go in the intermediate future." Thus, Mr. Ansbacher can sell options on the stock market which will be profitable for his clients if the market moves as The Ansbacher Index indicates it is likely to do.

The minimum account which Mr. Ansbacher accepts is US$100,000, and he accepts accounts from people residing anywhere in the world. Depending upon the type of account, the investor will receive monthly or quarterly statements giving the exact value of the account.

For more information contact:

Ansbacher Investment Management, Inc.
Attn: New Clients Information
45 Rockefeller Plaza, 20th Floor
New York NY 10111
telephone: (212) 332-3280
fax: (212) 332-3283; Attn: New Clients Information

Swiss Financial Experts

JML Swiss Investment Counselors

Swiss investment managers are experienced in working with investors from around the world. Most are fluent in English and have substantial experience in managing various types of investments. They are comfortable managing an investor's entire portfolio if he wishes; however, for investors who prefer to make their own financial decisions, Swiss advisers are happy to offer their expertise to the degree it is required. They can help you manage your investments, or manage them for you - whichever arrangement makes you feel more comfortable. For the entrepreneur who devotes much of his energy to building his venture, the efficiency and competence of Swiss investment managers can be a major attraction.

A fine example of a Swiss money management company is JML Swiss Investment Counselors. Founded by Jurg M. Lattman, who has been providing expert financial advice to investment professionals, bankers, economists, and private investors around the world since 1973, JML experts monitor global economic indicators and trends and provide their clients with some of the best financial advice available anywhere. They make it a simple matter to invest in Swiss annuities as well as take advantage of other global investment options.

One of the leaders in Swiss financial management is JML Swiss Investment Counsellors, a firm which offers a unique style of financial management. Clients can customize and control their own portfolios and still receive comprehensive management advice from some of the world's best experts on financial matters.

Recognizing that investors have differing goals, time frames, and tolerance for risk, JML's managers work with their individual clients to help them target their unique objectives. This naturally requires continued surveillance and analysis of worldwide economic trends, political events, financial markets, currencies, and other factors which could make some investments particularly attractive and others most unfavora•
ble. Few individuals have the time or

- expertise to undertake this kind of evaluation themselves.
- In any event, JML clumps the various opportunities that are available to investors into five separate categories for consideration by its Personal Portfolio Management Program clients:
- Cash Equivalents. Principal and interest are guaranteed for finite terms are provided.
- Blue Chips. The investment portfolio consists of high-quality securities purchased for long-term capital appreciation potential.
- Trading. The portfolio consists of securities which are bought and sold for short-term capital appreciation.
- Trends. Often referred to a cyclical portfolios, securities are selected on the basis of economic forecasts by industry, sector, or country. The investor normally needs to wait about six years to realize significant annual returns.
- Visions. The most speculative of the five categories, investments are selected from opportunities in emerging markets and new technologies. It may take ten or more years to realize larger annual yields.

For more information on JML write:

JML Jurg M. Lattmann AG
Swiss Investment Counsellors
Germaniastrasse 55, Dept. 212
CH-8033 Zurich, Switzerland
telephone: +41 1 368 8233
fax: +41 1 368 8299; marking the fax "Attn: Dept. 212"

Weber Hartmann Vrijhof & Partners

While there are many excellent Swiss investment financial managers, another one of particular note is the management firm of Weber Hartmann Vrijhof & Partners. Offering management services for the portfolios of both individuals and companies, the firm excels at providing personal attention to its clients. Weber Hartmann Vrijhof & Partners was established in 1992 by Hans Weber, Robert Vrijhof, and Adrian Hartmann. The three men have substantial experience in finance and investment. Weber managed Foreign Commerce Bank (FOCOBANK) in Switzerland for nearly 30 years as its president and CEO, Vrijhof was a former vice-president and head of FOCOBANK'S portfolio management group, and Hartmann was head of FOCOBANK'S North American subsidiary in Vancouver. Weber Hartmann Vrijhof & Partners offers specialized investment services designed to meet the individual needs of their clients.

The minimum opening portfolio to be managed by this firm is $250,000 or equivalent. The management team here normally recommends that a portion of the portfolio be invested in hard currencies other than the U.S. dollar including the Swiss franc, French franc, German mark, and Dutch guilder. Respected for their conservative approach to portfolio management, the partners assist clients with opening a custodial account at one of the major private Swiss banks, so that all client securities are held by the bank, not the investment manager.

A large percentage of their clients are based in the United States. One of their main goals has always been to get a certain portion of their clients' wealth out of the U.S. dollar and into European hard currencies such as Swiss francs, Deutschmarks, and Dutch guilders, and then build a portfolio with a mix of bonds and shares.

If you wish to learn more about the services the firm offers, contact them at:

Weber Hartmann Vrijhof & Partners, Ltd.
Attn: New Clients Department
Zurichstrasses 110B
CH-8134 Adilswil
Switzerland
Tel: +41 1 709-11-15
Fax: +41 1 709-11-13, please mark fax "Attn: New Clients Department"

Even though many investors recognize that Switzerland is a center of finance and investment, they do not realize the vast scope of the investment options offered by Swiss financial institutions and companies. Switzerland is a prime spot for investment for numerous reasons, most importantly for the strength of its currency, security of its financial system, and steady returns on investment.

Dunn & Hargitt: Offshore Managed Commodities Accounts

An offshore managed commodities account is typical of the type of investment that is available to an offshore corporation or trust, but is not available to Americans.

The Dunn & Hargitt International Group, founded in 1961, has specialized in doing research for developing Portfolio Management Programs that have the potential of providing investors with a high return on their capital by investing in a diversified portfolio trading in the commodity, currency, precious metals, and financial futures markets in the United States and throughout the world.

The Dunn & Hargitt group offers investors the possibility of participating in several of the different pools that are managed by them by investing through the investment programs that are offered by their affiliate, Winchester Life in Gibraltar, but which are actually managed by The Dunn & Hargitt International Group.

At the time of publication they are offering three possible investment alternatives, including The Winchester Life Umbrella Account (which allows 100% of a client's money to be invested in a diversified futures portfolio), The Winchester Life 100% Guaranteed Investment Account (in which Lloyds Bank acts as custodian trustee and US Government Zero Coupon Treasury Bonds are set aside to guarantee the client's capital), and The Winchester Life 150%

Guaranteed Investment Account (which is a similar program, but guaranteeing that the client will receive at least 150% of the value deposited with a maturity date at least ten years in the future).

The average net return for the 150% Guaranteed Investment Account over the last six years would have been 22% a year. The average net return on the 100% Guaranteed Investment Account over the last six years would have been 27% a year. The average annual net return for The Winchester Life Umbrella Account over the last twelve years would have been 35% a year.

The minimum accounts accepted are $20,000 for The Winchester Life Umbrella Account, $20,000 for The Winchester Life 100% Guaranteed Account, and $50,000 for The Winchester Life 150% Guaranteed Account.

Although commodities are a speculative form of investment, investors everywhere are diversifying part of their portfolios to take part in the considerable potential profit opportunities that are available in the commodity, currency, precious metals and financial futures markets. The programs devised by the Dunn & Hargitt International Group will make profits if significant trends develop in either direction; i.e. up or down. This does not mean that short term results are always profitable, however the Dunn & Hargitt proven trading systems can provide above average returns over the longer term. Their objective is to make a profit for their clients of between 20% and 40% per annum and their computer trading systems are geared to this level of performance.

For more information, contact:

The Dunn & Hargitt International Group
Department S-697
P.O. Box 3186
Road Town, Tortola
British Virgin Islands

The structure of the Dunn & Hargitt Group has been established so that no taxes are withheld from the client's investment on the international commodity, currency, precious metals and financial futures markets. Because of this they can only manage money for investors who are neither citizens nor residents of the United States, United Kingdom, or Belgium, and they will not mail their brochures to those countries.

The Dunn & Hargitt International Group offers complete confidentiality to all of its clients, and will not reveal any information on a client or on its accounts to any third parties.

Sources of Help in Forming Offshore Entities

Skye Fiduciary Services Limited

Skye Fiduciary Services Limited, based in the Isle of Man, are specialist consultants, designers and trustees and managers of offshore and international fiduciary structures.

They were established in 1991 by Charles Cain to provide specialist consultancy and management services in respect of offshore fiduciary structures, specializing in clients from or connected to the USA. The beginnings of Skye Fiduciary Services Limited go back over twenty

years. In 1972, their Executive Chairman, Charles Cain, after some years working in international banking in East Africa and the United Kingdom, returned to his native country as the managing director of a merchant bank. Three years later he resigned to start his own business, which became, by 1989, the largest corporate and trust management business in the Isle of Man. In 1989, however, as a consequence of an illness, he sold out to a large financial services group.

In 1991, fully recovered, he established Skye Fiduciary Services Limited.

From its executive office in the Isle of Man, Skye Fiduciary Services Limited provides a design and management service relating to offshore companies and trusts.

Unlike many firms that simply provide offshore corporations, one of Sky's major functions is to provide trade management services. These include:

- arranging and supervising appropriate banking and trade finance
- facilities and services.
- trade documentation
- exchange control planning
- double tax treaty planning.
- administration of trading entities
- arranging bank Letters of Credit and other financial instruments
- arranging leasing, invoice discounting and credit factoring
- arranging tax efficient vehicles for transferring royalties and other
- income flows derived from intellectual property rights.
- offshore joint venture vehicles and holding structures for US persons
- international trading structures.

For more information contact:

Skye Fiduciary Services Limited
Attn: New Clients Information
2 Water Street
Ramsey, Isle of Man 1M8 1JP
Great Britain
Telephone: +44 1624 816117
Fax: +44 1624 816645; attn: New Clients Information

ICS Trust (Asia) Limited

The other firm I can personally give my highest recommendation to is ICS Trust (Asia) Limited, based in Hong Kong.

The handover of the former British Crown Colony of Hong Kong to China is complete, and it is now called the Hong Kong Special Administrative Region, generally abbreviated to Hong Kong S.A.R., even on official documents.

As more than one local businessman has put it, "now that the politicians and journalists are gone (from covering the handover), we can get down to *business*." This attitude is typical of Hong Kong, still a true capitalist center. In fact, many of the wealthy who left to obtain second citizenships in Canada, Australia, and elsewhere, have now returned home to continue building their fortunes.

Offshore re-invoicing can be a very useful tool for exporters as well as importers, since it allows for the accumulation of tax-free profits in an offshore environment.

Through re-invoicing, an offshore corporation is established as an international intermediary between importers and their suppliers or between exporters and their customers. The offshore corporation can thus either 1) buy products, on behalf of the importer, at the negotiated price level and then sell, or re-invoice, these same products to the importer at a higher price, thereby accumulating profits offshore where there is no tax liability and significantly reducing profits in the country of destination where there is tax liability, or 2) buy products at discount prices from the exporter, thereby creating a very small profit in the exporting country with tax liability and sell, or re-invoice, these same products at market value prices to overseas buyers, thereby accumulating profits offshore where there is no tax liability.

In order to be profitable, offshore re-invoicing operations need to be situated in an environment where import-export transactions are either tax-free or low tax (in relation to the onshore portion of the operation).

Once the offshore company has been established, the management corporation needs to acquire the services of a post office box, a telex, a telephone, and a facsimile for its use. When all this is in place, the management company can begin re-invoicing. An offshore service provider can arrange these services.

The merchandise can be sent directly to the exporter's client or to the importer. The only functions performed in the offshore haven are the preparation and dispatch of the new invoice and the management of the funds in the way instructed by the client and complying with local regulations.

The major advantage of Hong Kong is simply that it is a real business center, not just a tax haven. One of the consequences of that is the ability to add value to services that are provided in only skeleton form in other tax havens. The reinvoicing business is a prime example. Most tax haven jurisdictions host a number of trading companies that do nothing more than reinvoicing. But one Hong Kong firm has now developed this traditional service into a "real" business mode, with an ability to arrange local trade financing. This is a healthy step away from traditional tax havenry into a true offshore **business** center.

ICS Trust Company Limited is part of the ICS International group of companies headquartered in Hong Kong. This highly successful entrepreneurial group was started by Elizabeth L. Thomson. Elizabeth describes herself as "a lawyer by profession" (2 law degrees, a member of 4 Law Societies internationally), "an entrepreneur by choice"! She has helped innumerable people start new enterprises in many parts of the globe and is well known in Hong Kong for her work with women entrepreneurs.

With a staff of 40 at ICS, every aspect of your business is covered — from deciding to incorporate, to obtaining financing from the bank, to managing your paper work including Letters of Credit, to investing your hard earned profits! ICS is truly a "one stop shop" for entrepreneurs.

Their clients range from multinational companies for whom they run Direct Import Programs worth millions of dollars to individuals who seek tax sheltering and estate planning on an international scale. As an entrepreneurial group, they attract many entrepreneurs as clients — business people who have grown their business to a level of maturity and profits that requires expansion into Asia for many diverse reasons.

Instead of just a paper thin traditional tax haven reinvoicing company, with ICS you can develop a real business in Hong Kong. With their extensive banking contacts, ICS professionals will "shop" for the best letter of credit facilities that Hong Kong's competitive banking scene can offer, likely better facilities than you can find at home. Depending upon the client, ICS can often arrange letter of credit banking facilities for clients with either a low or zero margin deposit, usually required by the opening bank. By freeing up your collateral and capital, they provide you with more purchasing power to increase sales and gain higher profits.

Most of these reinvoicing transactions are usually effected such that they are tax free in Hong Kong. There is no withholding tax on dividends so it is often possible to engage in international trade through a HK company and obtain dividends from that company tax free.

ICS will also work with international banks and factors in Hong Kong and overseas to arrange financing, secured primarily on the strength of purchase orders from your clients. Working with banks, factories, shipping companies and freight forwarders, ICS will structure a transaction to increase the likelihood of obtaining flexible, low cost facilities.

The goods do not need to go through HK for us to use a HK vehicle to pass title. Most of their clients ship from a third country direct to their own country.

Although the traditional Hong Kong focus is on firms who trade in goods, it is also possible to use these structures in cases where services are to be provided from overseas. For example, a firm could contract out a study to a company in Hong Kong. This Hong Kong company could then sub-contract out the work to a third party firm and the profit kept in Hong Kong, tax free.

If you import goods from Asia for sale to large chains, ICS can help you expand your credit facilities and increase your domestic sales by establishing and running a Direct Import Program for you. Combined with their international trade finance capabilities, the Direct Import Program is a powerful tool for generating more profits.

The primary goal of the Direct Import Program is to maximize your profits by making your customers perceive that they are buying "direct." This is achieved by:

- setting up a subsidiary company in Hong Kong
- getting your buyers to open their L/C or orders to this subsidiary
- liaising with suppliers to ensure goods are to specification.

The Direct Import Program works because of two powerful reasons:

- The trend in the retail industry is for buyers to "buy direct" from the Orient. Having a subsidiary in Hong Kong which receives orders or L/Cs greatly enhances this perception.
- Large retail chains often can obtain freight and insurance at significant savings because of their economies of scale. Selling FOB Asia can often result in a lower selling price for the importer but with the same profit.

ICS will set up and manage the subsidiary company for you, and prepare financing proposals for presentation to local banks. When everything is complete, goods are shipped directly from the Asian factory to the customer. The fact that you are now seen as an Asian supplier (and not the middleman) is often an important factor that clinches the deal. The added prestige of a Hong Kong office makes the customer think he or she is buying "direct" and therefore receiving the lowest price.

To get started, you should contact ICS with as much detail as possible about your business and its trading activities.

For further information, contact:

Mr. Kishore K. Sakhrani
Director
ICS Trust (Asia) Limited
Suite 605-6
Nine Queens's Road, Central
Hong Kong
Telephone: +852-2854-4544
Fax: +852-2543-5555

Britannia Corporate Management Limited

A consulting business specializing in the formation of offshore corporations and trusts is Britannia Corporate Management Limited, located in the Cayman Islands. Its president, Gary F. Oakley, is a Canadian with 17 years of Cayman Islands residency. Britannia is licensed to manage investment holding and trading companies, real estate holding companies, patent holding companies, and insurance holding companies. It is licensed to incorporate and manage corporations registered in the Cayman Islands. As such, the firm can service as the registered office of a corporation, provide its secretary, officers and directors, or undertake any day-to-day functions that may be required. More information can be obtained by writing the following:

Britannia Corporate Management Limited
Attn: New Clients Information
P. O. Box 1968
Whitewall Estates, Grand Cayman
Cayman Islands

Britannia can be reached by fax at +1 345 949 0716, marking your fax to "New Clients Information."

You will be well-advised and well-serviced in the hands of any of these fine companies.

About the Author

Over the past 25 years, Adam Starchild has been the author of over two dozen books, and hundreds of magazine articles, primarily on business and finance. His articles have appeared in a wide range of publications around the world -- including *Business Credit, Euromoney, Finance, The Financial Planner, International Living, Offshore Financial Review, Reason, Tax Planning International, The Bull & Bear, Trust & Estates*, and many more.

Now semi-retired, he was the president of an international consulting group specializing in banking, finance and the development of new businesses, and director of a trust company.

Although this formidable testimony to expertise in his field, plus his current preoccupation with other books-in-progress, would not seem to leave time for a well-rounded existence, Starchild has won two Presidential Sports Awards and written several cookbooks, and is currently involved in a number of personal charitable projects.

His personal website is at http://www.adamstarchild.com

www.ingramcontent.com/pod-product-compliance
Ingram Content Group UK Ltd.
Pitfield, Milton Keynes, MK11 3LW, UK
UKHW051456290926
15471UKWH00008B/1232

9 781893 713376